DATE DUE

NOV 2 6 2008		
OCT 2 8 2014		

PSYCHOLOGY OF FEAR

PSYCHOLOGY OF FEAR

PAUL L. GOWER
EDITOR

Nova Science Publishers, Inc.
New York

Senior Editors: Susan Boriotti and Donna Dennis
Coordinating Editor: Tatiana Shohov
Office Manager: Annette Hellinger
Graphics: Wanda Serrano and Matt Dallow
Editorial Production: Maya Columbus, Alexis Klestov, Vladimir Klestov,
                Matthew Kozlowski and Lorna Loperfido
Circulation: Ave Maria Gonzalez, Vera Popovic, Luis Aviles, Sean Corkery,
          Raymond Davis, Melissa Diaz, Meagan Flaherty, Magdalena Nuñez,
          Marlene Nuñez, Jeannie Pappas and Frankie Punger
Communications and Acquisitions: Serge P. Shohov
Marketing: Cathy DeGregory

Library of Congress Cataloging-in-Publication Data

Psychology of fear / Paul L. Gower, editor.
     p. cm.
Includes bibliographical references and index.
    ISBN 1-59033-786-7.
    1. Fear. I. Gower, Paul L.

BF575.F2P79 2003
152.4'6—dc22   2003014367

CONTENTS

PREFACE

Fear is a normal human emotional reaction - it is a built-in survival mechanism with which we are all equipped. Fear is a reaction to danger that involves both the mind and body. It serves a protective purpose - signaling us of danger and preparing us to deal with it. The major components of fear are sensations, feelings, cognitions and behaviors. Fear can be individual or collective such as expressed in the national fear in the United States related to terrorism. The Washington DC sniper attacks caused widespread fear in a large geographic region far out of proportion to the real danger. Individuals must cope with fear on a daily basis in a myriad of forms: financial fears, health fears, relationship conflict fears, dental appointments, fears about the future etc. This new book collects important research which helps shed light on important issues in this field which touches all of us each day.

Fear is a complex phenomenon. The complexity is manifested first and foremost in its being multi-component and multi-leveled. But it is also evident in the variety of forms it assumes, its multiple determinations, the variety of stimuli that may evoke it, and the multiplicity of functions it may serve. In chapter one the dynamics of fear and anxiety are discussed.

The purpose of chapter two is to explore current knowledge and concepts on the nature of emotion. The author mentions the different theories on emotion and the way emotion supposedly works. He then reviews the anatomy of brain circuits that produce and modulate emotional functioning. At last, the characteristics of rational and irrational fear and anxiety, its autonomic responses and the clinical disorders related to them are addressed.

Fear of falling (FOF) has been identified as a health problem of older adults, with greater prevalence in older age groups, women and those who were hospitalized. Many factors have been associated with FOF, including poorer health status, functional decline, and activity curtailment. Depression, anxiety and decreased quality of life also have been correlated with FOF. Various measurement tools, using different definitions and premises of FOF, have been developed and are compared in chapter three. Fear of falling needs to be assessed by health care providers as they work with older adults and other disease specific pathologies.

Fear is a very important emotion necessary for physical survival. It is a signal informing us that we are in danger. However, fear can also cause us many problems. We sometimes become aggressive and exploit others because of fear. One of the reasons why fear can be so problematic is that we learn to associate many things with fear through our experiences. Although our ability to associate various things through our experiences has many beneficial effects, it can also make us fear and react to people and events that are almost completely harmless in aggressive and hurtful ways. Because of our ability to associate, fear is considered to be an important factor in the development of problematic interpersonal patterns.

Chapter four focuses on the problems relating to the emotion of fear using from an interpersonal perspective.

Chapter five highlights how the concept of fear is an important element of the prison-based definition of bullying and yet has received little attention in the literature. In a prison, where physical escape from an aggressor is often not possible, fear responses can be magnified. Such responses can manifest themselves in a number of ways. This chapter shows the many types of ways in which a victim may react to bullying, and explores the extent to which these reactions may indeed be fear-motivated.

Dental fear in children is a wide spread and serious problem often interfering with effective dental treatment, having negative consequences for one's health. Its etiology is considered to be complex and multifactorial. Numerous studies have been published on factors associated with dental fear in children, resulting however in inconsistent findings, partly due to great variety in methodology and study populations used. Chapter six aims to provide an overview of research on the assessment, prevalence and etiology of child dental fear, and shed more light on important theoretical and practical developments in this area of research.

In chapter seven, the term dental fear is used to denote very strong fear together with phobic reactions. The patient experiences in such instances that the reaction can neither be explained nor reasoned away. They are largely beyond voluntarily control, and often lead to avoidance of dental treatment. Thus, many dental fear patients seek dental treatment only in cases of emergency, for instance when they are in pain. They often feel extremely nervous several days before the appointment, and if they show up in the dental office, they have extreme activation of fear.

The objective of chapter eight is to explain the increase in fears of childbirth and fear-related requests for cesarean sections (CS). Between 6 and 10% of Finnish first time parturients suffer from severe fear of childbirth. At its worst, it can overshadow the whole pregnancy, lengthen and complicate the labor and hamper the beginning of a good mother-infant relationship. The majority of parturients with fear wish to have CS. Psychoeducation for fear of childbirth aiming at alleviating the fear and helping the women to prepare for the future childbirth started at our hospital in 1996. During 1996-1999, a longitudinal randomized study of 90 nulliparous women with severe childbirth was conducted. Since 1998, nulliparous women with fear of childbirth were offered the possibility to participate in the psychoeducational group sessions, lead by a psychologist. Treatment of fear of vaginal childbirth remarkably reduced unnecessary cesareans, even more in group psychoeducation with relaxation and imaginary childbirth exercises. With better preparation and ability to relax, labors were also shorter.

In chapter nine it is argued that classical conditioning might result in two types of changes. First, one may learn that the conditioned stimulus (CS+) is a valid predictor for the occurrence of the biologically negative or positive event (US) (expectancy-learning), which may lead to fear or pleasure. Second, after acquisition one may perceive the conditioned stimulus itself as a negative or positive event, depending on the valence of the event it has been associated with (evaluative learning). Based on human research on evaluative learning, it has been suggested that unlike expectancy learning, such conditioned valences are resistant to extinction. In the present two experiments the authors were able to demonstrate that both outcomes can result from the same procedure. Moreover, the data of both experiments showed that whereas extinction returned expectancy learning to baseline, the acquired valence was unaffected by this procedure. It is suggested in this chapter that exposure (extinction) will lead to reduced US-expectancy and fear, but will leave the valence of the original stimuli/triggers unchanged.

When reviewing the psychological and electrophysiological literature on emotions, a discrepancy emerges. In fact, if behavioral studies have demonstrated that emotions are extracted pre-attentively and influence subsequent perception, many studies have found emotion-modulated event-related potentials (ERP) considerably later, typically between 250 and 600ms. In chapter ten the authors' created continua of morphed faces moving from one expression to the other (e.g., identity A "happy" to identity "A" fearful). The temporal course of fear and happiness facial expressions discrimination has been explored through ERPs. Three kinds of pairs were presented in a delayed same-different matching task: (1) two different morphed faces perceived as the same emotional expression (WITHIN-categorical differences), (2) two other ones reflecting two different emotions (BETWEEN-categorical differences), and (3) two identical morphed faces (SAME faces for methodological purpose). Following the second face onset in the pair, the amplitude of the bilateral occipito-temporal negativities (N170) and of the vertex positive potential (P150 or VPP) was reduced for WITHIN and SAME pairs relative to BETWEEN pairs. These results indicate that the categorical discrimination of human facial emotional expressions has an early perceptual origin, around 150 ms, in the bilateral occipito-temporal regions, maybe due to amygdalar connexions.

Recent theoretical and empirical work in evolutionary biology suggests that mammalian neurocognitive architecture is not necessarily a unified whole designed to further the interests of an individual organism. For example intragenomic conflicts may influence brain development and behaviour in accordance with probabilistic conflicts of interest between parental genomes over resources encountered by the descendant's mammalian ancestors. The phenomenon of genomic imprinting may be explained in part by conflicts of interest between parental genomes over developmental resources (e.g. growth). Genomic imprinting is differential gene expression depending upon the parental origin in which a gene was transmitted. Chapter eleven argues that psychological resources may be a battleground for intragenomic conflicts. Motivations and cognitions are instrumental resources for the production and suppression of fitness-related behaviours, which potentially have divergent costs for parental genes. For example, the traditional view of the fear response is that it is good for individual or species survival because it allows individuals to confront or avoid threats. This hypothesis is known as the "Fight-or-Flight" (FOF) response. Neuroscientists have located particular neural systems mediating FOF. A genomic conflict view may help elucidate FOF computational machinery.

The role of the cerebellum has been traditionally seen in coordination of limb movements and control of posture, gait, speech and gaze. However, results of the last decades of research suggest that the cerebellum is also crucially involved in implicit motor learning such as conditioning and habituation of specific aversive reflexes, adaptation of voluntary movements to external forces or changed visual cues and learning of complex motor skills. Recent studies provide evidence that specific cognitive processes may also rely on the integrity of the cerebellum. Moreover, it appears that the cerebellum is closely related to the autonomic nervous system. In chapter twelve patients with lesions involving the cerebellar vermis were tested for impairment of the fear-conditioned bradycardia and fear-conditioned potentiation of startle-reflex. Results demonstrated that controls, but not cerebellar patients, showed a significant decrease of heart rate during fear conditioning. In addition, the fear-conditioned potentiation effect of the blink reflex was significantly reduced in patients with medial cerebellar lesions compared with controls. To evaluate whether fear-conditioning or the potentiation itself are mediated by the cerebellum, a positron emission tomography (PET)-study of fear-conditioned potentiation of the startle reflex was performed in healthy human subjects. Results suggested that the left cerebellar hemisphere was activated by fear-conditioning, whereas the medial cerebellum showed a significant increase of the regional cerebellar blood flow attributable to the potentiation itself. Different parts of the human cerebellum appear to be involved in conditioning of fear.

Five hundred and twenty male and female Egyptian undergraduate students completed the 108 items of the Wolpe and Lang (1977) Fear Survey Schedule III in its Arabic version (A - FSS III). The correlation matrix was subjected to principal components analysis, followed by Varimax rotation. Three criteria for retaining factors were: (a) eigenvalue greater than one; (b) 0.4 or higher for a salient loading, and (c) a minimum of four variables with salient loadings. According to these criteria, nine interpretable factors were retained, which explained 40.3% and 40.5% of the variance for males and females, respectively. These factors are the fear of: (1) social inadequacy, (2) responsibility and authority, (3) death and surgical operations, (4) noise and violence, (5) sexual acts, (6) medical procedures, (7) agoraphobia, (8) heights and deep water, and (9) small animals. The factor of noise and violence in males becomes "noise" only in females. These factors were compared with both Wolpe and Lang's six conceptual categories and the five fear factors model of Arrindell (1980) and Arrindell et al. (1984). In chapter thirteen the nine factors were discussed in the light of specific characteristics of the Arabic culture.

In the past decade, research in the area of how individuals respond to pain has focused extensively on the cognitive and behavioral response domains. Consequently, most self-report instruments that are currently available to researchers and clinicians are limited to the assessment of pain-related cognitive and behavioral responses. To date, adequate attention has not been given to the development and validation of instruments for the assessment of emotional responses to pain. In the initial conceptualization of the Fear of Pain Questionnaire –III (FPQ-III) made extensive conceptual distinctions between the constructs of *fear of pain* and *anxiety related to the experience of pain.*

The Fear of Pain Questionnaire-III was designed by McNeil and Rainwater to assess three emotional components of pain-related responses: fear related of severe pain, fear related to minor pain, and fear related to medical pain. In chapter fouteen the authors generated the FPQ-III items from multiple sources to reflect the multidimensionality of the fear of pain response construct. Specifically, the initial items were designed to describe eight specific painful situations, as recommended in the behavioral-analytic principles. Items that were generated in response to these situations were submitted to content validity analyses by four independent judges. Additional items were developed and included in the initial pool of 151 potential items. The authors conducted two additional studies, with unselected undergraduates, to derive the final 30-item version of the FPQ-III. The factor-analytic study identified three correlated factors, each characterized by 10 items. Items on this instrument are scored on a 5-point Likert-type rating scale ranging from 1 (*not at all*) to 5 (*extreme*) in terms of how fearful the individual experiences pain associated with each item. The total score is obtained for each factor scale by summing ratings on the related items within the scale.

Chapter 1

THE DYNAMICS OF FEAR AND ANXIETY

Shulamith Kreitler
Ph.D. Department of Psychology, Tel-Aviv University
And Director, Psychooncology Unit, Tel-Aviv Medical Center

Fear is a complex phenomenon. The complexity is manifested first and foremost in its being multi-component and multi-leveled. But it is also evident in the variety of forms it assumes, its multiple determinations, the variety of stimuli that may evoke it, and the multiplicity of functions it may serve.

COMPONENTS OF FEAR

The major components of fear are sensations, feelings, cognitions and behaviors (Lader & Marks, 1973). Sensations and feelings represent the experiential aspect of fear. Characteristic sensations of fear reflect somatic (e.g. weakness in hands and feet, shaking and trembling) and autonomic manifestations (e.g., palpitations and tachycardia). Further physiological features of fear are difficulty swallowing, dry mouth, spasm in throat, difficulty breathing, flushes and chills, intestinal discomfort, numbing and tingling, sweating, dizziness, motor tension, enhanced arousal and frequent urination. Fear itself has been described as an ineffable and unpleasant feeling. Further feelings characteristic of fear are sense of foreboding, apprehension, tense expectation for the worst, worrying, helplessness, intrusive unpleasant thoughts, depersonalization and derealization. Fear includes also an element of irritability and may pass over into anger. The cognitive manifestations of fear are vigilance, scanning of the environment for signals of danger, difficulty concentrating, narrowed-down perceptual field, limited consideration of alternatives. The behavioral manifestations of fear have been classically defined as fight and flight. "Fight" may be manifested as attacking the danger or trying to destroy it whereas "flight" may be manifested in actual escape, avoidance, freezing ("being paralyzed"), or otherwise increasing the distance or dissociation between oneself and the fright-evoking object. Thus, each of the four components of fear is manifested through different elements. It is likely that at least some of the listed elements, particularly the behavioral ones, are inborn (Lang, 1984).

It is to be expected that not all elements and even not all components are active or fully deployed in all cases of fear. Though the different components are not isomorphic and cannot replace one another, one or another component may be weaker or stronger on a particular occasion or due to specific conditions (e.g., in combat due to training or habituation) (Rachman, 1978). Factor analytic studies of observed and self-reported symptoms suggested a division between somatic over-reactivity (e.g., flushing, palpitations) and cognitive or psychic anxiety (e.g., worrying, restlessness) (Schalling, Cronholm, & Åsberg, 1975). Thus, sometimes the physiological aspects may dominate the field, at other times the emotional-feeling aspect. For example, studies showed that panic can occur without physiological responses (Taylor, Telch & Havvik, 1982-1983) or sometimes without fear (Kushner & Beitman, 1990). Thus, fear is not a homogenous and fixed entity with invariable relations between its different manifestations, but rather a loosely interwoven network of manifestations that may or may not co-occur (Lang, 1978). None of the components is crucial for fear as long as the whole complex, however loosely organized it may be, is focused on the sense of threat or danger, regardless of whether it is known, defined or present.

VARIETIES OF FEAR

Fear comes in many shapes and forms, some of which have earned a special name or label. The most common forms are "fear" and "anxiety". There have been many attempts over the years to distinguish these two varieties. The best known attempt is the Freudian distinction in terms of the location and specificity of the evoking stimulus. The trigger for fear is assumed to be external, specific and known to the individual, whereas the trigger for anxiety is assumed to be internal, non-specific and often unidentified by the individual (Freud, 1926/1959). In more psychodynamic terms, fear is evoked under conditions of threat to physical existence whereas anxiety is evoked under conditions of threat to psychological existence which may be endangered by the activation of drives ("instincts") primarily the sexual and aggressive ones (Michels, Frances, & Shear, 1985). Other distinctions emphasize, for example, the core theme (imminent physical harm in the case of fear, and uncertain existential threat in anxiety) (Lazarus, 1991, pp. 234-5); the response (fight in regard to fear and avoidance in regard to anxiety) (Epstein, 1972); the function of the behavior (active avoidance by removing oneself from danger in the case of fear, and passive avoidance by facilitating entry into the danger area in the case of anxiety) (Gray & McNaughton, 2000); or the evolutionary substratum (reaction to "natural" dangers in the case of fear and threat to attachment in the case of anxiety) (Bowlby, 1973).

There are further differentiations concerning anxiety, elaborated in the DSM-IV manual. Some of these differentiations refer to the intensity of the phenomena. Thus, "panic attack" is defined as intense fear that reaches its peak within 10 minutes, and "generalized anxiety disorder" is excessive anxiety that persists for at least 6 months. Other forms of fear or anxiety are not mentioned in this context of psychopathology because they are relatively mild or moderate. They may include transient fear reactions and perhaps also what Horowitz (1985) calls "anxious or fearful states of mind", such as worried mood, apprehensive vigilance or excited disorganized.

Other differentiations are based on the eliciting stimuli. Thus, phobia is fear that is triggered by a specific stimulus, for example, animals or insects ("animal type"), blood or injection ("blood-injection-injury type"), cancer (cancerophobia) or a specific situation, such as being in a tunnel, elevator, airplane or bridge ("situational type"), social or performance situations ("social phobia") or more generally a location from which escape may be difficult ("agoraphobia"). A special name – hypochondriasis - has been reserved for a fear that is based on misinterpreting bodily symptoms.

It may be appropriate to mention also forms of fear and anxiety characterized by the time of onset, for example a startle reaction that occurs instantly as contrasted with delayed fear that may occur more than a day later (Izard, 1991, p. 300).

Finally, another familiar distinction is based on the circumstances in which the anxiety first occurred. If the anxiety followed exposure to a life-threatening stressor to oneself or others which involved intense fear or horror reactions, we are dealing with a stress disorder – acute (if the reactions last 2 days to 4 weeks and occur within 4 weeks of the event) or postraumatic (if the reactions last for more than 1 month).

Often fears are characterized in terms of the rationality or irrationality of the stimulus or the response of fear. Thus, fears that relate to commonly identified danger stimuli or fear reactions that are moderate or proportionate to the stimulus are considered "rational fears" or normal fears, whereas those that relate to stimuli of 'irrational fears' (e.g., personal fear stimuli such as yellow flickering light) or fear reactions that are excessive or disproportionate to the stimulus are considered irrational fears or abnormal (pathological) or disordered. This distinction may at times be difficult to uphold. For example, prior to the U.S. attack on Iraq on March 19, 2003 many people in Israel were paralyzed with fear for weeks (if not months) and spent thousands of dollars on protective means because they were afraid of a preemptive Iraqi attack on Israel with chemical or biological weapons. Since nothing of the sort happened, the fear may be judged to have been irrational, but it is still an open question whether it was irrational prior to the Iraqi war.

The different kinds of fears are organized by different researchers in line with their particular theories. Thus, Klein (1981) distinguishes between two forms of anxiety – panic attacks and anticipatory anxiety; Gray and McNaughton (2000, p. 45) present a functional classification of the responses to danger in line with the controllability of the situation: when the response is avoidance and the danger avoidable there is phobia but when it is unavoidable there is panic, while when the response is approach the avoidable variety of danger calls forth anxiety and the unavoidable – depression.

STIMULI OF FEAR

The variety of stimuli that may evoke fear responses is indeed astounding. From an ethological perspective, Bowlby (1969) defined four classes of events as "natural clues" to fear: pain or anticipation of pain, being left alone, sudden change of stimulation, and rapid approach. Some objects or input-patterns have been identified as inborn stimuli for fears, e.g., snakes that are fear-evoking also for monkeys (Mineka, Davidson, Cook, & Keir, 1984). Izard (1991, pp. 288-290) complemented the list by adding strangeness (or novelty) and heights. However, a survey of fears conducted by him with college students exposed many more fears not covered by the mentioned categories, e.g., fear of threat to self-esteem, of impending failure or feeling inadequate, of being caught using drugs or being drafted (Izard, 1991, p. 296). We may add to this, fear of success (Horner, 1972), of exams ("test anxiety"), of strangers, of being rejected, of being unpunctual, of commitments, of committing oneself, of losing love or a beloved one, etc.

Factor analyses of self-report questionnaires of fear, that found altogether 194 stimuli of fear, yielded four fear factors: (a) fears about interpersonal events or situations (e.g., fears of criticism, social interaction, conflicts, sexual aggression), (b) fears related to threats to physical and mental health (e.g., fears of death, injuries, illness, blood, surgery, disabilities, suicide, contaminations, homosexuality, losing control over oneself), (c) fears of animals (e.g., domestic, insects, creeping and crawling animals, many often harmless), and (d) agoraphobic fears (e.g., fears of entering public places, getting into open spaces, being in closed spaces, mingling with crowds, traveling alone in trains or buses (Arrindell, Pickersgill, Merckelbach, Ardon, & Cornet, 1991).

These lists barely exhaust the variety of fear-evoking stimuli. Every individual can easily think of further stimuli that evoke fear in him or her at present or have in the past, and of stimuli that in recent times have acquired fright potential for whole populations, such as terror acts, bombardments, anthrax, nerve gas, bubonic fever and other familiar specimen of chemical and biological warfare.

How can we explain the impressive proliferation of fear-evoking stimuli? Evolution and learning are two major factors that seem to play a role. First, humans seem to have been equipped by evolution with the tendency to associate fear with situations or stimuli threatening survival (Seligman, 1971). What exactly threatens survival has been partly determined innately but has been largely left unspecified. This absence of precise specification serves the needs of survival considering the dynamic nature of ever-increasing and changing dangers in the ecological and social environment. But, on the other hand, it leaves the sphere of fear-evoking stimuli open to the effects of the ever-broadening meanings of "threat" and "danger".

The number of dangerous stimuli seems to be large to begin with. It has been large in the prehistoric times of our ancestors and has increased a lot due to modern ecological and political hazards. When we add to these stimuli of actual danger the stimuli that present danger to "psychological" survival (e.g., our self-esteem, reputation and our belongings which we need for our self-esteem), the sphere of fear-evoking stimuli is largely expanded. Further extension takes place by including stimuli that do not actually endanger survival but merely injure or reduce our physical or psychological well-being. Moreover, since if danger materializes we stand to lose a lot (e.g., our physical or psychological existence), an attempt is made to reduce the risk by including in the sphere of fear-evoking stimuli also all those stimuli which may portend threat, which could be dangerous or which could be followed by dangerous stimuli (e.g., pain, blood). The tendency to reduce risk is probably also the reason why fear-evoking stimuli are rarely taken off the list. It is usually explained as due to resistance of extinction in cases of learning in the presence of aversive stimuli (Myers, 1971). But the common-sense consideration "why take a risk" may also contribute to the phenomenon.

Further, the proliferation of fears is also supported by learning. Many studies testify to the easy conditionability of fear. By means of conditioning, stimuli that had been completely neutral to begin with turn into fear-evoking stimuli in their own right after having been coupled a few times with fear-evoking stimuli. The coupling need not occur many times because aversive conditions such as fear hasten the process of conditioning. The process is further accelerated and fears are made less extinguishable if the original fear-evoking stimuli have a high fear potential (e.g., snakes, angry faces) (Öhman, 1993). This implies that many stimuli found in the presence of a fear response or even merely of fear-evoking stimuli will assume a fear-evocative potential. For example, people who have been exposed to painful stimuli in a medical setting, may be scared when they walk near the clinic or hospital where this has taken place; clothes worn on the occasion of a scary experience may assume a frightening potential; the melody of a voice that has announced to us some frightening news becomes fear-evocative in its own right.

Conditioning is only one form of learning. Fears proliferate also through other forms of learning, such as personal experience, hearing from others, watching others ("modeling"), or getting information from books and the media. Originally few people knew about anthrax but they learned to fear it when they learned about it from the media. Many people "inherit", so to say, fears of their parents about which they learn as children from the parents (e.g., "my mother told me that glass splinters are dangerous and may penetrate the skin"). This kind of learning is often called "warning". Fears acquired in that way are maintained often because we do not get a chance to test them. Some of the learning may be based on misunderstanding or lack of information. This is the basis for many childhood fears that get carried over into adulthood for reasons similar to those mentioned earlier (e.g., tendency not to take a risk, no opportunity to test them). Moreover, in many cases learning preserves only the "end-result" or the bottom line: 'X is scary', deleting with time the context, the reasons, the source and other details surrounding the acquisition of the fear. This deletion procedure is economical in terms of learning and memory storage but renders it difficult to critically examine the basis for a fear at a later time when we would have been ready for this cognitively and emotionally.

DETERMINANTS OF FEAR

Why the reaction of fear exists at all may be accounted for in terms of evolution and inborn tendencies of the species for self-preservation. On this level the answer would be that we react with fear because we have been endowed with the prewired reactions of fight or flight to certain types of stimuli. This answer, however, does not take account of the great inter-individual variability in the experience and response of fear. Therefore it is necessary to consider further levels, which will involve additional psychological systems. The major ones would be cognition and motivation.

THE COGNITIVE DETERMINANTS OF FEAR AND ANXIETY

The involvement of cognition in the determination of emotions is generally accepted. Indeed, emotion is commonly considered as the function of physiological changes and cognitions (Power & Dalgleish, 1997). However, there is much less unanimity concerning the kind of cognitions that are involved in emotions and their role. In the present context we will present the common views that focus on the proximal cognitive characteristics of fear stimuli and will complement them with the distal cognitive characteristics of fear stimuli based on meaning assignment tendencies.

The Proximal Cognitive Characteristics of Fear Stimuli

The common proximal cognitive characterizations of fear stimuli are based on the appraisal theory which assumes that there are different appraisals related to each emotion and that they precede and determine the evocation of emotion (Roseman & Smith, 2001). Accordingly, the appraisal approach is focused on the contents of the stimuli and attempts to present the contents in terms of more general features or variables. For example, fear is described as a reaction which expresses being *displeased* at the *prospect* of an *undesirable event*, whereby the variables affecting its intensity are the degree to which the event is undesirable and the likelihood of the event (Ortony, Clore, & Collins, 1988, pp. 112-8). Notably, this description sets fear as the direct opposite of the emotion of 'hope' which is described as being pleased at the prospect of a desirable event. Also other appraisal theorists agree in describing fear as unpleasant and obstructive to one's own goals, characterized by a high degree of uncertainty about whether one will be able to escape or avoid the anticipated unpleasant outcome (Ellsworth & Smith, 1988; Roseman, Antoniou, & Jose, 1996; Frijda, 1987). Accordingly, the dimensions these theorists define and apply are valence (negative), goal conduciveness (obstructive), relevance (high), specificity of event (high), certainty of event (considered by some high and by others low), one's own powerlessness (high), controllability (low), novelty (mostly considered high), agency (mostly considered as due to circumstances, sometimes – other person), urgency (high), legitimacy (low), and modifiability of the expected outcome (considered by most as low, by some as high).

This rational logical analysis of the conditions for the elicitation of fear assumes that the cognitive antecedents are essentially conscious, and amenable to voluntary control. It focuses on the interface between the stimulus qualities and the individual's tendencies without fully representing either. The attractive aspect seems to be the formal modeling character of this approach. However, the empirical support is still fragmentary (Scherer, Schorr, & Johnstone, 2001). Be it as it may, the appraisal approach deals merely with the surface of the fear stimuli and needs to be complemented by an approach that enables deeper insight into the involved cognitive processes.

Meaning Assignment Tendencies of Fear and Anxiety

From the point of view of psychology, it does not make sense to refer to stimuli or describe stimuli as detached from the human being who perceives these stimuli. In order to understand the impact of stimuli in a psychological framework, the bare minimum we have to consider is the manner in which the stimuli are processed by the individual's information-processing system. This is made possible within the framework of the psychosemantic approach, which describes how stimuli are assigned meanings (Kreitler & Kreitler, 1985b, 1990b).

Meaning is defined as cognitive contents focused on a referent. The referent can be any input, large or small, physical or psychological, concrete or abstract, internal or external, such as a person, an object, a concept, an event or a situation, a thought or a memory, or a whole historical period. The cognitive contents could describe the referent in terms of its structure, function, material, sensory qualities and so on. The referent and the cognitive contents together form a meaning unit which is characterized in terms of five classes of variables: (a)

Meaning Dimensions, which describe the contents assigned to the referent, e.g., the material of the referent, its parts, its structure, its sensory qualities and locational qualities; (b) Types of Relation, which describe the directness of the relation between the referent and the contents, e.g., an attributive relation, which is direct, or the comparative or metaphoric, which use the mediation of other referents; (c) Forms of Relation, which describe the form of the relation between the referent and the contents, e.g., positive or negative, total or partial, declarative or questioning; (d) Forms of Expression, which describe the mode of expression of the whole unit, e.g., verbal, motional, graphic; and (e) Shifts of Referent, which describe the relations between the referent of the meaning unit and the input or the previous referent, e.g., identical, opposite, partial. The five classes of characterizations are called meaning variables (see list of meaning variables in Table 1).

Table 1. Variables of the System of Meaning

1. Meaning Dimensions (DIM)			
1	Contextual allocation	13	Size and dimensionality
2	Range of inclusion: a. Subclasses; b. Parts	14	Quantity and number
		15	Locational qualities
3	Function, purpose and role	16	Temporal qualities
4	Actions and potentialities for action: a. By referent; b. To/with referent	17	Possession: a. By referent ; b. Of referent (belongingness)
5	Manner of occurrence and operation	18	Development
6	Antecedents and causes	19	Sensory qualities[e]: a. Of referent; b. Perceived by referent
7	Consequences and results		
8	Domain of application: a. Referent as subject; b. Referent as object	20	Feelings and emotions: a. Evoked by referent; b. Experienced by referent
9	Material	21	Judgments and evaluations: a. About referent; b. Of referent
10	Structure		
11	State and changes in state	22	Cognitive qualities: a. Evoked by referent; b. Of referent
12	Weight and mass		
Types of Relation[a] (TR)			
1	Attributive: a. Qualities to substance; b. Actions to agent	3	Exemplifying-Illustrative: a. Instance; b. Situation; c. Scene
2	Comparative: a. Similar; b.Different; c. Complementary; d. Relational	4	Metaphoric-Symbolic: a. Interpretation; b. Conventional metaphor; c. Original metaphor; d. Symbol
Forms of Relation[b] (FR)			
1	Propositional	5	Disjunctive
2	Partial	6	Normative (obligatory)
3	Universal	7	Questioning
4	Conjunctive	8	Desired
Shifts of Referent[c] (SR)			
1	Identical	8	Linguistic label
2	Opposite	9	Grammatical variation
3	Partial	10	Former meaning values combined
4	Input + addition	11	Superordinate
5	Former meaning value	12	Synonym a. Original language; b. Translated; c. Other medium
6	Associated on same level		
7	Unrelated	13	Former implicit meaning value
Forms of Expression[d] (FE)			
1	verbal	4	Auditory
2	Graphic	5	Object or situation
3	Motor		

[a] Modes of meaning: Lexical mode: TR1+TR2; Personal mode: TR3+TR4
[b] Each of the FRs has two forms: a. Positive; b. Negative
[c] Close SR: 1+9+12   Medium SR: 3+4+5+6+10+11   Distant SR: 2+7+8+13
[d] Each of the FEs has three forms: a. Direct; b. Described; c. By means of available materials. The studies described in this chapter did not make use of FEs.
[e] This meaning dimension includes a listing of subcategories of the different senses/sensations that may also be grouped into "external" and "internal".

The meaning variables represent forms of assigning meaning to inputs. Each person tends to use some more often than others. A meaning test enables assessing the frequency with which each person tends to use each of the meaning variables. The meaning test requests the individual to communicate the meaning of 11 stimulus words (e.g., street, bicycle). The meaning communications are analyzed into meaning units, each of which is coded in terms of the five classes of meaning variables. Summing the frequencies with which each meaning variable was used by the individual in the meaning test yields the meaning profile of the individual, namely, the set of frequencies with which that person tends to use each of the meaning variables.

The meaning profile is important because it provides information about the kind of meanings that the person tends to assign to various inputs. The meaning variables that have high frequency in the meaning profile are those that the person uses preferentially, or by default. Thus, if the meaning dimension Locational Qualities is salient in a person's meaning profile, we may conclude that the person will notice locations, will memorize easily routes and maps, will readily solve problems that have to do with locations, and so on. If for example the meaning dimension Temporal Qualities has a low frequency in the person's meaning profile, that person may be expected to have difficulties or fail in cognitive functions that require consideration of time or temporal cues.

In order to learn about the meaning variables that mediate the response of fear or anxiety, several studies were conducted (Kreitler & Kreitler, 1985a, 1987a, 1988). The studies were designed to identify the meaning variables characteristic of individuals high in anxiety or fear as compared with those low in anxiety or fear. In this set of studies anxiety and fear were assessed by means of standard questionnaires. Each group of participants responded to the meaning test and to one anxiety or fear scale. The results yielded a set of meaning variables that were used with high frequency or with low frequency by the anxious or fearful participants (see Table 2).

The findings show that anxious individuals tend to focus on their own sensations, feelings & state, on evaluations and cognitions, and on temporal cues, but overlook major aspects of interpersonally-shared reality, such as action possibilities, functions and consequences. Further, they have a restricted grasp of reality in general (viz., low on attributive type of relation and concrete examples) and tend to shift away from it (viz., shift away from the input) and flee into the metaphoric mode of experiencing. Notably, there is also evidence for narrowing down of cognitive activity (viz., lower number of meaning values).

The pattern of meaning variables characteristic for fear includes focusing on sensations, feelings and evaluations, that represent the internal sphere, coupled with focusing on different aspects of external reality, such as locations, size, objects involved in the situation (viz. range of application), while overlooking other aspects, mainly functions, consequences and temporal cues. In general they have a good grasp of reality (viz., high on attributive type of relation and concrete examples), and tend to deal with the input and its extensions (viz., shift to previous meaning values).

Table 2: Meaning Variables Correlated Significantly with Scales of Anxiety and of Fear

The scales of anxiety and fear[a]	Meaning variables correlated significantly with the scales
Anxiety scales: Correlations with all 7 anxiety scales; in all cases correlations in the same direction	**Meaning Dimensions:** Actions by referent [neg.] Sensory qualities experienced by referent Feelings & emotions experienced by referent Judgements & evaluations about referent Judgements & evaluations by referent Cognitive qualities of referent **Types of Relation:** Attributive: quality to substance or action to agent [neg.]
Anxiety scales: Correlations with 2-6 of the 7 anxiety scales; in some cases not all correlations in the same direction	**Meaning Dimensions:** Function, purpose & role [2 neg., 1 pos.] Consequences & results [2 neg., 1 pos.] State & possible changes in state [4 pos.] Locational qualities [1 neg., 1 pos.] Temporal qualities [4 pos.] Feelings & emotions evoked by referent [2 neg.,1 pos.] Cognitive qualities characterizing referent [4 pos.] **Types of Relation:** Comparative: similarity [2 pos.] Exemplifying-illustrative: exemplifying instance [2 neg.] Metaphoric-symbolic: metaphor [5 pos.] **Referent Shifts:** Identical with input or previous [3 neg.] Total number of meaning values: [3 neg.]
Fear scales: Correlations with all 5 fear scales; in all cases correlations in the same direction	**Meaning Dimensions:** Function, purpose and role [neg.] Results and consequences [neg.] Range of application Size and dimensions Locational qualities Temporal qualities [neg.] Sensory qualities experienced by referent Feelings and emotions experienced or evoked by referent Judgements and evaluations held or evoked by referent **Types of Relation:** Attributive: quality to substance or action to agent Exemplifying-illustrative: exemplifying instance **Referent Shifts:** To previous meaning value

[a] Anxiety scales: The IPAT Anxiety Scale Questionnaire (Krug, Scheier & Cattell, 1976), The Manifest Anxiety Scale (Taylor, 1953), The State-Trait Anxiety Inventory (STAI-2) (Spielberger, Gorsuch, Lushene & Vagg, 1977), The Self-Rating Anxiety Scale (SAS) (Zung & Cavenar, 1980), The Test Anxiety Scale (Sarason, 1978), The Zuckerman Inventory of Personal Relations ZIPERS (Zuckerman, 1979), The Anxiety Test MIHALI (adapted for adults) (Ziv, Levin & Israeli, 1974). Fear scales were those by Braun & Reynolds (1969), Geer (1965), Wolpe & Lang (1964), & two by Kreitler & Kreitler (1990b).

Comparing the patterns for anxiety and fear shows that they are different despite similarities in various respects. The pattern for anxiety is slightly more extensive (it includes 18 variables as compared with 15 in fear). The two patterns share an identical core that forms about a quarter of the patterns (22.2% of the anxiety pattern and 26.6% of the fear pattern). Further similar percentages of variables fulfill opposite roles in the two patterns, whereas the rest consists of meaning variables unique to anxiety or to fear. Notably, the core shared by anxiety and fear represents focusing on the internal sphere of sensations and feelings, but on the whole fear includes a more salient focus on interpersonally-shared reality than anxiety.

The relevance of the described meaning variables to anxiety and fear was confirmed in experiments which showed changes in the amount of anxiety following manipulation of the meaning variables (Kreitler & Kreitler, 1987a). After strengthening the tendencies for the meaning variables of anxiety in the course of a brief 30 minutes training session, participants had higher levels of anxiety (a mean increase of 19.5% in state anxiety scores) and, as expected, lower performance on logical problems (a mean decrease of 18.8% in correct solutions). Parallel findings were obtained after a training session designed to weaken the tendencies for the meaning variables of anxiety (mean decrease of 24.4% in anxiety and a mean increase of 21.9% in correct solutions). Similar procedures of weakening anxiety were applied for therapeutic purposes with individuals who had been struck by shock following terror acts and have subsequently been developed into a first-aid module for the treatment of fear or anxiety (Kreitler, 2001).

Accordingly, the meaning variables constituting the patterns of anxiety and of fear define meaning assignment tendencies that are used in the course of information processing in situations relevant for anxiety or fear. This indicates that individuals endowed with the meaning assignment tendencies of fear or anxiety use the described tendencies in identifying inputs. For example, when confronted with any stimulus they would focus on their own sensations, feelings and evaluations more than on the properties of the input itself. Further, in the case of anxiety they would shift away from the input itself, they would overlook the regular interpersonally-shared modes of attributing qualities to the stimulus, but would instead indulge in metaphors that may readily lead to a catastrophizing mood (e.g., "this is the end of the world", "I feel as if the earth is trembling under me", "My whole life is crumbling like a house of cards" etc.).

Fear and Anxiety and Meaning Assignment

Assigning meaning to inputs is not an act but a process. This implies that in the first phase only a few input features are perceived (viz. size, location) and are used for assigning a label to the input. In the second phase, following the determination of the label, further stimulus features are detected, in line with whether the label indicated an organic or nonorganic object. The amplification of the perceived information enables confirmation of the referent as well as a consolidation and expansion of its meaning. In the third phase, the meaning of the input is further elaborated in line with the available information and the meaning assignment tendencies characteristic of the individual. Thus, the first phase is input-driven, the second label-driven and the third meaning-driven (Kreitler & Kreitler, 1984).

It is likely that already in the input-driven phase a mechanism set to discover potential threat in the environment is operative. The features relevant for threat may be singled out as indicating threat on a hereditary basis or by conditioning (Öhman, 1993; Öhman & Soares, 1993). Two effects may be assumed in regard to such stimuli in the label-driven phase. First, such stimuli activate directly the arousal system, which may result in physiological responses. Second, such stimuli are selected for preferential treatment by the "significance evaluation system" which matches the label to a set of memory stored schemata in order to identify signals of danger or threat (Mathews, 1990). The physiological responses are likely to be perceived instantly by the anxiety- or fear-prone individuals in line with their meaning assignment tendencies (viz. focus on sensations and feelings). The matching process with stored schemata of danger stimuli is probably very fast in the case of anxiety- or fear-prone individuals because it is so habitual with these individuals. The enhanced arousal may contribute to the utility and speed of the process. The danger signals identified in the label-driven phase are likely to be elaborated to advantage in the meaning-driven phase in line with the individual's meaning assignment tendencies. Awareness of the physiological responses may be integrated with the identified danger signals to enhance the individual's anxiety or fear response. Thus, in each subsequent phase there occurs an enhancement of the anxiety or fear response in a spiral-kind mode.

In conclusion, fear and anxiety may occur in the different phases of elaborating the meaning of the input. It seems likely that they may occur already in the input-driven first phase of meaning elaboration, in the form of a startle reaction or a sudden surge of anxiety. These reactions would appear automatically, as manifestations of the identified input. They are in fact instances of "meaning action" which represents unconditioned or conditioned responses released by the mere identification of the input. They may be considered as meaning values of the input. In the label-driven second phase of meaning elaboration, fear and anxiety may occur in the form of a regular fear or anxiety feeling. They are dependent on the elaborated meaning of the label and include the feeling (experiential), physiological and cognitive components of fear or anxiety. These responses are much more personal and flexible than the startle responses since they depend on a more elaborate meaning generation. In the meaning-driven third phase of meaning elaboration, the meanings of the identified input, of one's own response and of the situation as a whole are taken into consideration in order to determine whether a behavioral act will ensue or not. The elaboration of meaning in this stage is focused, as it were, on questions, such as "Do I have to respond?", "Is action necessary?", "Am I involved in a manner that calls for a behavior on my part?" Passing from the experiential to the behavioral level of responding requires the involvement of further systems – the motivational and actional.

THE MOTIVATIONAL DETERMINANTS OF FEAR AND ANXIETY

The purely cognitive determinants of fear and anxiety refer to identifying the input as danger or threat signals. The identification of the input as danger or threat evokes fear or anxiety. It is of paramount importance to emphasize that the evocation of fear or anxiety is not followed or accompanied automatically or invariably by overt behavioral responses of fear or anxiety, let alone specific responses.

Following the identification of a threat signal, various response alternatives are possible. It is absolutely possible that the person will only experience fear or anxiety internally, but will not behave externally in line with fear or anxiety. That person may go on doing whatever she or he were doing as if there were no fear or anxiety at all. The standard response alternatives of fight or flight, namely, attacking the stimulus or escaping from it in some form, are possible. But they are not the only responses likely to be observed. Slowing down and watching vigilantly the developments are further responses that have been described. Another alternative is a behavior expressing despair and helplessness, namely, giving up any attempt to defend oneself. The list of possible behaviors should include also various more pathological responses, such as a generalized anxiety response or a panic attack.

The mere identification of threatening stimuli does not evoke responses of fear and anxiety. If a behavioral response is to occur, what is needed at this point is a motivational disposition to respond in line with fear and anxiety. If there is a motivational disposition, responses of fear or anxiety will be observed if appropriate behavioral programs are available. The motivation and behavioral programs will be described in terms of the cognitive orientation theory (Kreitler & Kreitler, 1976, 1982, 2003).

The Motivational Disposition

The motivational disposition for the behaviors of fear and anxiety is grounded in beliefs characterized in terms of their form and contents. In terms of form, they represent four types of beliefs: beliefs about goals, beliefs about norms (how one should behave), beliefs about oneself and beliefs about reality and others (how things usually are or happen). In terms of contents, the beliefs refer to themes representing underlying meanings of the behavior of interest, in our case - fear and anxiety.

The underlying meanings of fear and anxiety include, for example, the following: viewing the world as a hostile place, avoidance of getting help from others, mistrusting others, impossibility to rely on others, evaluating oneself as weak and helpless, placing high demands on oneself, assuming a lot depends on oneself and not merely on chance or circumstances, grasping oneself as responsible for events and situations, expecting that the worst possible scenario in any situation will actually occur, situations do not change, everything is deterministic, losses tend to occur according to the all or nothing principle (if they occur at all, then everything falls apart), evil to oneself or others can be averted by the right action.

The mentioned themes represent a general core of fear and anxiety responses. If a person assumes in general that situations do not tend to resolve themselves of their own accord, that expected evil is likely to occur, that one is responsible, and that right actions can produce good results – it is likely that the person will undertake action in response when fear or anxiety have been evoked. However, beliefs supporting the mentioned themes do not necessarily lead to the evocation of a particular response, but enable rather the evocation only of a general class of responses, probably of the more active fighting kind. In order to predict what kind of behavior will be actually manifested it is necessary to get information about additional beliefs. For example, responses of evasion, escape, fleeing, avoidance or hiding are grounded further in beliefs that confrontations are useless, that attacks and aggressive acts are to be avoided, that direct results are to be preferred to indirect ones, or that it is pointless to prove one is a hero or to gain the esteem of others. Again, responses of despair and helplessness may ensue when the underlying beliefs are that no one person can achieve anything, help is neither likely nor useful, one is not responsible, occurrences do not depend on the individual and fate rules all.

The themes relevant for different kinds of responses of fear and anxiety are identified by a standard procedure developed in the framework of the cognitive orientation theory (Kreitler & Kreitler, 1982). The themes themselves do not refer directly to fear or anxiety or danger or threat but to the underlying meanings of fear and anxiety. They appear in the form of beliefs of four types: about oneself, about rules and norms, about goals and about reality or others. Thus, after the themes are identified in pretests, they are presented in the form of beliefs of four types in questionnaire format for purposes of assessment. For example, the theme of getting help from others may be formulated as follows: 'I do not like others to help me in anything I do' (belief about self), 'One should not expect help from others' (belief about norms), 'I want to be able to do things by myself without the help of others' (belief about goals), and 'When others help you they actually interfere with your work and meddle things up' (belief about reality and others).

Not all beliefs are necessary for the emergence of a motivational disposition. What is needed is that a sufficient number of beliefs of at least three belief types supports the behavior of interest. A large body of data shows that if a person endorses a sufficient number of beliefs in at least three of the four belief types that behavior is likely to occur (e.g., Kreitler & Kreitler, 1982, 1987b, 1990a, 1991, 1993; Kreitler et al., 1994). In more theoretical terms, if there is sufficient support for a certain behavior in at least three belief types a motivational vector is formed (also called "behavioral intent"), which represents the motivational disposition for that behavior (see Figure 1). Thus, according to the cognitive orientation theory, behavior occurs not as a result of a conscious decision, a weighing of pros and cons in a rational manner, or comparing gains with losses. Behavior is the product of the integrated directionalities of meanings and beliefs that are clustered without the voluntary or conscious control of the individual. When there is a sufficient support of relevant beliefs it flows naturally without effort or obstacles. Conversely, when there is no sufficient motivational support through relevant beliefs, no amount of determined decision would bring forth the desired behavior and the individual would be left wondering why he or she are unable to act or do what they have decided to do.

Figure 1: The vector of the motivational disposition according to the cognitive orientation theory

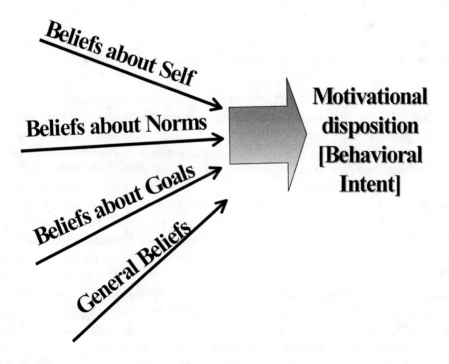

The Behavioral Program

The formation of a motivational disposition for a specific behavior is a necessary but still not a sufficient condition for the manifestation of the behavior. Also the actional system has to be involved. Accordingly, it is necessary to retrieve and adapt for application a behavioral program designed to implement the motivational disposition. Behavioral program is the term used to refer to schemes of action based on hierarchically structured sets of operational instructions that are, on the one hand, sufficiently stable to enable embedding of habits and other action components, and are, on the other hand, sufficiently flexible to be adaptable to varying situational conditions. Behavioral programs are operative in all action spheres, including the cognitive, emotional, behavioral and physiological. In the case of fear and anxiety a great variety of behavioral programs is usually available. Some of the behavioral programs are innate, such as the basic fight or flight behaviors, as well as freezing. Others are the joint products of inborn schemes and modifications provided by learning and modeling, such as panic attacks. Many forms of behavior in this context are largely or purely learned, whereas some may be ad-hoc formations in view of current needs and options. Part of the training of individuals expected to function under fear-evoking conditions consists in teaching them behavioral programs ready for enactment when necessary or possible. This refers not only to soldiers in preparation for combat but also to large numbers of civilians expected to be exposed to dangers.

However, the availability of action modes as such would not guarantee the enactment of the corresponding behaviors or, for that matter, the overcoming of fear and anxiety. It is necessary to make sure that in addition to the behavioral programs there is an understructure of meanings and beliefs adequate for the formation of the motivational disposition in the desired direction.

CONCLUDING REMARKS

In the course of centuries and in the framework of research, many descriptive terms have been attributed to fear and anxiety. They have been called basic, unpleasant, dangerous, difficult, "toxic", normal or pathologic, among other adjectives. We would like to add the epithet "complex" in order to emphasize the multiplicity of determinants that contribute to the evocation and determination of these emotions. For the evocation of fear or anxiety, the bare minimum that would be necessary is a stimulus, a full-fledged meaning assignment system making use of memory schemata and appraisal mechanisms, a motivational system, able to generate a motivational disposition, and an action system, disposing of a variety of behavioral programs. All this needs to be embedded in and integrated by an organism, with very special capacities, trained by evolution to maintain its survival and trained by culture to attain its goals so as to achieve a respectable and satisfying quality of life. It is evident that evolution and culture both contribute to the shaping of fear and anxiety and are shaped by them in turn.

However, beside the "big powers" that play a role in the scene of fear and anxiety, there are the more circumscribed psychological forces that provide more direct handles for investigating these phenomena and for manipulating them. Major among these are meanings and beliefs that may be trained and shaped individually, in groups and in masses not only for enhancing fears – as happens so often - but also for combating fears and overcoming them.

REFERENCES

American Psychiatric Association (1994). *Diagnostic and statistical manual of mental disorders* (4th ed.). Washington, DC: Author.

Arrindell, W. A., Pickersgill, M. J., Merckelbach, H., Ardon, M. A., & Cornet, F. C. (1991). Phobic dimensions: III. Factor analytic approaches to the study of phobic fears: An updated review of findingsobtained with adult subjects. Advances in Behavior Research and Therapy, 13, 73-130.

Bowlby, J. (1969). *Attachment and loss: Vol. I. Attachment.* New York: Basic Books.

Bowlby, J. (1973). *Attachment and loss: Vol. II. Separation, anxiety and anger.* New York: Basic Books.

Braun, P. R., & Reynolds, D. N. (1969). A factor analysis of a 100-item fear survey inventory. *Behavior Research and Therapy, 7,* 399-402.

Ellsworth, P. C., & Smith, C. A. (1988). From appraisal to emotion: Differences among unpleasant feelings. *Motivation and Emotion, 12,* 271-302.

Epstein, S. (1972). The nature of anxiety with emphasis on its relationship to expectancy. In C. D. Spielberger (Ed.). *Anxiety: Current trends in theory and research.* Vol. 2 (pp. 291-337). New York: Academic Press.

Freud, S. (1926/1959). Inhibitions, symptoms and anxiety. In *Standard edition of the complete psychological works Sigmund Freud* (Vol. 20). London: Hogarth Press.

Frijda, N. H. (1987). Emotion, cognitive structure and action tendency. *Cognition and Emotion, 1,* 115-143.

Geer, J. H. (1965). The development of a scale to measure fear. *Behavior Research and Therapy, 3,* 45-53.

Gray, J. A., & McNaughton, N. (2000). *The neuropsychology of anxiety* (2nd ed.). Oxford, England: Oxford University Press.

Horner. M. S. (1972). Toward an understanding of achievement-related conflicts in women. *Journal of Social Issues, 28,* 157-176.

Horowitz, M. J. (1985). Anxious states of mind induced by stress. In A. Hussain Tuma & J. Maser (Eds.), *Anxiety and the anxiety disorders* (pp. 619-631). Hillsdale, N.J.: Erlbaum.

Izard, C.E. (1991). *The psychology of emotions.* New York: Plenum

Klein, D. F. (1981). Anxiety reconceptualized. In D. F. Klein & J. Rabkin (Eds.), Anxiety: New research and changing concepts (pp. 235-265). New York: Raven Press.

Kreitler, H., & Kreitler, S. (1976). *Cognitive orientation and behavior.* New York: Springer Publishing.

Kreitler, H., & Kreitler, S. (1982). The theory of cognitive orientation: Widening the scope of behavior prediction. In B.A. Maher & W. A. Maher (Eds), *Progress in experimental personality research, Vol. 11. Normal personality processes* (pp. 101-169). NY: Academic Press.

Kreitler, S., & Kreitler, S. (1984). Meaning assignment in perception. In W. D. Froehlich, G. J. W. Smith, J. G. Draguns & U. Hentschel (Eds.), *Psychological processes in cognition and personality* (pp. 173-191). Washington: Hemisphere Publishing Corp./McGraw-Hill.

Kreitler, S., & Kreitler, H. (1985a). The psychosemantic determinants of anxiety: A cognitive approach. In H. van der Ploeg, R. Schwarzer & C. D. Spielberger (Eds.), *Advances in test anxiety research,* Vol. 4 (pp. 117-135). Lisse, The Netherlands and Hillsdale, NJ: Swets & Zeitlinger and Erlbaum.

Kreitler, S., & Kreitler, H. (1985b). The psychosemantic foundations of comprehension. *Theoretical Linguistics, 12,* 185-195.

Kreitler, S., & Kreitler, H. (1987a). Modifying anxiety by cognitive means. In R. Schwarzer, H. M. van der Ploeg & C. D. Spielberger (Eds.), *Advances in test anxiety research,* Vol. 5 (pp. 195-206). Lisse, The Netherlands and Hillsdale, NJ: Swets & Zeitlinger and Erlbaum.

Kreitler, S., & Kreitler H. (1987b). The motivational and cognitive determinants of individual planning. *Genetic, Social, and General Psychology Monographs, 113,* 81-107.

Kreitler, S., & Kreitler, H. (1988). Trauma and anxiety: The cognitive approach. *Journal of Traumatic Stress, 1,* 35-56.

Kreitler, H., & Kreitler, S. (1990a). Cognitive primacy, cognitive behavior guidance and their implications for cognitive therapy. *Journal of Cognitive Psychotherapy, 4,* 155-173. Kreitler, S., & Kreitler, H. (1990b). *The cognitive foundations of personality traits.* NY: Plenum.

Kreitler, S., & Kreitler, H. (1991). Cognitive orientation and physical disease or health. *European Journal of Personality, 5,* 109-129.

Kreitler, S., & Kreitler, H. (1993). The cognitive determinants of defense mechanisms. In U. Hentschel, G. Smith, W. Ehlers & J. G. Draguns (Eds), *The concept of defense mechanisms in contemporary psychology: Theoretical, research and clinical perspectives* (pp. 152-183). New York: Springer-Verlag.

Kreitler, S. (2001). Crisis intervention and psychological first-aid. *Psychosoziales Krisenmanagement und Notfallpsychologie* [International Symposium on Crisis Management and Emergency Psychology]. May 14-15, 2001, Vienna, Austria.

Kreitler, S. (2003). The cognitive guidance of behavior. In Jost et al. (Eds.), *The Yin and Yang of social cognition: Perspectives on the social psychology of thought systems.* Washington, DC: APA

Kreitler, S., Chaitchik, S., Kreitler, H., & Weissler, K. (1994). Who will attend tests for the early detection of breast cancer? *Psychology and Health, 9,* 463-483.

Krug, S. E., Scheier, I. H., & Cattell, R. B. (1976). *Handbook for the IPAT anxiety scale.* Champaign, IL: Institute for Personality and Ability Testing.

Kushner, M. G., & Beitman, B. D. (1990). Panic attacks without fear: an overview. *Behavior Research and Therapy, 28,* 469-479.

Lader, M., & Marks, I. (1973). *Clinical anxiety.* London: Heinemann.

Lang, P. J. (1984). Cognition in emotion: Concept and action. In C. E. Izard, J. Kagan & B. Zajonc (Eds.), Emotions, cognition, and behavior (pp. 192-225). New York: Cambridge University Press.

Lazarus, R. S. (1991). *Emotion and adaptation.* New York: Oxford University Press.

Mathews, A. (1990). Why worry? The cognitive function of anxiety. *Behavior Research and Therapy, 28,* 455-468.

Michels, R., Frances, A., & Shear, K. (1985). Psychodynamic models of anxiety. In A. Hussain Tuma & J. Maser (Eds.), *Anxiety and the anxiety disorders* (pp. 595-618). Hillsdale, N.J.: Erlbaum.

Mineka, S., Davisdson, M., Cook, M., & Keir, R. (1984). Observational conditioning of snake fear in rhesus monkeys. *Journal of Abnormal Psychology, 93,* 355-372.

Myers, J. S. (1971). Some effects of noncontingent aversive stimulation. In F. R. Brush (Ed.), *Aversive conditioning and learning* (pp. 469-536). New York: Academic Press.

Öhman, A. (1993). Stimulus prepotency and fear: Data and theory. In N. Birbaumer& A. Öhman (Eds.), *The organization of emotion: Cognitive, clinical and psychophysiologic perspectives.* Toronto, Canada: Hogrefe.

Öhman, A., & Soares, J. J. F. (1993). On the automaticity of phobic fear: Conditioned skin consductance responses to masked phobic stimuli. *Journal of Abnormal Psychology, 102.*

Ortony, A., Clore, G. L., & Collins, A. (1988). *The cognitive structure of emotions.* New York: Cambridge University Press.

Power, M., & Dalgleish, T. (1997). *Cognition and emotion: From order to disorder.* Hove, East Sussex, UK: Psychology Press.

Rachman, S. J. (1978). *Fear and courage.* London: Freeman.

Roseman, I. J., Antoniou, A. A., & Jose, P. E. (1996). Apprisal determinants of emotions: Contrasting a more accurate and comprehensive theory. *Cognition and Emotion, 10,* 241-277.

Roseman, I. J., & Smith, C. A. (2001). Appraisal theory: Overview, assumptions, varieties, controversies. In K. R. Scherer, A. Schorr & T. Johnstone (Eds.), *Appraisal processes in emotion: Theory, methods, research* (pp.3-19). New York: Oxford University Press.

Sarason, I. G. (1978).The Test Anxiety Scale: Concept and research. In C. D. Spielberger & I. G. Sarason (Eds.), *Stress and anxiety* (Vol. 5) (pp. 193-216). Washington, DC: Hemisphere.

Schalling, D., Cronholm, B., & Åsberg, M. (1975). Components of state and trait anxiety as related to personality and arousal. In I. Levi (Ed.), *Emotions: Their parameters and measurement.* New York: Raven Press.

Scherer, K. R., Schorr, A., & Johnstone, T. (Eds.), *Appraisal processes in emotion: Theory, methods, research.* New York: Oxford University Press.

Seligman, M. (1971). Phobias and preparedness. *Behavior Therapy, 2,* 307-320.

Spielberger, C. D., Gorsuch, R. L., Lushene, R. E., & Vagg, P. R. (1977). *The state-trait anxiety inventory: Form Y.* Tampa, Fl: University of South Florida.

Taylor, J. A. (1953). A personality scale of manifest anxiety. *Journal of Abnormal and Social Psychology, 48,* 285-290.

Taylor, C. B., Telch, M. J., & Havvik, D. (1982-1983). Ambulatory heart rate changes during panic attacks. *Journal of Psychiatric Research, 17,* 261-266.

Wolpe, J., & Lang, P. J. (1964). A fear survey schedule for use in behavior therapy. *Behavior Research and Therapy, 2,* 27-30.

Ziv, A., Levin, I., & Israeli, R. (1974). *MIHALI, an anxiety test for children.* Tel-Aviv: Tel-Aviv University Publications.

Zuckerman, M. (1979). *Sensation seeking: Beyond the optimal level of arousal.* Hillsdale, NJ: Erlbaum.

Zung, W. W. K., & Cavenar, J. O., Jr. (1980). Assessment scales and techniques. In I. L. Kutash, L. B. Schlesinger & Associates (Eds.), *Handbook on stress and anxiety.* San Francisco: Jssey-Bass.

Chapter 2

PSYCHOBIOLOGY OF FEAR

Erzsébet Marosi[‡], Guillermina Yañez,
Csilla Varga, Jorge Bernal and Mario Rodríguez
National University of Mexico,
FES Iztacala. Department of Neurosciences

ABSTRACT

The purpose of this chapter is to explore current knowledge and concepts on the nature of emotion. In a short historical review I mention the different theories on emotion and the way emotion supposedly works. Then, a short review on the anatomy of brain circuits follows that produce and modulate emotional functioning. At last, the characteristics of rational and irrational fear and anxiety, its autonomic responses and the clinical disorders related to them will be addressed.

Keywords: emotion, amygdala, anxiety disorders, therapy.

MEANINGS OF EMOTION

To understand the neural bases of fear and other emotional states and responses, it is necessary to understand the principles and mechanism by which emotion is acquired, stored and functioning in the brain. Emotion is a phenomenon of thousand aspects, either we fight against it because of our sufferings or we bless it because of our happiness or we blame it because of our distorted decisions, but life without it, is a colorless and tasteless boredom, as we can see it in patients with alexithymia.

If we want to understand it, maybe the first question to ask is: What might be the purpose or the role of emotion within the cognitive system?

Rolls (1995) determined its functions as follows:

[‡] Authors' address: Apartado Postal 82. Atizapàn de Zaeagoza, Estado de México. C.P. 52971. Phone: (525) 85016831; e-mail: marosi@servidor.unam.mx.

1. Elicitation of autonomic responses
2. Flexibility of behavioral responses to reinforcing stimuli.
3. Motivation
4. Communication
5. Social bonding
6. The current mood state can affect the cognitive evaluation
7. Emotion facilitates the storage of memories
8. Direct behavior
9. Triggers the recall of memories stored.

These points deserve serious consideration.

Elicitation of Autonomic Responses

Stretching back to a time when early mammals had to survive and breed in a hostile environment, full of deadly danger, survival meant acting rapidly.

As predators strike hard and fast, fear system had to be instantaneously activated. The autonomic responses prepared the body for an optimal condition that assured an efficient fight or an efficient flight. Autonomic responses are designated to make it possible. The autonomic nervous system is primarily an effector system. In its functions controls smooth muscle, heart muscle and exocrine glands. Sympathetic division governs the "fight-or-flight" reactions, whereas the parasympathetic system is responsible for rest and digest. Normally, autonomic adjustments are not accessible to consciousness, they are involuntary. As they accompany all emotional reactions, it is easy to identify them as the emotion itself. It is a frequent and common everyday experience that we feel galloping heart beat or "butterflies in the stomach" without any apparent reason and we seek for the motive. Based on that decision we make a hint of the emotion involved in this feeling. This reaction is quick and efficient, but permits erroneous identification of the feeling involved or wrong decisions. The conscious reconsideration is posterior to emotional reaction and is due to rectify the situation.

As LeDoux (1996) said: "False negatives" are more costly to nature than "false positives". The system makes more mistakes of responding to non-harmful stimulus, rather than refraining from responding. This is because conscious mental activity is slow, as it operates independently of consciousness. It explains why rational decisions are posterior to basic and quick emotional reactions.

Motivation

Sexual intercourse has an imperative importance for nature. It has to do with the perpetuation and maintenance of genetic material, so it is necessary to mark the event with some strong drive to be sure, that species do not take it with indifference. If nature permits free decisions on the topic of making sex or not, the number of off-springs would reduce dramatically. Strong emotion is a wonderful manner to make species interested in practicing sex, even in situations, when not to do it would be much more comfortable. It seems to be a very important reason that explains the necessity of emotions to be evolved.

Emotion Facilitates the Storage of Memories
and Triggers The Recall of Memories Store

Facilitation of storage and recall is the major profit of the emotional system and has the objective of having life-saving experiences in hand, to be more apt for survival. Emotion is a bridge that directly puts important information into the long-term memory and makes it easily available, when it is necessary. The ancient Greeks told: "The mother of the knowledge is the repetition". It is true, if we want to learn the date of Napoleon's birthday, we have to repeat it endlessly. Shortly after that the repetition is ceased, the information gets lost. This is not the case for the emotionally important information. We need not repeat the day, when our child was born, or the day when we first fell in love, because we never forget it. The best way of learning and recalling is being highly interested in the matter.

Emotional memories mediated by the amygdala system are indelible. The memories persist even after emotional behavior is extinguished. Extinction appears to involve cortical inhibition of indelible memories. The role of therapy may be to allow the cortex to establish more effective inhibition and efficient synaptic links with the amygdala. It is worth to consider the issue of infantile amnesia. It is considered that our inability to remember early experiences may be because the hippocampus is not sufficiently mature to allow us to form declarative or conscious memories until around the second or third year of the life; the system that encodes memories is not fully functional. At the same time, we know that early trauma can have long lasting influences on behavioral and mental states, which suggests that the system that encodes these unconscious traumatic memories is present and functional. There are several implications of these observations. 1.) Early memories may be emotional memories and not declarative ones. 2.) Early memories may be inaccessible to consciousness not because of active repression, but because of the time course of brain maturation and 3.) the extent to which one can gain conscious access may be limited (LeDoux, 1995).

Tooby and Cosmides (1995) said: The neural organization of the brain depends on understanding the functional organization of its cognitive devices. The brain originally came into existence, and accumulated its particular set of design features, only because these features functionally contributed to the organism's propagation. This brain organization has been carried out by natural selection.

Evolution has equipped mammals with a readiness to easily associate fear with recurrent threats and never forget it. There are certain stimuli that are pre-wired in the brain because they have been perennially dangerous to our ancestors. Ecological pressure during evolution has shaped emotion systems in animals, including humans, to prepare them to deal with problems encountered in their life. Emotional systems have their roots far back in mammalian evolution, their origin is with primitive organisms with much less neocortex than humans and without any linguistic capacity. Thus, they had functioned unconsciously for millions of years before they eventually came to exist in brains into which evolution gradually inserted capacities for language and conscious experience. Both evolution and social learning contributed to the establishment of those events which called forth one or another emotion (Öhman, 1999).

Social Bonding

This point has two important implications:

1. Mothers' identification has inherent meaning even without an opportunity for an infant to have learned it. Most animals have this information genetically printed, and maybe humans, too. However, child care is much longer in humans than in any other animal, emotional involvement helps to prolong the interest in it.

2. Highly developed animal groups have a hierarchical organization, where all group members give themselves in charge to the most strong, most intelligent and consequently the most apt member to help survival. Higher the rank on the evolutional scale, more emotion is necessary to keep the rule.

Communication

The speculation suggests that communication is a cognitive function not necessarily needs emotional involvement. The relation seems to be inversed. Apparently, emotion was not made to facilitate communication, but communication was made to facilitate expression of emotion.

Flexibility of Behavioral Responses to Reinforcing Stimuli. The Current Mood State Can Affect the Cognitive Evaluation and Direct Behavior

All these points do not seem to be functions, but by-products that can accompany emotional responses or not.

THEORIES

In order to deal with fear, it is necessary to give a short review to the way in which the theories of emotion developed and show the current state of ideas about it.

All emotions are impulses for action. The word "emotion" derives from the Latin verb "movere" that means move. The prefix "e" means away that refers to withdraw or retire from a possible danger.

Early philosophers were cognitivists. Plato divided the soul (or mind) in three functions: desire, reason and passion, and regarded the reason as the highest of them, as the moral agency holding destructive animal passions in check. The role of reason in the control of the passion implicates the concept of coping. This coping is an integral feature of emotion that later on, in the Middle Ages caused a lot of ethical and religious concerns.

Aristotle considered human nature as "matter in a structured form". For him, emotion and action depended on reason. He held the opinion, that reason must control the emotion, and the arousal of an emotion also depends on reason.

Stoics considered the emotion as the lack of virtue. The Epicureans saw emotion as a cognitively induced and directed feeling, which may or may not result in behavior. Aquinas placed the emotion in the body and Descartes placed it again in the soul. This dualistic point of view prevailed until this century in spite of the fact that numerous philosophers and scientists declared that it is a brain functions, like any other. Spinoza also called the emotion a bodily event: he seems to have held the view that, because of their subterranean sources in the conatus, our emotions are not blameworthy in themselves and so Puritanism and asceticism are foolish attitudes to adopt (Lazarus, 1999).

The Middle Ages were considered as Ages of cognitive darkness, where free thought and thinking in bodily events were subordinated to religious interests and were judged as sinful deeds.

New theories on emotion began to sprout, when Darwin published his book on emotions in 1872 and declared that the emotion is a function, a sign of preparation for action. He claimed that it is an inborn expressive behavior (postures, gestures and facial expression), and as such, it can be observed in inferior animals, in newborns, blinds from birth and in all races. It is evolutive in character; there are primitive emotions, like smile, fear and rage and posterior ones, like sadness and grief.

Later, William James and Carl Lange tried to give foundation to a really scientific theory. Based on the observed autonomic reactions, they declared that the emotion is the mirror-feeling of complex body actions and reactions. The hypothesis was that the changes in the body reactions accompany directly the perception of an exciting event. The sensation of these physiological changes (an increase or a decrease in blood pressure, in heart rate, and in muscular tension) constitutes the emotion. According to them emotional experience is the direct consequence of information arriving from the periphery in the cerebral cortex (Lyons, 1999). Cannon criticized the theory of James and Lange mentioning four serious arguments: 1.- Sherrington operated dogs cutting all the visceral connections that carry information from the periphery to the brain and the dogs still could show the typical emotional reactions of rage and fear; 2.- There are only a few autonomic responses that accompany a wide range of different emotions. It is not probable that they could be responsible for the highly differentiated emotional feelings. Obviously the autonomic responses are too similar, to produce the wide range of emotions, we are able to feel; 3.-Cannon also argued that the visceral organs like stomach, heart, guts etc. have a very limited sensibility and very slow reactions. Glandules or smooth muscles respond with the slow velocity of a quarter of seconds to some minutes. Emotional responses of fear are quicker than this rate; 4.- Cannon tried to induce visceral changes injecting adrenalin to people in order to produce artificially the same changes in heart rate, blood sugar, and so forth that are produced naturally during emotion. Yet, most of the people reported experiencing only the arousal and no emotion. Moreover, normally people were not aware of their visceral sensations.

Cannon not only criticized the James-Lange theory, but presented an alternative hypothesis to explain the relation between cerebral structures and emotions. Together with Baird, he observed emotional responses in decorticated animals, and noticed that such responses were lost, when the hypothalamus was removed. They proposed that hypothalamus and thalamus provide the motor command that regulates peripheral signs of emotion and they provide the cortex with the information required for the cognitive perception. They evoked sham rage with stimulating the hypothalamus, having demonstrated that emotional experience depends on the activation of certain cerebral structures (Cannon, 1929).

Freud viewed the unconscious mental mechanism as intimately connected to emotion. He sustained that repressed sexual impulses, and guilt worked in the subconscious and caused the problem in his hysterical patients. He treated his patients with hypnosis and using the technique of free associations, in order to help to reveal features of the subconscious. He never created a complete theory for emotion, however, in spite of the limitations; he gave a strong impulse to investigation (Freud, 1915).

Watson, who redefined psychology as "the science of behavior", also held that emotion is nothing but the pattern of physiological reactions or changes, adopting the theory of James. Behaviorist used the paradigm of conditioning and attributed the emotion to motivational factors (Lyons, 1999).

In 1937 J.W. Papez offered another theory contending that emotions depend on a circuit of brain structures called limbic system (or circuit of Papez). Papez did not assume that the actual feeling of emotion took place in the limbic system, but he did propose that the limbic system generates impulses to the cerebral cortex. According to him all kinds of sensory input are divided by the thalamus into three streams for different kind of processing: movement, thought and feeling (Kalat, 1980).

In his model Leventhal proposed that the components, which process emotion, are organized at three levels: a) sensorial-motor that includes a set of innate expressive-motor programs; b) schematic that provides a rapid, automatic, perceptual-emotional appraisal of current situation and includes memories of emotional experience; and c) conceptual that enables to reflect upon, abstract and draw conclusions (Teasdale, 1999).

The multi-level theories of emotion offer explanation at functional, anatomical and psychological levels of analyses. The most conspicuous of them is the model of Le Doux. This author distinguishes two classes of computation: cognitive and affective and studies their interaction in the brain. Using the technique of conditioned fear, he described the neural pathways involved in affective computation. According to LeDoux's neural model (1995, 1996), sensory, perceptual and cognitive inputs converge in the amygdala, where their affective significance is evaluated and emotional responses are generated. The amygdala plays a central role in the appraisal of danger, because it directly receives not only the "quick and dirty" sensory inputs via thalamus that allow rapid responses on the basis of limited stimulus information, but also the more detailed stimulus information via inputs from longer and slower neural pathways from hippocampus and cortical regions. Once the emotional response is on its way, fear activation becomes consciously represented, and an explanation for the arousal has to be found (Öhman, 1999, Teasdale, 1999). This theory clearly describes the sequence of events that occur between the appearance of the evoking stimulus and its consequence, the emotional response. It also clarifies the role of those cerebral structures that take part in the emotional behavior. It explains the interaction between automatic and controlled processes and sheds light on the coping process. Convention holds that an automatic process does not require cognitive capacity, does not require awareness and does not involve volition, meanwhile, a strategic process requires cognitive capacity, conscious attention and is amenable to voluntary control. Effortless processing or automatic processing usually does not interfere with concurrent processing and does not require effort or intentionality. It occurs by parallel processing. The human mind is par excellence a parallel processor. This could be the basis for a long-standing belief in Western culture that emotion is the enemy of reason. Social psychological research suggests that emotion often leads to bias and distortion, because it often focuses on the role of situationally irrelevant emotion. There is a complex interplay between the unconscious and consciousness. (Hirst, 1990).

We may resume that brain works like a chemical instrument that is shaped by genetics and tuned by early experience, determining in this way the exact quantity of neurotransmitters most advantageous for functioning in that exact environment. It is an instrument based on plasticity, evolved to keep pace with the ever changing medium. Education and experience transforms conscious, effortful mental activity into automatic activity. It gives optimally quick responses for the frequently repeated stimulus. This automatization guarantees that those stimuli that occur repeatedly in the calibration period (first 2-3 years of age) have a preferential treatment with automatically given, prompt responses. These responses that make the instrument so efficient cause us a lot of head-ache and costs in therapist's fees. This feature of emotional responses may be illustrated with an infantile joke: "How much is two times two"? And the answer comes: "Do you want velocity or precision?" If you are navigating by automatic pilot and we do it constantly, the response is prompt, but not precise. It must be a type of emotional priming, with connections previously done that opens the cortical dictionary of interrelated emotional solutions and suggest us the feeling of things that could be directly or maybe remotely related to the evoking stimulus.

We might think that personality consists of two basic characteristics: the quantity of neurotransmitters in certain critical parts of brain and the collection of primed solutions that are based on previous experience. Among the critical parts of brain, we should include frontal lobes that make possible to induce positive goal-directed emotions or make possible to inhibit distracters.

Ordinarily our feelings about something are hopelessly intertwined with our beliefs about it. Emotional influences are often mediated by emotional feelings themselves rather than by their associated cognitive content.

Finally, the difference between emotion and mood has to be considered. Moods and emotions differ in specificity partly because emotions have objects and mood do not. The presence of an object means that one can engage in problem-focused coping. When merely in a bad mood in which things in general seem unsatisfactory, it is unclear what steps might be taken. If moods are states of feeling, then emotions are states of feeling with specific objects and cognitive structure (Ketelaar and Clore, 1997).

ANATOMY OF FEAR

The first step in a neurobiological approach to any mental state or behavior is to identify the neural system that mediates the function in question. Previously, we have mentioned the limbic system, as the principal participant in emotional behavior, according to Papez. In 1937 he described a circuit of structures around the center of the brain, the limbic system (limbic comes from Latin limbus and means border) that includes the hypothalamus, the hippocampus, the amygdala, the olfactory bulb, parts of the thalamus and the cingulated gyrus of the cerebral cortex and other little parts. All limbic structures are richly interlinked with one another and receive a great deal of sensory input form the olfactory receptors. McLean revised Papez's theory and distinguished two basic subcircuits. One of these includes the cingulated gyrus, most of the hippocampus and the septum. This circuit seems to relate to pleasure versus displeasure or reward versus punishment. It is particularly important in sexual enjoyment. Olds (1962) found that monkeys, with electrodes implanted for auto-stimulation in the septum or medial forebrain bundle, pressed the lever as often as 8000 times per hour. However, this frenetic effect was not obtained in humans; they generally described self-stimulation as pleasant. The second circuit within the limbic system consists of the amygdala and those portions of cerebral cortex that are connected with it. This second circuit seems to be related to self-regulation and preservation (Kalat, 1980).

LeDoux described a network in the amygdala that goes directly from the thalamus. Through this way, the amygdala receives direct inputs from the visual, auditory, somatosensory, gustatory and olfactory areas, as well as inputs reflecting interoceptive sensory information. These connections make possible that the amygdala starts the response before this information is registered by the neocortex. The value of this quick and direct way is enormous, as it eliminates some critical milliseconds in moments of danger. This is the pathway that LeDoux called the "quick-and-dirty" way as it produces emotional responses that sometimes the reason does not justify. Cognitive inputs are fed to the amygdala from the hippocampus that keeps the episodic memories of events related to the stimulus (Armony and LeDoux, 1997).

Sophisticated cognitive neuroanatomical and electrophysiological studies suggest that the role of non-conscious processes may be far greater than is routinely supposed in cognitive and social psychology (Kitayama, 1997). A PET study of Morris et al. (1998) observed enhanced activity in the left amygdala, left pulvinar, left anterior insula and bilateral anterior cingulated gyri during the processing of fearful faces. People with brain injuries involving the amygdala are often poor at recognizing facial expressions of fear and a wide range of social signals that causes alteration of emotional experience (Sprengelmeyer et al. 1999).

In the past decades, the anatomical and structural bases of these functions have been more and more precisely delineated; in particular hippocampal system has been established as the support for the acquisition of explicit or declarative memory and the amygdala for retaining the emotional situation that accompanies these events. The hippocampus also has the capacity of integration and novelty detection and it has a critical importance in memory and learning. When information about the fully analyzed stimulus reaches amygdala via temporal cortex, it serves to confirm (or disconfirm) the activation that is already set in motion.

Meanwhile the amygdala works on the "dirty" response, other parts of the brain, the frontal lobes, are preparing a more meditated and supposedly more precise response. The enlarged neocortex is the most conspicuous feature of the human cerebral hemispheres and the most pre-eminent anatomical correlate of primate evolution. The neocortex is the part of the brain that is most closely associated with human cognitive function and appears to play an important role in emotion regulation, modulating the activity of the amygdala. A dynamic interaction between affect and cognition is carried out by it. Three aspects of prefrontal involvement in emotion-cognition interactions were described: a) prefrontal inhibition of posterior cortical zones b) prefrontal control of affect-relevant attentional processes and c) prefrontal inhibition of the amygdala and its role in regulation of negative affect (Davidson, 1999).

Damasio (1994) observed that frontal lobe damaged patients are unable to develop affective responses, which are suitable to a new situation, even though they have stable representations or factual knowledge of future outcomes. Maybe the marking of a positive or negative value is lacking, resulting in the inability to reject or accept a future outcome.

Temporal lobes also participate in emotional behavior. Biraben et al. (2001) studied temporal lobe epileptic patients with fear as the main symptom. They concluded that in ictal fear, the network involving orbitoprefrontal, anterior cingulated and temporal limbic cortices, interfered with information processing.

FEAR

There is a scientific debate concerning the biology of each of the different emotions and the idea is that there are much more overlaps than differences between the emotions and that our capacity to measure exactly the biological correlates of every emotion is still rudimentary to distinguish between them in a trustable way. In the light of this information all previously said on emotion, refers to fear, too.

Fear is an emotion that is particularly important to human and animal existence. It is a reaction to threatening events and is elicited when self-preservation goals are posed in danger during the pursuit of actions directed at other goals. In the face of possible harm or loss, responding with fear is surely adaptive to the extent that it motivates escape or avoidance.

When in fear, a person is likely to exhibit increased heart rate and blood pressure, to show pilo-erection, specific facial expressions and to try hard to get away from the dangerous situation. Sympathetic responses are activated through the nuclei of the lateral hypothalamus and startle modulation via the reticular nucleus of the pons and activation of facial muscles through the facial motor nerve (Davis, 1992). All autonomic manifestations have a specific function. When in fear, the blood irrigates the large skeletal muscles, like legs that facilitate movement. The face turns pale provided that all the blood is bombed to the heart and muscles. In the same time, there is a freezing behavior that allows time for taking decisions, if an attack or an escape is the most adequate to do. The attention is fixed on the threatening stimulus, maybe for a better evaluation of the situation. The central nervous system and the peripheral autonomic and endocrine activation put the organism in a general arousal to prepare the body for the following action. Fear is so fast, that it can be felt before the fear-evoking stimulus is eventually registered in consciousness. Due to this fast subcortical activation, persons can find themselves in a state of unexplained excitement.

Fear has multiple components, including a behavioral or expressive component, an experiential or verbal component and a physiological component. Expressivity reflects the extent to which individuals outwardly display their emotions. These behavioral changes, verbal or non verbal (e.g., facial, postural) typically accompany emotions and are particularly susceptible to modification by various social factors. There is an agreement amongst the theorist as to the existence of at least six facial expressions (happy, sad, surprise, fear, disgust, anger) of emotion which are recognized cross culturally (Ekman, 1993) and fear is one of them.

Fear seems to be organized by a neural network centered on the amygdala and providing efferent outflows to midbrain and brainstem regions controlling different aspects of manifest fear response. Stimulation of the amygdala in animals produces behaviors that appear fearful, such as piloerection and attempts to escape, rage, attack behavior, components of copulation sequences and vocalization. In human patients elementary experiences of fear are common, as are autonomic effects and sensations referable to the viscera (Brothers, 1995). Fear is not necessarily dependent on prior cognitive processing, but once the fear response is on its way, fear activation becomes consciously represented, and an explanation for the arousal has to be found.

LeDoux (1986) conditioned fear in rats through the application of a standard paradigm (presentation of an auditory stimulus followed by an electric shock), and studied fear responses by producing lesions at systematically chosen locations and measuring the electrical activity of neurons at different sites in the rat's brains. This research showed that fear in the rat could be elicited through neural activity involving the two above-mentioned pathways: subcortical and cortical. In both cases the amygdala played a central role in the evocation of fear responses. Le Doux (1996) distinguished between natural triggers and learned triggers of fear system. Natural triggers can be thought of as sign stimuli have been selected by evolutions and the represent a recurrent threat to survival. Learned triggers on the other hand have acquired their power to activate fear system through Pavlovian conditioning.

Antoniadis and McDonald (2000) found in the rat that freezing, locomotion, urination and preference are "fast" measures of fear that get established after a single training session (that may be responses to natural triggers), while ultrasonic vocalizations and defecation are "slow" measures following three training sessions (supposedly responses to learned triggers). They also underlined the contribution of the amygdala and hippocampus to this kind of fear learning.

Öhman (1986) distinguished fear of animals, fear of people, and fear of inanimate objects, suggesting that different actions may have evolved for fear of a predator as compared to social fears. In a later study, Öhman and Mineka (2001) proposed four characteristics for fear elicitation and fear learning: a) Fear is preferentially activated by stimuli in aversive context; b) Its activation to such stimuli is automatic; c) It is relatively impenetrable to cognitive control; and d) It originates in a dedicated neural circuitry, centered on the amygdala.

The most consistently documented findings include that fear decreases in prevalence and intensity with age and specific fears are transitory in nature. There are also predictable changes in the content of normal fear over the course of development. Such changes are characterized by a transition from infant fears, which are related to immediate, concrete and prepotent stimuli, and which are largely non-cognitive, to fears of late childhood and adolescence which are related to anticipatory, abstract, and more global stimuli and events (Gullone, 2000).

FEAR RELATED SYNDROMES

Normal fear has been defined as a normal reaction to a real or imagined threat and is considered to be an integral and adaptive aspect of development with the primary function of promoting survival (Gullone, 2000). However, we can suffer irrational fears of the same intensity. There are several mechanisms to become exposed to and perpetuate irrational fears: a) inborn vulnerability; b) learning c) erroneous self-beliefs and d) substitution.

A. Inborn Vulnerability

The synaptic network comes preset at birth with sensitivities to and biases for processing information in a certain way. Brain development is accelerated during childhood, when emotional habits became automatic. Results of research with normal infants suggest that hemispheric specialization for the perception and expression of emotion is already present within the first year (Nass and Koch, 1991). Nevertheless, through entire lifetime, these brain connections have plasticity and learning provokes changes, but these changes are of a smaller scale, than during infancy. These critical moments of brain development determine the exact quantity of neurotransmitters that establish the communication between nerve cells, and these connections are more or less stable during lifetime.

Differences in personality traits and varied reactions to emotional stimuli are manifested from birth. Research on personality and individual differences has focused on figuring out, why individuals respond differently to similar stimuli, process similar information in a different way and act differently in similar social situations. A study of Kagan (1984) done with shy children demonstrated that these children have more sensibility, more elevated blood pressure in rest, more dilated pupils, and more norepihephrine in urine from birth. So, we could suppose that a person's fate is his or her genetic equipment. A stable predisposition to negative emotions is inheritable. Although, due to plasticity of the brain, even genetically determined traits can be changed, reorganization is always possible. The fight against genetic predisposition may be difficult, but not hopeless.

B. Learning

It is a well known fact that most fear of adults is brought about by experiences during the first three years of life, the tendency for anxiety gets established in childhood. Frequently, it occurs by Pavlovian conditioning, when the presentation of a harmless stimulus is followed by a painful one. In this case, the harmless stimulus acquires the dangerous characteristics of the harmful one, and it is followed by the same reaction or avoidance. Randomly reinforced emotional stimuli may result in maintained automatic and frequently superstitious responses and posterior cognitive justification may or may not occur.

Another way to learn emotion is by imitation of the parents. In this case, not even a cognitive explanation is necessary; it works in an automatic way. Frequently, patients are not even aware of it, and its irrationality is not questioned.

One can suffer by irrational fear and anxiety due to the lack of learning. A newborn infant has to learn everything: how to walk, how to speak and how to feel. Overprotective mothers do not give the possibility to their children to have challenges, to cope with their frustrations and as a consequence, develop stronger connections with frontal lobes. If no later learning occurs, these persons will react with anxiety to every tiny problem of life.

C. Erroneous Self-Beliefs

Our feelings about something are intermingled with our beliefs about it. These beliefs may be adopted from other situations or conditions, where they represented practical solutions. However, erroneous or negative beliefs about subjective injustice and inferiority (for example: "I am a total failure.") can figure in the maintenance and perhaps the etiology of an emotional disorder. Pathologic reactions can be induced by these self-beliefs pertaining to goal failure or engaging in excessive processing of negative information or rumination. Negative automatic thoughts elicit characteristics response style, which serve to maintain psychopathology. The negative effect of the ruminative response style has been shown in depression and in anxiety disorder. Intrusive thoughts and images are the price that humanity pays for a flexible cognitive system. If it were possible to exercise absolute control over mental events, creativity in both art and science might be the first casualty. The repeated re-entry into awareness of unintended thoughts and images might reflect the operation of adaptive cognitive sub-routines alerting the organism with respect to future danger and facilitating distressing emotional information. In general, anxiety disorder, obsession and posttraumatic stress disorder can be understood as a loss of mental control, an effort to avoid "working through" emotional material that could result in continued disturbance and distress (Tallis, 1999).

Autonomic reactions that normally accompany emotional sensations sometimes can appear alone, or can be confused or mistakenly understood.

In these cases, when trying to find explanation to a peripherally provoked anxious feelings people usually react like this: "I feel that something tragic will happen to me" or "I always have bad luck, nothing is good in my life". This kind of justification of spontaneous feelings may act like reinforcement and a vicious circle can be established. More autonomic reactions result in more tragic beliefs and the anxiety is for ever.

D. Substitution

The subconscious proposed by Freud can be conceived as information kept in the long-term memory and we do not have the key for recalling, so it is lost for consciousness. It can be imagined like a huge library with millions of volumes in it. We can find easily all books that are in the catalogue. Once a volume does not figure in one of the catalogues, it is lost for ever. Unlike lost books in the library, unconscious information has the ability to distort our decisions without being aware of its intrusion. Specially, painful experiences behave in this way. They can be consciously forgotten, however, we substitute them with other phobias whose evocation is not so painful. It sounds odd, but the situation seems like that: Once, a certain quantity of neurotransmitters that mediate tragic reactions are secreted, they must be used. Apparently, it is not important for the brain, if it is used for the good or for the wrong business.

Anxiety Disorder

Anxiety disorder is relatively common and tends to be chronic, with the main symptoms of apprehensive expectations (schemata concerned with information relevant to threat or danger), muscle tension, autonomic hyperactivity, vigilance or scanning and enhanced recall of negative information (Barlow, 1988). Anxious persons also exhibit deficient inductive reasoning, slowed decision latencies, shallow depth processing, reduced memory span, impaired attentional control, problems in the execution of attentional inhibition and biased memory recall for negative events. Individuals who make little effort to interrupt the cognitive recycling process are apt to experience longer and more severe periods of anxiety or depression (MacLeod, 1999).

Drevets and Raichle, (1995) said that anxiety is an impairment of attention, bias of selective attention to threat related stimuli. When fear activates the emotional brain, the resultant anxiety fixes the attention on the threatening stimulus. The person gets obsessed how to resolve the situation and everything else is unnoticed. Anxiety states may involve activation of the limbic prefrontal cortex, demonstrated with PET imaging study. In the right amygdala, there is an increased flow during anxiety induced in normal subjects by the threat of a painful electric stimulus.

A study of Öhman (1999) demonstrated that expectancy ratings during the presentations of conditioned or unconditioned fear stimuli determined the responses. For example, fearful subjects were consistently faster to localize threatening stimulus, than normal subjects. Anxiety patients also responded faster to threatening words than to neutral ones, indicating that they selectively attended to threat. The emotional Stroop color naming paradigm showed that patients suffering by anxiety disorder, phobics and patients with post-traumatic stress disorder displayed disproportionately long color naming latencies on threatening words (MacLeod, 1999).

Panic Attack

Panic attacks are unexpected surges of terror accompanied by breathlessness, racing heart, chest oppression, nausea, dizziness, trembling, fear of dying, bewilderment, fainting, paresthesia or fear of "going crazy". The crisis of anxiety or panic attack is sudden in appearance and reaches its maximum expression very quickly, normally in 10 minutes or less.

The triggering stimulus for a panic attack may consist of an unconsciously perceived sudden increase in heart rate. Or in social interaction, socially anxious persons may construe threatening situations by rapidly passing stimuli in the form of individual facial gestures. An important feature of neural network memory system in these patients is that they can retrieve a complete memory from a partial stimulus. Through learned association, the subcortical circuit may be activated by any stimulus, and when activated it may control the persons behavior toward this stimulus without having explicitly revealed its influence to consciousness. Rational thought has little influence on strong fears (Le Doux, 1996).

There are three types of panic attacks: a) situational crisis, always related to the phobic stimulus b) non-situational crisis that are spontaneous, not triggered by the stimulus and c) delayed crisis that has more probability, when the patient is exposed to the evoking stimulus, however this relation between the triggering event and the panic attack is not always present, or the crisis can appear long after the exposure.

Frequently, a vicious circle begins with panic provoking more panic. Patients with panic attacks generally confess to have constant or intermittent anxious sensations that are not related to a specific situation or event. The frequency of crisis is varied widely, some people present it with periodicity, and others may have burst of several attacks and then a rest for weeks or months without it.

Drevets and Raichle (1995) observed elevated blood flow and metabolism in the right ventral prefrontal cortex, in subjects with panic disorder. It was also observed that panic patients did not report more cardiac events than normal control subjects did, but they became more anxious when they did detect them. People with panic disorder also showed better memory recalling for threatening events.

Phobias

Phobia is an irrational, wild fear that is capable to conceal the reasonable thoughts of a person. If a phobic situation is present (for example a snake or a stimuli reminding the phobic person a snake) the fear may reach an incontrollable level. People with specific phobia exhibit intense fear of circumscribed situations or objects. The upset is immediate, when the patient is exposed to the object of his fear. Phobics invariably admit that their feelings are exaggerated. When they do not accept it we are treating a psychotic patient.

We can distinguish different subtypes of phobias:

Animal type, when the fear is related to animals or bugs. Normally, this phobia begins in the childhood.

Environmental type, when the fear is associated with natural phenomena: tempest, precipices, heights, water, etc. It also begins in the childhood.

Blood-Injection type: Fear of blood-related cues, wounds, and injections. Its incidence is clearly familiar.

Situational type: Specific of places, tunnels, bridges, elevators, flying airplanes, cars or enclosed spaces.

Social phobia: is fear or avoidance of situations in which the person will be exposed to the scrutiny of other people. More specifically, they are concerned that they will embarrass or humiliate themselves by blushing, trembling, or otherwise behaving in a socially ungraceful way. When exposed to unavoidable critical scrutiny, people with social phobia may experience symptoms akin to panic attack. It can appear much before the phobic situation is present and can create a vicious circle. Usually, it appears in the adulthood with the antecedents of shyness and isolation.

Other type: fear of loud voices, of vomit or illnesses etc. An insight does not necessarily alleviate the phobia. Seventy-five percent of patients report multiple fainting episodes when exposed to the phobic stimulus. They frequently present shaking, stutter, trembling voice, cold and sticky hands, even paralysis. Seventy percent of the phobic persons are women.

Occasional panic attack and moderately intense fears are not uncommon in the general population.

Posttraumatic Stress Disorder

It is triggered by stimuli that involve real danger to the life or to the physical integrity of the patient, for example war situation, torture, violence, sexual aggression, armed robbery, kidnapping or car accidents etc. Any aspect of another stimulus that recalls this event can produce the same sentiment as the original trauma: the patient begins to sweat, tremble and shiver and has an attack of fear. The related aversive association is not avoidable.

This traumatic event can be re-experimented in different ways: It can be acute, when the symptoms appear within 3 months after the traumatic event. Or it can be chronic if its appearance is beyond three months. It also can appear with long latency, when the symptoms start to manifest 6 months after the traumatic event. This disorder can begin at any age. Patients with posttraumatic stress disorder are generally depressed and have low self-confidence.

It is difficult to separate these pathological entities, as they normally appear together and show as basic characteristic the creation of vicious circles. It is probable that the tendency toward pathology associated with "vicious circles" of appraisal and action serves to perpetuate the disorder. For example, depressed patients generate negative interpersonal cycles, which confirm their sense of missing self-worth. Similarly, panic disorder patients, by monitoring for signs of ill-health, progressively increase their sensitivity to somatic anxieties. In clinical practice, it is important to address failures to adapt to real-world environments directly, by reconstructing self-knowledge and reducing unrealistic goals and false negative appraisals. It is useful create plans for coping and meta-cognition in order to generate coping strategies (Matthews and Wells, 1999).

What can we offer to a patient who suffers one or several of the above mentioned disorders?

Pharmacotherapy with neuroleptic medication (mostly antidepressants) may give a breath of peace for the therapy, but generally is not a final solution. Treatments of anxiety and related pathologies often begin with assignment for self monitoring of the critical events. A good suggestion is to write stories about feelings related to fear. The act of writing down thoughts associated with changes in mood, can serve several purposes. It can direct attention to positive events, helps to avoid recalling biases often present in retrospective reports and can provide a more accurate picture for therapist and client. It may help to slow down the process of thinking about and of evaluating circumstances. The monitoring of variation in mood and cognition can also serve to reinforce the rationale and credibility by providing a first-hand demonstration of the correspondence between one's mood and interpretation of events (Segal et al. 1999).

Another helpful intervention is the desensibilization. The logic behind the exposure treatment is that people avoid what they fear. By exposing them to the threatening stimulus over a sustained period of time, their belief that they should avoid the threat to protect themselves from harm, will be disconfirmed. Kamphuis and Telch (2000) exposed claustrophobics to four conditions: a) exposure with guided threat appraisal, b) exposure with cognitive load distracter task, c) exposure with both guided threat reappraisal and cognitive load distracter task and d) exposure without guided threat appraisal and cognitive load distracter task. The authors observed, that the greatest level a fear reduction and the lowest level of return of fear were observed in the exposure condition involving guided threat appraisal without cognitive load. The cognitive load task had a detrimental effect on the fear reduction. The authors share Öhman's opinion that an irrational phobia cannot possibly be rationalized and these learned, automatic responses are relatively impenetrable to cognitive inhibition (2001).

The therapies have to be highly structured and directive in nature. Segal offers several techniques: consequential analysis (that examines the possible consequences of thinking or feeling certain thoughts), reattribution (generating alternative causal explanation to negative events), cost-benefit analysis (enumerating and comparing pros and contras of maintaining certain beliefs and behavior patterns) and instruction of problem solving strategies that may all serve to make information processing more efficient and emotionally beneficial. These techniques help to redirect attention away from self-focused worries and rumination, organizing information into balanced and meaningful units and provide strategies for problem solving. As core dysfunctional beliefs are identified and challenged, therapist may be surprised to discover that patients can be reluctant to give them up. Often, this persistence is due to the fact that the beliefs or rules had a self-protective function, or provided patients with some important benefits. Elaboration plays an important role in the establishment of new knowledge structure, there will be more competition within the system and the activation of earlier schematic elements may become less automatic over time. Adopting a graduated approach to the evaluation of experiences also helps patients to synchronize the rate at which change is occurring in their lives and the time needed for the consolidation of a new self-view (Segal, et al. 1999).

Modeling is also an efficient help against emotional disorders. Goleman (1995) suggests the following main objectives: 1) Know yourself 2) Learn to control your emotions 3) Direct your motivations 4) Learn to recognize the emotion of the others. 5) Social competence, satisfactory relationships.

Therapy based on emotional re-learning includes other tasks like learning relaxation, identification of prejudicial self beliefs, shifting attention from threatening cues, suppress catastrophic interpretations. Learning to narrow attention may also contribute to the common state of "self-focused" attention, in which anxious individuals focus inwardly upon their personal concerns and feelings, often neglecting the external environments.

To learn switching is also beneficial. There is nothing in this world that could be completely good or completely bad. Everything has multiple faces. Teaching the patient to switch attention and in moments of anguish focus on the profitable part of the event may be very helpful.

These re-learning techniques do not have to convince the patient to let worrying, because probably it serves as an effective strategy for dealing with their problems. The aim is to teach the patient the emotional self-regulation, an auto-imposed delay directed to an objective and to set in motion the inhibition voluntarily strengthening connections between the neocortex and the amygdala.

Obviously personality traits play an important role in coping with anxieties. Individuals who possess more openness are said to learn faster and be more willing to change their beliefs in the face of new information than those who do not. Extroverts can cope more easily as they develop beliefs about their competence within demanding situations which encourage them to enter those situations.

What emotion is, and how to handle it in moments of distress, are the big questions of life. Creating new theories and discussing underlying mechanisms allows us to make progress in understanding some fundamental aspects of emotions, and may some day also help us understand the essence of emotion as well.

REFERENCES

Antoniadis E.A., McDonald, R.J. (2000) Amygdala, hippocampus and discriminative fear conditioning to context. *Behavioral Brain Research*. 108:1-19.

Armony, J.L., LeDoux, J.E. (1997) How the brain processes emotional information. *Ann. N.Y. Acad. Sci.* 821:259-270

Barlow, D.H. (1988) Anxiety and Its Disorders. In *The Nature and Treatment of Anxiety and Panic.* Guilford, N.Y.

Biraben, A., Taussig, D., Thomas, P., Even, C., Vignal, J.P., Scarabin, J.M., Chauvel, P. (2001) Fear as the main feature of epileptic seizures. *Journal of Neurology, Neurosurgery and Psychiatry*, 70:186-91.

Brothers, L. (1995) Neurophysiology of the perception of intentions by Primates. In *The Cognitive Neurosciences*. (Ed). Gazzaniga. The Bradford Book. London, England

Cannon, W.B. (1929) Bodily changes in pain, hunger, fear and rage. Appleton, New York

Damasio, A.R. (1994) Descartes' error: *Emotion, research and the human brain.* New York Avon.

Davidson, R.J. (1999) Neuropsychological perspectives on affective styles and their cognitive consequences. In *Handbook of Cognition and Emotion* T. Dagleish and M Power (eds.) John Wiley and Sons Ltd.

Davis, M. (1992) The role of amygdala in conditioned fear. In *The Amygdala: Neurobiological Aspects of Emotion, Memory and Mental Dysfunction*, J.P. Aggleton (ed). New York: Wiley-Liss.

Drevets W.C. and Raichle M.E. (1995) Positron Emission Tomographic imaging studies of human emotional disorders. In In *The Cognitive Neurosciences*. (Ed.) Gazzaniga. The Bradford Book. London, England

Ekman, P. (1993) Facial expression and emotion. *American Psychologist*, 48:384-392.

Freud, S. (1915) The Unconscious. In S. Freud *Collected Papers,* Vol. IV. London, Hogarth Press, 1949.

Goleman D. (1995) *La Inteligencia Emocional* Javier Vergara Editor S.A.

Gullone, E. (2000) The development of normal fear: a century of research. *Clinical Psychology Review*, 20:429-51.

Hirst, W. (1990) On consciousness, recall, recognition and the architectures of memory. In *Implicit Memory*. K. Krisner, S. Lewandowsky and J.C. Dunn (eds) Hilldale, N.J. Erlbaum

Kagan, J. (1984) *The Nature of the Child*. New York: Basic Books.

Kalat, J.W. (1980) *Biological Psychology*. Wadsworth Publishing Company, Belmont Calif.

Kamphuis, J.H., Telch, M.J. (2000) Effect of distraction and guided threat reappraisal on fear reduction during exposure/based treatments for specific fears. *Behavioral Research and Therapy* 38:1163-1181.

Ketelaar, T., and Clore, G.L. 1997. Emotion and Reason: The Proximate Effects and Ultimate Functions of Emotions. In *Cognitive Science Perspectives on Personality and Emotion* eds. G. Matthews Elsevier

Kitayama, S., 1997. Affective Influence in Perception: Some Implications of the Amplification Model In *Cognitive Science Perspectives on Personality and Emotion* (ed) G. Matthews. Elsevier

Lazarus, R.S. (1999) The Cognition-Emotion Debate: A bit of History. In *Handbook of Cognition and Emotion* T. Dagleish and M. Power (eds.) John Wiley and Sons Ltd.

LeDoux, J.E. (1986) Sensory systems and emotion: A model of affective processing. *Integrative Psychiatry,* 4:237-248.

LeDoux, J.E. (1995) Emotion: Clues from the brain. *Annual Review of Psychology.* 46:209-235.

Le Doux, J.E. (1996) The Emotional Brain: *The Mysterious Underpinnings of Emotional Life.* New York: Simon and Schuster.

Lyons, W. (1999) Philosophy of cognition and emotion. In *Handbook of Cognition and Emotion* (eds) T. Dagleish and M.J. Power. John Wiley and sons.

MacLeod, C. (1999) Anxiety and anxiety disorder In *Handbook of Cognition and Emotion* T. Dagleish and M Power (eds.) John Wiley and Sons Ltd.

Matthews G. and Wells A., (1999) The cognitive science of attention and emotion. In *Handbook of cognition and emotion* (eds) T. Dagleish and M.J. Power. John Wiley and sons.

Morris, J.S., Friston, K.J., Büchel, C., Frith, C.D., Young, A.W., Calder, A.J., Dolan, R.J. (1998) A neuromodulatory role for the human amygdale in processing emotional facial expressions. *Brain,* 121(1):47-57.

Nass, R., Koch, D., (1991) Innate Specialization for Emotion: Temperament Differences in Children with early left versus right brain damage. In *Pediatric Neurology: Behavior and Cognition of the Child with Brain Dysfunction.* Basel Karger.

Olds, J. (1962) Hypothalamic substrates of reward. *Physiological Reviews,* 42:554-604.

Öhman, A. (1986) Face the beast and fear the face: animal and social fears as prototypes for evolutionary analysis of emotion. *Psychophysiology,* 23:123-145.

Öhman, A. (1999) Distinguishing unconscious from conscious emotional processes: methodological considerations and theoretical implications in In *Handbook of cognition and emotion* (eds) T. Dagleish and M.J. Power. John Wiley and sons.

Öhman, A, Mineka, S. (2001) Fears, phobias and preparedness: toward an evolved module of fear and fear learning. *Psychol. Rev.* 108:483-522.

Rolls, E.T. (1995) A Theory of emotion and consciousness, and its application to understanding the neural basis of emotion. In. *The Cognitive Neurosciences.* (Ed). Gazzaniga. The Bradford Book. The MIT Press London, England

Segal, Z.V. (1988) Appraisal of the self schema construct in cognitive models of depression. *Psychological Bulletin,* 103:147-162.

Sprengelmeyer, R., Young A.W., Schroeder, U., Grossenbacher, P.G., Federlein, J B., Büttner, T., Przuntek, H. (1999) Knowing no fear. *Proc. R. Soc. Lond. B. Biol. Sci,* 266:2451-56.

Tallis, F.(1999) Unintended Thought and Images In *Handbook of cognition and emotion* (eds) T. Dagleish and M.J. Power. John Wiley and sons.

Teasdale, J.D. (1999) Multi-level theories of cognition-emotion relations. In *Handbook of cognition and emotion* (eds) T. Dagleish and M.J. Power. John Wiley and sons.

Tooby J. and Cosmides, L. (1995) Mapping the Evolved Functional Organization of Mind and Brain In *The Cognitive Neurosciences* Gazzaniga (ed) Braford Book. The MIT Press. London, England.

Chapter 3

FEAR OF FALLING –
THE PSYCHOLOGY AND BEYOND

Kris Legters

ABSTRACT

Fear of falling (FOF) has been identified as a health problem of older adults, with greater prevalence in older age groups, women and those who were hospitalized. Many factors have been associated with FOF, including poorer health status, functional decline, and activity curtailment. Depression, anxiety and decreased quality of life also have been correlated with FOF. Various measurement tools, using different definitions and premises of FOF, have been developed and are compared in this chapter. As the causes of FOF are multifactorial, one instrument that reflects a comprehensive view of FOF has been difficult to develop. Further study is necessary to examine the reliability and validity of the current tools, with a need to establish threshold scores for specific populations. A multidimensional approach to intervention to decrease FOF was recommended throughout the literature. The primary components of the interventions discussed included education, environmental safety, discussion of risk-taking behaviors, assertiveness training and physical fitness. Minimal research has evaluated the results of these interventions and their impact on FOF. Recommendations for further research on FOF measurement and a comparison of individual components of intervention are enumerated. Fear of falling needs to be assessed by health care providers as they work with older adults and other disease specific pathologies. It is a pervasive health concern and must be viewed separately from falls and risk of falls.

INTRODUCTION

Since the identification of the post-fall syndrome[1] and use of the term "ptophobia"[2] (the phobic reaction to standing or walking) in the early 1980s, fear of falling (FOF) has gained recognition as a health problem of older adults. Tinetti and Powell[3] described FOF as an ongoing concern about falling that ultimately limits the performance of daily activities. Others have referred to FOF as a loss of confidence in his or her balance abilities.[4,5] Still other authors[6] defined FOF as a general concept that described low fall-related efficacy (low confidence at avoiding falls) and being afraid of falling.

In the early research, FOF was largely believed to be a consequence of falling. Researchers discussed FOF as resulting from the psychological trauma of a fall, leading to reduced activity and subsequent losses in physical capabilities.[2,7-9] This was confirmed by a strong correlation between falls and fear of falling,[8,10-13] with the circumstances surrounding the fall, the perceived need for others' assistance,[14] and the history of falls (recent or at a younger age) with a greater activity level[15] seeming to contribute to this relationship.

As research has evolved in the area of FOF, however, the original theory that FOF was a result of falls has been refuted. A relationship certainly exists between FOF and falls, as those people with a history of falling express a greater prevalence of FOF to the survey question "Are you afraid of falling?"[8,10] Howland et al[12] noted that the degree of FOF increased as a function of the number and seriousness of the falls experienced. In contrast, however, is ample evidence that those who have not fallen also report FOF.[4,5,11,14-17] Myers et al[14] found similar proportions of FOF, measured by the same question "Are you afraid of falling?," in people who reported falling versus people who had not fallen (56% and 58%, respectively) among an ambulatory group of community dwelling older adults.

Friedman et al[18] examined the temporal relationship of falls and fear of falling. In a large prospective study of older adults, they found that falls were a predictor of FOF and likewise, FOF was a predictor of falls. "An individual who develops one of these outcomes is at greater risk for developing the other."[18] Because each is a risk factor for the other, it may initiate a cycle of downward decline. They suggested that FOF was likely recognition of being at risk, both for falling and the adverse outcomes that result from falls.

Subjects in one study indicated they did not describe themselves as being "afraid of falling," but rather were "worried" about falling.[19] In a cognitive behavioral concept model put forth by Childs and Kneebone,[20] this worry about falling translated into fall related anxiety, reduced attention to the task at hand, and reduced activity participation. As these experiences altered the individual's self-perception of their ability to move and complete a task, there was a reduction in overall activity as a means to reduce their risk of falling. The resultant lack of activity was likely to lead to reduced body strength. This added to the research that has uncovered a relationship between FOF and physical, psychological and functional changes in older adults.[6]

Ongoing studies are focusing on the causes of FOF, dispelling misconceptions (e.g., FOF being a result of the normal aging process), and identifying the interventions that address FOF most effectively. The researchers, however, agree that FOF is multifactorial in etiology,[15,21] and they suggest that FOF may be a more pervasive and serious problem than falls in older adults[6,21] and thus deserves attention.

PREVALENCE

Fear of falling, to some degree, has been reported in 12% to 65% of older adults (those in sixth decade or older) who live independently in the community and do not have a history of falling.[8,10-12,15,22] In those who have fallen, FOF is 29%[12] to 92%.[23] A 30% prevalence has been noted in subjects, 65 and older and were hospitalized[6] and 47% prevalence in older adults who experience dizziness.[16] In older adults transitioning to frailty, FOF was present in almost half of these individuals.[24] In frail older adults living in nursing homes a 50% prevalence was noted.[25] In community dwelling older adults the prevalence of FOF was consistently higher among women than men.[5,10,13,21,22] The researchers, however, suggested that there was likely underreporting of FOF among men due to the perceived stigma attached to the reporting of their fears.[5,21] Increasing age was correlated with FOF in studies that compared age groups (>58 years old) with degree of FOF,[10,13,22] although increasing age was not correlated in 2 studies that used the mean age of the groups for analysis.[12,15] In one study with a small sample size, African Americans were twice as likely to be fearful of falling as were Caucasians.[24]

The variability in prevalence of FOF is likely due to the various definitions and instruments used to measure FOF. Lower prevalence was present when a dichotomous response ("no" versus some degree of fear) was required to answer the question "are you afraid of falling?"[13] Increased prevalence was evident when a response indicating a degree of fear was expected (e.g., "very afraid," "somewhat afraid" or "moderately fearful").[6,10-12,15] The highest prevalence was noted when FOF was assessed relative to an activity, such as "going out when it is slippery."[8] The suggestion has been made that these prevalence figures are at least a slight underestimation of the prevalence of FOF among community dwelling older adults, because those with the greatest fear probably did not agree to participate in the studies[5,14] or feared possible institutionalization.[6]

Research with disease specific populations is beginning to investigate FOF as a critical component of healthcare assessment and intervention. A measure of FOF was used to assess the success of movement therapy in individuals with multiple sclerosis to decrease FOF.[26] Similarly, FOF was examined in individuals post hip fracture rehabilitation.[27] Interestingly enough, although rehabilitation improved physical function following the hip fracture, FOF did not significantly change. Those with cerebrovascular accidents demonstrated lower balance confidence than the healthy older adult population, and the older stroke patients had lower balance confidence than the younger patients with stroke.[28] In adults with unilateral peripheral vestibular dysfunction, a moderate degree of FOF was found in 66% of the subjects reviewed.[29] Fear of falling was noted in 49% of adults with lower extremity amputations.[30]

FACTORS ASSOCIATED WITH FEAR OF FALLING

The factors that contribute to FOF seem to be multifactorial, similar to the causes of falls. Some researchers[12,15,16,22] have suggested that FOF may actually be an expression of generalized anxiety and/or part of a more generalized psychological disorder.[31] Howland et al[12] suggested that some degree of FOF was an expression of a more generalized fear. The Generalized Fearfulness Index was created to compare fear of falling with other typical fears of older adults, such as forgetting an important appointment, having financial difficulties, losing a cherished item, having a serious health problem or being a victim of robbery in the street.[15] This research confirmed that FOF, in those with a basic concern about falling, was an intense fear, and in comparison to the other fears examined, FOF was of greater concern to the older adult.[15]

Previously it may have been assumed that FOF was based on the fear of physical harm and functional incapacity. Evidence is emerging, however, that suggests that it is possible to distinguish between a number of fall-related fears, such as the fear of incapacity and loss of independence, and the fear of pain and suffering.[32] Yardley and Smith[32] examined the common consequences of falling and isolated two primary dimensions of negative consequences: loss of functional independence and damage to one's identity, such that social embarrassment is experienced with a fall. The complex nature of fear of falling was underscored in this study, providing further evidence that one's concern about the potential consequences of falling for personal identity reasons was critical to the older adult. The values of independence, sense of individuality and self-worth and freedom to decide what activities one wishes to undertake were also important to them.[32]

Psychological factors, specifically depression, have been examined relative to FOF. Three studies[16,24,27] have correlated depression with FOF. These investigations showed that depression decreased the performance of automatic daily behaviors, which in turn decreased the positive reinforcement that comes to a person. Kressig et al[24] found depressed older adults were more than twice as likely to be fearful of falling. Burker et al[16] identified that a decrease in positive reinforcement prompted a chain of events that led to increased focus on one's self, increased need for assistance, decreased participation in pleasurable activities and negative expectations. A relationship existed among depression and activity restriction,[31] social withdrawal and loss of independence.[33] In addition, fatigue often accompanies depression, which may make people less secure about their physical abilities and therefore fearful of falling.[16]

Consensus among the studies indicated that increased FOF was associated with decreased quality of life in older adults.[6,8,12,13,15,27] In studies by Cumming et al[6] and Lachman et al,[8] quality of life was measured by a health related quality-of-life measure, the Medical Outcomes Study 36-Item Short-Form Health Survey [SF-36].[34] Both groups of investigators noted that, with increased fear (Fall Efficacy Scale scores $\leq 75/100$) the subscale scores of the SF-36 decreased, especially the physical function and bodily pain subscales, which declined the most.[6] Lachman et al[8] noted that greater FOF was also associated with lower quality of life in mental health and social and leisure pursuits. Often this decrease in quality of life was associated with a decrease in the amount of social interaction that the person experienced, leading to fewer social contacts with friends and family, social isolation, depression and anxiety.[8,10,12] In this work it was unclear whether decreased quality of life led to FOF or whether FOF led to decreased quality of life.[8] Less well-known and well-tested quality of life measures were used in the other cited studies, although the investigators' conclusions about the relationship of FOF to quality of life concur with the findings of Cumming and Lachman.[12,13,15]

Several studies have confirmed that FOF is associated with poorer health status[6,10,12,15,22,23] and functional decline.[13,25,27] Cumming et al[6] completed a prospective study over a 12-month period with older adults who had received medical intervention, collecting data on fall history, fall-related self-efficacy using the Fall Efficacy Scale (FES) and the assistance required performing 10 ADL tasks. In addition to finding that those who had low fall-related self-efficacy tended to have poorer health, the researchers found that the poorer FES scores ($\leq 75/100$) were associated with greater declines in the ability to perform ADLs (.69 change in score) than those with higher FES scores (=100) (.04 change in score).[6] These results confirmed those found previously in a prospective study by Arfken et al[13] that asked

"At the present time, are you very fearful, somewhat fearful or not fearful that you may fall?" In those community-dwelling older adults who were very fearful of falling, 91% reported at least one characteristic of frailty, 85% had impaired balance and 22% described delay in getting up after a fall.[13]

Fear of falling has also generally been correlated to an increase in restriction of activity or activity curtailment.[10-12,27,31,35] The measures used to assess activity restriction due to FOF, however, are highly variable and therefore difficult to compare. Tinetti et al[11] assessed social activity participation with adaptations from the self-report tools, Established Populations for Epidemiologic Study of the Elderly interview[36] and physical activity using a modification of the Yale Physical Activity Survey.[37] Howland and colleagues[10,12] used self-report tools as well, although a smaller number of activities were investigated. Murphy et al,[31] using self-report and performance-based measures, found that indicators of poor health, physical and psychosocial function were most common in those with activity restriction and FOF. Lachman et al[8] used the Survey of Activities and Fear of Falling in the Elderly (SAFE) instrument, designed to discern the reasons for avoidance of activities. They found that the 2 activities most avoided because of FOF were "going out when it is slippery" and "reaching overhead." Reasons other than FOF (e.g., personal preference, physical limitations, external constraint) for avoiding other activities, such as "taking a tub bath" or "walking several blocks outside," were considered.[8] Lachman et al[8] suggested, based on this work, that there was evidence that people who experience FOF do not necessarily restrict their activities.

Activity restriction, poorer health status and functional decline have physical consequences. Kressig et al[24] found that fear of falling was increased by fourfold in those older adults transitioning to frailty that were using an assistive device. FOF was also noted to increase muscle stiffness, which resulted in inadequate compensatory postural strategies, and correlated with slow gait speed.[24] Slow timed physical performance was confirmed in those with activity restriction.[31]

Recent research has compared fall-related self-efficacy with FOF. Given that fall-related self-efficacy was a major premise for much of the early work on FOF, the terms were used interchangeably. Recently, however, the 2 entities have been evaluated separately. Self-efficacy, having a strong belief in one's self and perceived abilities, has been shown to be important for maintaining one's physical activity level and preventing functional decline.[38] Self-efficacy plays a definite role in FOF, although it is a different construct. It is concerned with what people think they can do, not their actual skill.[21] The role of self-efficacy becomes important in our society, where older people are often stereotyped as lacking independence and capabilities and frequently are offered aid when none is required. This may lead to a decreased sense of self and, in turn lead to a reluctance to carry out normal activities even when the skills are available to perform these tasks.[21] When fall-related efficacy and FOF were compared, fall-related efficacy was an independent correlate of physical function and ADL performance, whereas FOF was not.[11,39] When elderly people who were highly active were compared with elderly people who were less active, there was no difference in fall-efficacy between the groups, although the highly active group reported less FOF.[21]

Friedman et al[18] evaluated predictors for developing fear of falling and found that older age, female gender, use of greater than 4 medications, and history of falls were the most obvious. They proposed that efforts to reduce these predictive factors may reduce the fall risk, and in turn, decrease the risk of developing fear of falling. They also found that women with a history of stroke, those with Parkinson's disease and comorbidity were predictive of fear of falling.[18]

MEASUREMENT TOOLS

Fear of falling may be difficult to recognize in some older adults as they may have already eliminated the activities from their life that generate this fear. Some individuals may lack the awareness of their fear or avoid discussion of their fear, thus direct questioning has been a successful means to assess FOF.[20] The tools that have been developed over the past two decades to measure FOF use different definitions and premises. The simple question "are you afraid of falling?"[3,5,40] was used initially in research studies with a "yes/no" or "fear/no fear" response format,[14,21,33,40] and this format has the advantages of being straightforward and easy to generate prevalence estimates. This measure was later criticized for its limited ability to detect variability in degrees of fear[12,15] and because it may express a generalized state of fear that does not directly reflect FOF.[15] Various authors[15,21,41] have expanded the answer choices to this question to provide a hierarchy of responses (e.g., "not at all afraid," "slightly afraid," "somewhat afraid," "very afraid") to better reflect the degree of fear. Others have continued to advocate use of the simple question only as a screen for FOF in community dwelling older adults[14,42] or because of its ease of use with their specific population (i.e., patients in nursing homes).[25]

Tinetti et al[40] developed the Falls Efficacy Scale (FES) to examine older adults, under the premise that FOF could be measured by looking at fall-related self-efficacy, or a person's self-confidence in his or her ability to avoid falling while performing everyday activities (e.g., cleaning house, getting dressed, simple shopping). It is a 10-question scale, with questions such as "How confident are you that you can clean the house without falling?" Subjects rate each question on a scale of 1 to 10, and the scores are summed to give a total score between 0 and 100. Many authors have used this scale to quantify FOF or fall-related efficacy in community dwelling older adults[6,8,11,14,21,27,39] or they have modified it (MFES,[19] FES(S) for patients with stroke,[28] expanded FES,[43] Balance Self-Perceptions Test[44]) to meet the needs of their clients (See Table One). Because it measures only simple indoor activities, the FES is most usable with older adults who are homebound and have low mobility.[21,38]

Powell and Myers[42] developed the Activities-specific Balance Confidence (ABC) Scale for older adults with higher physical functioning, using the same premise of fall-related self-efficacy as the FES. It is a 16-item questionnaire that asks the subject to rate his or her balance confidence on a visual analog scale (0-100), with a response to the question "How confident are you that you will not lose your balance or become unsteady while ....?" Zero represents no confidence, and 100 indicates complete confidence in performing the activity. The authors chose activities and circumstances (e.g., reach into cabinets versus reaching for something at eye level) that were more specific than those of the FES to decrease the inconsistency of individual interpretation. Activities performed outside of the home and of greater difficulty than the FES (i.e. walking in a crowded mall, riding an escalator holding onto the railing) were also chosen because the FES tended to show a ceiling effect with active older adults.[3] (Table One) The ABC was found to have greater responsiveness for older adults who had higher functioning than the FES (ABC: range=21% -90%; FES: range=1.9-3.9), although the FES was better for adults who were frail (ABC: range=5%-84%; FES: range [conversion to percentages]=44%-84%).[42] Both of these scales could be used to discriminate between low and high mobility in older adults who avoided activity because of their FOF; the ABC showed greater usefulness in discriminating between those who were fearful or were avoiding activity (FES: M=43.4; ABC: M=30.8) and those who were not fearful or were not avoiding activity (FES: M=19.8; ABC: M=74.0).[14]

Table 1. Psychometric Properties of Fear of Falling Measures

Tool	Number of Subjects	Internal Consistency (Cronbach's alpha)	Reliability	Threshold Scores	Comments
Falls Efficacy Scale (FES)[40]	18 older adults	.91	.71	≤ 75 76-99 100[6]	
Modified Falls Efficacy Scale (MFES)[11,19]	216[19] older adults	.90-.93	-----	----	Two additional items added to the FES Revised scoring procedure with 1-4 rating scale
Falls Efficacy Scale Swedish Modification (FES(S))[28]	30 patients with stroke	----	.97*	----	Includes easier items than the FES to accommodate those with cognitive, motor and/or perceptual deficits
Expanded Falls Efficacy Scale[43]	179 older adults	.95	.95	----	Four outside activities added to FES Rating was on visual analog scale of 0-100%
Balance Self-Perceptions Test[44]	105 older adults	----	----	----	Modification to FES with 20 basic ADL and IADLs Rating scale of 1-5
Activities-specific Balance Confidence (ABC) Scale[42]	60 older adults	.96	.92*	≥80 50-80 <50[38]	-----
Survey of Activities and Fear of Falling in the Elderly (SAFE)[8]	270 older adults	.91	-----	-----	-----
Perceived Control of Falling[15]	392 older adults	.71	-----	-----	-----
Perceived Ability to Manage Falls and Falling[15]	392 older adults	.76	-----	-----	-----

* p < .001

Yet another measure, the Survey of Activities and Fear of Falling in the Elderly (SAFE)[8] was developed to assess FOF, using the premise that there are negative consequences to this fear, such as activity restriction or poor quality of life, that should be examined. This survey examines 11 activities of daily living (ADL), instrumental ADLs, mobility tasks, and social activities (e.g., taking a shower, going to the store, taking public transportation, and going to movies or shows, respectively). Lachman et al[8] included exercise activities and social activities, because they felt that avoiding these activities might signal early onset of FOF. For each task, the subjects were asked the following questions: 1. Do you currently do it? 2. If you do the activity, how worried are you that you might fall? 3. If you do not do the activity, do you not do it because you are worried that you might fall? 4. If you do not do the activity because of worry, are there other reasons that you do not do it? 5. For those not worried, what are the reasons that you do not do the activity? 6. Compared to five years ago, would you say that you do it more/the same/ less than you used to? A 5-point (0-4) response system was used for each of these questions and then totaled to give a FOF score. (Table One) Lachman and colleagues' study of older adults showed that the SAFE could be used to differentiate between different degrees of fear and those who do or do not restrict their activity level (afraid/restricted activity: M=1.27, afraid/no restriction: M=0.66, not at all afraid: M=.24), suggesting that the SAFE was useful for examining FOF as it relates to activity restriction.[8] A strong negative correlation was noted between the SAFE and the FES (r =-.76).[8] In addition to the need to assess the reliability of measurements obtained with the SAFE, further research should examine the relationship and discrimination abilities of the SAFE and ABC, because these tools are more similar to each other than to the FES and they address similar populations.

Lawrence et al[15] chose to further refine the premise of fall-related efficacy and developed 2 scales: Perceived Control over Falling and Perceived Ability to Manage Falls and Falling. The scales were developed to differentiate a person's ability to control the environment, mobility, and his or her ability to prevent and manage falls.[15] Perceived Control Over Falling has 4 items that focus on control over the environment and the person's mobility and ability to do things to prevent falls (e.g., "there are things I can do to keep myself from falling" or "falling is something I can control"). The scale's 5-point Likert-type response format ranges from "strongly disagree" to "strongly agree."[15]

Perceived Ability to Manage Falls and Falling is 5-item scale that assesses people's beliefs about managing falls, such as "finding a way to get up if they fall" or "protecting themselves if they do fall."[15] A 4-point scale ranging from "not at all" to "very sure" is used (Table One). Lawrence and colleagues' study demonstrated a lower level of FOF when the subjects had a higher perceived ability to manage falls.[15] They also found that FOF was a manifestation of a more generalized anxiety level, as measured by the Generalized Fearfulness Index (detailed in the report).[15] These findings raise important implications for the study of the causes of FOF and the interventions used to decrease the effects of FOF. Psychometric data relative to these tools, however, are needed.

Considerable effort has been made to construct user friendly tools that measure the underlying nuances of FOF. Because the causes of FOF are multifactorial, it may be difficult to develop an instrument that fully reflects a comprehensive view of FOF. Each of the tools described have strengths and weaknesses relative to the older adult population, although have not been studied with a younger population or with a population that has a different level of activity performance. Further study is needed to examine the reliability and validity of the measurements, establish threshold scores for the population studied, and consideration needs to be given to using these measures with other populations.

INTERVENTIONS FOR FEAR OF FALLING

As the factors that contribute to FOF seem to be multifactorial, a multidimensional approach to intervention to decrease FOF is often recommended. Minimal research, however, has examined the interventions or those who should be targeted for intervention.[18] The primary components of the interventions recommended include education, environmental safety considerations, discussion of risk-taking behaviors, assertiveness training and physical fitness.[19,34,43] Building confidence or fall-related efficacy was crucial[38] and was thought to be as important as physical training in decreasing FOF.[42] Tennstedt et al[19] conducted the only randomized control trial examining FOF intervention with older adults and concluded that cognitive-behavioral changes must occur for FOF to be reduced. This need for cognitive and behavioral changes has been confirmed in recent research and opinion. [15,20,32]

Childs and Kneebone[20] have suggested psychological management that adopts a philosophy of "fall reduction" rather than "fall prevention." The goal of their approach was to safely optimize the independence and increase the balance confidence of the individual, with direct consideration of their fear of falling. They proposed that the falls-reduction approach provides assurance to clients who may be skeptical about a complete fall prevention program. The approach encouraged open discussion, validated the client's fears, and gave the client permission to admit to falls without feeling that they will be blamed for a preventable incident. Education was provided, based on their cognitive-behavioral model, that explained how FOF may decrease activity and increased risk of falling, but also the relationships between the immediate and longer term risks of FOF.[20] The underlying theory of this method is supported by research evidence, although has not been tested.

Childs and Kneebone[20] recommended use of group intervention for those individuals where FOF was harder to establish or where the group of people have different levels of FOF. Individual intervention was suggested for those who have been clearly identified as having FOF. The goal of intervention in both scenarios was control of the anxiety associated with this fear, not eradication of fear. They recommended use of relaxation strategies, prepared self-coping statements when presented with a risky situation and a reminder list of the best means to manage the environment or their walking. Childs and Kneebone[20] advocated for clinical or health psychologists to be involved in falls management intervention, in conjunction with the healthcare team, typically composed of physical and occupational therapy, nursing and the physician.

Yardley and Smith[32] proposed that the interventions to decrease fear of falling be designed with caution, specifically that negative messages concerning one's identity need to be avoided. Oftentimes, in the fall reduction/prevention intervention with the individual, it is implied that one is no longer able to complete an activity independently or safely. There is increasing evidence that this negative approach may interfere in the investment and compliance of the older adult to follow-through on a fall reduction program.[45] Lawrence et al's[15] multifaceted approach concurred that the negative beliefs and attitudes must be altered for the intervention to be effective. Attending to the potential contribution of generalized fearfulness, enhancing physical functioning and including components to increase the ability to manage falls were found to be valuable components of the intervention.[15] Additionally, any depressive symptoms and the effects of multiple chronic conditions must be addressed as part of the management.[31] There must be acceptance and consistent implementation of the recommended interventions for fear of falling to be minimized.[19]

The goals of the education component of the majority of FOF interventions were to provide information and counseling on falls, fall-related injuries and fear of falls; to instill confidence in the older adults' abilities and perceived control over falling; and to train them to move from self-defeating to motivating thoughts on controlling this fear.[17,19] The focus was to educate older adults on a realistic assessment of their self-concept of falls and risk for falls, complemented by teaching them strategies to increase their perceived control over the environment to reduce fall risk and to increase their physical activity and exercise.[19] Some authors have included testimonials from those who had fallen and were comfortable discussing their fears, paired with advice from those who had appropriately overcome their FOF.[19,38] The need to instill confidence and perceived control of falls was considered critical,[38] including providing success in how to manage falls and gradual desensitization to the feared circumstances or environment.[2,15]

Environmental modification to reduce fall risk was a standard component of the education programs to reduce FOF, although the specifics were not detailed in the studies.[17,19,38] Home safety checklists were provided to the older adults, with suggestions presented for remedying the fall hazards.[17] In a recent home-based fall risk reduction program with rural older adults, researchers completed a home assessment (before and after intervention) for the subject and control groups, providing them with appropriate safety modifications that should be made in the home to reduce the fall risk.[46] Both groups were noted to have a decrease in environmental hazards in the home, although the difference was only significant for the intervention group (p =.002 when compared with the Bonferroni alpha = .10).[46] Providing older adults with information they could use to recognize and alter environmental hazards that increase fall risk allowed them to take control over this aspect of their fear.[19]

Assertiveness training and discussion of risk taking behaviors were critical components of this multifaceted approach, because the older adults needed to learn to ask for assistance when in a situation where they were fearful. They also needed to feel comfortable discussing their fear with family, friends, and health care providers. They could develop an appropriate support system, as part of the training process, to discuss their FOF, but they also had the opportunity to devise and carry out fall-prevention strategies.[17,19] Walker and Howland[17] noted that those who could talk about their FOF were less likely to restrict their activity level and they remained active. Encouragement from friends and family to ask for assistance and to discuss their FOF may have made the older adults more at ease in participating in the FOF interventions.[17,19]

Maintaining or improving the physical fitness levels of older adults has been the hallmark of many current fall-risk reduction and fall-prevention programs, the effectiveness of which have been supported by research.[44] Individualized exercise programs yielded significant improvements in balance measures (P<.001), mobility measures (P<.001), and decreased fall risk (P<.001).[44] This dimension of intervention remains important in programs to reduce FOF. Most programs included education that emphasized the benefits of exercise to improve strength and balance, but then provided specific strengthening exercises for extremities, balance and coordination activities, and mobility tasks.[17,19] Tai Chi exercise, with components of balance and flexibility, has been shown to significantly decrease fear of falling (P<.001).[47] Lawrence et al[15] and Tennstedt et al[19] suggested that more attention be paid to the skills in recovery from a fall and to management of the fall as part of the physical fitness program. Tennstedt et al[19] evaluated interventions for FOF, and noted that the subject group of older adults increased levels of activity and had a reduction in general physical dysfunction immediately after the intervention period that included physical fitness. The 6-month follow-up evaluation noted a decrease in both of these effects; therefore, they suggested a booster session a few months after the intervention.[19]

The results of multidimensional interventions for fall prevention have been mixed[19] and those that have specifically addressed FOF have been limited in number.[19,27] The primary emphasis of interventions has been on physical interventions rather than behavioral change, although the literature suggests that FOF is far more complex than a physical problem. Emerging evidence is increasing in support of cognitive and behavioral interventions.[20,32] Success in decreasing FOF apparently depends at least in part on the ability to restore a person's confidence in his or her mobility. Reducing the risk of falling may not reduce FOF, because this fear is, to some degree, independent of the risk of falling.[5] Successful mobility in activities that people need to perform on a regular basis may build their confidence,[14] when combined with knowledge about falls and fall risks and the assertiveness to ask for assistance when they need it. Researchers have not compared the individual aspects of this multidimensional approach to treating FOF (i.e. education versus physical fitness). Future interventions may want to place more emphasis on materials for instilling adaptive beliefs, greater confidence in one's abilities, and more realistic assessments of failures related to the management of falls and falling component prior to attacking the control of falling component.

FURTHER RESEARCH NEEDS

Most of the research that has been completed on fear of falling has been cross-sectional in nature; therefore, more longitudinal and prospective studies are needed. Research is difficult in this realm, however, because those potential subjects who are most fearful are those least likely to volunteer for studies. The samples used in previous research may underestimate the true effect of fall-related fear;[33] thus, creative sampling techniques are necessary.

Fear of falling is known to be multifactorial with, at a minimum, physical, psychological and functional influences. A complete understanding of the role of these factors is needed, including a clear delineation between fall-efficacy and FOF. The extent to which FOF is a protective mechanism versus a social dysfunction requires study.[10] The physical and psychological consequences of falling warrant further investigation, beyond the incidence of falls.[11] The degree to which generalized anxiety or the consequence of loss of identity or independence may contribute to FOF warrants further examination, as this may alter the direction of future interventions. The prevalence of FOF in other populations must be determined, including various age groups and pathology related groups. The ability to identify those at risk for developing FOF is also worthy of study,[25] because this may be the route for future preventative measures.

Further research is also needed in the area of measurement related to FOF. With the current instruments that are available, the reliability and validity of the SAFE and Perceived Control over Falling and Perceived Ability to Manage Falls and Falling scales need to be established. The relationship and discrimination ability of the ABC versus the SAFE should be examined for further clarity in the constructs the instruments assess. Threshold scores for these tools should also be determined for ease in use and communication among health care providers.

The interventions for FOF also require further examination. The individual aspects of the multidimensional programs need to be studied and compared with randomized controlled trials. Long term follow-up studies are a necessary part of these investigations. The role of vicarious experience in changing the activity levels of older adults is an area warranting study, to determine the underlying reasons for why older adults reduce their activity because of falls by other people.[10] The identification of strategies that foster a healthy degree of caution and risk taking rather than an unhealthy level of fear was recommended.[8] Isolation of those individuals that choose to engage in activities despite their fear would be helpful, as well as looking at whether changes in physical activity and self-efficacy actually bring about changes in balance and FOF.[21]

CONCLUSIONS

In the past two decades, much attention in research and the health care realm has focused appropriately on falls and fall prevention among older adults. As this research has evolved, FOF has emerged as an entity distinct from falls. Fear of falling is claimed to have an average prevalence of 30% or more in older adults who do not have a history of falling, and it is double that in those older adults who have fallen. It has long-term negative consequences to the physical and functional well being of older adults, to the degree that loss of independence is experienced with normally performed daily activities. The prevalence of FOF in other age and disease-related groups has not been thoroughly examined.

The factors contributing to FOF in older adults are numerous, although the exact causes remain unclear. Functional and physical decline and decreased quality of life are closely related to FOF, so that these factors may actually be causes of FOF or are caused by FOF. Specific measures based on a concise definition are needed, as further subtleties between fall-efficacy and FOF become evident. Multiple interventions have been recommended, with the key issue being cognitive-behavioral change in the older adult that results in bolstered self-confidence to perform daily activities.

Fear of falling needs to be assessed by health care providers as they work with older adults. Fear of falling should be viewed separate from falling, to be present in those who have not fallen, and as a pervasive health care concern in older adults. Prevention of this fear would be ideal, although, in lieu of this, education, dialogue and further research with this population may bring us closer to a full understanding of the causes and effective interventions for FOF, regardless of the population.

REFERENCES

1. Murphy J, Isaacs B. The post-fall syndrome. A study of 36 patients. *Gerontol.* 1982;28:265-70.
2. Bhala RP, O'Donnell J, Thoppil E. Ptophobia. *Phys Ther.* 1982;62:187-90.
3. Tinetti ME, Powell L. Fear of falling and low self-efficacy: A cause of dependence in elderly persons. *J Gerontol.* 1993;48:35-38.
4. Tinetti ME, Speechley M, Ginter SF. Risk factors for falls among elderly persons living in the community. *NEJM.* 1988;319:1701-07.
5. Maki BE, Holliday PJ, Topper AK. Fear of falling and postural performance in the elderly. *J Gerontol:Med Sci.* 1991;46:M123-31.

6. Cumming RG, Salkeld G, Thomas M, Szonyi G. Prospective study of in the impact of fear of falling on activities of daily living, SF-36 Scores, and nursing home admission. *J Gerontol:Med Sci.* 2000;55:M299-305.

7. Shumway-Cook A, Baldwin M, Polissar NI, Gruber W. Predicting the probability for falls in community-dwelling older adults. *Phys Ther.* 1997;77:812-19.

8. Lachman ME, Howland J, Tennstedt S, et al. Fear of falling and activity restriction: The Survey of Activities and Fear of Falling in the Elderly (SAFE). *J Gerontol:Psych Sci.* 1998;53:P43-50.

9. McKcc KJ, Orbcll S, Radlcy KΛ. Predicting perceived recovered activity in older people after a fall. *Dis Rehabil.* 1999;21:555-62.

10. Howland J, Lachman ME, Peterson EW, et al. Covariates of fear of falling and associated activity curtailment. *Gerontologist.* 1998;38:549-55.

11. Tinetti ME, Mendes de Leon CF, Doucette JT, Baker DI. Fear of falling and fall-related efficacy in relationship to functioning among community-living elders. *J Gerontol:Med Sci.* 1994;49:M140-47.

12. Howland J, Peterson EW, Levin WC, et al. Fear of falling among the community-dwelling elderly. *J Aging Health.* 1993;5:229-43.

13. Arfken CL, Lach HW, Birge SJ, Miller JP. The prevalence and correlates of fear of falling in elderly persons living in the community. *Am J Pub Health.* 1994;84:565-70.

14. Myers AM, Powell LE, Maki BE, et al. Psychological indicators of balance confidence: relationship to actual and perceived abilities. *J Gerontol: Med Sci.* 1996;51:M37-43.

15. Lawrence RH, Tennstedt SL, Kasten LE, Shih J. Intensity and correlates of fear of falling and hurting oneself in the next year. *J Aging Health.* 1998;10:267-86.

16. Burker EJ, Sloane PD, Mattingly D, Preisser J, Mitchell CM. Predictors of fear of falling in dizzy and nondizzy elderly. *Psych and Aging.* 1995;10:104-10.

17. Walker JE, Howland J. Falls and fear of falling among elderly persons living in the community: occupational therapy interventions. *Am J Occ Ther.* 1991;45:119-22.

18. Friedman SM, Munoz B, West SK, et al. Falls and fear of falling: Which comes first? A longitudinal prediction model suggests strategies for primary and secondary prevention. *JAGS.* 2002;50:1329-1335.

19. Tennstedt S, Howland J, Lachman M, Peterson E, Kasten L, Jette A. A randomized, controlled trial of a group intervention to reduce fear of falling and associated activity restriction in older adults. *J Gerontol:Psych Sci.* 1998;53:P384-92.

20. Childs L, Kneebone II. Falls, fear of falling and psychological management. *Br J Ther Rehabil.* 2002;9:225-231.

21. McAuley EM, Mihalko SL, Rosengren K. Self-efficacy and balance correlates of fear of falling in the elderly. *J Aging Phys Act.* 1997;5:329-40.

22. Vellas BJ, Wayne SJ, Romero LJ, Baumgartner RN, Garry PJ. Fear of falling and restriction of mobility in elderly fallers. *Age and Ageing.* 1997;26:189-93.

23. Aoyagi K, Ross PD, Davis JW, Wasnich RD, Hayashi T, Takemoto T. Falls among community-dwelling elderly in Japan. *J Bone Min Res.* 1998;13:1468-74.

24. Kressig RW, Wolf SL, Sattin RW, et al. Associations of demographic, functional, and behavioral characteristics with activity-related fear of falling among older adults transitioning to frailty. *JAGS.* 2001;49:1456-1462.

25. Franzoni S, Rozzini R, Boffelli S, Frisoni GB, Trabucchi M. Fear of falling in nursing home patients. *Gerontology.* 1994;40:38-44.

26. Stephens J, DuShuttle D, Hatcher C, et al. Use of Awareness through Movement improves balance and balance confidence in people with multiple sclerosis: a randomized controlled study. *Neuro Report.* 2001;25:39-49.

27. Petrella RJ, Myers PM, Chesworth B. Physical function and fear of falling after hip fracture rehabilitation in the elderly. *Am J Phys Med Rehabil.* 2000;79:154-60.

28. Hellstrom K, Lindmark B. Fear of falling in patients with stroke: a reliability study. *Clin Rehabil.* 1999;13:509-17.

29. Legters KS, Whitney SL, Porter RE, Buczek FL. The relationship between the Activities-specific Balance Confidence (ABC) Scale and Dynamic Gait Index (DGI) in peripheral vestibular dysfunction. *J Vest Res.* (In review)

30. Miller WC, Speeckley M, Deathe B. Ther prevalence and risk factors of falling and fear of falling among lower extremity amputees. *Arch Phys Med Rehabil.* 2001;82:1031-7.

31. Murphy SL, Williams CS, Gill TM. Characteristics associated with fear of falling and activity restriction in community-living older persons. *JAGS.* 2002;50:516-520.

32. Yardley L, Smith H. A prospective study of the relationship between feared consequences of falling and avoidance of activity in community-living older people. *Gerontologist.* 2002;42:17-23.

33. Maki BE. Gait changes in older adults: predictors of falls of indicators of fear? *JAGS.* 1997;45:313-20.

34. Ware JE. SF-36 Health Survey: Manual and Interpretive Guide. Boston, MA: Health Institute;1993.

35. Luukinen H, Koski K, Kivela S, Laippala P. Social status, life changes, housing conditions, health, functional abilities and life-style as risk factors for recurrent falls among the home-dwelling elderly. *Pub Health.* 1996;110:115-18.

36. Cornoni-Huntley J, Brock DB, Ostfeld AM, Taylor JO, Wallace RB. The Established Populations for the Epidemiologic Study of the Elderly: resource data book. NIH pub no. 86-2443. Bethesda, MD; National Institutes of Health, 1986.

37. DiPietro L, Caspersen CJ, Ostfeld AM, Nadel ER. A survey for assessing physical activity among older adults. *Med Sci Sports Exer.* 1993;25:628-42.

38. Myers AM, Fletcher PC, Myers AH, Sherk W. Discriminative and evaluative properties of the Activities-specific Balance Confidence (ABC) Scale. *J Gerontol: Med Sci.* 1998;53A:M287-M294.

39. Gill DL, Williams K, Williams L, Hale WA. Multidimensional correlates of falls in older women. *Intl J Aging Hum Dev.* 1998;47:35-51.

40. Tinetti ME, Richman D, Powell L. Falls efficacy as a measure of fear of falling. *J Gerontol: Psych Sci.* 1990;45:P239-43.

41. Turano K, Rubin G, Herdman SJ, Chee E, Fried LP. Visual stabilization of posture in the elderly: fallers vs. nonfallers. *Optom Vis Sci.* 1994;71:761-69.

42. Powell LE, Myers AM. The Activities-specific Balance Confidence (ABC) Scale. *J Gerontol:Med Sci.* 1995;50:M28-34.

43. Hill KD, Schwarz JA, Kalogeropoulus AJ, Gibson SJ. Fear of falling revisited. *Arch Phys Med Rehabil.* 1996;77:1025-29.

44. Shumway-Cook A, Gruber W, Baldwin M, Liao S. The effect of multidimensional exercises on balance, mobility, and fall risk in community dwelling older adults. *Phys Ther.* 1997;77:46-57.

45. vanHaastregt JC, Diederiks JP, van Rossum E, et al. Effects of preventive home visits to elderly people living in the community: Systematic review. *Br Med J.* 2000;320:754-781.

46. Yate SM, Dunnagan TA. Evaluation the effectiveness of a home-based fall risk reduction program for rural community-dwelling older adults. *J Gerontol: Med Sci.* 2001;56A:M226-M230.

47. Taggart HM. Effects of Tai Chi exercise on balance, functional mobility, and fear of falling among older women. *Appl Nurs Res.* 2002;15:235-242.

Chapter 4

FEAR AND THE DEVELOPMENT OF PROBLEMATIC INTERPERSONAL PATTERNS

Toru Sato[†]

Shippensburg University
Shippensburg, Pennsylvania, USA

ABSTRACT

Fear is a very important emotion necessary for physical survival. It is a signal informing us that we are in danger. However, fear can also cause us many problems. We sometimes become aggressive and exploit others because of fear. One of the reasons why fear can be so problematic is that we learn to associate many things with fear through our experiences. Although our ability to associate various things through our experiences has many beneficial effects, it can also make us fear and react to people and events that are almost completely harmless in aggressive and hurtful ways. Because of our ability to associate, fear is considered to be an important factor in the development of problematic interpersonal patterns. This paper will focus on the problems relating to the emotion of fear using from an interpersonal perspective.

Fear is a very important emotion necessary for physical survival. It is a signal telling us that we are or will be in danger. It is a basic emotion conducive to survival for all animal species including humans. Fear makes us alert and highly responsive to the environment. If we did not experience fear, we would not run away from dangerous predators or protect ourselves from natural disasters. Without fear, we would not protect our food and other resources from being taken away or lost. Fear is conducive to survival. It enables us to secure resources for survival and it also enables us to escape immediate life and health threatening dangers. Fear is an integral part of our will to survive.

However, fear can also cause us many problems. We sometimes become avoidant of others because of fear (Ainsworth, Blehar, Waters, & Wall, 1978). Moreover, we

---

[†] Correspondance address: Toru Sato, Dept. of Psychology, 204 Gilbert Hall, Shippensburg University, Shippensburg, PA 17257-2299, USA.

sometimes behave in aggressive and violent ways because of fear (Miller, Cowan, Cowan, Hetherington, & Clingempeel, 1993). Fear is one factor that causes drug abuse as well as hate and hateful behaviors (Simons, Conger, & Whitbeck, 1988). We also sometimes ignore and deny certain aspects of ourselves because of fear (Rogers, 1961). We fear because we anticipate pain or the increase of pain. Because pain is such a powerful negative emotion, we try almost everything we can to avoid it.

FEAR THROUGH ASSOCIATION

One of the reasons why fear can be so problematic is that we learn to associate many things with pain through our experiences. Our ability to associate things has many beneficial effects. It enables us to learn from our experiences and predict things in the future (Jaynes, 1976). It enables us to understand, control, and manipulate the environment. It also enables us to escape from dangerous situations. This ability to make associations, however, can also make us unhappy and distressed as well. For instance, a woman who has experienced rape may associate men in general with this painful experience and thus develop a general fear of men. A child scolded for failing in school may associate classrooms with pain. Fear can be overgeneralized from relatively insignificant events to very significant problems through associations in the mind.

Let us examine an example that we can all relate to. Many of us are commonly upset when we find out that we overpaid for a product. By overpaying, we feel that we lose more money than necessary. Losing money may be associated with not being able to pay the rent or mortgage. This may be associated with having no shelter, which may be associated with being cold and getting sick or being robbed. These things are associated with losing our health or even our lives. Because we have associated these things with overpaying for a product, one incident of slightly overpaying for a product may become a very serious problem for us. However, in most cases, many of the associations we make are so remote that the actual problem we are facing is almost completely unrelated to the larger problem that we are associating it with (e.g., overpaying - losing our lives). In this way, we often turn a small problem into a large problem by making seemingly unnecessary associations (Beck, 1976; Ellis, 1977; Sato, 2001).

Through our own experiences, many of us realize that almost all of the things we become distressed about in our lives are small unimportant problems (Beck, 1976; Ellis, 1977). The reason why we become so distressed about many things lies in the fact that we associate the insignificant problems with more profound problems that are only very remotely related to the actual small problem we are facing. This notion of blowing a small problem out of proportion applies to the distress we experience in many areas of our lives including everyday interpersonal experiences. For instance, we may become extremely upset about someone behaving in a very rude manner toward us. This incident in itself is not an extremely serious problem. In fact, most of us encounter rude behavior very often during our everyday lives. Why are we sometimes so upset at this? One probable reason why we are upset is because we associate this incident with more serious problems. We may associate others being rude to us with people not respecting us in general. We may associate people not respecting us with losing or not being able to obtain a job, which may be associated with not having any money. Not having money may be associated with not being able to obtain the resources for survival.

Or perhaps, other people not respecting us may be associated with people not caring for us, which may be associated with feeling emotionally deprived, lonely and isolated. This, in turn, may be associated with not being able to obtain the resources for survival as well.

Furthermore, we may even overgeneralize the other person's temporary rude behavior across time and think that this person will be rude to us for the rest of your lives and we may associate this with receiving no respect and attention from that person for the rest of our lives. In many cases, however, the rude behavior may be temporary and there may be no reason for us to become extremely upset. When we are upset, it is often useful to remind ourselves that whatever is bothering us is not anything as serious as we usually think. The problem seems serious only because we are making unnecessary associations in our mind. This may be difficult to do when we are highly emotional and highly involved in the interaction. Even when we are highly emotional, however, we can at least take some time out and distance ourselves from the situation to calm down (Goleman, 1995). After we calm down, we may be able to realize that what we are actually upset about is not as crucially important as we may have thought.

FEAR AND INTERPERSONAL PATTERNS

Fear can also be problematic in that it can adversely affect our interpersonal behavior patterns. Various theorists have discussed how various kinds of interpersonal patterns evolve through our life experiences (Berne, 1964, Bowlby, 1969; Harris, 1967; Stern, 1985). Interpersonal patterns represent a combination of the emotional and behavioral actions and reactions of one person to another (Leary, 1957; Safran, 1990). As an example, let us consider the following sequence of events: Every time Steve wants Eric to do some housework, he authoritatively demands it from him. As a result, Eric does the housework and Steve is rewarded for his demanding behavior. One the other hand, every time Eric wants some attention from Steve, Eric begins crying. When Eric cries, Steve provides him with attention and sympathy and therefore Eric is rewarded for his behavior. One can see from this example, that both Steve and Eric have specific interpersonal patterns that they have acquired from their past interactions with each other. Throughout our lives, we learn different ways of obtaining reinforcement from others. These methods of interacting with others are commonly referred to as interpersonal patterns or interpersonal behavior patterns (Kiesler, 1996). Although these interpersonal patterns develop and change throughout our lives, many interpersonal behavior patterns are considered to develop from early experiences in life (Bowlby, 1969; Stern, 1985).

Fear can adversely affect the development of our interpersonal behavior patterns in important ways (Kiesler, 1996). Many interpersonal patterns are considered to be acquired in childhood and tend to stay with us throughout our lives (Bowlby, 1969). One reason why we acquire many of these habits early on in life is because we are primarily in relatively powerless social positions when we are young children. As young children, most people we interact with are more powerful than us. During these early stages in our lives, we are dependent on powerful people such as parents and other caretakers for our comfort and survival. A newly born infant cannot feed him/herself. A young infant will have difficulty surviving without the support and protection provided by parents and other caretakers. Because we, as infants, are dependent on these people, these people are considered to be more powerful than us. They can refuse to feed us, they can refuse to provide us with shelter and clothing and they may even abuse us (both psychologically and physically) in some cases. In sum, infants and young children are at the mercy of their parents, babysitters, nannies, teachers, and anyone else who takes care of them because they have less social power than most people they interact with (Sato, 2001).

THE INTERPERSONAL CHAIN OF EXPLOITATION

Because infants are in relatively powerless positions, powerful people exploit them in subtle ways without awareness. The term "exploit" will be used here for the present purposes due to a lack of a better term. Although the term "exploit" often refers to extreme types of behaviors, this term is used here to include milder variations of this type of behavior. It includes all behaviors in which one demands more attention than one provides. In this context, the term "exploit" refers to situations in which one person's needs and desires are attended to more that those of the other person. Parents say "do this and don't do that", teachers send messages saying "you will fail if you don't do this". These people are essentially sending a powerful message claiming "I want you to be the way I want you to be, not the way you want to be. And if you are not the way I want you to be, I will make you suffer the consequences (by punishing you or by not accepting you or not caring for you properly)". Any behavior that contains this type of message is considered to be a form of exploitation in this context.

Even though it is not respectable to do so, any person in power has the opportunity to exploit less powerful individuals. In fact, most people in power end up exploiting less powerful individuals (often without awareness) to some extent. As a result, most infants end up being fearful of those people in power to varying extents. If certain people exploit us, we become afraid of those people. In many cases, we are afraid of the people that we are closest with during infancy, since the people closest to us are the ones we are dependent on.

Although some are more afraid than others because some are exploited more than others, we are all afraid of powerful people to a certain extent. This fear is sometimes generalized and associated with people in general and not just with certain individuals who have exploited and abused their power on us. The more fearful we become in our lives, the more we tend to feel that the world is a dangerous place and is a place full of people who will try to exploit us. Although fear is necessary in order to avoid danger and to ensure survival, it also has the effect of causing us desperation when taken to its extremes. The more we are exploited, the less powerful we feel and the less powerful we feel, the more desperation we experience. Many theorists contend that because of this sense of desperation, we tend to develop problematic interpersonal patterns (e.g., Bowlby, 1969; Carson, 1982).

The more fearful we are, the more desperate we become in trying to avoid painful or dangerous situations where we may possibly be exploited. Furthermore, not only do we avoid painful and dangerous situations, we also try to exploit others (sometimes in very subtle ways) in order protect ourselves and compensate for feelings of powerlessness (Adler, 1927; Ainsworth et al., 1978). We are all familiar with the notion of striking before being attacked as a common strategy to protect ourselves. Thus, the more fearful we are, the more we strike. Fear makes us try to capitalize on opportunities to feel powerful and important. Therefore, whenever the opportunity presents itself, we exploit others to compensate for our feelings of powerlessness. This enables us to temporarily escape from our fear. The more powerful we feel that we are, the less fearful we become (at least for a temporary period of time). This corresponds with recent findings on abusive behaviors such as bullying and violence among children and adolescents. Research indicates that abused children have a higher tendency for violence and other aggressive behavior (Dodge, Petit, & Bates, 1994; Emery, 1989; Patterson, Reid, & Dishion, 1992). Furthermore, research has suggested that bullying is more common among children who are neglected and thus feel powerless in their homes (Miller et al., 1993; Patterson et al., 1992; Widom, 1989).

Because some people have been in unfortunate circumstances where others have consistently exploited them, they develop this general belief that the world is a dangerous place full of people who are trying to take advantage of them. This general belief makes the person become more self-protective and look for opportunities to exploit others (Nolte & Harris, 1998; Dodge & Somberg, 1987). Unfortunately, these people often spend much of their energy and time protecting themselves and looking for victims and opportunities that allow them to exploit others. This behavior of exploiting others is commonly manifested as problematic interpersonal patterns.

VARIOUS FORMS OF EXPLOITATION

While some of these problematic interpersonal patterns such as bullying and violence are obvious forms of exploitation, other types of interpersonal patterns manifest themselves in more subtle ways. We often send subtle messages to others in order to control them and indicate that we are the one's in power. These types of behaviors have a tendency to make others feel disrespected and offended. Although various scholars have discussed numerous interpersonal patterns from different perspectives (Berne, 1964; Leary, 1957; Luborsky, 1984; Kiesler, 1996; Safran, 1990; Sullivan, 1953), four types of patterns seem to be common as less obvious forms of exploitation.

One common interpersonal pattern is conceptualized as criticism / high expectation. This behavior is characterized as being overly demanding of others. We expect others to be the way we want them to be regardless of how that person feels. We often criticize others, make sarcastic remarks, and make others feel inadequate. These are all mild forms of exploitation. The underlying message of this behavior pattern is, "I demand you to live up to my expectations and you are failing."

Another common interpersonal pattern is conceptualized as intimidation / anger. This behavior is basically characterized as making others fear the self through intimidation or expressing anger. Although this seems like an obvious form of exploitation, it can manifest itself in subtle ways. For example, we sometimes treat people with silence (in anger) if they are not the way we want them to be. The underlying message is, "I will punish you (even more) if you are not the way I demand you to be."

Self-pity / guilt infliction is another interpersonal pattern that we commonly use. This behavior is basically characterized as making others feel sorry for oneself or making others feel guilty for not being compassionate. We sometimes demand that others wallow with us in our pity. At other times, we manipulate others to do things by making them feel guilty if they do not attend to us. The underlying message is, "You are making me suffer even more if you don't attend to my needs."

The interpersonal pattern conceptualized as chainchatting is also one that we encounter quite often in our lives. This behavior is characterized as speaking incessantly without listening to others. We sometimes demand attention incessantly without letting others have their turn. This is a mild form of exploitation in that we demand the other person to attend to our own needs while ignoring the other person's needs. This type of behavior often makes others feel ignored and disrespected. The underlying message is, "What I think is more important than what you think."

Although there are many other forms of interpersonal patterns, the ones mentioned above may be some of the more common forms of interpersonal exploitation. Individuals tend to vary in the types of interpersonal patterns they tend to use due to differences in their past experiences. In addition to differences in the types of interpersonal patterns used, people also differ in the extent they use these patterns of exploitation. Some individuals engage in more extreme forms of exploitation while others may use milder variations of it. Moreover, some individuals may engage in these types of behaviors more often than others.

VARYING DEGREES OF EXPLOITATION

Although all of us exploit others to a certain extent, individuals who have experienced being victims of extreme forms of exploitation tend to engage in these types of behaviors more often. One reason for this is that these individuals tend to develop negative and rigid expectations about the characteristics of others and rigid beliefs concerning the ways in which they should behave in interpersonal situations (Carson, 1982; Kiesler, 1982). Consequently, individuals who have suffered from more exploitation tend to repeat similar negative interpersonal patterns across a wide range of different interpersonal situations more than other individuals (Kiesler, 1982, 1983; Leary, 1957; Safran, 1984). In sum, the more negative experiences we have, the more we fear. The more we fear, the more we use our rigid interpersonal patterns to exploit other people (Sato, 2001). Let us consider an example to illustrate this point.

Jerry and Jane are in a dating relationship. Jane is struggling to overcome a relationship with her father who was abusive to her during childhood. During Jane's childhood, her father had the habit of decorating their home with red roses. Jerry is unaware of this and takes the liberty to bring Jane some red roses on their date as a kind gesture. Seeing the red roses, Jane is reminded of her abusive relationship with her father and suspects that Jerry was doing this to make her feel uncomfortable. Jane becomes extremely upset at this and makes threatening remarks and intimidates Jerry. In this case, Jane is responding to her own fear that she has associated through her past experiences and not to Jerry's particular behavior and intentions. Because Jane is responding to her own unique associations that Jerry does not know about, her extreme reaction is surprising and out of proportion to Jerry's initial gesture (taking the liberty to bring Jane some roses) from Jerry's perspective. In this case, Jane's experience as an abuse victim caused her to become excessively fearful and behave in threatening ways toward Jerry. As discussed earlier, threatening behavior (intimidation) is a typical form of exploitation. Because of the fear experienced as a victim of abuse (an extreme form of exploitation), Jane has developed problematic interpersonal patterns such as intimidating others in order to protect herself.

Individuals who have experienced extreme types of exploitation (such as abuse) or consistent exploitation often develop various complex interpersonal patterns to protect themselves and make themselves feel more powerful and less fearful. These fearful individuals may look for people who are easy to take advantage of. The victims of these individuals are typically kind and giving or individuals who are particularly vulnerable. These fearful individuals may exploit others here and there every once in a while so that they are able to maintain relationships with the people they take advantage of. This enables them to maintain their relationships with the vulnerable individuals and allows them to come back to them when they become fearful again. These individuals usually have subconsciously developed very sophisticated game plans to exploit others in subtle ways so that their behavior seems socially acceptable on the surface. Unfortunately, this problem of fear is only resolved temporarily by exploiting others because the fear is based on one's own associations and expectations. As mentioned earlier, these individuals have this fear because they believe that everyone and everything is out to exploit us.

Sometimes this is referred to as "fighting your demons" because it is as if these people are constantly fighting their fear of being exploited (Ribi, 1990; Sato 2001). It is not anything in the real world that we are afraid of. As mentioned earlier, we are most often afraid of what we have associated with certain events and not the actual events themselves. Although we are fighting our own demons when we are afraid, we all have a tendency to see the demon in others and not in ourselves. In other words, we blame others for our fears. We think, "I am afraid or I am in pain because of this person" and we try to retaliate by exploiting others because we think that it is only fair to do so. Often times this only provides temporary relief and makes the situation even worse afterwards by adding momentum to the negative cycle of exploiting one another (Sato, 2001). This occurs because whenever we exploit others, we make those others fearful and this motivates them to exploit us back. In order to deal with this effectively, we need to realize that it is not anybody or anything else in the outside world that is causing this fear or pain. We need to recognize that in most cases, our own associations and expectations are the primary cause of the fear and pain that we experience.

CONCLUSIONS AND FUTURE DIRECTIONS

Although, we have focused on extreme cases, it is also important to remind ourselves that all of us engage in this type of exploitation to a certain extent. We all try to find opportunities to feel powerful and escape our fears. Individuals only differ in the how much we engage in this type of behavior. The more negative experiences that we have, the more we fear, and the more we exploit others. On the other hand, if we have experienced many negative experiences but have developed a consistent awareness that what we are fighting is our own associations with fear and not the outside force that we are actually facing, we may begin learning how to deal with this fear in a constructive way without exploiting others. Although work in the clinical field has explored the process of facing and dealing with this type of fear to some extent (e.g., Beck, 1967, 1976; Ellis, 1977; Rogers, 1961), we may benefit greatly from further future research focusing on the process of dealing with our fears in a constructive manner.

REFERENCES

Adler, A. (1927). *Understanding human nature*. New York: Greenberg.

Ainsworth, M. D. S., Blehar, M. C., Waters, E., & Wall, S. (1978). *Patterns of attachment*. Hillsdale, NJ: Erlbaum.

Beck, A. T. (1967). *Depression: Clinical, experimental, and theoretical aspects*. New York: Hoeber.

Beck, A. T. (1976). *Cognitive therapy and the emotional disorders*. New York: International Universities Press.

Berne, E. (1964). *Games people play*. New York: Random House.

Bowlby, J. (1969). *Attachment and loss* (Vol.1: Attachment). New York: Basic Books.

Carson, R. C. (1982). Self-fulfilling prophecy, maladaptive behaviour, and psychotherapy. In J. C. Anchin & D. J. Kiesler (Eds.), *Handbook of interpersonal psychotherapy* (pp. 64-77). Elmsford, NY: Pergamon.

Dodge, K. A., Pettit, G. S., & Bates, J. E. (1994). Socialization mediators of relation between socioeconomic status and child conduct problems. *Child Development, 65*, 649-655.

Dodge, K. A., & Somberg, D. R. (1987). Hostile attributional biases among aggressive boys are exacerbated under conditions of threat of self. *Child Development, 58*, 213-224.

Ellis, A. (1977). *Reason and emotion in psychotherapy* (2nd ed.). Saecaucus, NJ: Lyle Stuart.

Emery, R. E. (1989). Family Violence. *American Psychologist, 44*, 321-328.

Goleman, D. (1995). *Emotional Intelligence: Why it can matter more than IQ*. New York: Bantam Books.

Harris, T. A. (1967). *I'm OK-you're OK*. New York: Avon books.

Jaynes, J. (1976). *Origin of consciousness in the breakdown of the bicameral mind*. Boston: Houghton Mifflin.

Kiesler, D. J. (1982). Interpersonal theory for personality and psychotherapy. In J. C. Anchin & D. J. Kiesler (Eds.), *Handbook of interpersonal psychotherapy* (pp. 3-24). Elmsford, NY: Pergamon.

Kiesler, D. J. (1983). The 1982 Interpersonal circle: A taxonomy for complementarity in human transactions. *Psychological Review, 90*, 185-214.

Kiesler, D. J. (1996). *Contemporary interpersonal theory and research*. New York: Wiley.

Leary, T. F. (1957). *Interpersonal diagnosis of personality*. New York: Ronald.

Luborsky, L. (1984). *Principles of Psychoanalytic Psychotherapy: A manual for Supportive-Expressive Treatment*. New York: Basic Books.

Miller, N. B., Cowan, P. A., Cowan, C. P., Hetherington, E. M., & Clingempeel, W. G. (1993). Externalizing in pre-schoolers and early adolescents: A cross-study replication of a family model. *Developmental Psychology, 29*, 3-16.

Nolte, D. L., & Harris, R. (1998). *Children learn what they live: Parenting to inspire values*. New York: Workman

Patterson, G. R., Reid, J. B., & Dishion, T. J. (1992). *Antisocial boys*. Eugene, OR: Castalia.

Ribi, A. (1990). *Demons of the inner world: Understanding our hidden complexes* (trans. M. H. Kohn). Boston: Shambala.

Rogers, C. R. (1961). *On becoming a person: A therapist's view of psychotherapy*. Boston: Houghton Mifflin.

Safran, J. D. (1990). Towards a refinement of cognitive therapy in light of interpersonal theory: I. Theory. *Clinical Psychology Review, 10*, 87-105.

Sato, T. (2001). *Rhythms and relationships: Patterns in the complex web of life*. Manuscript in preparation.

Simons, R. L., Conger, R. D., & Whitbeck, L. B. (1988). A multistage social learning model of the influences of family and peers upon adolescent substance use. *Journal of Drug Issues, 18,* 293-316.

Stern. D. N. (1985). *The interpersonal world of the infant*. New York: Basic Books.

Sullivan, H. S. (1953). *The interpersonal theory of psychiatry*. New York: Norton.

Widom, C. S. (1989). Child abuse, neglect, and adult behavior. *American Journal of Orthopsychiatry, 59,* 355-367.

Chapter 5

BULLYING IN PRISONS: THE ROLE OF FEAR

*Jane L. Ireland**
Ashworth Hospital, Liverpool, UK
Department of Psychology, University of Central Lancashire,
Preston, Lancashire, UK.

ABSTRACT

The present chapter highlights how the concept of fear is an important element of the prison-based definition of bullying and yet has received little attention in the literature. In a prison, where physical escape from an aggressor is often not possible, fear responses can be magnified. Such responses can manifest themselves in a number of ways. This chapter highlights the many types of ways in which a victim may react to bullying, and explores the extent to which these reactions may indeed be fear-motivated. The chapter concludes with some directions for future research.

Experiencing fear is almost as an expected part of incarceration. This can include fear of what will happen to your family during your detention, fear that a relationship may dissolve and that you may lose contact with friends and family, and a fear of being stigmatised by society once released. Fear can also relate to a general fear about the prison environment and what you may be subjected to whilst you are detained there. In a setting where violence is perceived to be commonplace, a real fear for many prisoners is the possibility of being bullied (Ireland, 2002).

Bullying does occur in prisons, and there is ample evidence to suggest that it is both more frequent and more severe in these settings in comparison to that which occurs elsewhere such as in schools and in the workplace. For example, Ireland, Jarvis, Beck and Osiowy (1999) reviewed prison studies and reported estimates of self-reported bullying in the range of 20 to

---

* Dr Jane L. Ireland Ph.D., Chartered Forensic Psychologist, Psychology Department, Personality Disorder Unit, Ashworth Hospital, Parkbourn, Liverpool, L31 1HW; and the Psychology Department, University of Central Lancashire, Preston, PR1 2HE. EMAIL: Irelan-J@Ashworth.nwest.nhs.uk

70 per cent for young offenders and 0 to 62 per cent for adult offenders. The range for self-reported victims was 30 to 75 per cent for young offenders and 8 to 57 per cent for adult offenders. Thus, prisoners may be justified in fearing the possibility of being bullied.

It is also important to highlight how you do not need to experience bullying to be fearful of it; prisoners who have never been bullied report as much fear about future bullying as those who have actually been bullied (Grant, 1999). The intensity of fear reported by those who have been bullied regularly versus those who have been bullied 'once or twice' is also reported to be similar (Grant, 1999). This suggests that the *severity* of bullying (in terms of the frequency) may have little to do with the *level* of fear that victims experience. Similarly, even prisoners who have not been bullied will take 'precautions' to avoid becoming victims. McCorkle (1992) was one of the first researchers to explore the role of precautionary behaviours among prisoners, describing them as behaviours engaged in either following victimisation, or if the prisoner felt that it was likely to occur. Essentially they represent behaviours used by prisoners to make prison life safe. They include;

- Keeping more to themselves
- Avoiding certain areas of the prison
- Spending more time in their cells
- Avoiding activities
- Requesting protective custody
- Getting 'tough' to avoid victimisation
- Keeping a weapon nearby
- Lifting weights

McCorkle (1992) described these precautions as the behavioural consequences of fear in prison. Many of these precautions appear focused on limiting the opportunities that perpetrators have to bully, although some, such as 'getting tough', appear focused on being able to actively resist exploitation when it occurs. Interestingly, McCorkle (1992) found that up to 78 per cent of prisoners reported engaging in at least one precautionary behaviour. The most frequently reported precaution was 'kept more to self' (78 per cent), followed by 'had to get tough to avoid victimisation' (70 per cent). This perhaps gives an indication of the extent to which prisoners' feared victimisation. Indeed, Grant (1999) found that the prisoners who reported being most afraid of bullying were also the most likely to engage in precautionary behaviours. Fear also influences the *type* of precautionary behaviour that a prisoner displays, with fear representing the best predictor of passive precautions such as avoidance (McCorkle, 1992). McCorkle (1992) concluded from these findings that *"Fear appeared to be shaping the lifestyles of many of the many living at TSP [Tennessee State Prison]"* and that the relationship between fear, victimisation and personal precautions were markedly more pronounced in prisons than in community samples.

Fear also features in the different types of aggression that make-up bullying. Bullying can include both reactive and proactive aggression (Dodge, 1991). Reactive aggression occurs when an individual over-reacts to minor provocations. It has also been referred to as 'angry aggression' and has been described as a fear-motivated response (Weisfeld, 1994), one that includes defensive postures in response to perceived or actual threats. Proactive aggression involves more planning on the part of the perpetrator and is used instrumentally to obtain a goal through dominating or coercing others (Dodge, 1991). Ireland (2002) argues that the extent to which specific incidents of bullying contain elements of proactive and reactive aggression is dependent on the motivation of the aggressor and the social constraints of the environment in which it takes place. Ireland (2002) argues that pure bullies, namely those who only bully others and are not victims themselves, are more likely to represent proactive aggressors, whereas bully/victims, namely those who report both bullying others and being bullied themselves, are more likely to represent reactive aggressors.

The role of fear in bullying has, however, received little attention from prison-based researchers. This is surprising when it is considered that it has a crucial role to play, both in defining bullying, in encouraging bullying to take place by reducing the cost to the bully and in determining how victims may respond to the abuse. These areas will be the focus of the current chapter.

DEFINING BULLYING

School-based definitions of bullying describe it as an aggressive behaviour that must be repeated, intended to cause *fear* or harm to the victim, unprovoked, based on an imbalance of power and made up of physical, psychological or verbal aggression (Farrington, 1993). This definition has been used to measure the nature and extent of bullying in prisons although it has received criticism, largely because it does not reflect the specifics of the prison environment (see Ireland, 2000 and 2002).

The role of fear in this definition is determined by the intention of the bully, with no mention made of the victim's perspective. Fear does, however, have a central role to play in terms of *determining* whether or not an act of bullying has taken place, and should be linked more closely to the consequences of bullying for the victim. It should not be reliant solely on the intention of the bully. Indeed, the fear experienced by the victim may be more important in determining that an incident of bullying has occurred than the need for the aggression to be repeated. For example, it may not be physically possible for a prison bully to aggress towards a victim more than once; the population in prisons can be quite transient, with prisoners being moved to and from locations both within and outside of the prison on a fairly regular basis. This makes it difficult for an abusive relationship between individuals to develop. This does not mean, however, that bullying cannot take place. It is the victim's experience of fear that is crucial. If a prisoner is aggressed towards on a single occasion and then *fears* future aggression, regardless of how accurate this fear is, then that is bullying. The actual incidence of aggression therefore becomes irrelevant. Similarly, once a prisoner has been subjected to aggression, unless they defend themselves adequately, they risk becoming labelled as a 'victim' by other members of their peer group (Connell and Farrington, 1996). Once labelled as a victim they increase their chances of being victimised further by the same perpetrator or others. As stated by Ireland (2002), *"The 'fear' in this situation is not just limited to the possibility of being aggressed towards again by the same perpetrator, but is also a fear of becoming a viable target for other aggressors in the future"*. In a prison environment, where victims are offered little physical escape from their aggressor, the role of fear is perhaps magnified.

Not surprisingly, some researchers have applied broader definitions of bullying to prisons, definitions that make mention of the role of fear in determining whether or not bullying has taken place. For example; "*An individual is being bullied when they are the victim of direct and/or indirect aggression happening on a weekly basis, by the same or different perpetrator(s). Single incidences of aggression can be viewed as bullying, particularly when they are severe **and when the individual either believes or fears that they are at risk of future victimisation by the same perpetrator or others.** An incident can be considered bullying if the victim believes that they have been aggressed towards, regardless of the actual intention of the bully. It can also be bullying when the imbalance of power between the bully and his/her victim is implied and not immediately evident.*" (Ireland, 2002).

Fear should therefore be seen as central to how bullying is defined and this may be particularly true in a prison environment where it becomes a powerful tool for the bully.

FEAR AS A TOOL FOR THE BULLY

If a bully is able to engender fear in their victims, exploitation becomes easier. The more fearful a victim is of the bully the less likely they will retaliate towards them. However, some victims do become aggressive and this will be highlighted in the following section. This victim aggression is, however, often directed away from the bully and targeted towards other members of the peer group. Thus fear serves a protective function for the bully. It also helps to reinforce the consequences of bullying. Victims, for example, are often reluctant to tell staff that they are being bullied. This links into the 'inmate code', an intrinsic element of the inmate subculture that includes not informing on others and loyalty to the prisoner group (Tittle, 1969). This code also includes not backing down from conflicts, an approval of physical violence to protect oneself or one's possessions, a need to be tough and to resist exploitation and a need to maintain one's position in the prison 'pecking order'. In a prison setting, it has been suggested that bullying serves many functions one of which may be in controlling violations of this code (Ireland, 2002). Thus, if victims inform staff about bullying this may be construed as a violation, 'allowing' them to be bullied by their peers. Fear of violating this code and of becoming victimised even further prevents the victims from disclosing.

Fear may also influence the type of aggression displayed by bullies and their choice of victim. It could be speculated that until a bully has developed a reputation for violence, physical aggression may be needed to induce a fear response in their victims. Such aggression, although impacting significantly on the victim, carries the highest cost for the bully in terms of official sanctions if they are caught by staff e.g. segregation from their peers and/or days added onto their sentence. Once a bully's reputation is developed, however, the use of more subtle non-physical forms of aggression may be sufficient to ensure that others become fearful of them. This can include intimidation and threats, both of which carry the least cost to the bully in terms of getting caught. Thus, physical aggression may be used only by those bullies whose reputation is not yet developed, and for whom threats and indirect aggression are not sufficient to induce fear. Alternatively, it has also been suggested that indirect aggression is likely to be employed by an aggressor when they are fearful of retaliation (Beal O'Neal, Ong and Ruscher, 1998). It is certainly true that, in a prison setting, indirect aggression is used to the same extent, if not more so, than direct aggression (Ireland, 1999). The extent to which this is related to a fear of retaliation from the victim is not clear. Generally it is accepted that indirect aggression occurs more frequently among older age groups (Björkqvist, Lagerspetz and Kaukiainen, 1992), particularly in older adolescents and upwards, and thus would be expected to occur anyway in older samples, such as those found in prisons. It is, however, a more useful form of aggression to employ in a prison since it reduces the bully's risk of getting caught and being subjected to an official response from the prison authorities. Thus it may be important to clarify the target of this 'retaliation': it may be that the retaliation in this context is not a fear of retaliation from the victim but rather a fear of retaliation from the staff.

In terms of victim choice, bullies will aim to choose those prisoners whom they do not fear reprisals from. Prisoners 'early on' in their bullying career may have to carefully select victims to ensure that if they do retaliate that they can defend themselves adequately from them. Later, however, when their reputation for violence is well established and accepted by the peer group as a whole, bullies may not have to be so careful with their victim selection. In a sense, anyone can be at risk of being bullied. The implication of this is that identifying 'potential' victims becomes a futile activity. It could be speculated that the few victims who do retaliate towards the bully may be those that are new to the prison or wing and unfamiliar with the reputation of the bully. The reality is that few victims retaliate towards their aggressor.

Reacting to Bullying: the Role of Fear

Nesse (1999) describes how the characteristics of the 'fight-flight' reaction are well designed to cope with situations that require aggression or escape. Traditionally 'fear' is viewed as a motivation behind the flight reaction, although in some instances it could also apply to the 'fight' reaction. In a prison setting it could be argued that both fight and flight responses are equally motivated by fear.

The concept of 'fight-flight' is one of the oldest and its application to aggression is clear. Thus, it is perhaps surprising that the role of such responses in understanding bullying in prisons has received little attention in the research literature. This is even more surprising when it is considered that the bullying is occurring in an environment where the opportunities for escape are extremely limited and the ways in which victims respond extreme. Nesse (1999) states how *"emotions can be useful only if they influence the future"*. This sentiment applies well to the emotion of fear. In a prison setting, when the victim is fearful, this can lead to a range of responses that ultimately impact on their environment and influence the bullying. In some instances, depending on how the fear manifests itself, it can prove an adaptive response and help to prevent future victimisation.

In a prison setting, fear is one of the most common emotions reported by the victims of aggression (Lockwood, 1998). This fear is often intensified as the victims of bullying find themselves in a situation where they cannot report the abuse to staff for fear of violating the inmate code of 'not grassing'. This ensures that, ultimately, they are left living on the same unit as their aggressor. As stated by Ireland (2002) *"Undoubtedly if victims and their bullies remain in close proximity to each other following an incident of aggression, feelings of fear can persist and may even be intensified"*. These intense feelings of fear may manifest themselves in a number of ways, leading to increased feelings of anxiety, apprehension, feelings of paranoia and worthlessness (Ireland, 2002). The victim may then actively search for a solution to their situation and engage in a range of behaviours, some of which could be considered extreme. These 'extreme', and yet largely common, reactions will form the focus of the current section. They include aggression, self-injurious behaviour, avoidance and 'role-playing' and each, it will be argued, is aimed at preventing future aggression.

Aggression

Increasingly, it is acknowledged that the victims of bullying often use aggression as a way of responding to the abuse. The identification of a 'bully/victim' group, namely a group who report both bullying others and being bullied, is an acknowledgement that both aggression and victimisation may co-exist within the same individual. It has been suggested that 'bully/victims' represent those who have resorted to bullying their peers in order to prevent their own (future) victimisation. By bullying others they are communicating to the rest of the peer group that they are not 'easy targets', thus dissuading others from aggressing towards them. By displaying aggression they are also trying to increase their status among their peers and resist the stigma associated with being seen as a 'pure victim' (i.e. someone who is solely victimised and does not aggress towards their peers). It is, after all, less stigmatising to be seen as a victim who fights back than one who does not. By bullying others they are also drawing attention to themselves, and staff may begin to watch them more closely, thus indirectly reducing the opportunities that other prisoners have to bully them (Ireland, 2002). It is also recognised that bully/victims will aggress towards staff and show a range of negative behaviours towards the prison regime as a whole (Ireland, 2001). By behaving in this way they can quickly become labelled by staff as 'troublemakers' ensuring that staff will watch them more closely than the other prisoners. Being watched closely by staff reduces the opportunity that other prisoners have to bully them. Thus, behaving in this way serves a useful function for them.

Thus, 'bully/victims' are an interesting group whose aggression may be motivated more by a wish to prevent future victimisation than any real intention to cause harm and distress to others. They also make-up a sizeable proportion of the prisoner population, with 'bully/victims' reported more frequently than either pure victims or pure bullies (e.g. with one study reporting that 37 per cent of the sample were classified as bully/victims, 15 per cent as pure victims and 21 per cent as pure bullies; Ireland, 1999). The question then becomes, to what extent is the behaviour of the bully/victim motivated by fear? This question is best answered with reference to the prisoner subculture and the environment in which the bullying is taking place.

The emotion of fear, particularly with animals, inhibits the expression of aggression in certain situations e.g. *"Fear overshadows and inhibits any aggressive motivations that the individual animal may experience. This interpretation is consistent with a considerable body of experimental and observational evidence"* (Blanchard, 1990). This does not apply so readily to humans where an aggressive response is not necessarily inhibited by fear, but rather is dependant partly on whether or not an individual feels that they could *successfully* aggress towards another. It is also dependent on the penalties associated with *failing* to aggress, with the inhibiting function of fear decreased when the penalties for failing to attack are increased (Blanchard, 2000).

In a prison setting, where there is an inmate code that approves of violence in response to conflict and dictates that an individual *must* protect themselves and their possessions and resist exploitation, it could be expected that fear of the bully would not necessarily inhibit an aggressive reaction from the victim. Failing to actively resist bullying holds at least two penalties for the victim;

1. It increases the chance that they will be subject to further bullying.
2. It ensures that they become labelled as a 'victim' and stigmatised by the rest of the peer group. Once stigmatised, it then becomes very difficult for the victim to effectively resist further bullying.

A victim may be motivated to resist the bully aggressively in order to avoid these penalties, over-riding the usual aggression-inhibiting function played by fear. Part of this may also be the ability of the prisoner to assess the long-term consequences associated with failing to resist.

Thus, in a prison setting, aggression can be an effective response to bullying and perhaps is more appropriately described as a fear-motivated response. Fear in this sense should be considered an adaptive response. Such an argument is consistent with Cosmides and Tooby (1987) who provide the following example *"When a tiger bounds toward you, what should your response be? Should you file your toenails? Do a cartwheel? Sing a song? Is this the moment to run an uncountable number of randomly generated response possibilities through the decision rule?"*. In essence Cosmides and Tooby are emphasising how it is the adoption of certain responses over others that makes emotions adaptive. Experiencing fear in relation to being bullied motivates what could be considered an adaptive behaviour in a prison.

Equally, as mentioned earlier, 'fear' is traditionally viewed as a motivation behind the 'flight' reaction. It can, in the instance of defensive aggression, form part of the motivation behind a 'fight' reaction. In a prison setting however, the 'flight' options available to the victim are greatly diminished since physical escape is often not possible. Thus, it should not be a surprise that 'fight' responses are more common among victims, even if these responses are not targeted towards the bully and instead are targeted to other prisoners and staff. You could argue that these fight responses replace the flight response and are largely motivated by fear. However, the victim who chooses to aggress towards the peer group and staff may be engaging in a behaviour that could be construed as a 'delayed flight response'. By displaying aggression they are increasing their chances of being removed to another environment (i.e. another wing, unit) and/or being segregated from their peers (Ireland, 2002). In this way they are afforded some respite from the aggressor, but their aggression has served a function for them by affecting a 'flight' response.

Self-Injurious Behaviour

There is anecdotal and empirical evidence to support a link between being a victim of bullying and displaying self-injurious behaviour (including suicide), although the *magnitude* of this link remains unclear (Ireland, 2002), and in some instances has been exaggerated (O'Donnell and Edgar, 1996). Both 'bully/victims' and pure victims are reported to be at an equal risk of self-injury (Ireland, 1999). Self-injurious behaviour is, however, one of the most serious and extreme reactions to bullying. It could be speculated that, in some instances, self-injurious behaviour represents a fear response, in particular, a fear of future bullying. Some acts of self-injurious behaviour may serve an instrumental[1] function for the victim in that it helps them to avoid future abuse. By self-injuring, the victim ensures that they will receive the attention of staff, in the form of closer supervision, thus limiting the opportunities that

---

[1] not to be construed as a 'manipulative' function. The description of self-injurious behaviour as a form of manipulation is, in the author's opinion, both unhelpful and unethical.

other prisoners have to bully them. Victims may also be transferred to another environment where they can be watched more closely, affording them some respite. Thus, the self-injurious prisoner becomes similar to the aggressive prisoner; both ensure that through their behaviour they are watched more closely thus limiting the opportunities that others have to bully them and/or that they are sent to another environment where they receive some respite from their aggressor (i.e. the hospital wing for the self-injurious prisoner and the segregation unit for the aggressive prisoner). In many ways self-injury serves a similar function for the victim that aggression serves.

The self-injurious prisoner is also able to communicate their distress to staff without having to be specific about its cause (Livingston and Beck, 1997; Livingston and Chapman, 1997). In this way they avoid violating the inmate code of 'not informing' on the bully to staff. Self-injury, like aggression, could also be construed as a delayed 'flight' response to being bullied, particularly if the aim of the prisoner is to affect a move to another environment, even if only for a temporary period of time (i.e. the hospital). Self-injurious behaviour may actually be an effective way of coping in an environment where the options for physical escape are extremely limited. Ireland (2002) also describes how *"the potential for physical injury may be greater for the victim if they are unable to avoid the bully. At least if they self-injure they have some control over the extent of this injury"*.

It is also worth reflecting on the fear that the victim must have experienced in order to willingly inflict physical injury onto themselves. It is possible that they have exhausted all other avenues available to them, and that self-injury is their final desperate attempt to avoid a fearful situation, namely future interactions with the bully.

Avoidance

Many victims will isolate themselves from their peers in order to reduce the opportunities that others have to aggress towards them (Bolt, 1999; Ireland, 1999, 2002). Such reactions are perhaps appropriately described as 'flight' reactions in victims if they occur following an incident of bullying. Such a reaction may occur most frequently in those victims who are fearful that they will be aggressed towards again and are aimed at reducing this risk as much as possible.

Avoidance reactions can be both 'formal' or 'informal'. Formal reactions include requesting protective custody, to be locked in their cell or to be moved to another location within the prison. Informal responses include staying in their cell when they could be out, restricting the amount of time that they spend with other prisoners and avoiding certain areas of the prison (Ireland, 2002). Informal responses tend to be favoured over formal responses. This is undoubtedly due to victims endeavouring to involve staff in their situation as little as possible in order to avoid violating the inmate code of 'not informing'. By making a formal request to change location, victims will be subject to questioning from staff as to why this is the case. It could be speculated that those victims requesting a formal method of avoidance are those most fearful of being subjected to further bullying.

Avoidance is a common reaction to being bullied and has been termed 'secondary victimisation' to highlight the disruption that the aggression has caused to the prisoner's life (Lockwood, 1980). As stated by Ireland (2002), *"Fear can become a powerful emotion that ultimately places restrictions on the level of interaction that victims engage in with their peers"*. Victims who feel unable to defend themselves from the bully, or who feel that they have too much to lose by behaving aggressively may favour such reactions. Avoidance may thus represent an adaptive fear response to the threat of being bullied.

However, it also carries a hidden cost; prisoners who obviously isolate themselves from their peers may inadvertently be sending a signal to others that they are vulnerable and that they have few friends, increasing their 'victim potential' in the eyes of future aggressors (Ireland, 2002). As stated by Ireland (2002), *"The physical cost to victims preferring such avoidance behaviours may be reduced, although the social costs in terms of the limits that it places on peer interactions and the consequent support that they can receive from these are increased"*. In the long term isolation is unlikely to be adaptive as victims restrict the opportunities to gain support from their peer group and to increase their social network, with the latter being recognised as a protective factor for potential victims (i.e. the more friends they have, the less likely they are to be bullied as bullies fear the potential retribution from this peer group). As an alternative to avoidance, victims may instead choose to interact with their peers in order to avoid being seen as vulnerable. In such instances the interactions that they engage in with others may be carefully controlled and include 'role-playing'.

Role-Playing

If other, more aggressive, prisoners see that a prisoner is fearful, this increases their victim potential (Ireland, 2002). Hiding fear reactions from others becomes critical. In the short-term, this can be achieved via avoidance and self-imposed isolation. However, some prisoners may prefer to interact with others as 'normal', but the *quality* of their interactions may change. They may, for example, adopt a certain 'image' that will help them to avoid victimisation. This is not unusual and as stated by McCorkle (1992), *"Many [inmates] believe that unless an inmate can convincingly project an image that conveys the potential for violence, he [sic] is likely to be dominated and exploited throughout the duration of his sentence....violence and threats are...a form of pre-emptive self-defence"*. An example of such role-playing is captured in the following account from a male victim reported by Toch (1992);

> "All my motions, you know, like walking, you know, talking, and any movement at all, I always try to make myself look like if anyone would fuck with me I would kill them."

Adopting such roles means that essentially victims are 'acting' each and every time that they leave their cell and interact with others. Maintaining such role-playing is undoubtedly stressful and one could speculate that for some prisoners it becomes too difficult, leading to stress reactions and a need to limit the amount of interaction that they have with others by isolating themselves. It should be noted, however, that although there is anecdotal evidence for such reactions, there is a lack of empirical research addressing the extent to which prisoners take on a 'role' in order to prevent victimisation. This is certainly an area worthy of further research.

Thus fear can influence the type of response that is effected following, or prior to, an incident of bullying. A summary of how fear influences how prisoners respond to and prevent bullying is presented in figure 1.

Figure 1. The role of fear in responding to and preventing bullying

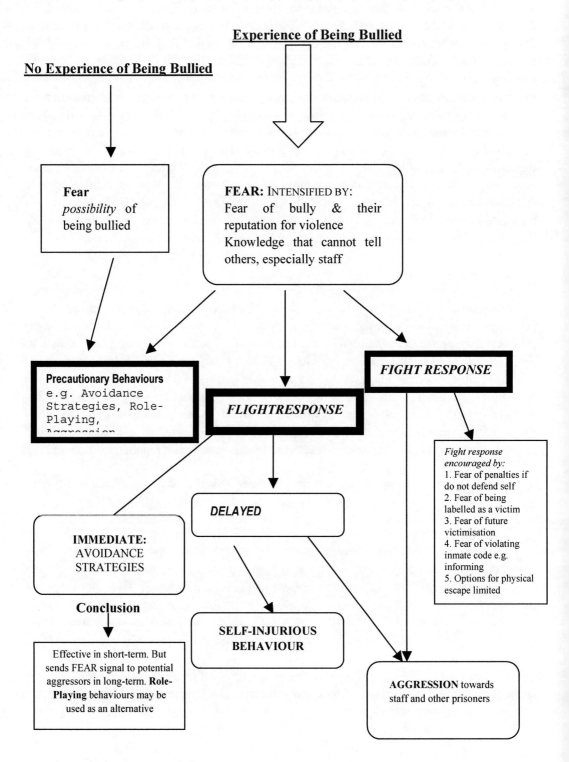

Fear plays a central role in understanding prison-based bullying behaviour. It exists both prior to an incident of bullying, as prisoners fear the possibility of being bullied and alter their behaviours accordingly, and also following an incident of bullying, as victims act in a way to prevent future victimisation. Despite this, the concept of 'fear' has received little attention in the prison-based research literature.

The way in which fear influences how victims react is particularly interesting. The types of fear reactions that victims can engage in are varied and may not, at least initially, be considered fear-motivated. Aggression is one such reaction. Whereas, in some environments, fear may inhibit an aggressive response, in a prison environment this inhibiting function is decreased as a result of the increased penalties associated with failing to resist the exploitation. Thus aggression can certainly represent a fear response, and one that is likely to be adaptive in a prison setting.

The notion of fear being an adaptive response is an important one. In some instances fear can certainly be a crippling emotion that inhibits any type of adaptive and proactive response in a victim. It can also impact negatively on those who have never experienced bullying and yet are fearful that it may occur. However, it can also represent a motivating drive where prisoners learn to take certain precautions against the possibility of being bullied (Ireland, 2002). This latter view of fear as a solution-focused emotion is not a new one. Such a reaction is well documented by evolutionary psychologists. Tooby and Cosmides (1990), for example, state how: *"Each emotional state.....fear of predators....and so on, will correspond to an integrated mode of operation that functions as a solution"*. In a prison setting these modes of operation can include aggression, self-injurious behaviour, self-isolation and role-playing.

This highlights the importance of acknowledging the environment in which fear responses are taking place. It also highlights the impact of this environment on understanding how the concepts of 'fight vs. flight' responses may relate to bullying. In a prison setting flight responses are reduced by the decreased opportunities available for physical escape. However, what may be reduced are *immediate* flight responses; flight responses will still exist but may be more subtle and *delayed*. This concept of a 'delayed flight response' is important and may help to explain both aggressive and self-injurious reactions. Both aggression and self-injury are argued here to function as delayed flight responses in certain circumstances.

There is undoubtedly a need for further research. Although the current chapter argues that aggression, self-injurious behaviour, avoidance and role-playing may be fear-motivated, empirical research is needed to test these assertions. It would also be worth exploring the extent to which other reactions to bullying, not explored here, relate to fear e.g. depression, anxiety and hopelessness etc. Similarly, exploring the emotional distress caused by fear would also be of interest. What the current chapter suggests is that the emotional distress caused by fear may be manifesting itself in 'objective symptomology' (Bagdasarian, 2000), namely aggression, self-injury, avoidance and role-playing. Discussing these behaviours as *symptoms* of fear may be more appropriate. Such symptoms may trigger a number of physical problems known to relate to stress such as peptic ulcers, tension headaches, asthma attacks, hypertension and a range of psychosomatic disorders (Bagdasarian, 2000). These symptoms may be increased if this fear remains unresolved. Looking at the existence of such physical symptoms in victims may be a valuable avenue for future research to pursue.

Finally, although not touched upon in the current chapter, addressing the role of sex differences in understanding fear responses both prior to or following bullying would also be useful. For example, there is evidence that women are generally more fearful than men, and that they tend to perceive a greater level of danger (Harris, 2000). Several factors have been hypothesised to explain this increased female fearfulness. This includes the lesser physical strength of women, an evolutionary bias for women to be more cautious, gender role stereotypes and schemas that ensure that women perceive incidents of violence as more serious and threatening than men (see Harris, 2000). Men, on the other hand, are more likely to deny being fearful, possibly because of the implications of reporting what is classically deemed a feminine trait. Researchers such as Dress (2000) argue that this decreased fearfulness among women may be behavioural. There is some evidence that the fear-related *behaviours* of women are less intense in comparison to men, that these responses are displayed in specific circumstances and are less tied to physiological arousal. Although both men and women share the capacity for fight or flight, women seem to use it less (Dress, 2000). Assessing how this applies to fight and flight responses following bullying would certainly be of value.

ACKNOWLEDGEMENTS

Many thanks to Emma Pearce who reviewed a draft of this chapter and provided many helpful comments.

REFERENCES

Bagdasarian, N. (2000). A prescription for mental distress: the principles of psychosomatic medicine with the physical manifestation requirement in N.I.E.D. cases. *American Journal of Law & Medicine*, Winter.

Beal, D. J., O'Neal, E. C. Ong, J., and Ruscher, J. B. (1998). The ways and means of interfacial aggression: Modern racists' use of covert retaliation. Unpublished manuscript.

Björkqvist, K, Lagerspetz, K.M.J. and Kaukiainen, A. (1992) Do girls manipulate and girls fight? *Aggressive Behaviour*, **18,** 117 – 127.

Blanchard, C. (2000). Emotions as mediators and modulators of violence: Some reflection on the 'Seville Statement on Violence', *Social Research*, Fall.

Bolt, C. (1999) 'A questionnaire survey to establish the incidence and nature of bullying at HMP Holme House', unpublished report, Psychology Dept, HMP Holme House: UK.

Connell, A. and Farrington, D. (1996) 'Bullying among incarcerated young offenders: developing an interview schedule and some preliminary results', *Journal of Adolescence* 19: 75–93.

Cosmides, L, and Tooby, J. (1987) 'From Evolution to Behavior: Evolutionary Psychology as the Missing Link,' In J. Dupre (Ed.) *The Latest on the Best: Essays on Evolution and Optimality*, Cambridge, MA: MIT press.

Dodge, K. A. (1991) 'The structure and function of reactive and proactive aggression' in D. J. Pepler and K. H. Rubin (Eds.) *The Development and Treatment of Childhood Aggression*, New Jersey, LEA: Hillsdale.

Dress, N (2000). Tend And Befriend (stress in females): Brief Article. *Psychology Today*, September.

Farrington, D. P. (1993) 'Understanding and preventing bullying' in M. Tonry (ed.) *Crime and Justice: A Review of Research,* Chicago: The University of Chicago Press.

Grant, K. (1999) 'Survey of the extent and nature of bullying among female prisoners and its relationship with fear and precautionary behaviours', *Prison Research and Development Bulletin* April: 5–6.

Harris, M. (2000). Gender and Perceptions of Danger. *Sex Roles: A Journal of Research,* December.

Ireland, J. L. (1999) 'Bullying among prisoners: A study of adults and young offenders', *Aggressive Behavior* 25: 162–178.

Ireland, J. L. (2000) 'Bullying among prisoners: A review of research', *Aggression and Violent Behaviour: A Review Journal* 5: 201–215.

Ireland, J. L. (2001) 'Bullying Behaviour Among Male and Female Adult Prisoners: A Study of Perpetrator and Victim Characteristics', *Legal and Criminological Psychology,* 6: 229-246.

Ireland, J. L. (2002) *Bullying Among Prisoners: Evidence, Research and Intervention Strategies.* Brunner-Routledge, London: UK.

Ireland, J. L, Jarvis, S, Beck, G, and Osiowy, S (1999). Recent research into bullying in prison. *Forensic Update,* **56**, 4 - 10.

Livingston, M. and Beck, G. (1997) 'A cognitive-behaviour model of self-injury and bullying among imprisoned young offenders' in G. J. Towl (ed.) *Suicide and Self-Injury in Prisons,* Issues in Criminological and Legal Psychology, 28, Leicester: The British Psychological Society.

Livingston, M. S. and Chapman, A. J. (1997) 'Bullying and self-injurious behaviour in young offenders', *Journal of Prison Service Psychology* 3: 78-81.

Lockwood, D. (1980) *Prison Sexual Violence,* New York: Elsevier.

McCorkle R. C. (1992) 'Personal precautions to violence in prison', *Criminal Justice and Behavior* 19: 160-173.

Nesse, R. M. (1999). The Evolution of Hope and Despair, *Social Research* Summer

O'Donnell, I. and Edgar, K. (1996a) *'The Extent and Dynamics of Victimization in Prisons (revised report)',* unpublished research paper, Centre for Criminological Research, University of Oxford: UK.

Tittle, C. R. (1969) 'Inmate organisation: Sex differentiation and the influence of criminal subcultures', *American Sociological Review* 34: 492–505.

Toch, H. (1992) *Living in Prison: The Ecology of Survival,* Washington, DC: APA.

Tooby, J, and Cosmides, L (1990), "The Past Explains The Present: Emotional Adaptations and the Structure of Ancestral Environments," Ethology and Sociobiology 11, 4/5, pp. 375-424.

Weisfeld, G. E. (1994) 'Aggression and dominance in the social world of boys', in J. Archer (ed.) *Male Violence,* London: Routledge.

Chapter 6

DENTAL FEAR IN CHILDREN: ASSESSMENT, PREVALENCE AND ETIOLOGY

M. Ten Berge [1, 2]

ABSTRACT

Dental fear in children is a wide spread and serious problem often interfering with effective dental treatment, having negative consequences for one's health. Its etiology is considered to be complex and multifactorial. Numerous studies have been published on factors associated with dental fear in children, resulting however in inconsistent findings, partly due to great variety in methodology and study populations used. This article therefore aims to provide an overview of research on the assessment, prevalence and etiology of child dental fear, and shed more light on important theoretical and practical developments in this area of research. At the end of this article, important results are summarised and a theoretical approach emphasising the potential importance of subjective treatment factors is proposed. In addition, implications for future research are discussed.

1. INTRODUCTION

In children dental fear is a wide spread phenomenon and often the main reason of behavioural management problems, interference with regular treatment and subsequent referrals to dental fear clinics. Other negative consequences of dental fear include avoidance of the dental situation and subsequently deterioration of dental health. This eventually may start a circle of avoidance, creating feelings of shame, guilt and inferiority, further maintaining this negative spiral by reinforcing one's fear and avoidance behaviour (Berggren, 1984). While for most children dental fear may be of a transitory nature, for some their fear

---

[1] Academic Centre For Dentistry Amsterdam, University of Amsterdam, The Netherlands E-mail: m.ten.berge@ acta.nl.

[2] Regional Institute For Mental Health Care, Dept. of Child And Adolescent Psychiatry, Rotterdam, The Netherlands.

reaction is thus maladaptive causing it to persist for a longer period of time, or even into adulthood.

The etiology of dental fear is considered to be complex and multifactorial; not only can various aspects be distinguished within its construct, also different factors are involved in the acquisition and development of dental fear in children (Ten Berge, Veerkamp & Hoogstraten, 2002a; Klingberg, Berggren, Carlsson, & Norén, 1995). More specifically, dental fear in children does not only concern fear of pain or of invasive procedures, but also entails separation from the parents, confrontation with unfamiliar people and surroundings, and the experience of loss of control. Closely related are potential etiological factors such as painful or negative dental experiences, parental fear or a child's temperament. In other words, several pathways of fear acquisition have been proposed; however, their relative contribution still remains to be determined, partly because of great variety in methodology and study populations used in research studies. This variety in study methods also seems to be the cause of great variety in prevalence estimates of dental fear in children, ranging from 3 up to 43% percent in studies.

The aim of this article is to provide an overview of practical and theoretical developments in the field of dental fear research among children, by discussing consecutively studies on the assessment, the prevalence and the etiology of dental fear. The article closes with a general discussion and recommendations for future research.

2. ASSESSMENT

Several measurement techniques have been proposed and used to assess dental fear in children, ranging from (self-report) questionnaires and projective techniques to behavioural and physiological registrations. Most of these instruments, however, entail serious disadvantages, often related to developmental changes in children.

Projective techniques (e.g., Children's Dental Fear Picture test (CDFP), Klingberg & Hwang, 1994) and *physiological registrations* (e.g., heart rate, skin conductance) may provide specific individual information, but are methodologically and practically difficult to use and process. For example, specific test situations and equipment may be needed for such measurements, and the administration may be time consuming or anxiety provoking in it self. In addition, it has been suggested that age and individual differences may influence the validity or efficacy of such registrations (Bastawi, Reid, & West, 1979; Benjamins, 1995; Klingberg, 1995). For example, it was discussed that some patients have larger variations in response to different procedures, meaning that physical responses could be obtained from a fearful child during all procedures, while a non fearful child might be disturbed only be procedures perceived as overtly threatening.

As to the *behavioural registrations*, (e.g., Frankl's rating scale, Frankl, Shiere & Fogels, 1962; Melamed's Behavior Profile Rating Scale (BPRS), Melamed, Weinstein, Hawes & Katin-Borland, 1975; see also Hosey & Blinkhorn, 1995), although these are easier to administer, also an important disadvantage is involved. That is, behaviour concerns more or other aspects than just dental fear and may be seen as the combined outcome of a child's dental fear, its temperament, its coping abilities and the dental situation. Behavioural registrations thus do not discriminate between actual dental fear and behavioural management problems. Not all children suffering from dental fear show behavioural management problems, while on the other hand, not all children displaying behavioural management problems have to be dentally fearful (Klingberg et al, 1995). For example, in certain instances behaviour management problems may essentially be a manifestation of a child's young age and its lack of capacities to understand and accept dental treatment, while having no actual relation to dental fear. With increasing age, fear and behaviour may begin to diverge even more as children learn to control the way they express their fears as they grow older. Thus for some of the younger children behavioural measures may provide a reasonable reflection of the child's dental fear, while the relation gets more clouded for older children. In other words, in research a distinction should be made between studies on behaviour management problems and studies on dental fear, since these should be considered as distinct phenomena in children.

Another closely associated disadvantage of behavioural measures is that of *observer bias*, which emphasises the need for trained observers and well-defined behavioural categories, which is however often lacking in studies, by using for example only a dichotomous overall classification. In addition, reliable behavioural registration requires registration during various time intervals or treatment situations. A review on behavioural measures suggest Melamed's BPRS (1975) to be preferred over other behavioural measures, although it was concluded that behavioural measures may not be the best option for assessing dental fear (Aartman, Van Everdingen, Hoogstraten & Schuurs, 1996).

Another option is *(self-report) questionnaires* (e.g., CFSS-DS, Cuthbert & Melamed, 1982; Dental Anxiety Scale (DAS, Corah, 1969). Questionnaires are, as opposed to some of the techniques discussed above, easy to administer and to process statistically. Also, extensive use of questionnaires in international research often provides normative data enabling for example cross-cultural comparisons. Self-report questionnaires often are adjusted for completion by the parents to enable to assess dental fear in younger children, a method that has been indicated to adequately reflect children's level of fear. In a review of self-report measurements on dental fear the CFSS-DS was preferred over the Venham Picture Test (VPT, Venham, Bengston & Cipes, 1977) and Corah's Dental Anxiety Scale for Children (DAS, Corah, 1969), with respect to its psychometric properties and available normative data (Aartman, Van Everdingen, Hoogstraten & Schuurs, 1998). That is, as opposed to some of the other measures, the scale has proven to be reliable and valid: both the internal reliability and test-retest reliability as well as its validity has proven to be satisfactory (Ten Berge, Hoogstraten, Veerkamp & Prins, 1998; Klingberg, 1994). In addition, normative data have been provided for US, Singaporean, Swedish, Finnish, Chinese and Dutch populations (Alvesalo, Murtomaa, Milgrom, Honkanen, Karjalainen & Tay, 1993; Chellappah, Vignesha, Milgrom & Lo, 1990; Ten Berge, Veerkamp, Hoogstraten & Prins, 2002c; Klingberg, Berggren & Norén, 1994; Milgrom, Jie, Yang & Tay, 1994; Milgrom, Mancl, King & Weinstein, 1995a). Table 1 shows different studies using the CFSS-DS in different populations and cultures.

Furthermore, the CFSS-DS was originally developed for assessment of dental fear in children, as opposed to the DAS, which is also frequently used in studies on child dental fear. Since measures designed for adults require other cognitive skills and may involve different (sub) constructs, adult measures may not be applied to children. That is, specific factors can be distinguished within the general construct of dental fear in children measured by the CFSS-DS, such as fear of strangers, fear of medical aspects and fear of invasive dental procedures (Ten Berge et al., 1998), which does not similarly apply for dental fear in adults.

In conclusion, (self-report) questionnaires (i.e., CFSS-DS) are recommended in the assessment of dental fear in children, above projective techniques and behavioural or physiological registrations. Behaviour management problems and dental fear should be regarded as distinct phenomena in children. In this context, it is important to note that although the CFSS-DS has been indicated to be of clinical value as a screening device of dental fear, it should not be used as an (predictive) indicator of fearful behaviour (Ten Berge, Veerkamp, Hoogstraten & Prins, 2002b).

3. PREVALENCE

Prevalence estimates of childhood dental fear vary considerably, from 3 to 43 percent in different populations (Alvesalo et al., 1993; Bedi, Sutcliffe, Donnan & McConnachie, 1992b; Ten Berge et al., 2002c; Chellappah et al., 1990; Gatchel, 1989; Holst & Crossner, 1987; Klingberg et al., 1994; Milgrom, et al., 1994; Milgrom et al., 1995a; Teo, Foong, Lui & Elliot, 1990). These differences in prevalence estimates may be due to several parameters such as methodological or cultural variables in the populations surveyed. As also discussed above, differences in assessment methods (e.g., DAS, CFSS-DS, clinical anxiety rating) and associated cut-off scores used often seem to influence the reported results. For example, some studies reporting on the prevalence of dental fear essentially seem to be assessing behavioural management problems in children (e.g, Holst & Crossner, 1987; Mejare & Mjones, 1989; Tuutti, 1986). Furthermore, different cut-off scores are used causing variety on the percentages of children described as fearful or highly fearful (see Table 1).

Another important issue is that of the selective nature of the study samples used. For example, among large samples in (Western-) European countries less variance in prevalence estimates and lower mean CFSS-DS scores have been reported (Alvesalo et al., 1993; Bedi et al., 1992b; Ten Berge et al., 2002c; Klingberg et al., 1994) than in Non-Western study samples (Chellappah et al., 1990; Milgrom et al., 1994), indicating possible cultural differences. In a large Dutch normative study significantly higher fear levels were found in children from a Non-Western cultural background (e.g., Morocco, Turkey) than in children from a Western cultural background (Ten Berge et al., 2002c). Socio-economic status has also been reported to be associated with higher fear levels in children (Wright & Alpern, 1972; Wright, Lucas & McMurray, 1980b; Bedi et al, 1992a), although its underlying cause remains unclear. It may be hypothesised that this relation again essentially involves children's behaviour instead of their actual fear level. It was indicated by some that the higher the education of the father, the better the child behaved, despite a high fear level (e.g., Tuutti, 1984). Townend et al. (2001) suggested that the relation between dental fear and social class may essentially be explained by another association: i.e., this relation may be due to different dietary and dental habits, possibly leading to more invasive treatment. Also, the age range and gender of the children constituting the samples appears to be of influence on the fear levels found and prevalence percentages reported. That is, repeatedly higher fear levels have been associated with younger age and female gender (e.g., Alvesalo et al., 1993; Bedi et al., 1992b; Cuthbert & Melamed, 1982; Klingberg et al., 1995; Milgrom et al., 1994, 1995a; Wright et al., 1990b). However, discussion about interpretation of these reported differences exists in literature (see also par. 4.2.1).

Table 1. Prevalence reports on childhood dental fear from studies using thee CFSS-DS

Authors	Country	N	Age	Sample	Assessment	Mean (SD)	Cut-off	%	Differences Gender	Age
Cuthbert & Melamed, 1982	USA	603	5-14	Schools	Self-report	28.7 (-)	--	--	x	y>o
Chellappah et al., 1990	Singapore	505	10-14	Schools	Self-report	30.6 (10.8)	≥ 42	17.7	g>b	-
Alvesalo et al., 1993	Finland	828	13 (median)	Schools	Self-report	22.1 (6.4)	Parental rating	21.0	g>b	x
Milgrom et al., 1994	Canadian Chinese	70	5-15	Dental program	Parents' version	31.9 (8.9)	≥ 38	21.4	x	x
	China	99	2.5-7	Paed. dept.	Parents' version	35.7 (8.9)	≥ 38	43.4	g>b	x
Klingberg et al., 1994	Sweden	3204	4-6, 9-11	Dental clinics	Parents' version	23.1 (8.1)	≥ 38	6.7	y: x y>o; o: b>g	
Milgrom et al., 1995	USA	895	5-11	Schools (low income)	Self –report	b: 31.1 (10.3) g: 34.2 (11.0)	> 40	19.5	g>b	y>o
Ten Berge et al., 2002	The Netherlands	2144	4-11	Dental practices	Parents' version	23.9 (8.1)	≥ 39	6% (8% at risk)	g>b	x

-- : no report

x : no relation

In conclusion, prevalence estimates seem to vary greatly due to variety in study populations and methods used. For example, age and socio-economic status seem to influence prevalence reports. Two studies among large, representative samples in Western-European countries using a similar assessment method (CFSS-DS) and study sample, however, yielded similar results. That is, around 6 or 7% of children between 4 and 11 years of age were found to be highly fearful, while another 8% seems to fairly fearful or 'at risk' of becoming high fearful (Ten Berge et al., 2002c; Klingberg et al., 1994). Studies in Non-Western countries have indicated higher percentages, even up to 43%.

4. ETIOLOGY

In the literature on the acquisition of fear and phobia, different pathways are described[1]. For example, Rachman (1977) has proposed three pathways: a) directly through direct conditioning or b) indirectly via vicarious learning (modelling) or the transmission of negative information.

Direct or classical conditioning refers to the association formed between an unconditioned stimulus (UCS) and a neutral stimulus. If an aversive UCS is paired with a neutral stimulus during a number of trials, this neutral stimulus (CS) alone can become sufficient to elicit a negative emotional reaction (UCR, CR). In the dental situation this means that pain experienced during a dental visit can cause a patient to associate the dental situation in general with pain, leading to aversive feelings and fear, and potentially also avoidance of the situation. Negative dental experiences other than pain may also cause such associations to develop. However, this conditioning theory does not seem to explain the acquisition of phobias entirely: the underlying mechanisms seem more complex. Several important refinements have therefore been made to the conditioning approach: e.g., the notion of 'preparedness' and of neo-conditioning (e.g., 'latent inhibition') (Lubow, 1973; Rachman, 1991; Seligman, 1971).

According to the *'preparedness'* hypothesis, aversive conditioning interacts with evolutionary processes in producing fear; certain stimuli may be more easily transformed into phobic stimuli than others. An association, which is readily acquired, is defined as "prepared" and one, which is acquired with difficulty as "unprepared". Dental fear might be seen as a readily acquired one, taking into account aspects such as lying on one's back in the dental chair (or losing control), sharp instruments in one's mouth and being examined by a stranger (Kent, 1997).

Another revision to the conditioning theory is that of neo-conditioning, which states that the conditioning process is not a reflexive but a cognitive process (e.g., Rachman, 1991). According to the *'latent inhibition'* theory, an association between a conditioned stimulus (CS) and an unconditioned stimulus (UCS) is formed less likely when the CS is presented alone on several occasions before it is paired with the UCS, than when there were no CS-alone trials before conditioning (Davey, 1989a). For the dental situation, this means that a history of positive or neutral dental experiences may serve as a defence against the development of traumatic associations or experiences, and subsequently against the

---

[1] See for general reviews Merckelbach, De Jong, Muris & Van Den Hout (1996); Ollendick, Hagopian & King (1997)

acquisition of high fears or phobias. Another interesting, though less studied revision to the conditioning theory is that of *'UCS inflation'* (Davey, 1989b). Briefly, this phenomenon refers to exposure to pairings of a CS and a mild UCS resulting in a weak conditioned fear response, which in a subsequent phase can become 'inflated' after exposure to a more aversive UCS than previous experience suggested.

The *modelling* pathway implies children's fears can be acquired by observing significant other reacting fearfully to a stimulus, while the transmission of *negative information* refers to learning via negative stimuli provided through anecdotes, books or television.

Other theories involve etiological processes not related to learning mechanisms, such as the non-associative account or the individual approach. The *non-associative account* claims that fear can be aroused by stimuli without previous direct or indirect associative learning (Menzies & Clarke, 1995). In this view, fears are innate or predictable at set stages of development, and habituation processes eventually cause a reduction in these fears. The *individual approach* considers that individual differences exist in the way people react to specific situations and that individual and temperamental characteristics may exacerbate a child's tendency to acquire fears.

In this article only theories and mechanisms empirically studied in relation to dental fear will be discussed: an extensive discussion of all the proposed theories is beyond the scope of this article. Below, several studies on the etiology of child dental fear will therefore be discussed by placing them within the following theoretical framework:

Conditioning mechanisms: direct conditioning (invasive dental procedures; dentist's behaviour) versus indirect conditioning (modelling; negative information),

Individual approach (temperamental factors; age-, gender- and SES-differences).

4.1.1 Direct Conditioning Pathway

In dental research many studies have reported a relation between dental fear and negative dental experiences (e.g., Klingberg et al., 1995; Liddell, 1990; Milgrom, Vignesha & Weinstein, 1992; Milgrom et al., 1995a). It has even been suggested that this conditioning pathway is particularly prominent in child-onset of dental fear (Locker, Liddell, Dempster & Shapiro, 1999a). It is, however, important to note that reported results depend on the method of assessing this conditioning. Most studies providing support for this pathway have been conducted retrospectively, often among adult patients (Bernstein, Kleinknecht & Alexander, 1979; De Jongh, Muris, Ter Horst & Duyx, 1995; Kleinknecht, Klepac & Alexander, 1973; Locker, Shapiro & Liddell, 1996). Studies among child patients using different research methods have yielded more inconsistent results. Most support for direct conditioning again stems from retrospective or 'subjective' reports on children's dental experiences, by using parental interviews or (self-report) questionnaires. Studies assessing conditioning by using 'objective' measures such as treatment records or dental pathology indices did not confirm the support for the important role of invasive dental procedures. Below studies using 'subjective' and 'objective' reports with respect to negative dental experiences are discussed separately.

Invasive dental procedures - Most of the child and adolescent *interview or questionnaire (subjective) studies* have reported a relation between high dental fear in children and negative or painful dental experiences. A relation between these experiences and uncooperative behaviour has also been reported. Experiences reported not only refer to re-called painful dental procedures, but also to negative dentist's behaviour perceived by children or more general invasive medical experiences (e.g., Holst, Hallonsten, Schröder & Ek, 1993; Holst, Schröder, Ek, Hallonsten & Crossner, 1988; Majstorovic, Skrinjaric, Glavina & Szirovicza, 2001; Neverlien & Backer Johnsen, 1991). For example, in an interview-study among children, they indicated as the cause of their fear: a painful experience (30%), a traumatic experience (24%), general fearfulness (22%), maternal dental fear (14%) and medical fears (Prins, 1985). In open-ended interview studies parents also most frequently attributed their child's fear or uncooperative behaviour to previous treatments or dentists' behaviour (Alwin, Murray & Niven, 1991; Ten Berge, Veerkamp, Hoogstraten & Prins, 2001; Holst & Crossner, 1984; Veerkamp, Gruythuysen, Van Amerongen & Hoogstraten, 1992). It should be noted, however, that results of these interview studies depend on the source of information. For example, in a study among parents as well as operating dentists, most parents (54%) attributed the child's uncooperative behaviour to previous dental treatment while the dentist often (44%) ascribed it to family attitudes or upbringing (Mejàre, Ljungkvist & Quensel, 1989).

Studies based on *treatment records or using dental pathology indices (objective)*, on the other hand, have resulted in inconsistent findings. Several reported a relation between oral health indices (*DMFT*: 'Decayed, Missing, Filled Teeth') and subsequent potential invasive procedures on the one hand and dental fear on the other hand, while others have shown an inverse relation (Alvesalo et al., 1993; Bedi, Sutcliffe, Donnan, Barrett & McConnachie, 1992a; Kruger, Thomson, Poulton, Davies, Brown, & Silva, 1998; Milgrom et al., 1995a). For example, Poulton, Thomson, Davies, Kruger, Brown and Silva (1997) found caries experience at the age of 15 to be positively related to dental fear at age 18, while a ratio of caries severity (*DMFS*: 'Decayed, Missing, Filled Surfaces') was inversely related to this dental fear. The authors suggested that relatively brief dental treatment occasioned by low levels of dental disease might result in the incubation of dental fear in some individuals while longer periods of treatment may facilitate fear habituation. In addition, a longitudinal study over a 3-year period reported children who did not receive invasive treatments to be more fearful than children who did experience such treatment (Murray, Liddell & Donohue, 1989). Moreover, it was concluded that '*receiving invasive treatment in the context of regular attendance may provide the best climate for the emotional processing of aversive dental experiences*' (p. 319), implying that exposure might act prophylactically. Similar results were reported by other authors (Brown, Wright & McMurray, 1986b; Brown & Wright, 1987). Other authors, on the other hand, did not establish a significant relation between dental fear and children's oral health status in children between the age of 7 and 14 years (Vignesha, Chellappah, Milgrom, Going & Teo, 1990; Wright, 1980a).

Interestingly, most studies examining the relative contribution of variables, showed factors such as perceived dentists' behaviour, general fears or maternal anxiety to be more important in the actual acquisition of dental fear than objective dental pathology (Ten Berge et al., 2002a; Klingberg et al., 1995; Townend, Dimigen & Fung, 2000). Townend et al. (2000) examined Rachman's pathways of fear acquisition in 7 to 14 year old children and suggested that subjective dental experiences may be decisive in the acquisition of dental fear, more important than dental pathology or maternal state anxiety. These subjective dental experiences were measured by parent reports on the number of "traumatic" visits and by child reports on perceived dentists' empathy. In another recent study (Ten Berge et al., 2002a) it was also indicated that experienced dental procedures only accounted for a small part of children's high dental fear in the age group between 5 and 10 years. It was suggested that subjective dental experiences (such as perceived dentist's behaviour and the use of behavioural management techniques) might play a more decisive role fear acquisition. Furthermore, in both studies support for the 'latent inhibition' theory was found: children with a longer history of non-invasive visits were found less likely to develop high dental fear than children who have experienced invasive treatment earlier in their dental history.

When interpreting these somewhat inconsistent results, it should be taken into consideration that reported results might depend on the specific measure of objective conditioning experiences (i.e., using oral health status (DMFT, DMFS) versus restorative treatment experience). In his proposed model of pain and anxiety associated with dental procedures, Litt (1996) criticised the use of oral health status as a method of assessing conditioning, since it does not automatically involve a similar, linear increase in frequency of invasive procedures experienced. Also, of course other factors such as age or attendance pattern seem to be mediating the conditioning process, causing comparison of results to be difficult.

Dentists' behaviour - As indicated before, in retrospective interview studies dentists' behaviour is often mentioned to be the cause for children's dental fear (e.g., Alwin et al., 1991; Ten Berge et al., 2001; Mejàre et al., 1989; Milgrom et al., 1992; Veerkamp et al., 1992). Studies on the immediate effect of specific dentists' behaviour have indicated behaviours such as direction, empathy and voice control to influence children's (fearful) reactions (Greenbaum, Lumley, Turner & Melamed, 1993; Greenbaum, Turner, Cook & Melamed, 1990; Melamed, Bennett, Jerrell, Ross, Bush, Hill, Courts & Ronk, 1983; Prins, Veerkamp, Ter Horst, De Jong & Tan, 1987; Weinstein, Getz, Ratener & Domoto, 1982a). Providing immediate direction and specific reinforcement in combination with working contact, for example, is reported to have a fear-reducing effect on children. Coercing, coaxing and criticism, on the other hand, are found to have the opposite effect (Melamed et al., 1983; Weinstein et al., 1982a). A study controlling for auto-correlations, however, has indicated that a child's fearful behaviour seems more closely related to its own previous behaviour than to this dentists' behaviour (Ter Horst, Prins, Veerkamp & Verhey, 1987). It should be noted that time lags in this study were very short (5 and 10 seconds), which of course may have influenced the auto-correlations found. Methodological problems thus seem to complicate the conclusions drawn from studying the immediate relation between a dentist's and a child's behaviour. Also, the effect of dentist's behaviour of course may depend on the child's age and level of dental fear (Alwin, Murray & Niven, 1994; Melamed et al., 1983; Weinstein, Getz, Ratener & Domoto, 1982b). In addition, in these studies child and dentist behaviour was observed and compared, while no information on the child's subjective perception of a dental visit or of the dentist's behaviour was included.

In a long-term study among highly fearful children referred to a dental fear clinic, not aimed at studying the immediate effects of dentist's behaviour, directive, controlling dentist's behaviour was found to have a fear-reducing long-term effect on children (Ten Berge, Veerkamp & Hoogstraten, 1999a). Moreover, recent studies (Ten Berge et al., 2002a; Townend et al., 2000) even suggested that perceived dentists' behaviour and subjective perception of treatment may be more decisive in the acquisition of dental fear than objective dental pathology. This perception of dentist and treatment might not only be influenced by the dentist's personal characteristics, but also by behaviour management techniques applied by the dentist. That is, the fear-eliciting effect of a painful treatment seems to be mediated by the dentists' behaviour: pain inflicted by a dentist perceived as "caring" may have less negative impact than pain inflicted by a "cold" or "uncaring" dentist (Bernstein et al., 1979; Milgrom et al., 1992). Furthermore, besides these dentist's characteristics also the application of conditioning mechanisms such as latent inhibition and gradual exposure during the course of treatment are found to have a fear reducing or even preventive effect on dental fear in children (Ten Berge et al., 2002a; Townend et al., 2000). In this context, also the effect of the lack of control on dental patients should be mentioned. That is, the perception of lack of control has been shown to have a negative effect on adolescent patients' level of arousal and perceived stress, and the use of strategies to enhance this sense of control by dental personnel was stressed (Milgrom et al., 1992).

4.1.2 Indirect Pathway: Modelling

Parental dental fear - Many studies have reported support for the modelling pathway in the acquisition of dental fear in children (Corkey & Freeman, 1994; Klingberg et al., 1995; Milgrom et al., 1995a; Winer, 1982). Several difficulties concerning the interpretation of this support, however, should be taken into consideration. First, most of these studies were based on simple correlations between parental and child fear (or behaviour), thus providing no information on its causality. That is, often no information on actual parental behaviour during dental visits, or on the way parents express their fears was included (Litt, 1996). For example, Townend et al. (2000) found maternal *state* anxiety to be strongly related to a dentist's rating of the child's dental anxiety but suggested that this might essentially be a sign of maternal empathy with their child's anxiety, instead of causing it. Another study reported that 45% of the children of parents with severe dental fear showed problem behaviours and the authors surprisingly concluded this to be indicative of a relation between child and parental dental fear (Klingberg & Berggren, 1992).

Moreover, it should also be noted that reported relations often are not very strong (Ten Berge et al., 2002a; Klingberg et al., 1995). It has been suggested that the parental influence may be strongest among dentally inexperienced children, and weakens or disappears as children have their own experiences to rely on (Ten Berge, Veerkamp, Hoogstraten & Prins, 2003; Townend et al., 2000; Winer, 1982). In other words, at a later age, the child's perception of dental treatment may be influenced more strongly by factors associated with actual dental treatment such as painful procedures or perceived dentist's behaviour. In his review, Winer (1982) stated that this relation might also be fragile because of moderating influences such as socio-economic variables. Furthermore, questions have also been raised whether the relation between parental and child dental fear may essentially be a shared genetic disposition, instead of a social learning process (Kent, 1997; Ollendick et al., 1997). Finally, the notion has been postulated that a fearful parent may be more sensitive to interpret his child's fearful behaviour (Veerkamp, 1994). In light of these seemingly conflicting results, a study on common childhood fears asking children retrospectively about their experiences should be noted (Muris, Merckelbach & Collaris, 1997). Although some of the children reported modelling experiences, none or only a small part of them actually ascribed the onset of their fear to this modelling.

Parental presence/behaviour - In medical situations, parental behaviour before and during stressful procedures has been found to influence the (coping) behaviour of children during these procedures (e.g., 'crisis parenting' model, Melamed & Siegel, 1985; for a review see Blount, Davis, Powers & Roberts, 1991). Contrary to medical situations in general, research on the effect of parental presence on the child's behaviour during dental treatment is limited. In general, only small effects of parental presence or behaviour during treatment were found, although some inconsistency in findings does occur (Bassin, Davis & Colchamiro, 1982; see Fenlon, Dobbs & Curzon, 1993; Holst et al., 1993; Koplik et al., 1992; Liddell, 1990; Townend et al., 2000; Winer, 1982). Logically, the effectiveness of parental behaviour depends on the nature of the child-parent interaction, the nature of dental visits and on the parent's own anxiety level (Milgrom, Weinstein, Kleinknecht & Getz, 1995b).

In some studies the uncooperative behaviour of children has been attributed to family attitudes and upbringing (Holst & Crossner, 1984; Mejàre et al., 1989; Varpio & Wellfelt, 1991). These results, however, stem from the dentists' point of view and were obtained by interviews or from dental records. Only one study actually provided empirical evidence for a relation of child rearing behaviour and child dental fear (Venham, Murray & Gaulin-Kremer, 1979). It was reported that coping skills and stress tolerance in children were facilitated when the home environment was structured, mothers were responsive and self-assured, and parents set limits and provide ample rewards and punishments. A recent study (Ten Berge et al., 2003), however, did not support such a relation; moreover, it was concluded that parents might play a more secondary, mediating role in the etiological process of child dental fear.

4.1.3 Indirect Pathway: Negative Information

The importance of negative information about dental stimuli in the etiology of dental fear has been repeatedly mentioned (Bernstein et al., 1979; Kleinknecht et al., 1973), although few studies have actually attempted to demonstrate a relation between dental fear and negative information provided by others. Reports are limited and findings inconsistent: some did find a significant relation with the number of fearful people or family members known to the child (e.g., Bailey, Talbot & Taylor, 1973; Townend et al., 2000; Bergius et al., 1997) while others did not report such a relationship. Moreover, it should be noted that no data on actual transmission of negative information is included in these studies. This shortcoming in research methodology may be due to the notion that this pathway is more difficult to study, since it is more implicit present in daily life. Milgrom et al. (1995a), for example, assumed that exposure to fearful images of dentists on television and in print are similar for all children, and concluded that there was no need to capture this aspect explicitly in their model.

4.1.4 Summary Conditioning Pathways

Mixed results have been found with respect to the role of direct conditioning experiences, depending on methods of investigating. In subjective reports dental fear repeatedly has been attributed to "traumatic" experiences, referring to painful, invasive treatment sessions or negative dentists' behaviour. Objective reports based on dental records or dental pathology, however, did not confirm the important role of painful procedures or restorative treatment. Furthermore, despite the fact that several studies have demonstrated a (moderate) relation between dental fear and oral health, recent studies eventually concluded other factors such as subjective dental experiences to be more important in the acquisition of dental fear. In some studies it has even been suggested that, in the context of regular attendance, the experience of restorative treatment might act prophylactically. This inconsistency in results may be related to differences in methods used but may also be a consequence of the relation between dental fear and oral health being mediated by other factors such as perceived dentists' behaviour or attendance pattern. The direct conditioning pathway thus does not seem to concern a simple linear relation between a child's oral health status (and subsequent potentially invasive procedures) and its level of dental fear. Recent studies seem to indicate that a distinction may be necessary between 'objective' (e.g., oral health, invasive procedures) and 'subjective' (e.g., perceived dentists' behaviour) dental experiences, and that the latter may be more important than the former in dental fear acquisition.

Of the indirect pathways, modelling has been studied extensively: repeatedly a relation between child dental fear and parental dental fear has been reported. The relative contribution of parental fear in the acquisition of dental fear, however, remains to be determined, due to the correlational nature of most studies. It has been proposed that parental influence may be limited to a child's initial dental experiences and thereafter is outweighed by other factors, leaving it to play a more secondary, mediating role. Few studies have been conducted on the influence of parental presence during treatment, general child rearing behaviour and transmission of negative information. Available results of studies in the dental situation are not impressive.

4.2.1 Individual Approach

Temperamental factors - Several closely linked temperamental qualities associated with responses or initial reactions to unfamiliar people and situations such as introversion, shyness and behavioural inhibition have been found to be related to high levels of dental fear in children. Particularly *general fearfulness* and *general emotional status* (e.g., introversion, negative emotionality and having difficulties coping with new situations or adapting to change) have been associated with high dental fear and uncooperative behaviour in children (Klingberg & Broberg, 1998; Williams, Murray, Lund, Harkiss, & De Franco, 1985; Winer, 1982). For example, Klingberg and Broberg (1998) found shyness in combination with negative emotionality to be a concomitant factor in the development of child dental fear and indicated this to be a risk factor. Beside this introversion or behavioural inhibition, other temperamental characteristics have been linked to dental fear in children. In light of the discussion of the potential role of *'attentional bias'* (hyper-attention to threatening stimuli; e.g., Kindt & Van Den Hout, 1999), an interesting relation with *distractibility* and *attention problems* has been reported for dentally fearful children. It has been speculated that dental phobia and associated behaviour management problems may develop more easily in children with a lower attention span (Alwin et al., 1991; Ten Berge, Veerkamp, Hoogstraten & Prins, 1999b; Liddell, 1990). In addition, children with uncooperative behaviour and higher dental fear were found to have increased pain expectations and lower *pain tolerance*. Others have found a significant positive correlation with emotional problems such as somatization, but concluded that this association is too weak to be regarded as a significant predictor of dental fear (Milgrom et al., 1994; Milgrom et al., 1995a; Raadal, Milgrom, Weinstein, Mancl & Cauce, 1995). A recent study on the potential influence of concomitant problems on children's further fear development, however, indicated that the presence of emotional or behavioural problems only has a small effect on a child's fear level after treatment in a dental fear clinic (Ten Berge & Veerkamp, submitted). It was concluded that the behavioural management approach at the clinic might suffice reducing the fear level for most children, regardless of the presence of concomitant problems.

Closely associated to these temperamental traits is the child's use of (negative) *coping styles*. For example, fearful children seem more focused on the negative consequences of dental treatment (catastrophising) than on the positive ones and engage in a more negative self-speech, possibly reinforcing their fear level (Brown, O'Keeffe, Sanders & Baker, 1986a; Prins, 1985). In addition, the use of cognitive coping strategies such as reality-oriented "working through" and "cognitive reappraisal", as well as the use of a greater variety and number of cognitive responses has been found to result in better adjustment to the dental situation. The use of behavioural strategies seem, however, to have an opposite effect (Curry & Russ, 1985; Curry, Russ, Johnsen & DiSantis, 1988). Other authors have studied the relation between child dental fear and coping and control strategies, but have reported inconsistent results (Weinstein, Milgrom, Hoskuldsson, Golletz, Jeffcott & Koday, 1996). Finally, monitoring has also been associated with increased anxiety. It has, however, been suggested that coping behaviour may vary with type of stressor and treatment phase (Miller, Roussi, Caputo & Kruus, 1995; Rape, Bush & Saravia, 1988).

Based on the above-mentioned results no causal conclusions can be drawn, since most studies are correlational. As a consequence of this lack of causality, in the literature a debate exists about whether dental fear is part of patients' general fearful nature or emotional status, or should be seen as a specific, isolated fear. It has been suggested that subgroups may exist within the adult fearful population. For example, Weiner & Sheehan (1990) made a distinction between *endogenous* and *exogenous* categories of fearful patients. The former refers to patients with a more general mood or anxiety disorder, while the latter refers to a simple conditioned fear. In addition, the Seattle system suggested four diagnostic types of adult patients: 1) simple conditioned fear, 2) anxiety about somatic reactions during treatment, 3) patients with generalised anxiety states and multiphobic symptoms and 4) distrust of dental personnel (Locker, Liddell & Shapiro, 1999b; Milgrom et al., 1995b). For child populations no such elaborated classifications have been proposed, although it has been suggested that subgroups of fearful children may exist within the child population (Arnrup, Broberg, Berggren & Bodin, in press; Ten Berge et al., 1999b, 2001; Klingberg et al., 1995; Klingberg & Broberg, 1998).

Age, gender and socio-economic status - Increased dental fear has repeatedly been associated with younger age groups and female gender (e.g., Alvesalo et al., 1993; Bedi et al., 1992b; Cuthbert & Melamed, 1982; Klingberg et al., 1995; Milgrom et al., 1994, 1995a; Wright et al., 1980b). However, reported age effects are not always very strong, possibly because of other developmental aspects affecting it or because it may not be a linear relation (Cuthbert & Melamed, 1982; Milgrom et al., 1995a; Raadal et al., 1995; Rape et al., 1988; Townend et al., 2000; Wright et al., 1980b). First, reported differences may well be associated with cultural factors or associated stigmas, i.e., being fearful still seems more socially accepted among younger children and girls. Second, it should be noted that the reported decline of fear with age seems to apply particularly to younger children while in late childhood and early adolescence opposite effects have been reported (Murray et al., 1989; Neverlien, 1994; Winer, 1982). Third, other developmental aspects may be involved in this association. For example, Milgrom et al. (1995a) found an age effect in fear level in children without or with possible caries but no such effect in children with frank or emergent caries, indicating that dental experience might be mediating this relation. Furthermore, lower fear levels in older children may essentially represent a general developmental change in children (Ten Berge et al., 2002c; Prins, 1994; Veerkamp, 1994; Winer, 1982). Increasing age in children is related to the development of cognitive abilities (Brown et al., 1986a; Curry & Russ, 1985), leading to a change in the expression of their fear (see also par. 2). That is, children may learn to control the way they exhibit fear as they grow older, and subsequently, this may lead to the decrease of inappropriate behaviour perceived and reported by others (Prins, 1994; Veerkamp, 1994; Winer, 1982). The question therefore arises as to whether it may actually be a child's developing coping abilities underlying this perceived decrease in fearful behaviour with increasing age, instead of an actual decrease in a child's level of fear. Comparisons between behavioural measures and anxiety ratings in children indeed have shown such a discrepancy: fearful behaviour has been found related to age whilst reported anxiety was not (e.g., LeBaron & Zeltzer, 1984; Koplik, Lamping & Reznikoff, 1992; Mekarski & Richardson, 1997; Milgrom et al., 1994). Herewith again the importance of using adequate assessment instruments is stressed. In addition, it should be noted that dental fear is associated with age-related general fears or pre-occupations. For younger children, dental fear may essentially reflect some degree of separation anxiety while older children may be merely pre-occupied by bodily harms or social standards. Developmental aspects are also important to the extent that cognitive biases or mechanisms may begin to play a role in children's fear acquisition or maintenance of this fear.

Some studies have found a negative relation between *socio-economic status* and dental fear or uncooperative behaviour in children (Bedi et al., 1992b; Klingberg et al., 1995, 1999; Townend et al., 2000; Wright et al., 1980b) (see also par. 3). However, others have not found a relation between dental fear and socio-economic status (Bergius, Berggren, Bogdanov & Hakeberg, 1997; Brown et al., 1986b; Corkey & Freeman, 1994; Lahti, Tuutti & Honkala, 1989; Koplik et al., 1992; Murray et al., 1989; Schwarz, 1990; Tuutti & Lahti, 1987; Wright, 1980a). Also, cultural factors have been mentioned to be of influence of children's fear level (Ten Berge et al., 2002c).

4.2.2 Summary Individual Approach

A specific cluster of temperamental traits associated with introversion and behavioural inhibition has been linked to dental fear in children. Subgroups of children may exist within the fearful population. For some children dental fear may be part of a general emotional status, while for others their fear may be a simple or specific conditioned fear. Dental fear in children also has been associated with moderating variables such as age, gender and socio-economic status. It has been indicated, however, that the proper management approach may have a fear reducing effect on fearful children, regardless of the presence of other problems.

5. GENERAL DISCUSSION

Several important theoretical and practical issues in the field of child dental fear research have been discussed. This article started with the discussion of assessment methods and associated problems in reported prevalence estimates. It was concluded that dental fear and behaviour management problems should be regarded as distinct phenomena in children, and therefore accordingly different assessment instruments should be used. For the assessment of dental fear, the CFSS-DS was indicated to be the most adequate instrument of screening dental fear in children, although it should not be used as a predictor of behavioural problems. Prevalence estimates in Western-European countries yielded a percentage of around 7% of children being high fearful, while another 8% may be 'at risk' for developing this. In Non-Western countries higher percentages were reported, varying from 18 up to 43%.

With respect to the etiology of dental fear in children, support for all the proposed pathways has been reported which seems to suggest that multiple pathways underlie a child's dental fear acquisition. From a practical point of view and for preventive purposes, however, it is important to distinguish causal and contributing factors. In this light it is important to note that for several pathways a causal relationship has not been demonstrated. The direct (conditioning) pathway is the only one that has been studied on a longitudinal and prospective basis. Support for the indirect pathways and temperamental factors, on the other hand, mainly stems from correlational and interview studies. Therefore, at this stage in research development modelling and temperamental factors such as negative emotionality or behavioural inhibition might have to be regarded as risk or mediating factors in the etiological process, while direct conditioning has been most frequently supported as the most important pathway.

The discrepancy in results between 'objective' and 'subjective' reports on this direct conditioning process is therefore of great interest. Most support for the conditioning pathway with respect to painful or invasive dental experiences stems from interview or questionnaire studies while several studies based on 'objective' treatment records did not confirm the importance of invasive dental procedures. Some of these studies did indeed demonstrate a (moderate) relation between child dental fear and oral health, while others reported an opposite effect and even concluded that invasive treatment might act prophylactically. Moreover, recent studies on the relative contribution of different pathways have indicated subjective dental experiences - such as perceived dentists' empathy and the use of behavioural management strategies - to be more important in the acquisition of dental fear than objective dental pathology or experienced dental procedures.

Herewith, an interesting shift in the focus in research on etiological factors is provided, that is, from objective (e.g., dental procedures) to more subjective (e.g., perceived dentists' behaviour) dental experiences. It might thus be hypothesised that painful procedures *per se* do not seem to be the direct cause of dental fear, but that the way these procedures are presented to the child might be decisive in this process. According to this view, factors such as temperament, experienced curative procedures and parental dental fear might need to be considered as risk factors attributing to dental fear instead of its direct cause. These risk factors may contribute to the conditioning process or predispose the child to a heightened risk for developing dental fear, though may not be responsible for the actual onset of this fear. In the end, the way children are managed and the way treatment is carried out by the dentist may be decisive in the acquisition or development of dental fear. This notion would have subsequent important implications for future research as well as for treatment of (fearful) children. That is, implementation of behavioural strategies such as gradual exposure could be helpful in reducing children's level of fear, while implementation of latent inhibition principles in a child's treatment course might help preventing the acquisition of dental fear. However, this hypothesised importance of treatment approach will need to be the focus in future research to determine its influence in the etiological process. Specific recommendations for future research are discussed below.

6. RECOMMENDATIONS FOR FUTURE RESEARCH

Although important indications have been demonstrated and discussed, more research is needed to further draw up a definite model of dental fear in children. As indicated above, especially studies on the specific contribution and most important aspects of treatment approach in the etiological process are needed. That is, the potential effects of modification of subjective, treatment-related, factors on the prevention and treatment of childhood dental fear should be explored further. More specifically, strategies and factors influencing a child's perception and subjective experience of dental treatment and of the operating dentist need to be a central issue in future studies, in order to eventually obtain information on the most effective treatment approach for subgroups of (fearful) children. With respect to practical implications of this most effective treatment approach, it is important to distinguish between situational and dispositional factors, since the former - as opposed to the latter - can be manipulated. In other words, research on treatment strategies needs to focus on the modification of situational factors such as implementation of conditioning mechanisms in treatment approach, while - with respect to dispositional factors such as temperament - it needs to be determined which subgroup of children benefits most from which specific treatment mode.

Furthermore, another important issue would be to examine the most effective way to include parents in the dental situation for children of different ages and developmental stages, as an additional, supportive method of helping a fearful child to cope with invasive dental treatments. Another interesting study would be to examine the potential role of temperamental characteristics, such as "attentional bias", in this etiological process more specifically. To summarise, in future research the emphasis should be on the child's subjective perception of treatment and dentists in order to determine the most important factors causing a visit to be experienced as invasive or traumatic.

REFERENCES

Aartman, I.H.A., Everdingen van, T., Hoogstraten, J., & Schuurs, A.H.B. (1996). Appraisal of behavioral measurement techniques for assessing dental anxiety and fear in children: a review. *Journal of Psychopathology and Behavioral Assessment, 18*, 153-171.

Aartman, I.H.A., Everdingen van, T., Hoogstraten, J., & Schuurs, A.H.B. (1998). Self-report measurements of dental anxiety and fear in children: a critical assessment. *ASDC Journal of Dentistry for Children, 65*, 252-258.

Alvesalo, I., Murtomaa, H., Milgrom, P., Honkanen, A., Karjalainen, M., & Tay, K-M. (1993). The Dental Fear Survey Schedule: a study with Finnish children. *International Journal of Paediatric Dentistry, 3*, 193-198.

Alwin, N.P., Murray, J.J., & Britten, P.G. (1991). An assessment of dental anxiety in children. *British Dental Journal, 171*, 201-207.

Alwin, N.P., Murray, J.J., & Niven, N. (1994). The effect of children's dental anxiety on the behaviour of a dentist. *International Journal of Paediatric Dentistry, 4*, 19-24.

Arnrup, K., Broberg, A.G., Berggren, U., & Bodin, L. (in press). Treatment outcome in subgroups of uncooperative child dental patients; an exploratory study. *International Journal of Paediatric Dentistry.*

Bailey, P.M., Talbot, A., & Taylor, P.P. (1973). A comparison of maternal anxiety levels with anxiety levels manifested in the child dental patient. *ASDC Journal of Dentistry for Children, 40*, 277-284.

Bassin, E.B., Davis, R.B., & Colchamiro, S. (1982). The preschool child's response to dental care when accompanied by day-care personnel. *Journal of Public Dental Health Dentistry, 42*, 345-352.

Bastawi, A.E., Reid, K.H., & West, G.A. (1979). Relative utility of different measures of stress induced by dental procedures. *Journal of Dental Research, 58*, 1484.

Bedi, R., Sutcliffe, P., Donnan, P.T., Barrett, N., & McConnachie, J. (1992a). Dental caries experience and prevalence of children afraid of dental treatment. *Community Dentistry and Oral Epidemiology, 20*, 368-371.

Bedi, R., Sutcliffe, P., Donnan, P.T., & McConnachie, J. (1992b). The prevalence of dental anxiety in a group of 13- and 14-year-old Scottish children. *International Journal of Paediatric Dentistry, 2*, 17-24.

Benjamins, C. (1995). Psychophysiological measurement of dental anxiety. PhD Thesis. University of Amsterdam, Enschede: Copyprint, 2000.

Berge ten, M., & Veerkamp, J.S.J. (submitted). Treatment outcome in a dental fear clinic: the role of emotional and behavioural problems in children.

Berge ten, M., Hoogstraten, J., Veerkamp, J.S.J., & Prins, P.J.M. (1998). The Dental Subscale of the Children's Fear Survey Schedule: a factor analytic study in the Netherlands. *Community Dentistry and Oral Epidemiology, 26*, 340-343.

Berge ten, M., Veerkamp, J.S.J., & Hoogstraten, J. (1999a). Dentists' behavior in response to child dental fear. *ASDC Journal of Dentistry for Children, 66*, 36-40.

Berge ten, M., Veerkamp, J.S.J., Hoogstraten, J., & Prins, P.J.M. (1999b). Behavioural and emotional problems in children referred to a centre for special dental care. *Community Dentistry and Oral Epidemiology, 27*, 181-186.

Berge ten, M., Veerkamp, J.S.J., Hoogstraten, J., & Prins, P.J.M. (2001). Parental beliefs on the origins of child dental fear in the Netherlands. *ASDC Journal of Dentistry for Children, 68*, 51-54.

Berge ten, M., Veerkamp, J.S.J., & Hoogstraten, J. (2002a). The etiology of childhood dental fear: the role of dental and conditioning experiences. *Journal of Anxiety Disorders, 16*, 321-329.

Berge ten, M., Veerkamp, J.S.J., Hoogstraten, J., & Prins, P.J.M. (2002b). The Dental Subscale of the Children's Fear Survey Schedule: predictive value and clinical usefulness. *Journal of Psychopathology and Behavioral Assessment, 24*, 115-118.

Berge ten, M., Veerkamp, J.S.J., Hoogstraten, J., & Prins, P.J.M. (2002c). Childhood dental fear in the Netherlands: prevalence and normative data. *Community Dentistry and Oral Epidemiology, 30*, 101-107.

Berge ten, M., Veerkamp, J.S.J., Hoogstraten, J., & Prins, P.J.M. (2003). Childhood dental fear in relation to parental child-rearing attitudes. *Psychological Reports, 92*, 43-50.

Berggren, U. (1984). *Dental fear and avoidance: a study of etiology, consequences and treatment*. PhD Thesis. University of Göteborg, Göteborg.

Bergius, M., Berggren, U., Bogdanov, O., & Hakeberg, M. (1997). Dental anxiety among adolescents in St. Petersburg, Russia. *European Journal of Oral Sciences, 105*, 117-122.

Bernstein, D.A., Kleinknecht, R.A., & Alexander, L.D. (1979). Antecedents of dental fear. *Journal of Public Health Dentistry, 39*, 113-124.

Blount, R.L., Davis, N., Powers, S.W., & Roberts, M.C. (1991). The influence of environmental factors and coping style on children's coping and distress. *Clinical Psychology Review, 11*, 93-116.

Brown, J.M., O'Keeffe, J., Sanders, S.H., & Baker, B. (1986a). Developmental changes in children's cognition to stressful and painful situations. *Journal of Pediatric Psychology, 11*, 343-357.

Brown, D.F., & Wright, F.A.C. (1987). Age-related changes in social and psychological models predicting dental care in children. *Preventive Medicine, 16*, 775-782.

Brown, D.F., Wright, F.A.C., & McMurray, N.E. (1986b). Psychological and behavioral factors associated with dental anxiety in children. *Journal of Behavioral Medicine, 9*, 213-218.

Corah, N.L. (1969). Development of a dental anxiety scale. *Journal of Dental Research, 48*, 596.

Corkey, B., & Freeman, R. (1994). Predictors of dental anxiety in six-year-old children: findings from a pilot study. *ASDC Journal of Dentistry for Children, 61*, 267-271.

Cuthbert, M.I,. & Melamed, B.G. (1982). A screening device: children at risk for dental fears and management problems. *ASDC Journal of Dentistry for Children, 49*, 432-436.

Curry, S.L., & Russ, S.W. (1985). Identifying coping strategies in children. *Journal of Clinical Child Psychology, 14*, 61-69.

Curry, S.L., Russ, S.W., Johnsen, D.C., & DiSantis, T.A. (1988). The role of coping in children's adjustment to the dental visit. *ASDC Journal of Dentistry for Children, 55*, 231-236.

Davey, G.C.L. (1989a). Dental phobias and anxieties: evidence for conditioning processes and modulation of a learned fear. *Behaviour Research and Therapy, 27*, 51-58.

Davey, G.C.L. (1989b). UCS revaluation and conditioning models of acquired fears. *Behaviour Research and Therapy, 27*, 521-528.

Fenlon, W.L., Dobbs, A.R., & Curzon, M.E.J. (1993). Parental presence during treatment of the child patient: a study with British parents. *British Dental Journal, 174*, 23-28.

Frankl, S.N., Shiere, F.R., & Fogels, H.R. (1962). Should the parent remain with the child in the dental operatory? *ASDC Journal of dentistry for Children, 29*, 150-163.

Gatchel, R.J. (1989). The prevalence of dental fear and avoidance: expanded adult and recent adolescent surveys. *Journal of the American Dental Association, 118*, 591-593.

Greenbaum P.E., Lumley, M.A., Turner, C., & Melamed, B.G. (1993). Dentists' reassuring touch: effects on children's behaviour. *Pediatric Dentistry, 15*, 20-24.

Greenbaum, P.E., Turner, C., Cook, E.W., & Melamed, B.G. (1990). Dentists' voice control: effects on children's disruptive and affective behavior. *Health Psychology, 9*, 546-558.

Holst, A., & Crossner, C-G. (1984). Management of dental behaviour problems. *Swedish Dental Journal, 8*, 243-249.

Holst, A., & Crossner, C-G. (1987). Direct ratings of acceptance of dental treatment in Swedish children. *Community Dentistry and Oral Epidemiology, 15*, 258-263.

Holst, A., Hallonsten, A-L., Schröder, U., Ek, L., & Edlund, K. (1993). Prediction of behavior-management problems in 3-year-old children. *Scandinavian Journal of Dental Research, 101*, 110-114.

Holst, A., Schröder, U., Ek, L., Hallonsten, A-L., & Crossner, C-G. (1988). Prediction of behavior management problems in children. *Scandinavian Journal of Dental Research, 96*, 457-465.

Horst ter, G., Prins, P.J.M., Veerkamp, J.S.J., & Verhey, H. (1987). Interactions between dentists and anxious child patients: a behavioral analysis. *Community Dentistry and Oral Epidemiology, 15*, 249-252.

Hosey, M.T., & Blinkhorn, A.S. (1995). An evaluation of four methods of assessing the behaviour of anxious child dental patients. *International Journal of Paediatric Dentistry, 5*, 87-95.

Jongh de, A., Muris, P., Horst ter, G., & Duyx, M.P.M.A. (1995). Acquisition and maintenance of dental anxiety: the role of conditioning experiences and cognitive factors. *Behaviour Research and Therapy, 33*, 205-210.

Kent, G. (1997). Dental phobias. In G.C.L. Davey (Ed.), *Phobias – A handbook of theory, research and treatment*. Chichester: John Wiley & Sons.

Kindt, M., & Hout van den, M. (1999). Anxiety and selective attention for threatening information. *Nederlands Tijdschrift voor Psychologie, 54*, 63-72.

Kleinknecht, R.A., Klepac, R.K., & Alexander, L.D. (1973). Origins and characteristics of fear of dentistry. *Journal of the American Dental Associaton, 86*, 842-848.

Klingberg, G. (1994). Reliability and validity of the Swedish version of the Dental Subscale of the Children's Fear Survey Schedule, CFSS-DS. *Acta Odontologica Scandinavia, 52*, 255-256.

Klingberg, G. (1995). *Dental fear and behavior management problems in children. A study of measurement, prevalence, concomitant factors, and clinical effects*. PhD Thesis. University of Göteborg, Göteborg: Public Dental Service.

Klingberg, G., & Berggen, U. (1992). Dental problem behaviors in children of parents with severe dental fear. *Swedish Dental Journal, 16*, 27-32.

Klingberg, G., Berggren, U., Carlsson, S.G., & Norén, J.G. (1995). Child dental fear: cause related factors and clinical effects. *European Journal of Oral Sciences, 103*, 405-412.

Klingberg, G., Berggren, U., & Norén, J.G. (1994). Dental fear in an urban Swedish child population: prevalence and concomitant factors. *Community Dental Health, 11*, 208-214.

Klingberg, G., & Broberg, A.G. (1998). Temperament and child dental fear. *Pediatric Dentistry, 20*, 237-243.

Klingberg, G., & Hwang, C.P. (1994). Children's dental fear picture test (CDFP): a projective test for the assessment of child dental fear. *ASDC Journal of Dentistry for Children, 61*, 89-96.

Klingberg, G., Sillén, R., & Norén, J.G. (1999). Machine learning methods applied on dental fear and behavior management problems in children. *Acta Odontologica Scandinavica, 57*, 207-215.

Koplik, E.K., Lamping, D.L., & Reznikoff, M. (1992). The relationship of mother-child coping styles and mothers' presence on children's response to dental stress. *Journal of Psychology, 126*, 79-92.

Kruger, E., Thomson, W.M., Poulton, R.G., Davies, S., Brown, R.H., & Silva, P.A. (1998). Dental caries and changes in dental anxiety in late adolescence. *Community Dentistry and Oral Epidemiology, 26*, 355-359.

Lahti, S., Tuutti, H., & Honkala, E. (1989). The relationship of parental dental anxiety and child's caries status. *ASDC Journal of Dentistry for Children, 56*, 191-195.

LeBaron, S., & Zeltzer, L. (1984). Assessment of acute pain and anxiety in children and adolescents by self-reports, observer reports and a behavior checklist. *Journal of Consulting and Clinical Psychology, 52*, 729-738.

Liddell, A. (1990). Personality characteristics versus medical and dental experiences of dentally anxious children. *Journal of Behavioral Medicine, 13*, 183-194.

Litt, M.D. (1996). A model of pain and anxiety associated with acute stressors: distress in dental procedures. *Behaviour Research and Therapy, 34*, 459-476.

Locker, D., Liddell, A., Dempster, L., & Shapiro, D. (1999a). Age of onset of dental anxiety. *Journal of Dental Research, 78*, 790-796.

Locker, D., Liddell, A., & Shapiro, D. (1999b). Diagnostic categories of dental anxiety: a population-based study. *Behaviour Research and Therapy, 37*, 25-37.

Locker, D., Shapiro, D., & Liddell, A. (1996). Negative dental experiences and their relationship to dental anxiety. *Community Dental Health, 13*, 86-92.

Lubow, R.E. (1973). Latent inhibition. *Psychological Bulletin, 79*, 398-407.

Majstorovic, M., Skrinjaric, I., Glavina, D., & Szirovicza, L. (2001). Factors predicting a child's dental fear. *Collegium Antropologium, 25*, 493-500.

Mejàre, I., Ljungkvist, B., & Quensel, E. (1989). Pre-school children with uncooperative behaviour in the dental situation. Some characteristics and background factors. *Acta Odontologica Scandinavica, 47*, 337-345.

Mejàre, I., & Mjones, I. (1989). Dental caries in Turkish immmigrant primary schoolchildren. *Acta Paediatric Scendinavica, 78*, 110-114.

Mekarski, J.E. & Richardson, B.A. (1997). Toward convergent validation of children's dental anxiety and disruptiveness ratings. *Perceptual and Motor Skills, 85*, 1155-1162.

Melamed, B.G., Bennett, C.G., Jerrell, G., Ross, S.L., Bush, J.P., Hill, C., Courts, F., & Ronk, S. (1983). Dentists' behavior management as it affects compliance and fear in pediatric patients. *Journal of the American Dental Association, 106*, 324-330.

Melamed, B.G. & Siegel, L.J. (1985). Children's reactions to medical stressors: an ecological approach to the study of anxiety. In A.H. Tuma & J. Maser (Eds.), *Anxiety and the anxiety disorders*. Hillsdale, NJ: Erlbaum.

Menzies, R.G., & Clarke, J.C. (1995). The etiology of phobias: a non-associative account. *Clinical Psychology Review, 15*, 23-48.

Merckelbach, H., Jong de, P.J., Muris, P., & Hout van den, M.A. (1996). The etiology of specific phobias: a review. *Clinical Psychology Review, 16*, 337-361.

Milgrom, P., Jie, Z., Yang, Z., & Tay, K-M. (1994). Cross-cultural validity of the Dental Fear Survey Schedule for children in Chinese. *Behaviour Research and Therapy, 32*, 131-135.

Milgrom, P., Mancl, L., King, B., & Weinstein, P. (1995a). Origins of childhood dental fear. *Behaviour Research and Therapy, 33,* 313-319.

Milgrom, P., Vignesha, H., & Weinstein, P. (1992). Adolescent dental fear and control: prevalence and theoretical implications. *Behaviour Research and Therapy, 30,* 367-373.

Milgrom, P., Weinstein, P., Kleinknecht, R.A., & Getz, T. (1995b). *Treating fearful dental patients: A patient management handbook.* Seattle: University of Washington, Continuing Dental Education.

Miller, S.M., Roussi, P., Caputo, G.C., & Kruus, L. (1995). Patterns of children's coping with an aversive dental treatment. *Health Psychology, 14,* 236-246.

Muris, P., Merckelbach, H., & Collaris, R. (1997). Common childhood fears and their origins. *Behaviour Research and Therapy, 35,* 929-937.

Murray, P., Liddell, A., & Donohue, J. (1989). A longitudinal study of the contribution of dental experiences to dental anxiety in children between 9 and 12 years of age. *Journal of Behavioral Medicine, 12,* 309-320.

Neverlien, P.O. (1994). Dental anxiety, optimism-pessimism, and dental experience from childhood to adolescence. *Community Dentistry and Oral Epidemiology, 22,* 263-268.

Neverlien, P.O., & Backer Johnsen, T. (1991). Optimism-pessimism dimension and dental anxiety in children aged 10-12 years. *Community Dentistry and Oral Epidemiology, 19,*342-346.

Ollendick, T.H., Hagopian, L.P., & King, N.J. (1997). Specific phobias in children. In: G.C.L. Davey (Ed.), *Phobias – A handbook of theory, research and treatment.* Chichester: John Wiley & Sons.

Poulton, R.G., Thomson, W.M., Davies, S., Kruger, E., Brown, R.H., & Silva, P.A. (1997). Good teeth, bad teeth and fear of the dentist. *Behaviour Research and Therapy, 35,* 327-344.

Prins, P.J.M. (1985). Self-speech and self-regulation of high- and low-fearful children in the dental situation: an interview study. *Behaviour Research and Therapy, 23,* 641-650.

Prins, P.J.M. (1994). Anxiety in medical settings. In T.H. Ollendick, N.J. King & W. Yule (Eds.), *Handbook of phobic and anxiety disorders in children and adolescents* (p. 267-290). New York: Plenum Press.

Prins, P.J.M., Veerkamp, J.S.J., Horst ter, G., Jong de, A., & Tan, L. (1987). Behavior of dentists and child patients during treatment. *Community Dentistry and Oral Epidemiology, 15,* 253-257.

Raadal, M., Milgrom, P., Weinstein, P., Mancl, L., & Cauce, A.M. (1995). The prevalence of dental anxiety in children from low-income families and its relationship to personality traits. *Journal of Dental Research, 74,* 1439-1443.

Rachman, S. (1977). The conditioning theory of fear acquisition: A critical examination. *Behaviour Research and Therapy, 15,* 375-387.

Rachman, S. (1991). Neoconditioning and the classical theory of fear acquisition. *Clinical Psychology Review, 11,* 155-173.

Rape, R.N., Bush, J.P., & Saravia, M. (1988). Development of children's dental fears: an observational study. *Journal of Clinical Child Psychology, 17,* 345-351.

Schwarz, E. (1990). Dental anxiety in young adult Danes under alternative dental care programs. *Scandinavian Journal of Dental Research, 98,* 442-450.

Seligman, M.E.P. (1971). Phobias and preparedness. *Behavior Therapy, 2,* 307-320.

Teo, C.S., Fooong, W., Lui, H.H., Elliot, J. (1990). Prevalence of dental fear in young adult Singaporeans. *International Dental Journal, 40*, 37-42.

Thomson, W.M., Poulton, R.G., Kruger, E., Davies, S., Brown, R.H., & Silva, P.A. (1997). Changes in self-reported dental anxiety in New Zealand adolescents from ages 15 to 18 years. *Journal of Dental Research, 76*, 1287-1291.

Townend, E., Dimigen, G., & Fung, D. (2000). A clinical study of child dental anxiety. *Behaviour Research and Therapy, 38*, 31-46.

Tuutti, H. (1986). Dental anxiety in children and adolescents. Thesis. Kuopio: University of Kuopio.

Tuutti, H., & Lahti, S. (1987). Oral health status of children in relation to the dental anxiety of their parents. *The Journal of Pedodontics, 11*, 146-150.

Varpio, M., & Wellfelt, B. (1991). Some characteristics of children with dental behaviour problems. Five-year follow-up of pedodontic treatment. *Swedish Dental Journal, 15*, 85-93.

Veerkamp, J.S.J. (1994). *Nitrous oxide: happy air or hot air?* PhD Thesis. University of Amsterdam, Amsterdam.

Veerkamp, J.S.J., Gruythuysen, R.J.M., Amerongen van, W.E., & Hoogstraten, J. (1992). Dental treatment of fearful children using nitrous oxide part 2: the parents' point of view. *ASDC Journal of Dentistry for Children, 59*, 115-119.

Venham, L.L., Bengtson, D., & Cipes, M. (1977). Children's responses to sequential dental visits. *Journal of Dental Research, 56*, 454-459.

Venham, L.L., Murray, P., Gaulin-Kremer, E. (1979). Child-rearing variables affecting the preschool child's response to dental stress. *Journal of Dental Research, 58*, 2042-2045.

Vignesha, H., Chellappah, N.K., Milgrom, P., Going, R., & Teo, C.S. (1990). A clinical evaluation of high- and low-fear children in Singapore. *ASDC Journal of Dentistry for Children, 57*, 224-228.

Weiner, A.A., & Sheehan, D.J. (1990). Etiology of dental anxiety: psychological trauma or CNS chemical imbalance? *General Dentistry, 22*, 39-43.

Weinstein, P., Getz, T., Ratener, P., & Domoto, P. (1982a). The effect of dentists' behavior on fear-related behaviors in children. *Journal of the American Dental Association, 104*, 32-38.

Weinstein, P., Getz, T., Ratener, P., & Domoto, P. (1982b). Dentists' responses to fear and non-fear-related behaviors in children. *Journal of the American Dental Association, 104*, 38-40.

Weinstein, P., Milgrom, P., Hoskuldsson, O., Golletz, D, Jeffcott, E., & Koday, M. (1996). Situation-specific child control: a visit to the dentist. *Behaviour Research and Therapy, 34*, 11-21.

Williams, J.M.G., Murray, J.J., Lund, C.A., Harkiss, B., & De Franco, A. (1985). Anxiety in the child dental clinic. *Journal of Child Psychology and Psychiatry and Allied Disciplines, 26*, 305-310.

Winer, G.A. (1982). A review and analysis of children's fearful behaviour in dental settings. *Child Development, 53*, 1111-1133.

Wright, F.A.C. (1980a). Relationship of children's anxiety to their potential dental health behaviour. *Community Dentistry and Oral Epidemiology, 8*, 189-194.

Wright, F.A.C., Lucas, J.O., & McMurray, N.E. (1980b). Dental anxiety in five-to-nine-year-old children. *Journal of Pedodontics, 4*, 99-115.

Chapter 7

DENTAL FEAR: IN SEARCH OF EFFICIENT TREATMENT PRINCIPLES

Tiril Willumsen[*]
Institute of Clinical Odontology,
University of Oslo, Norway

INTRODUCTION

Dental fear refers to a response out of proportions with the realistic dangers connected to dental treatment. It may vary from mild avoidance to phobic reactions. The terms dental fear, dental anxiety and dental phobia have all been used. In the present chapter, the term dental fear is used to denote very strong fear together with phobic reactions. The patient experiences in such instances that the reaction can neither be explained nor reasoned away. They are largely beyond voluntarily control, and often lead to avoidance of dental treatment. Thus, many dental fear patients seek dental treatment only in cases of emergency, for instance when they are in pain. They often feel extremely nervous several days before the appointment, and if they show up in the dental office, they have extreme activation of fear. Dental fear is difficult to measure objectively. Thus, questionnaires tested for reliability and validity are the instruments used to measure dental fear in research (e.g. Corah, 1969, Kleinknect et al., 1978).

Despite innovations in dental equipment and treatment procedures as well as increased knowledge of dental fear and its consequences, the prevalence of dental fear has been relatively constant during the last 20 years. About 5% of the population in Western countries suffers from severe dental fear and 20 - 30% has moderate dental fear (Milgrom et al., 1988, Thomson et al., 1996, Weinstein et al., 1993, Kaufman et al., 1992, Stouthard & Hoogstraten, 1990, Hakeberg et al., 1992, de Jongh, 1995, Moore et al., 1993, Neverlien, 1990,).

[*] Institute of Clinical Odontology, University of Oslo, Boks 1109 Blindern, 0317 Oslo, Norway. Phone 22-85-22-88; Fax: 22-85-23-86; E-mail: tiril@odont.uio.no.

Dental fear has been classified as a specific phobia. In about 20 % of the patients, it has been found to be part of a more complex psychological problem (Moore et al., 1993). The fear has negative consequences for both the patients' psychosocial and oral health.

In the search for new treatment methods, the author and coworkers in the Oslo Dental Fear Program stated that the following principles are of importance: (a) The treatment methods should be based on previous research of both dental fear and comparable psychological conditions. (b) The treatment methods should be treatment principles used in modern psychological treatment. (c) Treatment manuals should be developed for all treatment conditions to ascertain treatment consistency and differentiability. (d) In order to increase generalization to dental general practice, psychological interventions and dental treatment should be conducted in the same session with a minimum of technical equipment.

The present chapter aims to give a summary on the psychological and interpersonal aspects of dental treatment, development of dental fear and dental fears' psychosocial and oral health consequences. Further, it will present descriptions of new treatment methods used in the Oslo Dental Fear Program, summarize the major findings concerning treatment outcome from these methods and finally discuss principles behind the various new treatment methods.

PSYCHOLOGICAL AND INTERPERSONAL ASPECTS OF DENTAL TREATMENT

Dental treatment does not constitute any real danger. However, it seems as though some situations are easier learned more fearful than others. This learning does not follow rational principles. Darwinian theory claims that the liability to experience fear may be part of an evolutionary process. Situations that enhanced survival in the past are more readily learned to be fearful even today (Marks, 1987, Nesse and Williams, 1994). Dental treatment seems to trigger instinctive survival mechanisms and it seems to be more fear provoking than comparable situations (e.g. medical consultations, minor surgery on other parts of the body). This may be one reason why dental fear has such a high prevalence. In a study by Agras (Agras et al., 1969) dental fear was rated as the fifth most common fear, and the ninth most intense fear. Fear of doctors or medical procedures were not included among the 11 most common intense fears.

In order to understand the nature of dental fear, it is important to consider psychological and interpersonal aspects of the dental consultation that may affect the patient's appraisal, feelings and coping in the situation. These aspects are important to all patients but of special relevance to the fearful patient.

The dentist often has to perform operations on soft and mineralized human tissue with a high demand for precision. To be able to perform this work, the dentist must have a convenient field of work with good light and possibilities to reach any pathological tissues with adequate instruments. This may require a bodily position that challenges the patients' feeling of control.

Another essential feature of dental treatment is the intimacy of the oral area. Most people experience shyness when strangers or even acquaintances come too close. In a personal conversation the proper distance between two people is about 1-1.5 meters. If anyone come closer than this, a feeling of unpleasantness or stress easily arises, and a defense reaction (e.g.

stepping back to reach a comfortable distance) is often observed. To provide dental treatment the dentist must operate within this zone of intimacy.

The mouth has several basic physiological functions. Our taste organs are responsible for identifying food elements and are involved in decision-making concerning whether food should be swallowed or expectorated. For example an unknown bitter taste is often associated with toxic food elements. In addition the mouth is important in keeping free air space, especially for patients with enlarged adenoids or other obstructive conditions in the nasopharynx. It is normal to react with defense mechanisms if one feels that these basic functions are threatened. In dental fear patients, who are liable to feel a lack of control and distrust in the dentist in the treatment situation, these feelings of threat are easily triggered.

Pain

Dental tissues are highly innervated with pain receptors, and almost any dental operation is likely to cause pain in some patients. In a study of a representative sample of the Norwegian adult population, about 20-30 % reported their last dental visit as moderately painful or worse, and 60% reported having had at least one very painful experience (Vassend, 1993). It is a common clinical observation that local anesthesia is less effective in patients who show extreme fear than in relaxed and confident patients (Fiset et al., 1989, Kaufman et al., 1984), and it may be speculated that fear make the effect of local anesthesia less potent. Another hypothesis is that patients who are difficult to give adequate anesthesia (e.g. due to anatomical variations in the mandible) may develop dental fear mainly for this reason.

In contrast to the speculative theories of the association between effect of local anesthesia and dental fear, the relation between remembered experience of pain and dental anxiety is well documented. In one study, a group of patients with high dental fear anticipated more pain during treatment than a group of patients without dental fear (Kent, 1985). Immediately after treatment, the experience of dental pain was almost the same for the two groups. After three months the patients rated their memory of pain during the dental treatment. The patients with dental fear remembered the treatment as more painful than the patients without dental fear.

Several retrospective studies have shown that patients with dental fear more often have experienced painful dental treatment than patients with no dental fear (Davey, 1989; Vassend, 1993). It is uncertain whether these reported experiences of pain are cognitive appraisals due to anxiety, or whether the patients actually have experienced more painful episodes during dental treatment.

Control

Dental treatment causes some degree of stress in most patients. Experiments have demonstrated that when test subjects experienced high degree of control in a stressful situation (whether they actually possess this control or not), the level of stress is reduced (e.g. Moreland and Logan, 1989, Thompson, 1981, Law et al., 1994). The dental setting can be unfamiliar for the patient. Without a clear and intelligible explanation of the different sequences in the treatment and the consequences of refusing it, it may be difficult for the patient to comply with and accept the treatment. According to e.g. Piaget's theories (Inhelder and Piaget, 1958) it may be assumed that children have to be at least 10-12 years old before they fully understand the reasons for dental treatment, and the consequences of not receiving treatment. This may theoretically be a component in the development of dental fear, as most dental fear seems to originate in childhood. Prevention and treatment of early stages of dental fear is consequently a challenge for all pediatric dentistry.

In a study by Logan et al. (1991) patients with a high desire for control and an experience of a low feeling of control during treatment, scored significantly higher on dental fear than patients who had a high desire for control and an experience of high control. They also scored higher than patients with a low desire for control. A desire for control is dependent on a person's previous experiences, and his/her personality. The degree of perceived control during treatment is dependent on both the patients' individual needs and the dentist's mode of treatment (e.g. practical arrangements for stopping the treatment and predictability). Milgrom and Weinstein (1985) found that limited experience of control in the dental treatment situation is a predictor of dental fear.

In a study of patients' fear and anxiety when treated in an oral surgery department more than half of the patients reported moderate or severe anxiety before the treatment (Petersen et al., 1978). The author concluded that the dominating cause of anxiety was uncertainty and lack of knowledge about the treatment due to insufficient information from the dentists.

Transference

Many dental fear patients feel helpless during dental treatment and characterize dentists as authoritarian (Berggren, 1984). According to psychodynamic theories this kind of situation may evoke so-called transference phenomena, which means that the patients tend to transfer emotions, conflicts, frustrations and negative expectations from various sources (e.g. early relationship with their parents), onto their therapist (dentist). A patient may subconsciously feel related to the dentist, as a child to a parent. For instance, he/she may regard the dentist as e.g. an omnipotent, magical helper who will solve all his /her problems or as an authority who never listens to any objections. According to cognitive theory, the same phenomena may be regarded as activation of irrational and unconscious interpersonal schemata.

According to Moulton (1955) the dental treatment situation can initiate psychological processes in the patient such as dependence, sexual attraction and phobic avoidance on a scale otherwise only met by obstetricians and psychologists.

Regression

During dental treatment many dental fear patients have described a desire to scream, to cry, or to run out of the office (Willumsen, 1999). They find these urges incomprehensible and frightening. Such reactions may be explained, at least partly, as regression phenomena. Regression is a psychological state where the person reacts in an immature way, often in a similar way as earlier in life when a traumatic event has happened (Gill, 1972). The patient may also recall the size of an object as unrealistic big, for example the size of the injection syringe or the dentist's hands (Todes, 1972).

For example, one patient gave the following description: "When I sit in the dental chair I feel like I am about 5 years old and helplessly abandoned. I was hospitalized for long periods at that age. When my parents were together with me, I was happy. They always left me while I was occupied with playing, and I did not really observe that they left. When I observed that they were gone, I had these helpless and abandoned feelings and it was extremely frightening" (Willumsen, 1999).

A second patient claimed "The dentist told me that my teeth were very bad and that my mother had given me sweets and not taken care of my teeth. I felt this as a strong accusation towards my mother. After this event, I always felt defensive in dental clinics. As soon as I was old enough, I withdrew from contact with dentists and I never told my mother the reason. Even if I intellectually understand that the dentist did not intend to accuse my mother, I still feel a strong distrust against dentists" (Willumsen, 1999)

Personality

Patients suffering from dental fear often report early negative experiences with dentists (Liddell and Gosse, 1998). However, there are patients with early negative experiences with dentists who do not develop dental fear and patients with dental fear who have no previous negative dental experiences. Obviously there are differences in how an experience is assessed. Some individuals need more intense stimuli than others to learn that something is dangerous. For instance, some children will not get scared even after excessive and painful dental surgery whereas others learn that dental treatment is dangerous by listening to playmates describing their experiences.

It may be that persons with specific personality traits experience negative stimuli as more threatening and therefore have an enhanced risk of developing dental fear. This has not yet been confirmed in longitudinal studies. However, patients with dental fear differ from a normative population by having elevated scores on tests of neuroticism in personality tests (Schuurs et. al, 1988).

DEVELOPMENT OF DENTAL FEAR

The development of dental fear is best understood as vicious circles (see Figure 1).

The patient experiences the dental treatment situation or the thought of this situation as threatening. He/she will respond to this with increased muscular tension and a set of bodily changes induced by the autonomic nervous system, e.g. increased blood pressure, sweating, and increased heart rate. The patients tend to misinterpret these bodily sensations as signs of imminent physical and mental disaster. This results in thoughts with catastrophic content, which in turn increase the feelings of threat, dread and terror.

After a fearful dental treatment situation, the risk of canceling or postponing the next appointment increases. Cancelled and no-show appointments cause practical, emotional, financial and motivational problems for the patient as well as for the dental staff. When the patient later shows up, the dental staff may consciously or unconsciously react negatively. This further increases the risk of a tense interpersonal atmosphere and a negative experience for the patient. Cancellation of the next appointment is often the result, and the risk of avoiding all dental treatment, increases. When a patient with dental fear starts to avoid dental treatment, this often leads to a deterioration of the dentition. Bad teeth create negative feelings such as shame, guilt and embarrassment. These feelings are likely to reinforce avoidance behavior, and the vicious circle is established (Berggren and Meynert, 1984).

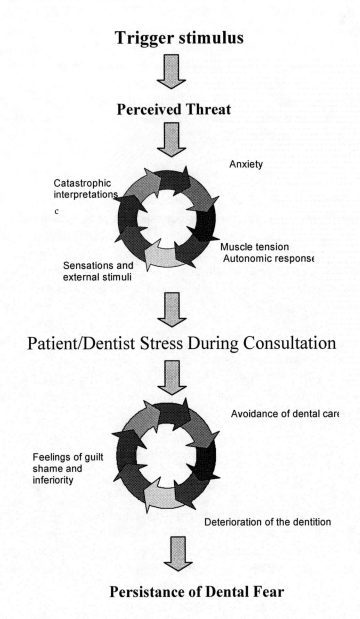

Figure 1. Theoretical model for development and persistence of dental fear.

When dental fear is established, it can last a lifetime, or it can vanish after some time.

Dental fear may vanish as a part of a natural extinction process occurring without exposure to the phobic stimulus. For instance, when a child with dental fear matures he/she sees the benefit of dental treatment and gets more motivated for managing dental treatment. Another spontaneous cure may occur when the fear appears as a secondary problem (e.g. depression or anxiety disorder) and which will disappear when the main problem is successfully treated.

Resistance

The patients may exhibit resistance towards treatment of their dental fear. Resistance is a psychodynamic concept. Cognitive–behavioral theory conceptualizes the problem as one of treatment non-compliance (Safran and Segal, 1990). Resistance is a frequently registered problem in patients with dental fear. They acknowledge their fear, but are not capable of trying to overcome it. Often these patients see general anesthesia as the only acceptable solution for their problem.

Lazarus and Fay (1982) identified four reasons for resistance: (i) the patient's individual characteristics, (ii) the patient's interpersonal relationships (network or family processes), (iii) the therapist and (iv) the state of the art (Safran and Segal, 1990). The following examples of resistance illustrate these reasons of resistance: First, the patient may loose secondary gains from his or her maladaptive behavior. Second, someone in the patient's network may sabotage the therapy. Third, the therapist's communication skills may cause failure in the patient-therapist relationship. Forth, elements in the treatment process e.g. homework assignments may be perceived as too threatening or irrelevant.

The causes of the patient's resistance may vary from mild motivational problems to severe psychological disorder.

ORAL AND PSYCHOSOCIAL HEALTH CONSEQUENSES

As avoidance is a prominent feature of dental fear, dental fear is a predictor of oral health. Dental fear patients have more dental problems than others. They have more missed and decayed teeth than others (Unell et al. 1999, Schuller et al., 2003).

Typically some teeth are seriously damaged, whereas the others are intact. If a tooth has a cavity, it will deteriorate if it is left untreated. This is not the case for teeth without caries lesions. In an epidemiological study from Norway, it was found that the median number of functional teeth in the age group 55-64 was 7.5 for individuals with strong dental fear compared to 22 for individuals without dental fear (Schuller et al., 2003). This makes a substantial difference with respect to oral health, both chewing ability and aesthetic functioning.

It has been shown that dental fear patients have increased level of general psychological distress (Aartmann et al., 1997, Eli at al., 1997, Vassend et al., 2000).

Dental fear patients are often unsatisfied with the appearance of their teeth and many patients report that they never smile freely. The socio-psychological consequences never smiling has not been properly investigated, but most probably the consequences for the interpersonal relationships are severe.

It is a clinical observation that many dental fear patients feel shameful of their fear. It is not unusual for dental fear patients to be too embarrassed of their dental fear to tell even their closest family or, if they receive psychotherapy, their therapist about it.

TREATMENT METODS OF DENTAL FEAR AND THE OSLO DENTAL FEAR PROGRAM

Different types of sedative medications, e.g. benzodiazepines or nitrous oxide sedation cause reductions in dental anxiety (Weinstein et al., 1988, Berggren, 1984, Makkes et al., 1987; Hallonsten, 1988, Hakeberg et al., 1990, Veerkamp et al., 1991, 1993).

Various behavioral treatment techniques, particularly systematic desensitization (gradual exposure combined with relaxation) have proved to be effective (Klepac, 1975, Carlsson et al.1984, Berggren and Linde 1984, Liddell et al. 1994, Carpenter et al., 1994). The effect of clinical rehearsal (gradual exposure to threatening dental situations by simulated dental treatment) seems to be equally effective as video training (videotaped dental episodes watched by the patient, accompanied by relaxation) (Moore, 1991). Various cognitive intervention techniques such as those described by Kent (1987), Kent and Gibbons (1987), de Jong et al. (1995a; 1995b) and de Jongh (1995) have also given promising results. Other specialized treatment principles that have resulted in reduction of dental fear are distraction (Corah et al., 1979), audio taped rehearsals (Horowitz, 1992) and desensitization in combination with nitrous oxide sedation (Weinstein et al., 1988). In treatment of children, favorable results have been demonstrated with techniques such as tell-show-do (Varpio and Wellfelt, 1991) and modeling by use of video (Ter Horst et al., 1987).

Systematic desensitization and cognitive preparation have given the best results in well-designed trials. (for reviews, see Hallonsten, 1988; van der Bijl, 1992, Berggren et al., 2000).

However, when establishing the Oslo Dental Fear Program the author and coworkers searched for treatment methods that fulfilled the criteria mentioned in the introduction of this chapter. The use of treatment manuals and a design that made the treatment able to generalize for use in general dental practice was considered essential. None of the previously reported studies fulfills all our intensions. In addition, many of these published treatment methods have methodological shortcomings (e.g. lack of control, not randomized trials) and few have follow-up studies. Thus, new treatment methods founded on previous research of both dental and comparable psychological conditions (agoraphobia) were developed and tested.

In the following, these methods are presented. (Willumsen et al. 2001a, 2001b Willumsen and Vassend 2003).

General Treatment Principles

In the Oslo Dental Fear Program, several general principles are common in all treatment conditions:

1. Education about fear is emphasized. Theoretical models of anxiety and avoidance is introduced, using the patients' former experiences in dental settings as a basis. Dental staff demonstrates equipment used for dental treatment to the patient.

2. To ensure that the patient has an adequate understanding of treatment principles before treatment start, each patient gets a written description (1-2 pages) of the treatment method.

3. The patient's emotional state and experience of control in the treatment situation is emphasized. All patients should be aware of what to expect during treatment. At the end of each session, the next dental treatment is discussed and decided upon in a collaborative fashion. Use of behavioral control procedures (e.g. the patient decides when he/she is ready to start each procedure and the use of a stop signal) are encouraged.

4. Effective pain control is important. Local anesthesia should be used in those parts of the treatment that is expected to be painful. Patients are encouraged to give feedback when the anesthetic is effective.

5. Positive feedback is important. Examples of positive feedback are small comments by the dentist like "When you are as relaxed as you are now, it is easy for me to give you an injection with minimal discomfort", as well as more elaborated comments and evaluations during and after treatment sessions.

6. Relaxing music is used if the patient wants it.

7. To avoid postponing treatment sessions, all appointments (preferably at the same time every week) are scheduled at the start of the treatment.

Cognitive Therapy (CT)

The fundamental assumption in cognitive therapy is that maladaptive thinking is decisive for the development and maintenance of most emotional problems.

In cognitive therapy of patients with anxiety, the patient's problem is understood as related to anxiety management. The patient is encouraged to develop a mental way of identifying and correcting his/her thoughts after a stimulus perceived as threatening in a way that makes him/her able to master the anxiety.

The treatment model for dental fear presented in this chapter is based on the cognitive model for treatment of panic with agoraphobia, developed by Beck and Emery (1985) and Clarke (1986). As this treatment method includes both cognitive interventions and exposure it could more precisely be called a cognitive behavioral treatment method. However, in the present chapter it will be called cognitive treatment (CT).

According to Beck and Emery it is crucial to consider anxiety as a cognitive process. The central form is a combination of Socratic dialogue and behavioral experiments. Socratic dialogue means a conversation between patient and therapist where the therapist, through adequate questions, acts as a "midwife" for the patient's own thinking process.

People with irrational phobic reactions have dysfunctional assumptions (general beliefs) e.g. about dental treatment. These assumptions operate without one being aware of them and are embodied in so-called schemata. When a person is confronted with a phobic situation, automatic thoughts or images appear and activate the schemata. These schemata may be understood as the unconscious link between the perception of the stimulus and the reaction in the person. Schemata may be activated by automatic thoughts initiated by bodily symptoms alone, pain or interpersonal relations. The sensations or interpersonal relations are judged much more dangerous than they really are (Clark, 1986). Such automatic thoughts are called catastrophic thoughts. Once the schemata are activated, they will determine the person's emotions and the physical reactions. In a phobic situation they lead to a wave of anxiety.

Cognitive therapy aims to show the patients that the schemata are unconscious and irrational. When the patient understands this, and through therapy learns to assess his/her automatic thoughts, schemata and dysfunctional assumptions, his/her reaction to a stimulus can better be understood and coped with.

In the Oslo Dental Fear Program, the rationale of the treatment is introduced and explained to the patient. The theory of cognitive therapy should be illustrated using the patients' own experiences. To test the hypothesis that thoughts create fear when one is facing a threatening stimulus (stimulus/ thought/ emotion); a set of catastrophic thoughts written on paper is shown to the patient, e.g. "drilling in the nerve/ extreme pain" or "injection/ faint". Almost all patients experience that the sight of the words (stimulus/ thought) makes them feel fearful (emotion).

To illustrate the theory of automatic thoughts and schemata the patients is given examples like: Three schoolchildren, 7 years of age, are to be collected by car by their mothers at the end of the school day. After the last lesson, no mothers are present. Based on their general beliefs, their automatic thoughts differ and different schemata are activated. One child may think:" Great, now I can play football", and he feels pleased. The other think, "She may have had an accident", and he feels frightened. The third may think, "She may have forgotten me", and he feels sad. In the same way, in a given dental situation, automatic thoughts will activate different schemata in people based on their general beliefs.

Each treatment session consists of three parts. The first part, the pre-exposure interview, is conducted in a neutral room. The patient's experiences from homework assignments and his or her preparations for the planned exposure to a dental situation are investigated. The question" What is the worst event that may happen during today's treatment?" is asked. Cognitive techniques (Clark 1986, Salkovskis et al., 1991 and Hoffart et al.,1993) help the patients to identify and change misinterpretations of bodily sensations. Questions like "What could happen if the injection causes pain?" are asked and the chain of catastrophic thoughts explored, using the "Downward Arrow" technique. In this technique, the therapist by use of Socratic dialogue encourages the patients to explore their chains of thoughts. An example of such a chain of thoughts was revealed is a woman: she feared she would experience a general state of panic, which would make her flee from the dentist's office and never return. Lack of dental treatment would lead to deterioration of her teeth and she would have to wear full dentures. Furthermore, she would not dare to take her child to the dentist and his teeth would be ruined as well. A second example was a man whose worst expectation was to be unable to breathe. He could then suffocate and he felt he could actually die.

Belief ratings for the various dangers that could occur are recorded on a scale from zero (no chance) to 100 (it will certainly happen). Almost all patients are afraid of pain, and the expected pain during treatment is rated from zero to 100.

Alternative non-harmful "hypotheses" are asked for, such as "If you feel pain while having an injection are there any possibilities other than loosing consciousness?" or "If you feel that you panic, is there anything else that can happen to you other than fleeing from the office?" Often the patient is unable give suggestions and the therapist then suggests alternative responses such as: "If you feel pain during treatment, would it be possible for you to tell me about it and to demand more anesthetic?" The patient's evidence for and against the catastrophic expectation is examined.

The second part of the treatment session is the exposure to the dental treatment previously planned by the patient and dentist together.

In the third part of the session, the post-exposure interview, the experience gained from the exposure is discussed. The most frightening moment of the treatment, the catastrophic thoughts associated with it, and the connection between these thoughts and the anticipated thoughts are discussed. Patients answer questions like: "What was the most frightening moment during treatment?" "What were you thinking about at that moment?" "How much did you believe in this thought?" Moreover, if the catastrophic thoughts during exposure were different from the anticipated thoughts: "How much did you believe in the original catastrophic thought at that moment?" Belief ratings for these experienced catastrophic events are recorded.

Furthermore, the reaction, which the patient would anticipate if he/she were exposed to the same event again, is examined. The belief rating for this is estimated: "How much do you believe in today's anticipated catastrophic event, if you were to go through a similar treatment once more?"

The differences in anticipation are investigated through questions such as "What makes you think differently concerning an injection now?" The reasons for a different belief rating are examined and the patient is asked: "Are today's experiences anything you may use in future preparation for the same type of treatment?"

Finally, the patient is encouraged to summaries what he/she has learnt during the exposure and this is compared to the expectations for the session. The dentist and patient then jointly plan the dental treatment in the next session.

Homework

Between each treatment session, the patients are given various homework assignments concerning their anticipated fear and their bodily sensations. They record all fearful feelings related to dental treatment as well as other situations. The following is recorded: 1. Date and time of the event. 2. What were you afraid of? 3. How strong was the feeling of fear (0-10)? 4. What were you doing at the moment this thought struck you? 5. What were your most important bodily sensations?

In addition, the patients write arguments for and against catastrophic thoughts about their next dental treatment. During the last weeks in the treatment program the homework focus on catastrophic thoughts related to future treatment done in another dental clinic.

Applied Relaxation (AR)

The second new treatment method used in the Oslo dental fear program is an approach based upon applied relaxation developed by Lars Goran Öst in Sweden (Öst, 1986; 1988). Although it is modified from the methods used by Öst and coworkers and could more precisely be call a modified version of applied relaxation, the term applied relaxation (AR) is used.

Applied relaxation (AR) is theoretically founded on the assumption that panic starts with a small and insignificant change in bodily sensations. The patient experiences negative thoughts about these sensations and is led into a vicious circle of panic. In AR, the patient is trained to recognize the early signs of anxiety, and to use relaxation techniques to cope with, or eliminate, the phobic stress response. Relaxation in AR is regarded as a skill, which the patient learns in the same way as swimming or cycling. When the skill has been learned, the patient is capable of producing a state of relaxation in short time (Öst, 1986, 1988).

The treatment manual of this method instructs the patient to practice relaxation at home every day. The treatment outcome depends on regular practice.

Every treatment session starts with a relaxation procedure introduced by the dentist. In the last sessions of treatment the patients are given time before the treatment starts in order to perform the relaxation exercises by themselves. He/she tells the dentist when an acceptable level of relaxation had been reached and the treatment can start. Throughout treatment, emphasis is placed on the patient's state of muscular tension. If the patient experiences a rise in muscular tension, treatment is stopped and relaxation re-established before treatment proceeds.

Homework

The patients practice relaxation training according to a CD- recorded program of progressive relaxation every day. They record the day and the time of their relaxation training, as well as their level of relaxation (scored 0-10) before and after training. They also record early signs of anxiety in everyday life, and their bodily sensations associated with them.

TREATMENT OUTCOME FROM THE OSLO DENTAL FEAR PROGRAM

To test the effects from the above described new treatment methods, cognitive therapy and applied relaxation were compared to a traditional treatment method, nitrous oxide sedation, in a controlled and randomized trial.

Methodological Considerations

After being at least one month on a waiting list, the patients were randomly assigned to the three treatment methods and scheduled for 10 treatment sessions over a period of 10 weeks. A trained dentist (the author) conducted all treatment. In the first session, the dentist interviewed all patients and performed an oral examination. In the second session, all patients received education in fear reactions and the use of dental equipment. In the third to ninth session, the patients received treatment according to their randomization. Finally, in the tenth session all patients were again interviewed and afterwards referred to general practitioners. One and five years after the patients (n=62) completed the dental fear treatment, they received follow-up questionnaires by mail.

The aims of the different interventions are summarized in Figure 2.

AIMS of Intervention:		
Nitrous oxide sedation	**Cognitive therapy**	**Applied relaxation**
1. To be able to receive dental treatment in a sedated and relaxed condition.	1. To learn to identify catastrophic thoughts during dental treatment.	1. To learn to identify early signs of fear /anxiety during dental situations.
2. After some time, if possible, to manage treatment without sedation.	2. To learn to use one's own knowledge and one's own experience in talking to oneself (an inner dialogue) to re-schedule catastrophic thoughts.	2. To learn to cope with this anxiety by initiating relaxation instead of being overwhelmed by it.

Figure 2. Aims of intervention

Treatment Manuals

Formalized treatment manuals have seldom been used in studies on dental fear. Detailed treatment manuals were developed and adhered to in all treatments in the Oslo Dental Fear Program. Two conditions have to be fulfilled in order to make a treatment method identifiable: (i) treatment integrity, that is the extent to which the treatment is conducted according to the criteria of the manual, and (ii) treatment differentiability, which, is the extent to which the treatment method is unique and can be differentiated from other treatment methods (Hoffart, 1994). Treatment manuals are important tools to verify these conditions. In most treatment today using cognitive therapy, detailed treatment manuals are routinely used (Dobson & Shaw, 1988).

In the treatment manual explicit treatment principles are described and instructions for interventions in critical situations are given. The manual also has a role in education and training of therapists.

The treatment manual in the Oslo Dental Fear Program contributes to treatment integrity in four ways: (1) Specification of the theoretical models of development and maintenance of dental fear. These theories are explained to the patient. (2) Specification of the techniques used by the dentist to achieve the overall goals of the therapy. (3) Incorporation of new clinical experiences gained during pilot treatments, in order to improve the way implementation into actual practice. (4) It is important that the therapist is relaxed while providing treatment. This demands that the therapist master the treatment method so well that it is possible to act spontaneously while providing treatment, and at the same time to have the aim of the therapy clearly in mind (Hoffart, 1994).

Treatment Differentiability

In order to make a treatment method identifiable, treatment differentiability is important. To accomplish this we (i) performed a theoretical contrast analysis between the therapies, and (ii) highlighted the different aspects of the actual treatment procedures (Hoffart, 1994).

Figure 3 shows the contrast analyze where the three treatment methods were compared with regard to theoretical aspects: the focus of treatment intervention, the anxiety arousal during exposure, the level of learning, indicators of change, medium of change and the therapist's role.

The level of learning was based on a conceptualization developed by Bateson (1972) and Hoffart (1994). Learning at level I concerns associations between stimuli and responses, and learning at level II concerns thinking schemata.

	Nitrous Oxide sedation	Cognitive Therapy	Applied relaxation
Focus	Effect of NO-relaxation /indifference	Symptoms –thoughts	Symptoms-relaxation
Anxiety arousal	Unwanted	Necessary	Unwanted
Level of learning	Positive experiences from similar situations (Level I)	Schema Shift (Level II)	Positive experiences from similar situations (Level I)
Indicators of change	Reduction of fear response	Reduction of catastrophic beliefs	Ability to relax
Medium of change	Behavior	Dialogue and behavior	Behavior
Therapist role	Administering NO	Socratic Dialogue Partner	Induction of Relaxation

Figure 3. Contrast analyses between nitrous oxide sedation, cognitive therapy and applied relaxation

An identical situation is acted upon differently according to the principles of each treatment method. Example: The patient may say: "I don't know if I am able to go through the planned treatment today". In all treatment condions, the dentist/therapist will first give an empathic response e.g., "I understand that you feel frightened." The further response will differ according to treatment condition: Cognitive Therapy: "What are you afraid of might happen if you go through the treatment?" Nitrous oxide sedation: "I will give you nitrous oxide so that you will probably experience a state of calm and indifference, and then you will feel different about today's treatment." Applied relaxation: "We will go through the relaxation exercises, and then we will try to do the dental treatment. If you feel your anxiety level rise, please tell me, and we will take a break and do some more relaxation exercises. Then we will try again."

Summary of Results

Sixty-five patients who had a score on the Corah Dental Anxiety Scale indicating very high dental fear (Corah et al. 1978) were enrolled in the treatment program. Three dropped out and 38 women and 24 men finished dental fear treatment. All were invited to participate in the one-year and the five-year follow-up questionnaire studies. Data were available from 58 at one-year follow-up and 40 at five-year follow-up. The mean age at the start of dental fear treatment was 33.4 years (range 17-56 years), and the patients had avoided dental treatment for a mean period of 11.7 years (range 1-30 years). The non-responders in the 5-years follow-up study were compared to those who did respond. Non-responders were younger persons with more decayed, missed or filled teeth at the start of treatment and they had lower dental fear level after the treatment program. However, they did not differ from the responders with regard to dental fear or general distress at enrolment.

Dental fear was measured using three widely used tests for dental fear: Corah's Dental Anxiety Scale (CDAS), a 4 item's test measuring anticipatory fear with a range from 4(no) to 20 (extreme) (Corah, 1969). Kleinknecht's Dental Fear Scale (DFS) is a 20 item's test that have a range from 1(no) to 5 (extreme) and measures dental fear in several dimensions e.g.

specific situations (Kleinknecht and Bernstein, 1978). The Dental Belief Scale (DBS), measures distrust in dentists and have a range from 1(no) to 5 (extreme) (Smith et al., 1987).

Effect sizes were calculated according to the formula M1-M2/ SD where M1 was the mean of the treatment group at the time of testing, M2 was the mean of the treatment group before treatment and SD was the pooled standard deviation (Kazdin, 1998). The effect sizes concerning dental fear were substantial at the end of the treatment program as well as at five-year follow-up for all dental fear measurements. Particularly favorable were effect sizes concerning anticipatory fear (CDAS) and fear of specific dental situations (DFS-Situation). Effect sizes at five-year follow-up are presented in Table 1. The effect sizes of all dental fear measures were acceptable in all treatment conditions. At five-year follow-up the AR group had higher effect sizes than the NO and the CT groups.

Table 1. Effect sizes of dental fear assessments in each treatment condition five years after treatment

	Nitrous oxide sedation	Cognitive therapy	Applied relaxation
CDAS	2.5	2.3	3.0
DBS	1.2	1.2	2.2
DFS	2.6	1.9	2.5

CDAS scores after treatment in each of the present treatment groups were compared to CDAS scores obtained in Berggren's study of systematic desensitization (1984), and Moore's study of video training, and clinical rehearsals (1991). Results from z-tests showed significantly (p<0.05) higher CDAS scores in the NO group compared to any of the three treatment conditions in other studies. However, no significant differences between the AR and CT groups on the one hand, and the external groups on the other, were found. Compared to the Berggren (1984) and Moore (1991) studies, the dropout rate in the present study was the lowest. Moreover, after treatment the dental fear levels in the three intervention groups were comparable to reported normative Norwegian populations, mean 7.5 (SD=3.1) for CDAS (Neverlien, 1990) and mean 2.2 (SD=1.0) for DFS (Kvale et al. 1997).

A CDAS score above 12 has been used as cut-off point for dental fear. Five years after treatment about three quarters (74.4%) of the participants reported a CDAS below 13 (78% in the NO group, 58.3% in the CT group, and 82.4% in the AR group). In comparison, Aartman et al. (2000) reported 11.8% below the cut-off point for patients who had received intravenous sedation, 39.0% after nitrous oxide sedation, and 51.6% after behavioral management. Seven patients (15.9 %) had a CDAS score above 14, indicating a relapse of very high dental fear (21.4 % in the NO group, 16.7% in the CT group, and 11.8% in the AR group).

The patients who had a relapse of dental fear (CDAS> 14) scored significantly higher than the rest on the dental fear measures DFS [T (35) = 3.2, p < 0.05] and DBS [T (37) =1.82, p < 0.05], but not on general psychological distress [T (32) = 0.90, p = 0.32].

No significant correlations between dental fear measures five years after treatment and level of general distress before or five years after treatment were found.

General psychological distress was measured by the Symptom Checklist 90 Revised SCL-90-R, a 90 items test with a range from 0 (no) to 5 very much) (Derogatis, 1983). The mean score on general distress (0.83, SD= 0.64) was statistically significant higher than the normal population at enrolment in the treatment program. The score decreased during therapy

(F = 40.30, p < 0.001) and five years after the scores were still in the normative range (mean 0.35, SD= 0.3) five years after treatment. No between group differences were found.

One year after they had finished dental fear treatment, all participants had been to the dentist. Five year after treatment, more than half of the patients (61.9%) had regular controls and were non-symptomatic users of dental services. The rest (38.1%) reported that they were symptomatic attenders (53.8% in the NO group, 33.3% in the CT group, and 29.4% in the AR group). No significant differences between the treatment groups were found. Compared with the symptomatic users, the non-symptomatic users of dental services scored significantly lower on the CDAS [T (40) = 2.55, p < 0.05], the DFS [T (34) = 2.41, p < 0.05], and the DBS [T (35) = 4.55, p < 0.05.

Five years after the treatment intervention, a majority of patients (75.6%) assessed improvement in their dental health (64.4% in the NO group, 80.4% in the CT group, and all the patients in the AR group).

Moreover, after five years, 94.5% of the participants still reported the dental fear treatment as very beneficial or beneficial (92.9 % in the NO group, 91.7% in CT group, and all the patients in the AR group). A majority (76%) found that the dental fear treatment five years ago had a positive impact on other parts of their lives (78.6% in the NO group, 75% in the CT group, and 82.2% in the AR group). Nobody had experienced negative consequences of the treatment.

Principles behind the Various New Treatment Methods

In the Oslo program, we use different approaches of interventions. Cognitive therapy aims to change the patient's cognitive schemata whereas applied relaxation aims to control anxiety by reduction of stress.

To test out these principles we evaluated changes in the patients' cognitions and feelings of stress in all treatment condions.

1. Book an appointment with a dentist
2. Sit in a waiting room
3. Sit down in a dental chair
4. The dentist examines your teeth
5. The dentist gives you an injection
6. The dentist uses a dental drill in your anaesthetized tooth
7. The dentist extracts an anaesthetized tooth

Figure 4. The seven dental treatment situations in the imagine enactment test

The patients registered their cognitive mechanisms in three ways:

1. Coping abilities was explored in an imagine enactment test (imagining oneself doing it) (Bandura, 1977, Williams, 1990). In this test, the patients were asked to judge their ability to endure seven concrete situations (Figure 4) of dental treatment rated on a scale from 0 (can certainly not do it) to 100 (absolutely sure I can manage this).

2. Catastrophic thoughts were tested by the Agoraphobic Cognition's Questionnaire (ACQ) (Chambless et al., 1984). The ACQ examines thoughts (not specific for dental situations) of negative consequences of experiencing anxiety in there dimensions physical, control and social (see Figure 5) (Clark et al. 1994, and Hoffart 1994).

3. The patients' assessments of cognitions concerning fear, pain and stress were explored by asking how much pain and fear they expected to experience immediately before each of the first five exposures to dental treatment.

Physical dimension	I will vomit I will faint I must have a brain tumor I get a heart attack	I will be strangled to death I will be blind I will have a brain stroke
Control dimension	I will loose control I will hurt someone I am going to be insane	I will scream I will talk strangely I will be paralyzed by anxiety
Social dimension	I will behave stupidly People will see my anxiety People will stare at me	People will laugh at me I will make a scandal People will think I am silly

Figure 5. Dimensions of the Agoraphobic Cognition's Questionnaire

The patients' feelings of stress were explored by asking them to assess their level of stress during the first five exposures to dental treatment immediately after the treatment.

The imagine enactment test showed that the patients increased their imaginations of coping with all seven situations significantly during the dental fear treatment. At enrolment the mean score of the seven situations were 22.9 (SD= 19.7 and after dental fear treatment 75.5 (SD = 22.4). No difference between the groups was found.

Concerning catastrophic thoughts a decrease in scores were found for all dimensions too. No between groups were found. At enrolment the patients' mean score was 17.5 (SD= 19.5) on the social dimension. This is significantly higher than both the physical dimension (7.2 SD= 9.9) and the control dimension (11.3 SD=13.9), (social-control: t=3.60, p=0.001; social physiological: t=4.51, p<0.001). After treatment the patients continued to scored statistically significant higher on the social dimension (mean 12.5, SD = 19.5) than both the physical (mean 6.0, SD= 7.6) and control dimension (mean7.9, SD=11.6).

Table 2. The patients' anticipations and experience of fear, pain and stress during exposure sessions

	Fear				Pain				Stress	
	Expected		Experienced		Expected		Experienced		Experienced	
	Mean	SD	Mean	SD	Mean	SD	Mean	SD	Mean	SD
1.exposure	56	23	36	25	42	25	4	5	39	32
2.exposure	49	30	30	24	48	73	6	10	29	26
3.exposure	40	28	33	28	30	25	7	14	31	27
4.exposure	33	24	26	27	23	19	7	12	28	28
5.exposure	26	23	18	19	15	19	7	9	18	18

Before exposure: How much fear/pain do you expect to experience during treatment today (0-100)
After exposure: How much fear/pain /stress did you experience during treatment today (0-100)

This cognitive pattern with higher scores on the social dimension supports the assumption that shame and feelings of inferiority are important concomitants of dental fear (Berggren, 1984, de Jongh 1995)).

Table 2 shows the patients' assessments of their cognitions concerning expectations of fear and pain before each exposure, and how much fear and pain they actually experienced. Although the dental treatment successively became more fear- provoking the experienced pain decreased statistically significant from exposure session 1 to 5. Thus, the patients had more negative anticipations before the first exposure (usually an injection of local anesthesia) than the fifth exposure (usually an extraction or a filling in the molar region).

Concerning the patients' feelings of stress, they experienced a significant decrease during the first five exposures. There were no differences between the groups.

Thus, after the dental fear treatment the patients' imaginations of coping abilities in dental situations were significantly higher and their tendency to catastrophic thoughts significantly lower than at the beginning of the treatment. The patients' assessment of expectations and perceived fear, pain and stress showed that even if the experienced pain increased, the expectations reached a more realistic level in all conditions. As changes in all three facets of registered cognitions changed in similar ways in all three treatment condions, one could imagine that the effect, at least partly, had been exerted via the same cognitive mechanism. Similarly, the change in experienced stress decreased in all treatment conditions, which could imply that the effect was additionally exerted via similar mechanism stress reduction.

CONCLUDING REMARKS

Dental fear patients tend to avoid dental treatment for many years. When they admit that, they have a problem and realize that they want to do something about it; most patients can be successfully treated. The reasons for treatment of dental fear are many. Most important are the positive effects from treatment on both oral and psychosocial health. Dental fear patients seldom seek dental treatment, but almost all visit physicians and some consult psychotherapists. Thus, dentists, physicians and psychotherapists are all important for detecting dental fear in a patient. A dentist who treats acute dental problems in a stressful patient with poor dental health should explore whether the patient has dental fear. Similarly, when a physician inspects a patient's oral cavity and observes poor oral health or a psychotherapist treats patients with anxiety disorders, he /she should consider dental fear.

Many dental fear patients are reluctant to talk about their dental fear. The first step for a dentist, physician, or psychotherapist may be to help the patient to be more open and think and talk constructively about their dental fear.

Unrealistic fear of pain is often prominent (Kent 1985). The patient cannot imagine a situation where dental treatment is conducted with a minimum of pain and he/she feels in control of the situation. Since cognitions of great danger seem to play a critical role in fear evocation, diminishing catastrophizing ideation may motivate patients for dental fear treatment. An emphatic response is often crucial in the meeting with patients who are embarrassed and who have negative beliefs about themselves. The patient should be inspired to challenge his/ her cognitive stereotyping. An interlocutor may do this by asking questions like: "Which parts of the dental treatment that are the most threatening?", "How would you think dental treatment could be performed without pain?", "What can the dentist do to make the dental treatment less threatening?" and "What can you do yourself to make the dental treatment less threatening?" By using such cognitive explorations, the patients may increase their belief in their coping abilities and get motivated for seeking dental fear treatment.

Treatment Methods

It seems that quite different treatment methods are all suitable for treatment of dental fear. In a study by Berggren et al. (2000), they found that relaxation – oriented treatment resulted in more significant reduction in dental fear than cognitive interventions. This result is supported by the Oslo Dental Fear Program. Although all treatment methods displayed satisfying effect sizes, both the CT and the NO group scored less favorable on dental fear tests than the AR group five years after dental fear treatment (Willumsen and Vassend, 2003). In Berggren et al.'s study a clinical psychologist conducted the psychological interventions. Exposure to dental situations was viewing of video-recorded dental treatment sessions. Moore et al. used exposure by clinical rehearsals (gradual exposure to threatening dental situations by simulated dental treatment). Research with dentists as the only therapists has shown that both video training and clinical rehearsals are effective in combination with relaxation training (Moore et al. 1991). Taken together, these studies clearly indicate that especially variants of relaxation training represent a robust and effective treatment principle. Compared to Berggren and Moore's studies, the new treatment methods presented here are characterized by using dental treatment according to the patient's individual needs for exposure and by less use of special technical equipment. In addition, treatment manuals specifying both general and specific treatment principles were used. These advantages make the new treatment methods in the Oslo Dental Fear Program more applicable for use in general practice.

The patients in the Oslo Dental Fear Program were randomly assigned to the treatment methods. It could be assumed that if the dentist and the patient jointly chose treatment method, results would improve. Furthermore, combination therapies should be seriously considered. For example, it may be that relaxation – nitrous oxide sedation and relaxation – cognitive therapy, could be favorable combinations for many dental fear patients. However, relaxation therapy requires substantial motivation for home practice. It should be emphasized that for patients who do not have this motivation, CT or NO treatment may be the most appropriate treatment methods.

In the search for better treatment method, we tested three different methods in the Oslo Dental Fear Program. There were all over few significant differences between the groups. Several explanations may be given for this. Firstly, the power of the between-group analyses was generally weak and may indicate that the sample size was too small to detect actual, albeit small, differences. The lack of between-group differences may also be explained as a "ceiling and floor" effect. As one of the inclusion criteria was extreme dental fear (ceiling effect) and all treatment groups scored within the range of the normative mean score after treatment (floor effect), the absence of differences between the groups may result from limits in the range of scores obtained (Kazdin 1998).

The present results indicate that the decline in negative expectation is similar across equal for all treatment conditions. Patients from all three treatment groups equally increase their coping abilities, reduce negative cognitions concerning social, control and physiological disasters and change their anticipation of stress and pain during the first exposures. One explanation of this may be the possibility that all three treatment methods exert their effects via the same cognitive mechanisms.

However, the findings may also be explained by the effect of the so-called non-specific factors. Common elements like exposure to dental situations, practical procedures (e.g. fixed appointments), and hearing a logical procedure that describes the origin of one's problem may exert influence on patient performance and generate therapeutic effects. As in psychotherapy research, such common factors may not be trivial in the processes they mobilize in the dental fear patient or in the changes they produce (Kazdin 1998). Friedman and Wood (1998) who achieved a positive treatment outcome from an iatrosedative interview, and Berggren et al. (2000) who found motivation to be predictive for successful dental fear treatment support this assumption. Furthermore, Freeman (1998, 1999a, 1999b) highlights the importance of the patient-dentist relationship, and Kulich et al. (2000) the importance of dentist-patient communication.

It can be concluded that patients with dental fear represent a problem of considerable proportion and treatment of dental fear constitute an improvement in patients' oral as well as psychosocial health. Programs to solve or reduce dental fear would be a sound investment in public dental health (Halvorsen and Willumsen, in press).

ACKNOWLEDGEMENTS

I would like to thank Professor Olav Vassend, Professor Asle Hoffart, Professor emeritus Bjarne Svatun for contributions to the study and to Dr. Med. Peter Kjær Graugaard for careful reading of the manuscript.

REFERENCES

Aartman, I., de Jong, A., and van der Meulen, M.R. Psychological characteristics of patients applying for treatment in a dental fear clinic. *Eur.J.Oral Sci.* 105(5):384-388, 1997.

Aartman, I., de Jongh, A., Makkes, P.C., Hoogstraten, J. Dental anxiety reduction and dental attendance after treatment in a dental fear clinic: a follow-up study. *Community Dent Oral Epidemiol.* 28:435-42, 2000.

Agras, S., Sylvester, D., and Oliveau, D. The epidemiology of common fears and phobias. *Comprehens Psych* 10:151-156, 1969.

Bandura, A., Adams, N.E., and Beyer, J. Cognitive processes mediating behavioural change. *Journal of Personality and Social Psychology* 35:125-129, 1977.

Bateson, G. *Steps to an ecology of mind.* New York:Ballantine, 1972.

Beck, A.T., Emery, G., and Greenberg, R.L. *Anxiety Disorders and Phobias. A Cognitive Perspective*, New York: Basic Books, 1985.

Berggren, U. *Dental Fear and Avoidance.Faculty of Odontology,*University of Gøteborg Sweden, 1984. Thesis

Berggren, U. Long-term effects of two different treatments for dental fear and avoidance. *J.Dent.Res.* 65(6): 874-876, 1986.

Berggren, U., Linde, A. Dental fear and avoidance: a comparison of two modes of treatment. *J.Dent.Res.* 63(10): 1223-1227, 1984.

Berggren, U.,Meynert, G. Dental fear and avoidance: causes, symptoms, and consequences. *J.Am.Dent.Assoc.* 109(2): 247-251, 1984.

Berggren, U., Hakeberg, M., Carlsson, S.G. Relaxation vs. cognitively oriented therapies for dental fear. *J Dent Res.* 79:1645-51, 2000.

Carlsson, S.G., Linde, A., and Ohman, A. Reduction of tension in fearful dental patients. *J.Am.Dent.Assoc.* 101(4):638-641, 1980.

Carpenter, D.J., Gatchel, R.J., and Hasegawa, T. Effectiveness of a videotaped behavioral intervention for dental anxiety: the role of gender and the need for information. *Behav.Med.* 20(3):123-132, 1994.

Chambless, D., Caputo, G.C., Bright, P., and Gallagher, R. Assessment of Fear of Fear in Agoraphobics: The Body Sensations Questionnaire and the Agoraphobic Cognitions Qustionnaire. *J.Consult.Clin.Psychol.* 52(6):1090-1097, 1984.

Clark, D.M. A cognitive approach to panic. *Behav.Res.Ther.* 24(4):461-470, 1986.

Clark, D.M., Salkovskis, P.M., Hackmann, A., Middleton, H., Anastasiades, P., and Corah, N.L. Development of a dental anxiety scale. *J.Dent.Res.* 48(4):596, 1969.

Corah, N.L., Gale, E.N., and Illig, S.J. The use of relaxation and distraction to reduce psychological stress during dental procedures. *J.Am.Dent.Assoc.* 98(3):390-394, 1979.

Corah, N.L., Gale, E.N., and Illig, S.J. Assessment of a dental anxiety scale. *J.Am.Dent.Assoc.* 97(5):816-819, 1978.

Davey, G.C. Dental phobias and anxieties: evidence for conditioning processes in the acquisition and modulation of a learned fear. *Behav.Res.Ther.* 27(1):51-58, 1989.

de Jongh, A., Muris, P., ter Horst, G., van Zuuren, F., Schoenmakers, N., and Makkes, P. One-session cognitive treatment of dental phobia: preparing dental phobics for treatment by restructuring negative cognitions. *Behav.Res.Ther.* 33(8):947-954, 1995.

de Jongh, A., Muris, P., ter Horst, G., and Duyx, M.P. Acquisition and maintenance of dental anxiety: the role of conditioning experiences and cognitive factors. *Behav.Res.Ther.* 33(2):205-210, 1995.

de Jongh, A. *Dental Anxiety: A cognitive Perspective.* Academic Centre of Dentistry Amsterdam, 1995. Thesis.

Dobson, K.S. and Shaw, B.F. The use of treatment manuals in cognitive therapy: experience and issues. [Review] [64 refs]. *J.Consult.Clin.Psychol.* 56(5):673-680, 1988.

Derogatis, L.R. SCL-90-R. Administration, scoring and procedures manual. Balimore: *Clinical Psychometric Research*, 1983.

Eli, I., Uziel, N., Baht, R., and Kleinhauz, M. Antecedents of dental anxiety: learned responses versus personality traits. *Community.Dent.Oral Epidemiol.* 25(3):233-237, 1997.

Fiset, L., Getz, T., Milgrom, P., and Weinstein, P. Local anesthetic failure: diagnosis and management strategies. *Gen.Dent.* 37(5):414-417, 1989.

Friedman, N. Fear reduction with the iatrosedative process. *J Calif Dent Assoc.* 21:41-4, 1993.

Freeman, R. A psychodynamic theory for dental phobia. *Br Dent J.* 184:170-2, 1998.

Freeman, R. A psychodynamic understanding of the dentist-patient interaction. *Br Dent J.* 186:503-6, 1999.

Freeman, R. Barriers to accessing and accepting dental care. *Br Dent J.* 187:81-4, 1999.

Friedman, N., Wood, G.J. An evaluation of the iatrosedative process for treating dental fear. *Compend Contin Educ Dent.* 19:434-6, 1998.

Gill, M.M. Hypnosis as an altered and regressed state. *International journal of clinical and experimental hypnosis* 20:224-337, 1972.

Hakeberg, M., Berggren, U., and Carlsson, S.G. A 10-year follow-up of patients treated for dental fear. *Scand.J.Dent.Res.* 98(1):53-59, 1990.

Hakeberg, M., Berggren, U., and Carlsson, S.G. Prevalence of dental anxiety in an adult population in a major urban area in Sweden. *Community.Dent.Oral Epidemiol.* 20(2):97-101, 1992.

Hallonsten, A.L. Sedation by the use of inhalation agents in dental care. [Review] [29 refs]. *Acta Anaesthesiol.Scand.Suppl.* 88:31-35, 1988.

Halvorsen, B., Willumsen, T. Willingness to Pay for Dental Fear Treatment: Is Supplying Fear Treatment Social Beneficial? Eur Jour of Health Economics, In press.

Hoffart, A. A Comparison of Cognitive and Guided Mastery Therapy of Agoraphobia. *Behav.Res.Ther.* 4:423-434, 1995.

Hoffart, A. Use of Treatment Manuals in Comparative Outcome Research: A Schema-Based Model. Journal of Cognitive Psychotherapy 8(1):41-54, 1994.

Hoffart, A., Hauge, T., Hedley, l., Larsen, S., Olsen, B., Simarud, J., and Vestergård, L. Kognitiv terapi ved panikk med agorafobi. Tidsskift for norsk psykologforeneing 30:742-748, 1993.

Horowitz, L.G. Audiotaped relaxation, implosion, and rehearsal for the treatment of patients with dental phobia. *Gen.Dent.* 40(3):242-247, 1992.

Inhelder, B. and Piaget, J. The growth of logical thinking from childhood to adolescence, New York: New York: Basic Books, 1958.

Jacobson, N.S. Variation of blood pressure with skeletal muscle tension and relaxation. *Ann. Int. Med,* 12:1194, 1939.

Jacobson, N.S. Variation of pulse rate with skeletal muscle tension and relaxation. Ann. Int. Med, 13:1619, 1940.

Kaufman, E., Rand, R.S., Gordon, M., and Cohen, H.S. Dental anxiety and oral health in young Israeli male adults. *Community.Dent.Health* 9(2):125-132, 1992.

Kaufman, E., Weinstein, P., and Milgrom, P. Difficulties in achieving local anesthesia. *J.Am.Dent.Assoc.* 108(2):205-208, 1984.

Kazdin, A.E. Research Design in Clinical Psychology, Boston, USA: Allyn and Bacon, 1998.

Kent, G. and Gibbons, R. Self-efficacy and the control of anxious cognitions. *J.Behav.Ther.Exp.Psychiatry* 18(1):33-40, 1987.

Kent, G. Cognitive processes in dental anxiety. *Br.J.Clin.Psychol.* 24(Pt 4):259-264, 1985b.

Kent, G. Memory of dental pain. *Pain 21*(2):187-194, 1985a.

Kent, G. Self-efficacious control over reported physiological, cognitive and behavioural symptoms of dental anxiety. *Behav.Res.Ther.* 25(5):341-347, 1987.

Kent, G.G. Thinking about anxiety. *Br.Dent.J.* 169(5):133-135, 1990.

Kleinknecht, R.A. and Bernstein, D.A. The assessment of dental fear. *Behavior Therapy* 9:6626-6634, 1978.

Kleinknecht, R.A., Thorndike, R.M., McGlynn, F.D., and Harkavy, J. Factor analysis of the dental fear survey with cross-validation. *J.Am.Dent.Assoc.* 108(1):59-61, 1984.

Klepac, R.K. Successful treatment of avoidance of dentistry by desensitization or by increasing pain tolerance. *J.Behav.Ther.Exp.Psychiatry* 6:307-310, 1975.

Krochak, M. and Rubin, J.G. An overview of the treatment of anxious and phobic dental patients. [Review]. *Compendium.* 14(5):604, 1993.

Kulich, K.R., Berggren, U., Hallberg, L.R. Model of the dentist-patient consultation in a clinic specializing in the treatment of dental phobic patients: a qualitative study. *Acta Odontol Scand.* 58:63-71, 2000.

Kvale, G., Berg, E., Nilsen, C.M., Raadal, M., Nielsen, G.H., Johnsen, T.B., and Wormnes, B. Validation of the Dental Fear Scale and the Dental Belief Survey in a Norwegian sample. *Community.Dent.Oral Epidemiol.* 25(2):160-164, 1997.

Law, A., Logan, H., and Baron, R.S. Desire for control, felt control, and stress inoculation training during dental treatment. *J.Pers.Soc.Psychol.* 67(5):926-936, 1994.

Lazarus, A.A. and Fay, A. *Resistance or rationalization?* A cognitive behavioral perspective, Plenum Press, New York, 1982.pp. 115-132.

Liddell, A., and Gosse, V. J Characteristics of early unpleasant dental experiences.Behav *Ther Exp Psychiatry* 1998 Sep;29(3):227-37.

Liddell, A., Di Fazio, L., Blackwood, J., and Ackerman, C. Long-term follow-up of treated dental phobics. *Behav.Res.Ther.* 32(6):605-610, 1994.

Logan, H.L., Baron, R.S., Keeley, K., Law, A., and Stein, S.Desired control and felt control as mediators of stress in a dental setting. *Health Psychol.* 10(5):352-359, 1991.

Makkes, P.C., Schuurs, A.H., van Velzen, S.K., Duivenvoorden, H.J., and Verhage, F. Effect of a special dental program upon extreme dental anxiety. *Community.Dent.Oral Epidemiol.* 15(3):173, 1987.

Marks, I.M. Fears, Phobias and Rituals, New York:Oxford University Press, 1987.

Mathews, A. and Rezin, V. Treatment of dental fear by imaginal flooding and rehearsal of coping behaviour. *Behav.Res.Ther.* (15):321-328, 1977.

Milgom, P. and Weinstein, P. Treating fearful dental patients, VA: Reston:Reston, 1985.

Milgrom, P., Fiset, L., Melnick, S., and Weinstein, P. The prevalence and practice management consequences of dental fear in a major US city. *J.Am.Dent.Assoc.* 116(6):641-647, 1988.

Miller, A.A. Psychological considerations in dentistry. *JADA* 81:941-946, 1970.

Moore, R. Dental fear treatment: Comparison of a Video Training Procedure and Clinical Rehearsals. Sand J Dent Res 99:229-235, 1991.

Moore, R. The Phenomenon of Dental Fear, University of Århus, Denmark. 1991a Thesis.

Moore, R., Berggren, U., and Carlsson, S.G. Reliability and clinical usefulness of psychometric measures in a self-referred population of odontophobics. *Community.Dent.Oral Epidemiol.* 19(6):347-351, 1991b.

Moore, R., Birn, H., Kirkegaard, E., Brødsgaard, I., and Scheutz, F. Prevalence and characteristics of dental anxiety in Danish adults. *Community.Dent.Oral Epidemiol.* 21(5):292-296, 1993.

Moore, R., Brødsgaard, I., Berggren, U., and Carlsson, S.G. Generalization of effects of dental fear treatment in a self-referred population of odontophobics. *J.Behav.Ther.Exp.Psychiatry* 22(4):243-253, 1991c.

Moreland, M. and Logan, H. The role of sensory information and perceived control on distress. *J.Dent.Res.* 69:961, 1989.

Moulton, R. Oral and Dental Manifestations of Anxiety. Psychiatry 18:261-273, 1955.

Nesse, R. and Williams, G. *Why We Get Sick- The New Science of Darwinian Medicine*, New York: Times Books, 1994.pp. 66-69.

Neverlien, P.O. Normative data for Corah's Dental Anxiety Scale (DAS) for the Norwegian adult population. *Community.Dent.Oral Epidemiol.* 18(3):162, 1990.

Ning, L. and Liddell, A. The effect of concordance in the treatment of clients with dental anxiety. *Behav.Res.Ther.* 29(4):315-322, 1991.

Öst, L.G. Applied relaxarion: Descripion of a coping technique and review of controlled studies. *Behav.Res.Ther.* 25(5):397-409, 1986.

Öst, L.G. Applied relaxation vs progressive relaxation in the treatment of panic disorder. *Behav.Res.Ther.* 26(1):13-22, 1988.

Petersen, J.K., Therkildsen, P., Ritzau, M., Skjødt, O., and Nielsen, E. "Tandlægeskræk" på en kirurgisk avdeling. Tandlægebladet, 1978.(Danish)

Safran, J.D. and Segal, Z.V. *Interpersonal Process in Cognitive Therapy*, New York, United States of America:Basic Books, Inc, 1990.

Salkovskis, P.M., Clark, D.M., and Hackmann, A. Treatment of panic attacks using cognitive therapy without exposure or breathing retraining. *Behav.Res.Ther.* 29(2):161-166, 1991.

Schuller AA, Willumsen T, Holst D. Differences oral health and oral health behaviour between individuals with high and low dental fear *Community Dent Oral Epidemiol.* In press.

Schuurs, A.H., Duivenvoorden, H.J., Makkes, P.C., Thoden van Velzen, S.K., and Verhage, F. Personality traits of patients suffering extreme dental anxiety. *Community.Dent.Oral Epidemiol.* 16(1):38-41, 1988.

Seligman, M.E.P. Helplessness: On depression, development, and death, San Francisco: Freeman, 1975.

Smith, T., Getz, T., Milgrom, P., and Weinstein, P. Evaluation of treatment at a dental fears research clinic. *Spec.Care Dentist.* 7(3):130-134, 1987.

Teo, C.S., Foong, W., Lui, H.H., Vignehsa, H., Elliott, J., and Milgrom, P. Prevalence of dental fear in young adult Singaporeans. *Int.Dent.J.* 40(1):37-42, 1990.

Ter Horst, G., Prins, P., Veerkamp, J., and Verhey, H. Interactions between dentists and anxious child patients: a behavioral analysis. *Community.Dent.Oral Epidemiol.* 15(5):249-252, 1987.

Thompson, S. Will it hurt less if I can control it? A complex answer to a simple question. *Psychological Bulletin* 90(1):89-101, 1981.

Thompson, W.M., Stewart, J.E., Carter, K.D., and Spencer, A.J. Dental Anxiety among Australians. *Int.Dent. J* 46(4):320-324, 1996.

Todes, C.J. The child and the dentist: a psychoanalytical view. *Br.J.Med.Psychol.* 45:45-55, 1972.

Unell L, Soderfeldt B, Halling A, Birkhed D Explanatory models for clinically determined and symptom-reported caries indicators in an adult population. *Acta Odontol Scand* 1999;57:132-8.

Van der Bijl, P. *The benzodiazepines in dentistry: a review*. [Review]. Compendium. 13(1):46-50, 1992.

Varpio, M. and Wellfelt, B. Some characteristics of children with dental behaviour problems. Five-year follow-up of pedodontic treatment. *Swed.Dent.J.* 15(2):85-93, 1991.

Vassend, O. Anxiety, pain and discomfort associated with dental treatment. *Behav.Res.Ther.* 31(7):659-666, 1993.

Vassend, O., Willumsen, T., & Hoffart A. Effect of dental fear treatment on general distress: The role of personality variables and treatment method. *Behav Modif.* 24: 580-99, 2000.

Veerkamp, J.S., Gruythuysen, R.J., Hoogstraten, J., and van Amerongen, W.E. Dental treatment of fearful children using nitrous oxide. Part 4: Anxiety after two years. *ASDC.J.Dent.Child* 60(4):372-376, 1993a.

Veerkamp, J.S., Gruythuysen, R.J., van Amerongen, W.E., and Hoogstraten, J. Dental treatment of fearful children using nitrous oxide. Part 2: The parent's point of view. *ASDC.J.Dent.Child* 59(2):115-119, 1992.

Veerkamp, J.S., Gruythuysen, R.J., van Amerongen, W.E., and Hoogstraten, J. Dental treatment of fearful children using nitrous oxide. Part 3: Anxiety during sequential visits. *i* 60(3):175-182, 1993b.

Veerkamp, J.S., van Amerongen, W.E., Hoogstraten, J., and Groen, H.J. Dental treatment of fearful children, using nitrous oxide. Part I: Treatment times. ASDC.J.Dent.Child 58(6):453-457, 1991.

Weinstein, P., Domoto, P.K., and Holleman, E. The use of nitrous oxide in the treatment of children: results of a controlled study. *J.Am.Dent.Assoc.* 112(3):325-331, 1986.

Weinstein, P., Milgrom, P., and Ramsay, D.S. Treating dental fears using nitrous oxide oxygen inhalation and systematic desensitization. *Gen.Dent.* 36(4):322-326, 1988.

Weinstein, P., Shimono, T., Domoto, P., Wohlers, K., Matsumura, S., Ohmura, M., Uchida, H., and Omachi, K. Dental fear in Japan: Okayama Prefecture school study of adolescents and adults. *Anesth.Prog.* 39(6):215-220, 1993.

Williams, S.L. *Guided mastery treatment of agoraphobia: Beyond stimulus exposure*. Process in Behaviour Modification (26): 89-121, 1990.

Willumsen, T., Vassend, O. *Effects of Cognitive Therapy, Applied Relaxation and Nitrous Oxide Sedation*. A Five-year Follow-up Study of Patients Treated for Dental Fear. Acta Odontol Scand. In press

Willumsen, T., Vassend, O., Hoffart, A. A comparison of cognitive therapy, applied relaxation, and nitrous oxide sedation in the treatment of dental fear. *Acta Odontol Scand.* 2001a ;59:290-6.

Willumsen, T., Vassend, O., Hoffart, A. One-year follow-up of patients treated for dental fear: effects of cognitive therapy, applied relaxation, and nitrous oxide sedation. *Acta Odontol Scand.* 2001b;59:335-40.

Wolpe, J. *Psychotherapy by resiprocal inhibition*. Stanford, CA: Stanford University Press , 1958.

Chapter 8

ALLEVIATING FEAR OF VAGINAL CHILDBIRTH IN NULLIPAROUS WOMEN

*Terhi Saisto**

Department of Obstetrics and Gynecology
Helsinki University Central Hospital

Objective: The increase in fears of childbirth and fear-related requests for cesarean sections (CS), call for new forms of treatment for future mothers. Between 6 and 10% of Finnish first time parturients suffer from severe fear of childbirth. At its worst, it can overshadow the whole pregnancy, lengthen and complicate the labor and hamper the beginning of a good mother-infant relationship. The majority of parturients with fear wish to have CS.

Material: Psychoeducation for fear of childbirth aiming at alleviating the fear and helping the women to prepare for the future childbirth started at our hospital in 1996. During 1996-1999, a longitudinal randomized study of 90 nulliparous women with severe childbirth was conducted. Since 1998, nulliparous women with fear of childbirth were offered the possibility to participate in the psychoeducational group sessions, lead by a psychologist.

Methods: First, 90 nulliparous women experiencing severe fear of childbirth were randomized at the 25th gestational week either to have intensive (4 sessions with obstetrician and one with midwife) or conventional therapy (2 sessions with obstetrician), and followed 3 months postpartum. Therapy in the intensive therapy group consisted of provision of information and routine obstetric check-ups to assure the normal course of the pregnancy, combined with cognitive therapy. Therapy in the conventional therapy group consisted of standard information distribution and routine obstetric check-ups.

Later, 76 nulliparous women at their 31st gestational week experiencing severe fear of childbirth intended 5 group sessions with psychologist and one with midwife during

---

* Department of Obstetrics and Gynecology, Helsinki University Central Hospital, P.O. Box 140 FIN-00029 HUS (Helsinki) Finland.

pregnancy and one 3 months postpartum. Psychotherapeutic group sessions and psychoeducation was incorporated with relaxation and imaginary childbirth exercises.

Results: In a randomized trial, after intervention, 79.5% in the intensive treatment group and 76.1% in the conventional treatment group choose to have a vaginal delivery. In a group psychoeducation and relaxation study, 86.9% choose to have a vaginal delivery, and labors were shorter than in nulliparous in general (mean 9.4 ± 3.9 hours (standard deviation SD)). Also in a randomized trial, labors were shorter than in nulliparous in general, in intensive therapy group 9.0 ± 3.9 hours (mean ±SD) and in conventional therapy group 9.6 ± 3.6 hours (NS).

Conclusion: Treatment of fear of vaginal childbirth remarkably reduced unnecessary cesareans, even more in group psychoeducation with relaxation and imaginary childbirth exercises. With better preparation and ability to relax, labors were also shorter.

* * *

Fear of childbirth and consequent cesarean sections have been increasing in recent years in all western countries (1,2). After enthusiastic studies in Finland and Sweden, it has estimated that between 6 and 10% of parturients suffer from severe fear of childbirth (3-5), expressed as nightmares, physical complaints, and difficulties in concentrating on work or on family activities (6). At its worst, fear of childbirth can overshadow the whole pregnancy, lengthen and complicate the labor in the form of fetal growth restriction, and asphyxia (7-10) and high risk for emergency cesarean (11), and hamper the beginning of a good mother-infant relationship (12-14). The majority of parturients with fear wish to have cesarean section (15-17). Fear of childbirth was the reason for 8% of all cesarean sections at the Helsinki University Central Hospital, Department of Obstetrics and Gynecology in 2002 and represented 2% of all pregnancies. Thus, to reduce fear and anxiety, and the morbidity both of women and infants due to obstetric complications and unnecessary cesareans, treatment for fear and anxiety should be organized and established in modern antenatal outpatient clinics.

In this report two consequent studies on the treatment of fear of vaginal childbirth in nulliparous women are reviewed. First, we randomized women referred for antenatal consultation because of fear of childbirth to receive either intensive or conventional treatment (17). Later, nulliparous women with fear of childbirth have been offered the possibility to participate in the psychoeducational group sessions, lead by a psychologist (18). The primary goal for these studies was to evaluate the possibility of reducing requests for cesarean without coercing the women into vaginal delivery.

MATERIALS AND METHODS

Fear of childbirth was diagnosed by a specific questionnaire, a Revised Version of a fear-of-childbirth questionnaire (19,20) (Cronbach alpha reliability coefficient 0.76). The original questionnaire was revised based upon a pilot study (n=45) done at our out-patient maternity clinic. The cut-off point for diagnosis of fear of childbirth was five or more affirmative answers to ten questions or request for cesarean.

Between August 1996 and July 1999, a total of 90 obstetrically low-risk and physically healthy primigravida women were referred to the outpatient clinic of Department of

Obstetrics and Gynecology in Helsinki University Central Hospital because of fear of vaginal childbirth (Table 1). At the time of the first appointment, the women were randomized either to an intensive therapy group or a conventional therapy group.

Table 1. Characteristics of the Study Population (represented as mean ± SD (range))

	Randomized study		Group psychoeducation n=76
	Intensive treatment n=44	Conventional treatment n=46	
Maternal age	31.2 ± 5.1(21-43)	31.9 ± 4.8 (21-41)	33.1 ± 4.6 (20-40)
Gestation at enrollment	24.9 ± 1.7 (18-30)	24.9 ± 1.8 (19-30)	30.8 ± 3.7 (18-36)
Score for fear of delivery*	6.0 ± 1.7 (1-9)	5.7 ± 1.8 (1-9)	6.2 ± 1.9 (2-10)

*According to (20)

Therapy in the intensive therapy group consisted of provision of information and conversation regarding previous experiences as a patient, feelings, and misconceptions. The appointments were based on routine obstetric check-ups to assure the normal course of the pregnancy, combined with cognitive therapy, the main principles of which is focus on one target problem involving the active role of the therapist and reformulation of the problem during a limited time. An appointment with the midwife and personal obstetric ward visits were recommended to provide more practical information about pain relief and possible interventions (vacuum, scalp blood sample, etc.) during labor and delivery. Written information was given at the first session regarding the pros and cons of vaginal delivery and of cesarean as well as information about alternative modes of pain relief available at our hospital. At the last appointment before delivery, the woman's personal written wishes related to delivery were discussed and attached to her records.

Therapy in the conventional therapy group consisted of standard information distribution and routine obstetric check-ups, as well as provision for written information about the pros and cons of vaginal delivery and of a cesarean, and the pain relief that is offered at our hospital.

Between November 1998 and October 2002, group psychoeducation was offered to 105 nulliparous women referred for consultation because of fear of vaginal delivery, 76 of which accepted to join the group. Each group consisted of six nulliparous women. The women met each other weekly for a total of five times. Each session lasted for 120 minutes and was led by a psychologist with a degree of psychotherapy. Group sessions consisted of discussions, visualization exercises and relaxation exercises. Each of the five meetings had a theme for discussion: stages of delivery, effects of relaxation, pain relief, parenthood and changes in the family. During the third session (theme pain relief), a midwife specialized in fears of childbirth described the course of labor and gave information on pain relief.

All the women in both studies were from Finnish background, Finnish-speaking, middle or upper social class, and from the urban capital area of Helsinki. The main outcome measure was the percentage of women choosing vaginal delivery after the appointments, and the duration of their vaginal delivery, which was defined from initiation of regular contractions more often than once in 10 minutes to the delivery of the infant.

RESULTS

In a randomized trial, 35 of the 44 primigravidas in the intensive treatment group and 38 out of 46 primigravidas in the control group choose vaginal delivery (79.5% vs. 82.6%, χ^2 NS). In a psychoeducation group, 66 primigravidas out of 76 choose vaginal delivery (86.8%, χ^2 NS compared to other groups). (Table 2)

In women delivering vaginally, the time from the beginning of the regular contractions more often than once in 10 minutes to the delivery of the infant was in the intensive therapy group (mean 9.0 ± 3.9 (SD) hours) and in the conventional therapy group (9.6 ± 3.6 hours, NS). In the group psychoeducation group, the mean duration of vaginal delivery was 9.4 ± 3.9 hours (NS compared to other groups). No difference existed between the groups in the use of epidural analgesia: it was used in 85% of vaginal deliveries in the intensive therapy, in 82% in the conventional therapy group, and in 82% in the group psychoeducation group (Table 2).

In comparison of the two studies referred here, vaginal delivery succeeded in 57.8% (in 52 women of out 90) in randomized study and in 71.5% (in 54 women out of 76) in group psychoeducation study (χ^2 P=0.032).

Table 2. Characteristics of the deliveries

Mode of delivery (n (%))	Randomized study, intensive group n=44	Randomized study, conventional group n=46	Group psychoeducation study n=76
Choosing vaginal delivery after appointments	35 (79.5%)	38 (82.6%)	66 (86.8%)
Successful vaginal delivery	25 (56.8%)	27 (58.7%)	54 (71.1%)
Emergency cesarean	5 (11.4%)	8 (17.4%)	9 (11.8%)
Elective cesarean for obstetric reasons	5 (11.4%)	3 (6.5%)	3 (3.9%)
Elective cesarean for fear of vaginal childbirth	9 (20.5%)	8 (17.4%)	10 (13.1%)
Duration of labor and delivery	Mean (range)		
Total length (hours))	9.0 (3.1-19.9)	9.6 (3.6-18.4)	9.4 (2.9-20.9)
Length of the first stage (hours)	8.2 (2.3-19.2)	8.7 (2.8-16.4)	8.4 (2.1–20)
Length of the second stage (minutes)	50 (12-138)	57 (5-173)	54 (13-220)
Epidural analgesia during vaginal delivery (%)	85%	82%	82%%

DISCUSSION

Conversely, to pregnant women in general, our patients were very anxious about the delivery, one third of them having nightmares and every fourth of them considering childbirth unnatural (17,18). In our earlier study, in unselected pregnant population only 6% of women had nightmares about childbirth and 4-5% considered it unnatural (20). Further, in this unselected pregnant population the mean score for fear of delivery was low (2.1 ± 2.1 as compared to 5.7-6.2 (±1.9) in the two studies referred here), and a third of those women were totally unafraid of delivery (score for fear of delivery being 0) (4). Our patients in two studies referred here can thus be regarded as a sample of women with abnormal and exceptional fear of childbirth. In Finland, for the last decade, severe fear of childbirth has been considered as an indication for cesarean, and in year 2002 8% of all cesareans carried out in Helsinki University Hospital were done for this reason.

Studies on the treatment for fear of childbirth are scanty, and no consensus exists on how, where and by whom the possible treatment should be given. Childbirth preparation and support both during pregnancy and delivery are the principal elements for every pregnant woman. Different kinds of psychotherapies could be useful, and can be combined with either simple or specific counseling (psychoeducation). Medical treatment is usually avoided, unless clinical anxiety, depression, or panic disorder calls for it. Employees at different health care levels can treat women with fear of childbirth.

Childbirth preparation, consisting of education and training of methods to cope with pain, aims at gaining control over fear of labor and delivery (21). Education and information reduce concerns on the infant's health, but the training of relaxation and methods of coping with pain are needed to alleviate general anxiety (22,23). This leads to improved confidence, which in turn is a significant predictor of satisfaction with the childbirth experience (23-26). The effects of treating anxiety and fear of childbirth could be measured in terms of alleviation of perceived stress and better adjustment during pregnancy, but also in terms of withdrawal of the request of cesarean section. No studies on the two previous factors exist, and the studies on the latter subject are also scarce. Treatment for fear of childbirth mostly includes individual psychosomatic support, given by an obstetrician (15-17).

One of the most common fears with nulliparous women is the fear of losing control. A woman with fear of childbirth has typically a pronounced need to control new situations through careful preparation and planning. The unexpected nature of childbirth, and giving way to a process, which cannot be controlled and the course of which cannot be predicted, can cause anxiety. The future mother might suspect such enormous pain, that she would be unable to control herself in the way she would like to. This often leads to a request for cesarean section even in normal pregnancy without any medical indication for operative delivery.

The therapy in our randomized study was based on the approach of cognitive therapy, which suitable to treatment for fear of childbirth because of its short duration and focus on one target problem. The cognitive-behavioral approach teaches the patient constructive thinking, which reduces anxiety both directly and indirectly by reducing perception of stress(27), and increases positive adaptation to pregnancy, which is significantly related to general well-being. (27,28). Positive cognitive adaptation is achievable also in group sessions (27).

Group therapy is an effective mode of treatment for fear of childbirth. The parturients felt less fearful and 87% of them chose vaginal delivery. The number of elective cesarean sections performed on the participants of the group psychoeducation was smaller than in randomized study (13.1% vs. 18.9%). In other previous studies where nulliparous patients with fear have been given individual counseling, 41.5 % and 60% chose CS after intervention (15,16). In addition in our studies the labors were shorter and safer than with first-time parturients on the average (2,29). The treatment for fear of childbirth probably has a more extensive therapeutic effect on the lives of these women. For example, it is probable, that women who were prepared for their first childbirth may benefit from it also in their subsequent delivery (23).

The idealization of motherhood may make a mother with fear of childbirth feel inferiority, inability and shame because of her fear. Central issues discussed in the psychoeducation group were experiences of shame and inferiority. However, discussing and sharing the feelings of shame can be crucial in psychological recovery and relieving anxiety (30,31). Actually, the group participants felt they benefited most from discussions with others in the same situation (18).

Also limitations should be considered when generalizing the findings of these studies. They were carried out in a country with highly emancipated, mostly full-time working women with nearly equal rights with men, and with public health services which encourage women to express their feelings and wishes openly. This enables, on the one hand, the permission to request cesarean but on the other hand, our public health system does not approve of cesarean purely on maternal request. This calls for discussion and new forms of treatment to care for future mothers. In Finland, fear of childbirth is considered an indication for cesarean if it cannot be relieved by some kind of psychoeducation during pregnancy.

In childbirth preparation, training in relaxation and learning methods of coping with pain are essential and help to lead to a successful labor (21,32). In our studies, shorter labors in less anxious women can be seen as a consequence of better relaxation and self-assertion. These effects can have an impact on long-term health and thus even positive economical consequences, as general well-being among these women increases.

Treatment for fear of childbirth should be planned individually bearing in mind the psychological makeup of the pregnant woman, her life situation as a whole, her family situation and the support networks at her disposal. Intervention can be carried out both at the general and specialized health care levels. Multidisciplinary (medicine, psychology, nursing and social sciences) education and cooperation is needed on all levels.

REFERENCES

1. Ryding EL: Psychosocial indications for cesarean section. A retrospective study of 43 cases. *Acta Obstet Gynecol Scand* 1991 70:47-49.
2. Saisto T, Ylikorkala O, Halmesmaki E: Factors associated with fear of delivery in second pregnancies. *Obstet Gynecol* 1999 94:679-682
3. Areskog B, Uddenberg N, Kjessler B: Fear of childbirth in late pregnancy. *Gynecol Obstet Invest* 1981 12:262-266.
4. Saisto T, Salmela-Aro K, Nurmi JE, Halmesmaki E: Psychosocial characteristics of women and their partners fearing vaginal childbirth. *Br J Obstet Gynecol* 2001 108:492-498.
5. Melender HL: Experiences of fears associated with pregnancy and childbirth: a study of 329 pregnant women. *Birth* 2002 29:101-111.
6. Jolly J, Walker J, Bhabra K: Subsequent obstetric performance related to primary mode of delivery. *Br J Obstet Gynaecol* 1999 106:227-232.
7. Barnett B, Parker G: Possible determinants, correlates and consequences of high levels of anxiety in primiparous mothers. *Psychol Med* 1986 16:177-185.
8. Wadhwa PD, Sandman CA, Porto M, Dunkel-Schetter C, Garite TJ: The association between prenatal stress and infant birth weight and gestational age at birth: a prospective investigation. *Am J Obstet Gynecol* 1993 169:858-865.

9. Paarlberg KM, Vingerhoets AJ, Passchier J, Dekker GA, Heinen AG, van Geijn HP: Psychosocial predictors of low birthweight: a prospective study. *Br J Obstet Gynaecol* 1999 106:834-841.

10. Kurki T, Hiilesmaa V, Raitasalo R, Mattila H, Ylikorkala O: Depression and anxiety in early pregnancy and risk for preeclampsia. *Obstet Gynecol* 2000 95:487-490.

11. Ryding EL, Wijma B, Wijma K, Rydhstrom H: Fear of childbirth during pregnancy may increase the risk of emergency cesarean section. *Acta Obstet Gynecol Scand* 1998 77:542-547.

12. Avant KC: Anxiety as a potential factor affecting maternal attachment. *JOGN Nurs* 1981 10:416-419.

13. Murray L: The impact of postnatal depression on infant development. *J Child Psychol Psychiatry* 1992 33:543-561.

14. Fowles ER: Relationships among prenatal maternal attachment, presence of postnatal depressive symptoms, and maternal role attainment. *J Soc Pediatr Nurs* 1996 1:75-82.

15. Ryding EL: Investigation of 33 women who demanded a cesarean section for personal reasons. *Acta Obstet Gynecol Scand* 1993 72:280-285.

16. Sjögren B, Thomassen P: Obstetric outcome in 100 women with severe anxiety over childbirth. *Acta Obstet Gynecol Scand* 1997 76:948-952.

17. Saisto T, Salmela-Aro K, Nurmi JE, Kononen T, Halmesmaki E: A randomized controlled trial of intervention in fear of childbirth. *Obstet Gynecol* 2001 98:820-826.

18. Toivanen R, Saisto T, Salmela-Aro K, Halmesmäki E: The treatment of fear of childbirth with a therapeutic group and relaxation exercises. *Finnish Medical Journal* 2002 45:4567-4572 (english abstract).

19. Areskog B, Kjessler B, Uddenberg N: Identification of women with significant fear of childbirth during late pregnancy. *Gynecol Obstet Invest* 1982 13:98-107.

20. Saisto T, Salmela-Aro K, Nurmi JE, Halmesmaki E: Psychosocial predictors of disappointment with delivery and puerperal depression. A longitudinal study. *Acta Obstet Gynecol Scand* 2001 80:39-45.

21. Triolo PK: Prepared childbirth. *Clin Obstet Gynecol* 1987 30:487-494.

22. Klusman LE: Reducation of pain in childbirth by the alleviation of anxiety during pregnancy. *J Consult Clin Psychol* 1975 43:162-165.

23. Crowe K, von Baeyer C: Predictors of a positive childbirth experience. *Birth* 1989 16:59-63.

24. Thune-Larsen K-B, Moller-Pedersen K: Childbirth experience and postpartum emotional disturbance. *J Reprod Infant Psychol* 1988 6:229-240.

25. Waldenstrom U, Bergman V, Vasell G: The complexity of labor pain: experiences of 278 women. *J Psychosom Obstet Gynaecol* 1996 17:215-228.

26. McCrea BH, Wright ME: Satisfaction in childbirth and perceptions of personal control in pain relief during labour. *J Adv Nurs* 1999 29:877-884.

27. Affonso DD, De AK, Korenbrot CC, Mayberry LJ: Cognitive adaptation: a women's health perspective for reducing stress during childbearing. *J Womens Health Gend Based Med* 1999 8:1285-1294.

28. Salmela-Aro K, Pennanen R, Nurmi J-E: Self-focused goals: what they are, how they function, and how they relate to well-being, in Schmuck P, Sheldon K (eds): *Life goals and well-being: Towards A Positive Psychology of Human Striving*. Seattle: Hogrefe & Huber Publishers 2001, p 148-166.

29. Russell K: The course and conduct of normal labor and delivery, in Pernoll M, Benson R (eds): *Current obstetric & gynecologic diagnosis and treatment* (ed 6). Norwalk, Appleton & Lange, 1987, p 178-203.

30. Beardslee WR, Swatling S, Hoke L, Rothberg PC, van de Velde P, Focht L, Podorefsky D: From cognitive information to shared meaning: healing principles in prevention intervention. *Psychiatry* 1998 61:112-129.

31. Ehrmin JT: Unresolved feelings of guilt and shame in the maternal role with substance-dependent African American women. *J Nurs Scholarsh* 2001 33:47-52.

32. Jenkins MW, Pritchard MH: Hypnosis: practical applications and theoretical considerations in normal labour. *Br J Obstet Gynaecol* 1993 100:221-226.

Chapter 9

EXPECTANCY-LEARNING AND EVALUATIVE-LEARNING IN HUMAN CLASSICAL CONDITIONING: DIFFERENTIAL EFFECTS OF EXTINCTION

Dirk Hermans,[1] Geert Crombez,[2] Debora Vansteenwegen,[1] Frank Baeyens[1] and Paul Eelen[1]

[1] University of Leuven, Belgium
[2] Ghent University, Belgium

ABSTRACT

It has been argued that classical conditioning might result in two types of changes. First, one may learn that the conditioned stimulus (CS+) is a valid predictor for the occurrence of the biologically negative or positive event (US) (expectancy-learning), which may lead to fear or pleasure. Second, after acquisition one may perceive the conditioned stimulus itself as a negative or positive event, depending on the valence of the event it has been associated with (evaluative learning). Based on human research on evaluative learning, it has been suggested that unlike expectancy learning, such conditioned valences are resistant to extinction. In the present two experiments we were able to demonstrate that both outcomes can result from the same procedure. Moreover, the data of both experiments showed that whereas extinction returned expectancy learning to baseline, the acquired valence was unaffected by this procedure. The presence of an (unchanged) evaluative difference between CS+ and CS- after extinction was not only demonstrated in the verbal ratings, but could also be corroborated by the results of an affective priming procedure. Given that some anxiety disorders are based on expectancy learning, it is suggested here that exposure (extinction) will lead to reduced US-expectancy and fear, but will leave the valence of the original stimuli/triggers unchanged. This might be a potential source of relapse.

* * *

Although conditioning models of anxiety have known a chequered history (Davey, 1997) and cognitive approaches to the understanding of the etiology of clinical anxiety have recently received a lot of interest (Arntz, 1997; Mogg & Bradley, 1998; Wells, 1997), contemporary cognitive models of human classical conditioning still provide a rich conceptual framework for the understanding of the etiology, maintenance and treatment of human fears and phobias (see also, Davey, 1989, 1992, 1997; Eelen, Van den Bergh, & Baeyens, 1990; Lovibond, Davis, & O'Flaherty, 2000; Mineka & Zinbarg, 1996; Rachman, 1991, 1998). Based upon recent insights from both animal and human conditioning research and enriched with knowledge gathered from information processing research (e.g. Mogg & Bradley, 1998), these models have been successful in addressing most of the criticisms that have been associated with old behaviouristic accounts of classical conditioning and the acquisition of clinical fear.

According to these contemporary models, classical conditioning can be conceptualized as the acquisition of associations between the representations of stimuli/events. A Pavlovian conditioning preparation, for example, in which a tone is used as CS and an electrocutaneous stimulus as US, will result in the establishment or strengthening of an associative link between the memory representations of both stimuli. As a consequence, after acquisition the presentation of the CS will activate the CS representation. And through mechanisms of spreading of activation also the representation of the US will be activated, which will again lead to the activation of associated response units and hence observable CRs.

Within this framework, a distinction has been made between two qualitatively distinct outcomes that could result from such a classical conditioning procedure; *expectancy-learning* and *merely referential learning* (Baeyens, 1998; Baeyens, Eelen, & Crombez, 1995). CS-US expectancy learning is inferred when presentation of the CS activates the expectation of real US occurrence in the here-and-now of the immediate future. For example, a tone CS may activate the expectation of the immediate deliverance of an electrocutaneous US. Likewise, an internal or external cue may become established as a CS activating the expectation of a panic attack (US; e.g. Wolpe & Rowan, 1988), or specific social situations (CS) might lead to the active expectation of rejection or panic (US) in persons with a social phobia or public speaking anxiety (Hofmann, Ehlers, & Roth, 1995; Mineka & Zinbarg, 1995). Merely referential CS-US learning is inferred when the CS makes the subject 'think of' the US, without generating an active expectancy of the US. Presentation of the CS activates a memory of the US, without the active expectancy of real US occurrence in the here-and-now of the immediate future.

One particular type of referential learning that has been studied extensively over the last decade is evaluative conditioning (EC). Evaluative conditioning refers to the observation that the mere contingent presentation of a neutral stimulus (CS) with a positively or negatively valenced stimulus (US) results in the originally neutral CS itself acquiring a valence congruent with the affective value of the US (Baeyens, Eelen, Crombez, & Van den Bergh, 1992; Levey & Martin, 1987). For example, after a neutral picture of a human face has repeatedly been paired with a liked (or disliked) picture of another face, research participants typically demonstrate an acquired liking (or disliking) for the originally neutral face (e.g. Baeyens, Eelen, Crombez, & Van den Bergh, 1992; for an overview of the evaluative conditioning literature, see Baeyens, Vansteenwegen, Hermans, & Eelen, 2001).

Although expectancy learning and evaluative learning have traditionally been studied separately, employing different types of paradigms, a series of studies from different labs demonstrate that both outcomes can co-occur as a result from an aversive conditioning preparation. For example, in a study by Hamm, Greenwald, Bradley, and Lang (1993), who used the startle blink as a measure of evaluative learning and skin conductance responses as a measure of expectancy-learning, it was demonstrated that stimuli that had previously been coupled with an electrocutaneous stimulus (CS+), did not only result in higher SCRs but also led to stronger blink responses than stimuli that had previously not been associated with an electrocutaneous stimulus (CS-). Similar results have been obtained by Hamm and Vaitl (1996), Hodes, Cook, and Lang (195), Lipp, Sheridan, and Siddle (1994), and Hardwick and Lipp (2000).

Similarly, in a recent series of studies study at our laboratory (Hermans, Vansteenwegen, Crombez, Baeyens, & Eelen, in press; Hermans, Spruyt, & Eelen, in press), we were able to demonstrate the co-occurrence of both outcomes within a differential aversive conditioning procedure with human participants. During the acquisition phase, neutral pictures of human faces served as CSs of which one (CS+) was contingently followed by an unpleasant electrocutaneous stimulus (US), while a second picture (CS-) was never followed by the US. After a semi-randomized presentation of 8 CS+/US trials and 8 CS-/no-US trials, participants were asked to provide expectancy ratings (expectancy-learning) as well as affective ratings (evaluative learning) for both CSs. Results showed that the acquisition procedure had altered the meaning of the CS+ in several ways. First, after acquisition and as compared to the CS-, the CS+ was now experienced as a valid predictor for the US. In other words, participants now actively expected an electrocutaneous stimulus after presentation with the CS+. Besides the fact that the CS+ had become a meaningful predictor for the occurrence of the US, the acquisition procedure has also led to significant shifts in the evaluation of the CS+, as this stimulus was now rated significantly more negative than before acquisition. An important aspect of the results was that this evaluative shift could also be corroborated by the data from an affective priming procedure (Hermans, Crombez, & Eelen, 2001) that was administered after the conditioning phase, and that can be considered as a response-latency based index of stimulus valence.

The observation that evaluative learning and expectancy learning can co-occur might have interesting clinical implications. To the extent that the acquisition of clinical anxiety (e.g. agoraphobia) is based on the contingent presentation of an originally neutral stimulus (e.g. open spaces) and an aversive event (e.g. a panic attack), this might not only result in the CS becoming a valid predictor for the US, but also in an affective shift for the CS. Open spaces not only predict an aversive panic attack, but become negative in their own right.

In this context research on the functional characteristics of expectancy learning and evaluative learning is highly relevant. In fact, research has shown that evaluative conditioning demonstrates a number of properties that differ from expectancy-learning (Baeyens & De Houwer, 1995). For example, unlike expectancy-learning, evaluative learning has been demonstrated not to depend on awareness of the CS-US pairings (e.g. Baeyens, Eelen, & Van den Bergh, 1990; for an overview, see Baeyens, De Houwer, & Eelen, 1994), not to be sensitive to either modulation (see Baeyens, Crombez, De Houwer, & Eelen, 1996; Baeyens, Hendrickx, Crombez, & Hermans, 1998), CS-US contingency (Baeyens, Hermans, & Eelen, 1993), or extinction (see Baeyens, Eelen, & Crombez, 1995). Conversely, evaluative learning resembles expectancy-learning in being sensitive to US-revaluation (Baeyens, Eelen, Van den Bergh, & Crombez, 1992; but see Baeyens, Vanhouche, Crombez, & Eelen, 1998).

With respect to clinical practice, particularly the resistance to extinction that has been observed for acquired evaluative meaning is attention-grabbing. Given that extinction can be viewed as a laboratory-equivalent of exposure treatment (e.g. Eelen, Hermans, & Baeyens,

2001), this observation would suggest that exposure treatment for clinical fear might successfully reduce the expectancy component in clinical fear, but would leave the acquired affective meaning unaltered. Clinical experience indicates that this differential outcome can indeed be observed (Marks, 1987).

With respect to extinction in evaluative learning, Baeyens, Crombez, Van den Bergh, and Eelen (1988) found that 5 or even 10 unreinforced presentations of the CS did not have any influence on the evaluative value that was acquired as the result of 10 previous CS-US pairings. Moreover, if Baeyens et al. (1988) added a delayed test two months after this first study, based on the rationale that participants would no longer remember their initial ratings, the evaluative conditioning effect was still evident (see also Baeyens, Eelen, Van den Bergh, & Crombez, 1989). And, in light of a possible artifact identified by Field and Davey (1997,1999) with respect to the assignment of CS-US pairs on the basis of perceptual similarity, it is important to note that resistance to extinction has also been demonstrated using randomized CS-US assignment (De Houwer, Baeyens, Vansteenwegen, & Eelen, 2000). Moreover, in the flavor-flavor variant of the evaluative conditioning paradigm, which is not susceptible to this possible artifact, it was observed that post-acquisition unreinforced CS presentations do not attenuate the acquired flavor dislike (Baeyens, Crombez, Hendrickx, & Eelen, 1995; Baeyens et al., 1996; 1998b).

As mentioned before, the resistance to extinction that has been observed for evaluative learning is in clear contrast with what is typically observed for expectancy-learning (Mackintosh, 1983). The paradigms that have been used in the study of extinction in evaluative learning are, however, markedly different from traditional expectancy-learning paradigms. This latter form of learning is typically studied in traditional conditioning studies wherein biologically significant stimuli (food, aversive stimuli) are used as US, and wherein the organism essentially learns that the CS is a valid predictor for the US. Based on this knowledge, the organism is capable of anticipating this event, and to (behaviorally) prepare for it. Therefore, it is not at all surprising that once the CS is no longer followed by the US, the former looses its signal-value, which leads to the diminishing of the conditioned, anticipatory responses (extinction).

In the present studies, we wanted to further test the observations concerning extinction and evaluative learning in the context of an aversive conditioning procedure. Building on the idea that expectancy-learning and evaluative learning can be observed within one single conditioning preparation, the aim of the study was to investigate whether both forms of learning differentially respond to extinction procedures. It was predicted that the differential aversive conditioning procedure would lead to both expectancy-learning as well as evaluative learning, and that the former but not the latter form of learning would be affected by a procedure of extinction. It needs to be stressed that it was not our intention to demonstrate that evaluative learning is completely resistant to extinction. This would call for more extensive series of extinction trials. It was, however, our intent to test the *differential* impact of extinction on expectancy learning and evaluative learning. More specifically, we were interested in whether an evaluative difference can still be observed when US-expectancies are completely extinguished. This research question is also clinically inspired. In fact, if it can be demonstrated that extinction has a differential influence on expectancy learning and evaluative learning, this might indicate that when exposure therapy has successfully reduced US-expectancies, the formerly phobic stimulus might nevertheless be experienced as a negative stimulus. As will be discussed later, this unaltered negative valence might function as a source of relapse.

In the two studies that are reported here, reductions in US-expectancy were obtained by CS-only presentations as well as by verbal instructions about the absence of the US. Although the instructions add more to the extinction phase than what is traditionally viewed as an extinction procedure, the purpose of combining the CS-only presentations with these verbal instructions was to arrive at powerful reductions in US-expectancy. Expectancy learning was evaluated by ratings of US-expectancy (i.e. a rating of the extent to which the presentation of the CS⏋ or CS- evokes an active expectancy of the UCS to occur). The acquired stimulus valence was not only assessed by verbal ratings but also by means of the proposed affective priming procedure. Given that the conditioning procedure that is employed in this kind of studies is rather transparent[1], the priming procedure has the advantage that it is not susceptible to demand characteristics.

In a standard affective priming study (e.g. Fazio, Sanbonmatsu, Powell, & Kardes, 1986; Hermans, De Houwer, & Eelen, 1994, 2001), a series of positive or negative target stimuli is presented, which have to be evaluated as quickly as possible as either 'positive' or 'negative'. Each target is immediately preceded by a prime stimulus, which can be positive, negative, or neutral, and which has to be ignored by the participant. Nevertheless, results show that the time to evaluate the target stimuli is affected by the affective meaning of the primes. If targets are preceded by an evaluatively congruent prime, response latencies are significantly smaller than on evaluatively incongruent trials. This effect is based on the automatic processing of the valence of the prime (see Klauer, 1998; Klauer & Musch, in press, for details). Hence, the affective priming paradigm is an excellent method to assess the (newly acquired) valence of the CS+ in a way that is unobtrusive and -in contrast to standard evaluative ratings- is not easily biased by demand effects (Hermans, Baeyens & Eelen, in press; Hermans, Van den Broeck, & Eelen, 1998). Given this underlying principle, evaluative changes in the studies by Hermans et al. (in press b, c) were evident from the fact that when, after conditioning, the CSs were introduced as primes in this affective priming task, a significant differential impact of the CS+ and CS- was observed on the time needed to evaluate positive and negative target words. When the CS+ was used as prime, response latencies were faster for negative as compared to positive targets, while this pattern was reversed when the CS- was used as prime.

EXPERIMENT 1

In Experiment 1 an individually selected neutral picture (CS+) was contingently followed by an electrocutaneous stimulus. The other picture (CS-) was never followed by the US. Before and after acquisition verbal ratings of stimulus valence were obtained. Additionally, after acquisition, US-expectancy was assessed. The extinction procedure consisted of the removal of the electrodes and the explicit statement that no more electrocutaneous stimuli

---

[1] Traditionally, the number of CS's used in evaluative conditioning studies is relatively large. Given this fact, it has repeatedly been demonstrated that evaluative changes are present, even for the CS's for which the participant fails to recognize the associated US, and even when the participant does not remember whether the associated US was positive or negative. This provides strong evidence that E.C. can occur independent from the (verbal) awareness of the original CS-US relationship, and that the observed effects are not a mere product of demand

would be administered (Hughdal & Öhman, 1977; Vansteenwegen, Crombez, Baeyens, & Eelen, 1998), subsequently followed by a series of unreinforced CS+ and CS- presentations. After the extinction phase, participants were asked again to provide US-expectancy ratings and evaluative ratings. Finally, participants were asked to accomplish the affective priming procedure.

In addition to the measures of expectancy and evaluation, the Fear Thermometer (Malloy & Levis, 1988) was administered (i.e. a rating of the amount of fear elicited by the presentation of the CS+ or CS-). Also, self-reports for arousal were obtained for both stimuli. Although it is to be expected that after conditioning the CS+ will induce more fear and will be rated as more arousing than the CS-, the status of both measures with regard to the distinction between expectancy-learning and referential/evaluative learning is not very clear at present. As suggested by Hermans et al. (in press c), this issue might be resolved experimentally by the extinction procedures that are introduced in the subsequent experiments. Because it is predicted that extinction will have a strong influence on expectancy-learning, but will have less or no influence on the amount of referential learning, the impact of an extinction procedure on the conditioned arousal ratings would then be indicative of their nature: expectancy-based, merely referential, or both.

Method

Participants

Twenty first-year psychology students (5 men, 15 women) and twenty-two first-year economics students (5 men, 17 women) participated for partial fulfillment of course requirements. All participants gave informed consent and were instructed that they could decline further participation at any time during the experiment.

Materials

The pictures that were used as CS+, CS-, and as additional primes for the priming procedure were selected on an individual basis from a set of 60 color pictures of human faces. Half of the pictures in this set showed the face of a man, while the other half showed the face of a woman. Pictures varied in the age of the portrayed persons and in their affective expression. None of the faces displayed a strong emotional expression. Targets for the affective priming procedure were a fixed set of six positive (bouquet, melody, art, applause, game, cake) and six negative (hunger, offence, nervousness, weeds, worms, dirt) Dutch nouns selected from Hermans and De Houwer (1994). Positive and negative targets differed significantly on the affective dimension, $t(10) = 26.30$, ($M_{positive} = 5.39$; $M_{negative} = 2.63$), but not for word length, $t(10) = 1.09$, *n.s.*, ($M_{positive} = 5.67$; $M_{negative} = 6.83$), subjective familiarity, $t(10) = 0.23$, *n.s.*, ($M_{positive} = 4.82$; $M_{negative} = 4.92$), or affective extremity, $t(10) = 0.13$, *n.s.*, ($M_{positive} = 1.39$; $M_{negative} = 1.37)^2$.

---

characteristics. The latter can however not be excluded in studies that employ only a few CS's and in which the possibility of awareness of the correct CS-US pairs is rather high.

[2] Affective extremity refers to the (absolute) extent to which the affective rating of a specific word deviates from the mean of the affective rating scale. For example, a word for which the affective score is 2.7, has an affective extremity of 1.3 (with '4' being the theoretical mean of these seven-point rating scales).

During the stimulus selection phase, each color picture was mounted on a separate card (9 x 13 cm). All photographs were digitized as 256 colors, 640 x 480 resolution image files. During the acquisition phase, the extinction phase, and the priming phase, pictures and target words were presented against the black background of a SVGA computer monitor. The pictures were presented 13 cm by 19 cm; target words were presented in white uppercase letters (8 mm high, 5 mm wide).

Electrocutaneous stimuli with duration of 1500 ms were delivered by Fukuda standard Ag/AgCl electrodes (1.2 cm diameter). The electrodes were filled with electrode gel and were attached to the left wrist. Administration of the electrocutaneous stimulus, and presentation of primes and targets on the 15" VGA computer screen was controlled by a Turbo Pascal 5.0 program operating in SVGA graphics mode. Response times were registered by a voice key that stopped a highly accurate Turbo Pascal timer (Bovens & Brysbaert, 1990) upon registration of a sound. The experiment was run on an IBM compatible Pentium 150 Mhz computer.

Procedure

The procedure, and more specifically the individual selection and use of the electrocutaneous stimulus, was explained in detail. The experiment started after the participant had given informed consent. The experiment consisted of four major phases: the stimulus selection phase, the acquisition phase, the extinction phase, and the affective priming phase.

During the *stimulus selection phase* participants were handed over the 60 color pictures of faces, and were asked to evaluate them on a 21-category scale (-100 = very negative / very unpleasant; 0 = neutral; +100 = very positive / very pleasant). The experimenter stressed that they should rely on their first, spontaneous reaction towards the picture. To get an idea about the kind of pictures that were included in the set, participants took a quick look at the pictures before starting to rate them. When all 60 pictures had been evaluated (E.R.1, Evaluative Rating 1), the participant was invited to fill out the Dutch version (Crombez, Eccleston, Baeyens, & Eelen, 1998) of the Pain Catastrophizing Scale (PCS; Sullivan, Bishop, & Pivik, 1995), which was used as filler task. Meanwhile, out of the participant's sight, the experimenter selected six neutrally rated stimuli. First, pictures with a '0' score were selected. If this category did not contain six stimuli, pictures were selected from the categories '-10' and '+10', and so on. On a random basis, two stimuli were designated as CS+ and CS-, and four stimuli as neutral filler primes for the priming phase. Next, the participant was asked to rate the future CS+ and CS-, together with the four neutral filler primes on the arousal dimension (A.R.1; Arousal Rating 1). This was done for each picture on a separate 11-point (0, 10, ... , 100) graphic rating scale, anchored by 'very calm' (0) and 'very aroused' (100).

During the second part of the stimulus selection phase, the intensity of the US was determined. The wrist of the participant was cleaned with Brasivol Nr 1 peeling cream, and the electrodes were attached. Next, during a work-up procedure, the experimenter increased the level of the electrocutaneous stimulus gradually until the participant reported that it was 'unpleasant and demanding some effort to tolerate'. This stimulus was used as the US in the acquisition phase.

During the *acquisition phase* the participant was invited to take place at a distance of about 60 cm from the computer screen. The CS+ and the CS- were each presented eight times for the duration of eight seconds. The order of the presentations was semi-randomized, in the sense that a stimulus could never be presented on more than two successive trials. The inter trial interval (ITI) was either two, three, four, or five seconds and was semi-randomized in a similar fashion. The offset of the CS+ was immediately followed by a 1500 ms presentation of the US. Participants were provided with the information that one stimulus (CS+) would always be followed by the US, while the second stimulus (CS-) would never be followed by the US. They were also instructed to attentively watch this series of presentations.

After the electrodes were removed, the participant was asked to rate each of the six pictures (including the CS+, CS-, and the four neutral filler primes) for a second time on the evaluative dimension (E.R.2) and the arousal dimension (A.R.2). It was stressed that their rating could have remained the same or could have changed as compared to their previous ratings during the stimulus selection phase (E.R.1 & A.R.1), and that we were only interested in how they rated these stimuli at this very moment. Next, *contingency awareness* was tested by asking them to select the CS+ and the CS- from this set of six pictures and to indicate which of both had been followed by an electrocutaneous stimulus. In addition, they were asked to provide *US-expectancy* and *Fear Thermometer* ratings for each of both stimuli using 11-point graphic rating scales. US-expectancy was assessed by indicating to what extent they had expected a US following the presentation of the CS+, and following the presentation of the CS- during the acquisition phase. The rating scale was anchored by 'never' (0) and 'always' (100). Fear was assessed by indicating the extent to which they had felt fearful or anxious during the presentation of the CS+ and the presentation of the CS-. This rating scale was anchored by 'not anxious at all' (0) and 'very anxious' (10). Finally, participants rated the US for three characteristics. First, the (un)pleasantness of the US was rated on an 11-point numerical graphic scale, with '-5/unpleasant' and '+5/pleasant' as extremes. The intensity of the US was assessed by a verbal rating scale with *weak, moderate, intense, enormous,* and *unbearable* as labels. The extent to which they were startled by the US was appraised on a similar verbal rating scale with *not, lightly, moderately, strongly,* and *very strongly* as labels.

At the start of the *extinction phase,* the participants were asked to again take place at the computer screen. It was told that no electrodes would be attached, and that no more electrocutaneous stimuli would be presented for the rest of the experiment. Next, the CS+ and CS- were presented eight times each. The presentation parameters were the same as for the acquisition phase, with the only exception that no USs were presented. Subsequently, the participants were asked again to provide evaluative (E.R. 3) and arousal ratings (A.R. 3) for the same set of six stimuli that had been rated before, as well as US-expectancy ratings and fear ratings for both the CS+ and CS-.

Finally, in the *affective priming phase,* the experimenter explained that pairs of stimuli would be presented on the computer screen, the first of which would always be a picture of a face (the prime), while the second would always be a word (the target). It was instructed to attend to the word and to evaluate it as quickly as possible by saying aloud 'POSITIVE' or 'NEGATIVE'. It was told that they could look at the picture, but that all attention had to be directed at the word for which a response had to be given. The experimenter explained that the primes were only presented to make the task more difficult. Finally, the use of the voice key was explained.

The affective priming task consisted of two blocks of 72 experimental trials, preceded by 12 practice trials. Each trial started with a warning tone (200 ms, 1000 Hz), followed by the presentation of the prime word for a duration of 200 ms. Either 100 ms (SOA 300) or 800 ms (SOA 1000) after the offset of the prime, the target word was presented. For half of the participants, the first experimental block was presented with an SOA of 300 ms, while for the second block the SOA was 1000 ms. For the other participants the order was reversed. This SOA-manipulation was introduced because prior research (Fazio et al., 1986; Hermans et al., 1994) has shown that automatic affective priming effects can be obtained at short (e.g. 300 ms) but not at long (e.g. 1000 ms) SOAs, which is a strong, but indirect indication for the automaticity of the affective priming effect.

The target stayed on the screen until the participant gave a response or 2000 ms elapsed. The inter trial interval was always 2 s. Participants were given the opportunity to take a brief break after the first experimental block.

In both blocks, all 72 combinations of the 6 primes and 12 targets were presented once. The presentation order of these 72 trials was semi-randomized for each block and each participant separately. The restrictions of this randomization were that the same prime should not be presented on more than two consecutive trials, and that two successive trials should not contain the same target. Thus, in each block there were 12 trials in which the CS+ was used as the prime, and 12 trials in which the CS- was used as prime. For each of both types, there were six trials with a positive target and six trials with a negative target. The remaining 48 trials consisted of one of the four neutral filler primes being followed by a positive (24 trials) or a negative (24 trials) target.

Results

Data Reduction and Analysis

The data from the verbal reports were analyzed using 2 X 2 univariate analyses of variance (ANOVA) with CS-type (CS+/CS-) and moment (combinations of pre-acquisition, post-acquisition, and post-extinction) as within-subjects variables. The results were further examined using a priori contrasts (two-tailed).

For the affective priming procedure, the data from trials on which a voice key failure occurred or on which an incorrect response was given were excluded from the analysis. In addition, all response latencies shorter than 200 ms or longer than 1500 ms were excluded to reduce the influence of outlier responses. Because we had strong directional hypotheses with respect to the affective priming effects at SOA 300 and SOA 1000, we will only report the crucial (one-sided) a priori contrasts concerning the difference between affectively congruent and affectively incongruent trials for both levels of the SOA-variable separately.

An alpha-level of .05 was used for all statistical tests. p-Values will only be reported in the case of marginally significant effects ($.05 < p < .10$).

Acquisition Data

After acquisition, participants rated the US as unpleasant ($M = -3.27$), intense ($M = 5.6$), and indicated that they were moderately to strongly startled by the US ($M = 5.9$). All participants were able to correctly select the CS+ and the CS- from the set of six pictures. Therefore, we can conclude that participants experienced the US as a rather aversive stimulus and that they were fully aware of the CS+/US and CS-/no-US contingency.

Moreover, during acquisition the CS+ had become a valid predictor for the US. The mean US-expectancy score was 97.4 for the CS+ and 6.42 for the CS-, $F(1, 41) = 2046$.

In addition to the fact that the CS+ had become a meaningful predictor for the occurrence of the US, the acquisition procedure had also led to significant shifts in the *evaluation* of the CS+ and CS- (see Figure 2).

After acquisition there was a highly significant difference between the *valence ratings* of the CS+ (M = -27.6) and the CS- (M = 9.05), $\underline{F}(1, 41)$ = 28.6, whereas there was no difference before acquisition, $\underline{F}(1, 41)$ = 2.1, *n.s.*, M_{CS+} = 0.71, M_{CS-} = -0.24. The significant CS-type (CS+/CS-) X Moment (E.R.1/E.R.2) interaction, $F(1, 41)$ = 28.0, can be attributed to the CS+ becoming more negative from E.R.1 to E.R.2, $\underline{F}(1, 41)$ = 32.31, as well as to the CS- becoming more positive, $F(1, 41)$ = 5.44.

Finally, conditioning was also apparent from the data of the *Fear Thermometer*, which showed that the CS+ elicited significantly more fear (M = 5.74) than the CS- (M = 0.60), $F(1, 41)$ = 155.4. Also, there was a significant interaction between CS-type and moment of assessment (A.R.1/A.R.2) for the arousal ratings, $F(1, 41)$ = 7.17 (see Figure 4).

A priori contrasts showed that during acquisition the CS+ had become more *arousing*, $F(1, 41)$ = 27.8, while a similar shift for the CS- did not occur (F < 1). This resulted in the CS+ being significantly more arousing than the CS- at the post-acquisition ratings, M_{CS+} = 46.9, M_{CS-} = 22.4, $F(1, 41)$ = 35.42.

Extinction Data

After the extinction phase, the participants were asked to provide US-expectancy ratings for the CS+ and the CS- for the second time. As expected, there was a significant interaction between CS-type and moment (post-acquisition/post-extinction), $F(1, 41)$ = 260.64 (see Figure 1).

The extinction procedure led to a dramatic change in the extent to which a US was expected following the CS+, $F(1, 41)$ = 299.63, $M_{post-acquisition}$ = 97.4, $M_{post-extinction}$ = 20. The US-expectancy ratings for the CS- that were already very low at post-acquisition ratings, even dropped somewhat further, $F(1, 41)$ = 6.9, $M_{post-acquisition}$ = 6.42, $M_{post-extinction}$ = 1.93. It is however important to note that even though the extinction procedure had a tremendous impact on the extent to which the CS+ led to the active expectancy of the US ($\underline{F}$ = 299), there remained a small, but nevertheless significant difference between the CS+ and CS- at the post-extinction ratings; $F(1, 41)$ = 22.99.

In contrast, extinction had no impact at all on the conditioned *stimulus valence*. The relevant CS-type (CS+/CS-) X Moment (E.R.2/E.R.3) interaction was not significant, $F(1, 41)$ = 1.39, n.s. (see Figure 2). And, although the CS+ became more positive from E.R.2 to E.R.3, $F(1, 41)$ = 6.29, a similar non-significant tendency was observed for the CS-, $F(1, 41)$ = 1.46, resulting in a highly significant difference in the evaluative ratings of both stimuli after extinction, M_{CS+} = -17.86, M_{CS-} = 12.38, $F(1, 41)$ = 18.12. Also, the interaction between CS-type and moment, in which the pre-acquisition and post-extinction ratings were included, was still highly significant, $F(1, 41)$ = 18.77.

With respect to the *arousal ratings,* the extinction procedure led to a significant decrease in the arousal ratings for the CS+, $F(1, 41)$ = 21.33, but not for the CS-, F < 1 (comparison between A.R.2 and A.R.3), which resulted in a significant interaction between CS-type and moment (A.R.2/A.R.3), $F(1, 41)$ = 10.56. In fact, the extinction procedure totally erased the acquisition effect in the arousal ratings. The interaction between CS-type and moment, in which the pre-acquisition and post-extinction ratings were entered, was no longer significant, $F(1, 41) = 1.98$, $n.s.$[3] (see Figure 3).

For the *Fear Thermometer*, there was also a significant interaction between CS-type and moment (post-acquisition/post-extinction), $F(1, 41) = 66.35$ (see Figure 4). The CS+ no longer elicited as much anxiety after extinction ($M = 1.86$) as compared to the post-acquisition ratings ($M = 5.74$), $F(1, 41) = 103.6$, while a similar shift was absent for the CS-, $F(1, 41) = 1.40$, $n.s.$, $M_{post-acquisition} = 0.60$, $M_{post-extinction} = 0.33$. Nevertheless, there remained a significant difference between the CS+ and CS- for both measures at the post-extinction ratings; US-expectancy: $F(1, 41) - 22.99$, Fear Thermometer: $F(1, 41) - 15.23$.

Affective Priming Data

As the affective priming procedure was intended as a second, and unobtrusive test of stimulus valence, shorter response latencies for affectively congruent trials as compared to affectively incongruent trials were predicted at the SOA 300 level, while no difference was expected at the SOA of 1000 ms. Against expectations, however, at neither of both SOA levels there was a significant difference in the response latencies for affectively congruent and affectively incongruent trials; SOA 300: $t(40) = 0.978$, $n.s.$; $M_{congruent} = 654$, $M_{incongruent} = 661$; SOA 1000, $t(40) = 0.51$, $n.s.$: $M_{congruent} = 669$, $M_{incongruent} = 663$.

In line with the absence of an affective priming effect at SOA 300, there was also a general tendency for the evaluative conditioning effect to be less strong in the present experiment as compared with previous research (Hermans et al., in press b, in press c). One reason for this less robust evaluative learning, as indicated by the verbal evaluation ratings and the response latency data, might have been that the selected US was not sufficiently aversive for all participants. Indeed, although these experiments did not differ in the mean unpleasantness ratings for the US, there was a larger variability in the ratings of the present experiment. Whereas the US was rated as very unpleasant by some participants (e.g. -5 on the '-5 to +5' scale), others rated the US as rather neutral (e.g. -0.4). It will be obvious that for the latter participants no evaluative conditioning or affective priming should be expected.

Therefore, it was decided to conduct a median split on the basis of the (un)pleasantness ratings of the US after acquisition. Additional analyses showed that for the group ($N = 21$) who had experienced the US as unpleasant ($M = -4.21$), the results of the affective priming data were clearly in line with our predictions. For the SOA 300 ms condition, response latencies were significantly shorter, $t(40) = 2.41$, for affectively congruent ($M = 674$) as compared to affectively incongruent trials ($M = 695$), while a similar effect was absent for the SOA 1000 condition, $t(40) = 0.62$, $n.s.$, $M_{congruent} = 681$, $M_{incongruent} = 692$. For the participants ($N=21$) who rated the US less extremely negative or even neutral ($M = -2.35$), the affective congruency effect was present at neither of the two SOA levels, SOA 300: $t(40) = 0.958$, $n.s.$, SOA 1000: $t(40) = 1.34$, $p = .10$.

Of course, a post-hoc median split based on the pleasantness ratings of the US is a rather crude measure of the extent to which the selected electrocutaneous stimulus is aversive enough to be a real US. Therefore, correlations might provide supplementary information. It

---

[3] Nevertheless, there was still a significant difference between the arousal ratings of the CS+ and the CS- after extinction, $M_{CS+} = 35.23$, $M_{CS-} = 20.95$, $\underline{F}(1, 41) = 13$. However, for unknown reasons, a similar difference was already present in the baseline measures (A.R.1), $F(1, 41) = 3.23$. Hence, given the absence of a significant Moment X CS-type interaction, the difference in the post-extinction ratings should not be viewed as an effect of conditioning, but as the result of an initial baseline difference.

could be demonstrated that a general index of affective priming at SOA 300 ($M_{incongruent}$ - $M_{congruent}$) correlated significantly with the degree to which the participants experienced the US as unpleasant, $r(42) = .48$, or startling, $r(42) = .39$, and with the amount of fear elicited by the CS+ during acquisition, $r(42) = .33$.

Finally, it is worthwhile mentioning that there was a significant correlation between a general index of evaluative learning and the general index of affective priming at SOA 300, $r(42) = .40$[4]. No such correlation could be observed for affective priming at SOA 1000, $r(42) = .19$, *n.s.*.

Discussion

In the present experiment, we obtained evidence for both expectancy-learning as well as evaluative learning in the verbal ratings after acquisition. Confirming our prediction, the extinction procedure had a differential impact on both types of learning. Whereas there was a massive impact on the expectancy-ratings ($\underline{F} = 260$), the acquired difference in valence ratings between the CS+ and the CS- was unaffected by this procedure. And, although this unaltered evaluative difference was not instantaneously reflected in a general effect of affective priming, a median split on the basis of the rated intensity of the US showed that for those participants who had indeed experienced the US as intense, the affective priming effect emerged as predicted. For those however, who had experienced the electrocutaneous stimulus as only mild, or even neutral, the affective priming effect was absent. This is also in line with the expectations, because if the US did not have aversive characteristics (intense, startling), no evaluative learning should occur. Finally, the strong correlation between the verbal evaluative responses and the affective priming data not only demonstrates that the verbal evaluative responses are not entirely based on demand effects, but is also remarkable given the usually low correlations between the different response systems (e.g. Öhman & Bohlin, 1987).

Pertaining to the status of the arousal and fear ratings it is important to note that although the extinction procedure reduced the arousal ratings back to the baseline level, there remained a significant difference between the CS+ and the CS- after acquisition with respect to the fear ratings. Given this sensitivity to the extinction procedure, we would be inclined to characterize the arousal ratings as an index of expectancy-learning. The fact that there was no complete reduction in the fear ratings after extinction might be attributed to an insufficient number of extinction trials. On the other hand, if one assumes that fear is based on a combination of high arousal and negative valence (Lang, Bradley & Cuthbert, 1990), it might be that the residual difference between CS+ and CS- after extinction is the mere reflection of the acquired difference in valence.

Although the results of the present experiment are consistent with our theorizing, there was some room for improvement. First, and in contrast to what we observed in previous research (Hermans et al., in press b, in press c), the priming effect could only be obtained after a post-hoc splitting up of the group based on their evaluation of the US. Only for those participants who had experienced the US as an intense negative stimulus the affective priming effect emerged. Although this post-hoc analysis and the conclusions derived from it are

---

[4] The general index of evaluative learning was calculated as follows: ($E.R.2_{CS-}$ - $E.R.1_{CS-}$) - . ($E.R.2_{CS+}$ - $E.R.1_{CS+}$)

certainly justified, we would nevertheless have a stronger case if we could present similar results without the necessity of such a posteriori analyses. Second, even though the extinction procedure had a very strong impact on the extent to which the CS+ led to the active expectancy of the US, there remained a significant difference between the CS+ and CS- at the post-extinction ratings. Although the point we are making is a differential one – namely that expectancy learning and evaluative learning are *differentially* affected by an extinction procedure – and not an absolute one, we would nevertheless have a more solid argument if we could demonstrate the endurance of an evaluative shift in spite of a complete extinction of the conscious active expectancy of the US. Finally, although the CS+ and CS were randomly selected from the set of pictures that were rated as neutral by the participant, there was nevertheless a significant difference between both stimuli in the baseline arousal ratings in the previous study. Although these ratings do not pertain to the central questions of the reported research, analysis and interpretation of the arousal data would nevertheless be more straightforward if such baseline differences were absent. In the planning of Experiment 2, these elements were taken into account.

EXPERIMENT 2

The main aim of Experiment 2 was to replicate the findings of Experiment 1. In addition, the procedure was slightly modified in three ways in order to increase the robustness of the findings. First, the number of trials for the crucial SOA 300 condition was doubled, while simultaneously leaving out the SOA 1000 trials from the priming procedure. This way we wanted to increase the sensitivity of the affective priming procedure to capture the acquired stimulus valence. Also, during the working-up phase, the importance of a sufficiently unpleasant (but not necessarily painful) electrocutaneous stimulus was stressed some more. Second, with respect to the amount of US-expectancy that could still be observed after extinction, a small modification was introduced in the questioning of the US-expectancy ratings. In the course of Experiment 1 we noticed that participants differed in the way the question concerning the US-expectancy ratings was interpreted. It was our impression that whereas most participants indeed based their answer on the extent to which they actually expected a US after seeing the CS+, a relatively high number of participants also (or even exclusively) relied on the extent to which the CS made them think of the US. If this indeed had been the case, the US-expectancy ratings, which were intended as a measure of 'expectancy learning', were also contaminated by a mere 'referential' component. And, because it is assumed that whereas a procedure of extinction will reduce the extent to which the CS+ leads you to actively expect the presentation of the US (expectancy learning), it will not affect its capacity to 'make you think of' the US (referential learning). Hence, to prevent such contamination of the expectancy measure by a merely referential component, we slightly adapted the way in which the questions were formulated. Finally, with respect to the baseline difference in the arousal data that was observed in Experiment 1, the CSs were now not only selected on the basis of their neutral valence, but also on the basis of their low arousal ratings.

Method

Participants

Twelve female second-year psychology students participated for partial fulfillment of course requirements. All participants gave informed consent and were instructed that they could decline further participation at any time during the experiment.

Materials and Procedure

The stimuli and apparatus were the same as in Experiment 1. Also, the procedure was almost identical to Experiment 1. One modification was that participants now received two blocks of trials in which an SOA of 300 ms was used, instead of one block with SOA 300 trials and one with SOA 1000 trials. The second difference was that participants were told that the US-expectancy question did not pertain to the extent to which the CS 'reminded them of the US, or made them think of it' but to the extent to which they actually had expected that the CS would be actually followed by the US. Finally, to prevent baseline differences, CSs were now not only selected on the basis of their neutral evaluation, but also on account of their low arousal ratings. All other instructions and presentation parameters were identical to Experiment 1.

Results

The data were analyzed as in Experiment 1.

Acquisition Data

After acquisition, participants rated the US as unpleasant ($M = -3.49$), intense ($M = 5.6$), and indicated that they were moderately to strongly startled by the US ($M = 5.8$).

As in Experiment 1, the CS+ had become a valid predictor of the US (see Figure 1). The mean *US-expectancy* score was 95 for the CS+ and 5 for the CS-, $F(1, 11) = 381.9$.

Besides the support for expectancy-learning, there was again clear evidence for evaluative learning in the present experiment (see Figure 2). After acquisition there was a significant difference between the *valence ratings* of the CS+ ($M = -22.5$) and the CS- ($M = 32.5$), $F(1, 11) = 14.84$, whereas there was no difference before acquisition, $F = 1$, $M_{CS+} = 1.67$, $M_{CS-} = 0$. The significant CS-type (CS+/CS-) X Moment (E.R.1/E.R.2) interaction, $F(1, 11) = 14.6$, can be attributed to the CS+ becoming more negative from E.R.1 to E.R.2, $F(1, 11) = 8.87$, as well as to the CS- becoming more positive, $F(1, 41) = 15.45$.

Finally, conditioning was also apparent in the fear ratings. The CS+ elicited significantly more fear ($M = 5.5$) than the CS- ($M = 1$), $F(1, 11) = 42.43$ (Figure 4). Also, there was a significant interaction between CS-type and moment of assessment (A.R.1/A.R.2) for the arousal ratings, $F(1, 11) = 5.71$ (Figure 3). After acquisition, there was a significant difference in the arousal ratings for the CS+ and the CS-, $M_{CS+} = 50$, $M_{CS-} = 25$, $F(1, 11) = 6.6$, whereas no such difference was present before conditioning, $M_{CS+} = 10$, $M_{CS-} = 9.17$, $F = 1$. Additional a priori contrasts showed that the observed interaction was due to the fact that during acquisition the CS+ had become more *arousing,* $F(1, 11) = 24.56$, while a similar, but significantly less strong shift for the CS- could be observed, $F(1, 11) = 6.76$.

Extinction Data

After the extinction phase, the participants were now asked to provide *US-expectancy* ratings for the second time. As predicted, there was a significant interaction between CS-type and moment (post-acquisition/post-extinction), $F(1, 11) = 288.78$. The US-expectancy ratings for the CS- that were already very low at post-acquisition ratings, even dropped further to the zero-level, $F(1, 11) = 3.66$, $p = .08$, $M_{post-acquisition} = 5$, $M_{post-extinction} = 0$. More dramatic, however, was the impact of the extinction procedure on the extent to which a US was expected following the CS+, $F(1, 11) = 1078$, $M_{post-acquisition} = 95$, $M_{post-extinction} = 1.67$. US-expectancy was even reduced to the level that there was no longer any significant difference between CS+ and CS- after extinction, $F(1, 11) = 2.2$, $p = .16$ (see Figure 1).

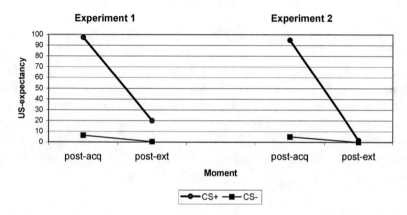

Figure 1. Mean US-expectancy ratings for CS+ and CS- as a function of the moment of assessment (post-acquisition, post-extinction) for experiments 1 and 2.

In contrast, extinction had no impact at all on the conditioned *stimulus valence* (see Figure 2)

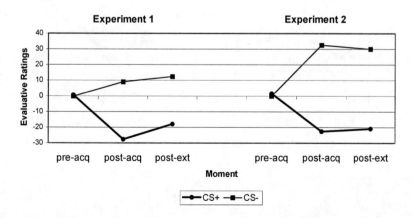

Figure 2. Mean evaluation ratings for CS+ and CS- as a function of the moment of assessment (pre-acquisition, post-acquisition, post-extinction) for experiments 1 and 2.

The relevant CS-type (CS+/CS-) X Moment (E.R.2/E.R.3) interaction was not significant, $F<1$. For neither the CS+ or the CS- there was a significant change from the post-acquisition ratings to the post-extinction ratings, $F < 1$ for both comparisons. So, there remained an unaltered evaluative difference between both stimuli at the end of extinction phase, M_{CS+} = -20.83, M_{CS-} = 30, $F(1, 11)$ = 13.38. Also, the interaction between CS-type and moment, in which the pre-acquisition and post-extinction ratings were included, was still highly significant, $F(1, 11)$ = 13.66.

As was the case for the US-expectancy-ratings, the extinction procedure had a strong influence on data of the *Fear Thermometer* (see Figure 4), $F(1, 11)$ = 14.77. The CS+ no longer elicited so much anxiety after extinction (M = 2.5) as compared to the post-acquisition ratings (M = 5.5), $F(1, 11)$ = 62.66, while a similar shift was absent for the CS-, $F(1, 41)$ = 2.85, p = .11, $M_{\text{post-acquisition}}$ = 1, $M_{\text{post-extinction}}$ = 0.83. It is however important to note that even though the extinction procedure had a strong impact on the amount of fear elicited by the CS+, there nevertheless remained a significant difference between the CS+ and CS- at the post-extinction ratings; $F(1, 11)$ = 10.38.

With respect to the *arousal ratings* (see Figure 3), the extinction procedure led to a significant decrease in the arousal ratings for the CS+, $F(1, 11)$ = 7.86, but also for the CS-, $F(1, 11)$ = 9.13 (comparison between A.R.2 and A.R.3). Nevertheless, given that the absolute reduction was larger for the CS+, there was no longer any significant difference between the arousal ratings for both CSs after extinction, M_{CS+} = 25, M_{CS-} = 19.17, $F(1, 11)$ = 1.96. In addition, the interaction between CS-type and moment, in which the pre-acquisition and post-extinction ratings were entered, was not significant, $F(1, 41)$ = 1.13.

Affective Priming Data

The data of these verbal evaluative ratings could be corroborated by the results from the affective priming procedure. Response latencies for affectively congruent pairs (M = 680 ms) were significantly shorter as compared to affectively incongruent pairs (M = 708 ms), $t(9)$ = 1.90.

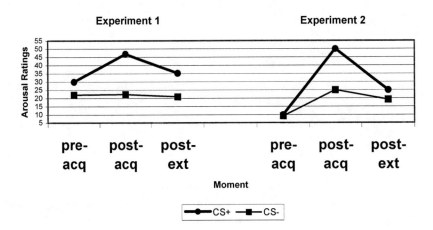

Figure 3. Mean arousal ratings for CS+ and CS- as a function of the moment of assessment (pre-acquisition, post-acquisition, post-extinction) for experiments 1 and 2.

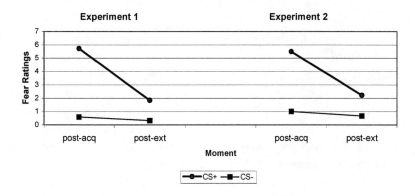

Figure 4. Mean fear ratings for CS+ and CS- as a function of the moment of assessment (post-acquisition, post-extinction) for experiments 1 and 2.

DISCUSSION

The procedural changes that were introduced in Experiment 2 were successful. Not only could the general pattern of results of Experiment 1 be replicated, but the results are also more straightforward. As can be seen from Figure 2, the overall evaluative conditioning effect was more outspoken than in the previous study. Moreover, this evaluative conditioning effect was not affected by the extinction procedure. Also, the significant difference in the evaluative ratings for the CS+ and CS- after extinction could be corroborated by the results of the affective priming task. In contrast with Experiment 1, there was no longer a need for a post-hoc analysis based on the appropriateness of the US for the individual participants.

This study further demonstrated that expectancy learning is highly sensitive to extinction procedures, including CS-only presentations and verbal instructions. Moreover, due to extinction the US-expectancy ratings were now reduced to the point that there was no longer any significant difference between the CS+ and CS-. These data lead to a fine and important demonstration of the persistence of acquired valence in the absence of reported US-expectancies. This can be considered as a laboratory equivalent of the patient who, after successful exposure treatment, no longer expects to have a panic attack in the supermarket and hence no longer avoids to do the shopping over there, but nevertheless still (somewhat) dislikes this place. As we will argue later, this might be an affective-motivational source for the return of fear.

Finally, with respect to the status of the arousal and fear ratings, the pattern of the results was similar to that of Experiment 1. Extinction reduced arousal ratings to the baseline level, whereas there remained a significant difference in the fear ratings between the CS+ and CS-after extinction. Based on these results we would be inclined to repeat our conclusion that arousal ratings are mainly a reflection of expectancy learning, whereas the fear ratings might be based on a combination of expectancy learning (arousal) and referential learning (valence).

GENERAL DISCUSSION

In general, the results from both experiments can be summarized as follows: (a) they confirm the observation that signal-learning and evaluative learning can co-occur (e.g. Hermans et al., in press b, in press c), and (b) they provide empirical support for the hypothesis that extinction has a differential impact on both types of learning. In what follows we will elaborate on both aspects of the results.

With respect to the first conclusion, it can be affirmed that the experience of repeated contingent presentations of a previously neutral face (CS+) and an aversive electrocutaneous stimulus (US) altered the meaning of the CS+ in two different ways. First, the CS+ became a valid predictor for the US as it elicited the active expectation of the US, whereas the CS- was even experienced – according to the comments of several participants – as a safety signal that indicated the nonappearance of the US (signal-learning). On the other hand, the CS+ by itself became a more negative stimulus, as evidenced by the evaluative ratings and the affective priming data. Correspondingly, the CS- became more positive.

An interesting observation is that these shifts in the evaluative ratings for the CS+ and CS- could be confirmed by the data of the affective priming procedure. This measure is particularly interesting within the present conditioning paradigm because it is regarded to be not susceptible to demand characteristics. An additional advantage of this procedure in the context of the present extinction studies is that it is most likely less sensitive to changes in arousal as compared to the eye blink startle response that was used in related studies (e.g. Hamm et al., 1993). This latter response is most often implemented and defined as a defensive reflex to an unexpected noise that has been shown to vary linearly with the judged emotional valence of a pictorial foreground slide (Vrana, Spence, & Lang, 1988). Although often employed as an index of stimulus valence, results from our laboratory (Vansteenwegen et al., 1998) demonstrated that while the startle modulation might be a good measure of valence at the end of acquisition, it is probably not a valid measure to study subsequent effects of extinction on acquired valence. This is because substantial startle modulation is only found for pictures with high levels of judged arousal (Cuthbert, Bradley, & Lang, 1996), which will be present after acquisition, but which habitually vanishes over extinction trials. In a recent report by Sabatinelli, Bradley, & Lang (2001), it was demonstrated that the startle reflex is modulated by hedonic valence in studies that involve mere picture perception, but is modulated by emotional arousal in a task context involving anticipation. Hence, although startle modulation can be regarded as a highly interesting measure of affective meaning, it does not seem to be the best alternative to study differential effects of extinction on mere stimulus valence. With respect to the affective priming procedure, however, no such mediating influence of arousal has been demonstrated.

In addition to further substantiation of the idea that evaluative learning and expectancy learning can co-occur, the present data also demonstrate a differential impact of extinction manipulations on both types of learning. Drastic changes in US-expectancy that were induced by CS-only presentations and verbal instructions were not accompanied by a similar decrease in acquired evaluative meaning. In fact, the evaluative ratings showed no impact of these manipulations at all.

It will be obvious that we do not interpret the present data as evidence for the 'absolute' hypothesis that evaluative learning is unaffected by extinction. As pointed out before, our hypothesis was a differential one rather than an absolute one: Do extinction manipulations differentially affect evaluative learning and expectancy-learning? Although this issue can be answered affirmatively, it still leaves open the question of whether evaluative learning is completely resistant to extinction. It remains to be tested whether a drastically increased number of extinction trials would eventually not lead to a (complete) extinction of the acquired valence. Pertaining to this possibility, there is now recent evidence from our laboratory (Francken et al., 2001) that even when the number of extinction trials is increased up to three times the number of acquisition trials (8 acquisition trials versus 24 extinction trials for each of both CSs), the acquired evaluative difference between the CS+ and CS- remained significant after the elaborate extinction phase as evidenced by the evaluative ratings as well as an affective priming procedure that was scheduled both after acquisition and extinction. Future studies could include even more extinction trials or consist of a parametric analysis of the number of extinction trials to further investigate this issue.

The present results are framed within the distinction between evaluative learning and expectancy learning (Baeyens, Eelen & Crombez, 1995). Although it is sometimes argued that both forms of learning are also based on qualitatively different processes, it might well be that the crucial difference not so much involves a difference in the associative knowledge base or associative processes on which behavior is founded, but relates to a difference in the way in which this acquired knowledge is translated into behavior (for further discussion concerning different computational views of the referential/expectancy distinction, see De Houwer, Thomas & Baeyens, in press). Awaiting further experimental evidence concerning the exact nature of the difference between both forms of learning, we prefer to situate our observations at the 'outcome'-level of a conditioning procedure, rather than at the process level. This leaves open the possibility that changes in US-expectancy and evaluative meaning are based on one and the same process. In fact, it is rather plausible that both are based on the most primitive form of associative learning: the acquisition of an associative link between memory representations based on a simple learning rule that increases the strength of the association whenever the stimuli co-occur but leaves the association strength intact when one of the two stimuli are presented in isolation. Innovative research with respect to expectancy-learning (Bouton, 1998; Rescorla, 1996) suggests that this latter type of learning might also essentially be based on the same basic mechanism. These studies demonstrate that although an extinction procedure results in a decrease of conditioned responses, it does not seem to affect the strength of the underlying association. In fact, extinction is assumed to add new associations on top of the existing association (see Rescorla, 1996). To the extent that future evidence would point to a similar learning process for expectancy learning and evaluative learning, research will need to focus on the nature of the performance rules that drive differential effects in measures of valence and expectancy as a function of specific manipulations like extinction procedures and contingency manipulations. Also, in the past, other authors have introduced the notion that human classical conditioning involves two or more simultaneous levels of learning (e.g. Mandel & Bridger, 1973; Öhman, Hamm, & Hugdahl, 2000; Razran, 1955). Comparison of these models with the two-level account that encompasses evaluative learning and referential learning, raises a number of questions concerning the way in which these models can be related to each other and the differential predictions that would result from them. It is our conviction that future research and theorizing should be aimed at addressing these questions.

Finally, given that both expectancy-learning and evaluative learning are involved in the acquisition of many fears and phobias (see Eelen, Hermans, & Baeyens, 2001), and given that extinction differentially influences both types of learning, the present results might have important clinical implications. In fact, we predict that interventions such as exposure will reduce the signal-value of the CSs and will therefore lead to diminished fear reactions, but might leave (most often negative) evaluative reactions towards the stimulus unchanged (Marks, 1987). For instance, most therapists will regard an exposure treatment as effective and will stop further exposure sessions when the original fear reactions towards the phobic stimulus/situation have been substantially reduced and the patient no longer exhibits any avoidance behavior. Although this might reflect a significant reduction in US-expectancy, the subjective evaluative appraisal of this stimulus/situation might still be unaffected. An example would be the patient who no longer expects a panic attack when entering a large supermarket, and after the apparently successful exposure treatment again frequents these superstores, but still somehow dislikes them. Given that stimulus valence – together with arousal – is one of the two basic dimensions of emotion (Lang, Bradley, & Cuthbert, 1990), we believe that such unaltered negative valence might form an affective-motivational source for the re-emergence of the original phobic fear. Hence, it does not seem unlikely that if this person later again enters such a supermarket that is still endowed with negative valence, and is aroused for reasons that are unrelated to this situation (e.g. bad news, too much coffee), this combination might lead to enhanced fear or even a new panic attack. Future experimental and clinical studies are necessary to substantiate this point.

REFERENCES

Arntz, A. (1997). The match-mismatch model of phobia acquisition. In G.C.L. Davey. (Ed.), *Phobias. A handbook of theory, research and treatment (pp. 375 - 395)*. Chichester: John Wiley and Sons.

Baeyens, F. (1998). Koele witte wijn als plots de deurbel rinkelt: Referentie en evaluatie versus verwachting en voorbereiding bij Pavloviaans leren. [Cool white wine when suddenly the doorbell goes: Reference and evaluation versus expectancy and preparation in Pavlovian learning]. *Gedragstherapie, 31,* 7-47.

Baeyens, F., Crombez, G., De Houwer, J., & Eelen, P. (1996). No evidence for modulation of evaluative flavor-flavor associations in humans. *Learning and Motivation, 27,* 200-241.

Baeyens, F., Crombez, G., Hendrickx, H., & Eelen, P. (1995a). Parameters of human evaluative flavor-flavor conditioning. *Learning and Motivation, 26,* 141-160.

Baeyens, F., Crombez, G., Van den Bergh, O., & Eelen, (1988). Once in contact, always in contact: Evaluative learning is resistant to extinction. *Advances in Behaviour Research and Therapy, 10,* 179-199.

Baeyens, F., & De Houwer, J. (1995b). Evaluative conditioning is a qualitatively distinct form of classical conditioning: A reply to Davey (1994). *Behaviour Research and Therapy, 33,* 825-831.

Baeyens, F., De Houwer, J., & Eelen (1994). Awareness inflated, evaluative conditioning underestimated. *Behavioural and Brain Sciences, 17,* 396-397.

Baeyens, F., Eelen, P., & Crombez, G. (1995c). Pavlovian associations are forever: On classical conditioning and extinction. *Journal of Psychophysiology, 9,* 127-141.

Baeyens, F., Eelen, P., Crombez, G., & Van den Bergh (1992). Human evaluative conditioning: Acquisition trials, presentation schedule, evaluative style, and contingency awareness. *Behaviour Research and Therapy, 30,* 133-142.

Baeyens, F., Eelen, P., & Van den Bergh, O. (1990). Contingency awareness in evaluative conditioning: A case for unaware affective-evaluative learning. *Cognition and Emotion, 4,* 3-18.

Baeyens, F., Eelen, P., Van den Bergh, O., & Crombez, G. (1989a). Acquired affective-evaluative value: Conservative but not unchangeable. *Behaviour Research and Therapy, 27,* 279-287.

Baeyens, F., Eelen, P., Van den Bergh, O. & Crombez, G. (1992). The content of learning in human evaluative conditioning: Acquired valence is sensitive to US-revaluation. *Learning and Motivation, 23,* 200-224.

Baeyens, F., Hendrickx, H., Crombez, G., & Hermans, D. (1998). Neither extended sequential nor simultaneous feature positive training result in modulation of evaluative flavor-flavor conditioning in humans. *Appetite, 31,* 185-204.

Baeyens, F., Hermans, D., & Eelen, P. (1993). The role of CS-US contingency in human evaluative conditioning. *Behaviour Research and Therapy, 31,* 731-737.

Baeyens, F., Vanhouche, W., Crombez, G., & Eelen, P. (1998). Human evaluative flavor-flavor conditioning is not sensitive to post-acquisition US-inflation. *Psychologica Belgica, 38,* 83-108.

Baeyens, F., Vansteenwegen, D., Hermans, D., & Eelen, P. (2001). Chilled white wine, when all of a sudden the doorbell rings: Mere reference and evaluation versus expectancy and preparation in human Pavlovian learning. In F. Columbus (Ed.), *Advances in Psychology Research, Vol. 4, (pp. 241-277).* Huntington, NY: Nova Science Publishers, Inc.

Bouton, M.E. (1998). The role of context in classical conditioning: Some implications for cognitive behavior therapy. In W.T. O'Donahue (Ed.), *Learning and Behaviour Therapy,* Boston, MA.: Allyn & Bacon Inc.

Bovens, N., & Brysbaert, M. (1990). IBM PC/XT/AT and PS/2 Turbo Pascal timing with extended resolution. *Behavior Research Methods, Instruments, and Computers, 22,* 332-334.

Crombez, G., Eccleston, C., Baeyens, F., & Eelen, P. (1998). When somatic information threatens, pain catastrophizing enhances attentional interference. *Pain, 75,* 187-198.

Cuthbert, B.N., Bradley, M.M., & Lang, P.J. (1996). Probing picture perception: Activation and emotion. *Psychophysiology, 33,* 103-111.

Davey, G.C.L. (1989). UCS revaluation and conditioning models of acquired fear. *Behaviour Research and Therapy, 27,* 521-528.

Davey, G.C.L. (1992). Classical conditioning and the acquisition of human fears and phobias: A review and synthesis of the literature. *Advances in Behaviour Research and Therapy, 14,* 29-66.

Davey, G.C.L. (1997). A conditioning model of phobias. In G.C.L. Davey. (Ed.), *Phobias. A handbook of theory, research and treatment (pp. 301-322).* Chichester: John Wiley and Sons.

De Houwer, J., Baeyens, F., Vansteenwegen, D., Eelen, P. (2000). Evaluative conditioning in the picture-picture paradigm with random assignment of conditioned stimuli to unconditioned stimuli. *Journal of Experimental Psychology: Animal Behaviour Processes, 26,* 237-242.

De Houwer, J., Thomas, S., & Baeyens, F. (in press). Associative learning of likes and dislikes: A review of 25 years of research on human evaluative conditioning. *Psychological Bulletin.*

Eelen, P., Hermans, D., & Baeyens, F. (2001). Learning perspectives on anxiety disorders. In E.J.L. Griez, C. Faravelli, D., Nutt, & J. Zohar (Eds.), *Anxiety disorders: An introduction to clinical management and research (pp. 249-264).* London: John Wiley and Sons.

Eelen, P., Van den Bergh, O., & Baeyens, F. (1990). Fobieën: Leertheorieën. [Phobias: Learning theories]. In J.W.G Orlemans, P. Eelen, & W.P. Haajman (Eds.), *Handboek voor gedragstherapie. (C 15.4, pp. 1-28).* Deventer: Van Loghum Slaterus.

Fazio, R.H., Sanbonmatsu, D.M., Powell, M.C., & Kardes, F.R. (1986). On the automatic activation of attitudes. *Journal of Personality and Social Psychology, 50,* 229-238.

Field, A.P., and Davey, G.C.L. (1997). Conceptual conditioning: evidence for an artifactual account of evaluative learning. *Learning and Motivation, 28,* 446-464.

Field, A.P. & Davey, G.C.L. (1999). Reevaluating evaluative conditioning: A nonassociative explanation of conditioning effects in the visual evaluative conditioning paradigm. *Journal of Experimental Psychology: Animal Behaviour Processes, 25,* 211-224.

Francken, G. Vansteenwegen, D., Hermans, D., Van Calster, B., Declercq, A., & Eelen, P. (2001). *Differential effect of extinction on evaluative conditioning and conventional Pavlovian conditioning: Affective priming and skin conductance responses.* (submitted for publication).

Hamm, A.O., Greenwald, M.K., Bradley, M.M., & Lang, P.J. (1993). Emotional learning, hedonic change, and the startle probe. *Journal of Abnormal Psychology, 102,* 453-465.

Hamm, A.O., & Vaitl, D. (1996). Affective learning: Awareness and aversion. *Psychophysiology, 33,* 698-710.

Hardwick, S.A., & Lipp, O.V. (2000). Modulation of affective learning: An occasion for evaluative conditioning? *Learning and Motivation, 13,* 251-271.

Hermans, D., Baeyens, F., & Eelen, P. (in press a). On the acquisition and activation of evaluative information in memory: Evaluative learning and affective priming combined. In J. Musch & K.C. Klauer (Eds.), *The psychology of evaluation: Affective processes in cognition and emotion.* Mahwah, NJ: Lawrence Erlbaum.

Hermans, D., Crombez, G., & Eelen, P. (2000). Automatic attitude activation and efficiency: The fourth horseman of automaticity. *Psychologica Belgica, 40,* 3-22.

Hermans, D., & De Houwer (1994). Affective and subjective familiarity ratings of 740 Dutch words. *Psychologica Belgica, 34,* 115-139.

Hermans, D., De Houwer, J., & Eelen, P. (1994). The affective priming effect: Automatic activation of evaluative information in memory. *Cognition and Emotion, 8,* 515-533.

Hermans, D., De Houwer, J., & Eelen, P. (2001). A time course analysis of the affective priming effect. *Cognition and Emotion, 15,* 143-165.

Hermans, D., Spruyt, A., & Eelen, P. (in press b). Automatic affective priming of recently acquired stimulus valence: Priming at SOA 300 but not at SOA 1000. *Cognition and Emotion.*

Hermans, D., Van den Broeck, A., & Eelen, P. (1998). Affective priming using a colour-naming task: A test of an affective-motivational account of affective priming effects. *Zeitschrift für Experimentelle Psychologie, 45,* 136-148.

Hermans, D., Vansteenwegen, D., Crombez, G., Baeyens, F., & Eelen, P. (in press c). Expectancy- learning and evaluative learning in human classical conditioning: Affective priming as an indirect and unobtrusive measure of conditioned stimulus valence. *Behaviour Research and Therapy*.

Hodes, R.L., Cook, E. W., & Lang, P. (1985). Individual differences in autonomic response: Conditioned association or conditioned fear? *Psychophysiology, 22,|545-560*.

Hofmann, S.G., Ehlers, A., & Roth, W.T. (1995). Conditioning theory: A model for the etiology of public speaking anxiety ? *Behaviour Research and Therapy, 33,* 567-571.

Hugdahl, K. & Öhman, A. (1977). Effects of the instruction on acquisition and extinction of electrodermal responses to fear-relevant stimuli. *Journal of Experimental Psychology: Human Learning and Memory, 3(5),* 608-618.

Klauer, K.C. (1998). Affective priming. In W. Stroebe & M. Hewstone (Eds.), *European Review of Social Psychology* (pp. 67-103). New York: Wiley.

Klauer, K. C. & Musch, J. (in press). Affective Priming: Findings and Theories. In J. Musch & K. C. Klauer (Eds.) *The Psychology of Evaluation: Affective Processes in Cognition and Emotion.* Mahwah, NJ: Lawrence Erlbaum.

Lang, P.J., Bradley, M.M., & Cuthbert, B.N. (1990). Emotion, attention, and the startle reflex. *Psychological Review, 97,* 377-395.

Levey, A.B. & Martin, I. (1987). Evaluative conditioning: A case for hedonic transfer. In H.J. Eysenck & I. Martin (Eds.), *Theoretical foundations of behavior therapy.* New York: Plenum.

Lipp, O.V., Sheridan, J. & Siddle, D.A.T. (1994). Human blink startle during aversive and nonaversive Pavlovian conditioning. *Journal of Experimental Psychology: Animal Behavior Processes, 20,* 380-389.

Lovibond, P., Davis, N.R., & O'Flaherty, A.S. (2000). Protection from extinction in human fear conditioning. *Behaviour Research and Therapy, 38,* 967-983.

Mackintosh, N.J. (1983). *Conditioning and associative learning.* Oxford: Oxford University Press.

Malloy, P., & Levis, D.J. (1988). A laboratory demonstration of persistant human avoidance. *Behavior Therapy, 19,* 229-241.

Mandel, I.J., & Bridger, W.H. (1973). Is there classical conditioning without cognitive expectancy? *Psychophysiology, 10,* 87-90.

Marks, I. (1987). *Fears, phobias, and rituals. Panic, anxiety, and their disorders.* New York: Oxford University Press.

Mineka, S., & Zinbarg, R. (1995). Conditioning and ethological models of social phobia. In R.G. Heimberg, M.R. Liebowitz (Eds.), *Social phobia: Diagnosis, assessment, and treatment (pp. 134-162).* New York: The Guilford Press.

Mineka, S., & Zinbarg, R. (1996). Conditioning and ethological models of anxiety disorders: Stress-in-dynamic-context anxiety models. In D.A. Hope (Ed.). *Perspectives on anxiety, panic, and fear. Vol. 43 of the Nebraska Symposium on Motivation. (pp. 135-210).* London: University of Nebraska Press.

Mogg, K, & Bradley, B. (1998). A cognitive-motivational analysis of anxiety. *Behaviour Research and Therapy, 36,* 809-848

Öhman, A., & Bohlin, G. (1987). Barry's unification of matter, mind, and body: one mental process for each polygraph channel. *Advances in Psychophysiology, 2,* 259- 270.

Öhman, A., Hamm, A., & Hugdahl, K. (2000). Cognition and the autonomic nervous system. Orienting, anticipation, and conditioning. In J.T. Cacioppo, L.G. Tassinary, & G.G.

Berntson (Eds.), *Handbook of psychophysiology, 2nd ed. (pp. 533-575)*. Cambridge: Cambridge University Press.

Rachman, S. (1991). Neo-conditioning and the classical theory of fear acquisition. *Clinical Psychology Review, 11,* 155-173.

Rachman, S. (1998). *Anxiety.* Hove: Psychology Press.

Razran, G. (1955). Conditioning and perception. *Psychological Review, 62,* 83-95.

Rescorla, R.A. (1996). Preservation of Pavlovian associations through extinction. *Quarterly Journal of Experimental Psychology, 49B,* 245-258.

Sabatinelli, D., Bradley, M.M., & Lang, P.J. (2001). Affective startle modulation in anticipation and perception. *Psychophysiology, 38,* 719-722.

Sullivan, M.J.L., Bishop, S.R., & Pivik, J. (1995). The Pain Catastrophizing Scale: Development and validation. *Psychological Assessment, 7,* 524-532.

Vansteenwegen, D., Crombez, G., Baeyens, F., & Eelen, P. (1998). Extinction in fear conditioning: Effects on startle modulation and evaluative self-reports. *Psychophysiology, 35,* 729-736.

Vrana, S.C., Spence, E.L., & Lang, P.J. (1988). The startle probe response: A new measure of emotion ? *Journal of Abnormal Psychology, 67,* 487-491.

Wells, A. (1997). Cognitive therapy of anxiety disorders. A practice manual and conceptual guide. Chichester: Wiley.

Wolpe, J., & Rowan, V.C. (1988). Panic disorder: A product of classical conditioning. Behaviour Research and Therapy, 26, 441-450.

AUTHOR NOTE

Dirk Hermans, Frank Baeyens and Debora Vansteenwegen are postdoctoral researchers for the Fund for Scientific Research (Flanders, Belgium), Department of Psychology, University of Leuven, Belgium; Paul Eelen, Department of Psychology, University of Leuven, Belgium. Geert Crombez, Department of Psychology, Ghent University, Belgium.

Correspondence concerning this article should be addressed to Dirk Hermans, Department of Psychology, University of Leuven, Tiensestraat 102, B-3000 Leuven, Belgium. Electronic mail may be sent to Dirk.Hermans@psy.kuleuven.ac.be

Chapter 10

ERP CORRELATES OF HAPPINESS AND FEAR: FACIAL EXPRESSIONS DISCRIMINATION

Salvatore Campanella[†]
Catholic University of Leuven (UCL),
Cognitive Neurosciences Unit (NESC),
Louvain-la-Neuve, Belgium

ABSTRACT

When reviewing the psychological and electrophysiological literature on emotions, a discrepancy emerges. In fact, if behavioral studies have demonstrated that emotions are extracted pre-attentively and influence subsequent perception (Kunst-Wilson & Zajonc, 1980; Murphy & Zajonc, 1993), many studies have found emotion-modulated event-related potentials (ERP) considerably later, typically between 250 and 600ms (Münte, Brack, Grootheer, Wieringa, Matzke & Johannes, 1998).

In the present study, we created continua of morphed faces moving from one expression to the other (e.g., identity A "happy" to identity "A" fearful). The temporal course of fear and happiness facial expressions discrimination has been explored through ERPs. Three kinds of pairs were presented in a delayed same-different matching task: (1) two different morphed faces perceived as the same emotional expression (WITHIN-categorical differences), (2) two other ones reflecting two different emotions (BETWEEN-categorical differences), and (3) two identical morphed faces (SAME faces for methodological purpose).

Following the second face onset in the pair, the amplitude of the bilateral occipito-temporal negativities (N170) and of the vertex positive potential (P150 or VPP) was reduced for WITHIN and SAME pairs relative to BETWEEN pairs. These results indicate that the categorical discrimination of human facial emotional expressions has an

---

[†] Correspondance: Université Cathloique de Louvain, Faculté de Psychologie – Unité NESCC, Place du Cardinal Mercier, 10, B-1348 Louvain-la-Neuve. Tel: +32 10 473808; Fax: +32 10 473774; email: Salvatore. Campanella@psp.ucl.ac.be.

early perceptual origin, around 150 ms, in the bilateral occipito-temporal regions, maybe due to amygdalar connexions.

1. INTRODUCTION

The environment provides a large amount of various stimulations that the human brain cannot exhaustively process. One method to simplify our perception of events is to categorize stimuli. The categorization process is a highly complex cognitive function (e.g., Almassy, Edelman & Sporns, 1998), and its end-products, categories, are particularly important because they will determine how we will see and act upon the world. A *categorical perception effect* was initially observed on unidimensional stimuli, such as speech sounds and colour perception (Liberman, Harris, Hoffman, Griffith, 1957; Bornstein & Korda, 1984). Even if humans are confronted with physical linear changes, they perceive both phonemes and hues categorically. Accordingly, a physical change in a stimulus is taken into account when it occurs at the boundary between two categories while it is neglected when it occurs within a given category. For instance, if we looked at color categories, a continuous range of light frequencies represents the color spectrum. Nevertheless, we perceive bands of colors rather than a gradual continuum of color change. Categorization reflects a process by which linear physical changes of a stimulus have non-linear perceptual effects. Moreover, it appears that two colors straddling a category boundary (green-yellow) are easier to discriminate than two colors stemming from the same category (green-green), even though the physical differences in wavelength are identical within both pairs (Bornstein & Korda, 1984). This phenomenon, which consists in enhancing "between-category" differences while "within-category" differences are reduced, is known as the categorical perception (CP) effect (Harnad, 1987).

In the last decade, developments in computer graphics have made it possible to explore categorical perception effects with multidimensional stimuli, such as faces (see Figure 1 for illustration). Studying CP effects on face reveals to be of particular relevance because faces were particularly important in social interactions, as they allow an observer to derive the identity, gender, age, emotional status, race of the face's bearer, influencing also the attribution of personality characteristics to persons. With this in mind, facial expressions constitute an excellent way to explore the categorical perception with multidimensional stimuli (Calder, Young, Perrett, Etcoff & Rowland, 1996). Indeed, the investigation of categorical perception of facial expressions turns out to be of the greatest conceptual relevance, as we know little about the *perceptual* representation of facial affect, and the mechanisms used to decode it (Calder et al., 2000). One of the fundamental issues that is still discussed concerns whether facial expressions are perceived as varying continuously along underlying dimensions or as belonging to qualitatively discrete categories, as one might use existing theories to argue either way (Calder et al., 1996). Indeed, the idea of basic universally recognized emotions would suggest categorical perception, whereas dimensional accounts would not.

Etcoff and Magee (1992) carried out the first study on categorical perception of facial expressions. They converted photographs from the Ekman and Friesen (1976) series of pictures of facial affect into line drawings and used a computer program to generate drawings of equal interpolated steps between two different facial expressions posed by the same individual. These authors used a two-step procedure. First, subjects were confronted with an ABX *discrimination* task, during which two drawings (A, B) were successively presented, followed by a third one (X). Subjects had to decide whether X was the same as A or B. Second, subjects were confronted with an *identification* task, during which they had to categorize all the randomly interpolated faces falling along a particular expression continuum (e.g., from happiness to fear). Although the expression information was linearly manipulated, sharp boundaries appeared in the subjects' responses between regions of each continuum perceived as corresponding to one expression, and a region corresponding to the other expression. Moreover, results of the ABX task showed that subjects discriminated more easily two pairs of drawings crossing a subjective category boundary (such as a drawing seen as happy in the identification task and one seen as fearful) as compared to pairs of drawings separated by an equal physical distance but laying within a category (e.g., two drawings identified as happy). This clearly demonstrated a categorical perception of facial expressions. By using photograph-quality morphed images of expression continua, Calder et al. (1996), Granato, Bruyer, & Revillon (1996), Young, Rowland, Calder, Etcoff, Seth & Perrett (1997), Bimler & Kirkland (2001) replicated Etcoff and Magee's (1992) findings in that field, these results being extended to 7-month-old infants and 9- to 10-year-children respectively by Kotsoni, de Haan & Johnson (2001) and de Gelder, Teunisse & Benson (1997).

These results lead to two main considerations. First, the categorical perception effect needs two stages to be assessed: (1) *an identification task*, showing non-linear responses to linearly manipulated stimuli and allowing to define boundaries within each continuum, and (2) *a discrimination task*, defining the hallmark of categorical perception effect and which has to evidence an enhanced discriminability for BETWEEN- as compared to WITHIN-categorical differences. Second, findings of categorical perception of facial expressions were inconsistent concerning the emotion perception in terms of a two-dimensional model (such as pleasant-unpleasant and rejection-attention; e.g., Woodworth & Schlosberg, 1954) but provided strong evidence that facial expressions are perceived as belonging to discrete categories (Young et al., 1997; see also Calder, Burton, Miller, Young & Akamatsu, 2001 for discussion).

The above review shows that CP gives rise to the following behavioral phenomena: stimuli from the centre of categories are classified faster than those at the edges (Bornstein & Monroe, 1980), discrimination of stimuli and same/different judgements are more accurate and faster across than within categories (Etcoff & Magee, 1992). At this point, it was a challenge for neurophysiologists to assess where and mainly *when* does the categorical perception of facial emotional expressions occur. Due to better temporal resolution (as compared to positron emission tomography or functional magnetic resonance), even-related potentials (ERPs) allow us to investigate the temporal course and the various stages of cognitive processing with a temporal resolution of 1ms. Moreover, when reviewing the psychological and electrophysiological literature on emotions, a discrepancy emerges. In fact, if behavioral studies have demonstrated that emotions are extracted pre-attentively and influence subsequent perception (Kunst-Wilson & Zajonc, 1980; Murphy & Zajonc, 1993), only one study (Pizzagalli, Regard & Lehmann, 1999) has found neurophysiological correlates for these processes. Pizzagalli et al. (1999) showed that personal affective judgments of face images significantly modulated ERP responses at early stages, 80-116ms after right hemisphere stimulation and 104-160ms after left stimulation. However, prior studies found emotion-modulated ERP components considerably later, typically between 250 and 600ms (Münte, Brack, Grootheer, Wieringa, Matzke & Johannes, 1998). Subjects of Potter & Parker (1989) had to decide whether the second face of a pair matched the first one in terms of expression. The ERPs showed a later difference in the 490-540ms time range, only for a right parietal site. Accordingly, Hautecoeur, Debruyne, Forzy, Gallois, Hache & Dereux (1993) showed a modulation of a parietal P400 when subjects were asked to look for emotional expression of the face (smiling or non-smiling) in comparison with a recognition task (known or unknown). Several studies, as ours (Campanella et al., 2002a) limited *a priori* their analyses around the P300 component by investigating emotional processing using oddball paradigms (e.g., Oroczo & Ehlers, 1998). Finally, by using intracranial recordings, Halgren & Marinkovic (1995) showed that significant differentiation among waveforms evoked by different facial emotions appears frontocentrally in the 400-600ms latency range. With this in mind, we wonder whether earlier modulations due to emotional categories could be found by using ERPs. This would suggest that our brain was able at early perceptual stage to discriminate between different facial expressions. This seems to us particularly plausible if we consider the status of an emotional expression such as fear. A large and growing body of evidence points towards the amygdala, a small structure in the temporal lobes, as being crucial for the expression and the recognition of fear emotion. Indeed, neural representations of sensory events are susceptible to selective attentional modulation: the act of paying attention to one particular stimulus may result in the inhibition of the representation of the stimuli in the cortex (Treue & Maunsell, 1996). However, we have to be able to react as quickly as possible to threatening stimulations in order to furnish fast and adapted responses. As a fearful face could represent a signal warning of immediate danger, we need to be able to interrupt and set aside ongoing programs when real-time needs are encountered. Nowadays, it is thought that the amygdala may interrupt the attentional process and redirect the attention of the cortex, and its resources, to the threatening stimuli (Ledoux, 1995).

In the next section, we will describe an ERP experiment showing that our brain is able to discriminate between happy and fearful faces as early as about 170 ms (Campanella et al., 2002 b). This gives further support to the hypothesis that direct neural pathways, involving the amygdala, could enhance our attentional resources when we are confronted with a potential dangerous situation, such as fearful faces.

2. NEUROPHYSIOLOGICAL CORRELATES OF FEAR AND HAPPINESS DISCRIMINATION

Stimuli

Three male faces with happy and fear expressions were taken from Ekman & Friesen series (1976). Three continua of pairs were therefore possible ("A happy" to "A fear", "B happy" to "B fear" and "C happy to C fear"). Five morphed images were created for each continuum. They were prepared by blending two faces in proportion 90:10 (i.e., 90% "A happy" and 10% "A fear"), 70:30, 50:50, 30:70 and 10:90. We will refer to these as 90%, 70%, 50%, 30% and 10% morphs along the appropriate continuum (see Figure 1 for illustration).

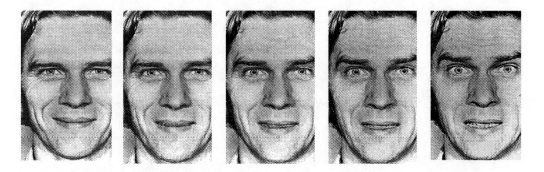

Figure 1. Illustration of a continuum of morphed faces illustrating the manipulation of emotional information. These morphed faces are respectively constituted by 90%/10%, 70%/30%, 50%/50%, 30%/70% and 10%/90% of endpoint faces.

Behavioral Pre-Experiments

The aim of the behavioral pre-experiment was to identify the categorical boundary of the 3 face continua in order to prepare pairs of faces for the ERP experiment.

An identification task allowed the determination of the categorical boundary of the 3 continua. Eighteen subjects were confronted with the 15 morphed faces, randomly presented and repeated 4 times each. Their task consisted in deciding to which expression (happy or fear) the presented morphed face was more similar. As shown previously (Etcoff & Magge, 1992; Calder et al., 1996; Young et al., 1997), this task allows us to define for each of the 3 continua the categorical boundary, which is necessary to create BETWEEN and WITHIN pairs that will be used in the delayed same-different matching task during the ERP recording. The generation of these pairs is necessary to assess, in a discrimination task, an enhanced discriminability for BETWEEN-categorical differences (two morphed faces perceived as two different emotions, i.e. happy and fear) as compared to WITHIN ones.

Procedure

Data of the behavioral pre-experiments were used to define boundaries between categories. For example, Figure 2 shows the percentages of "happy" and "fear" responses for each stimuli (10%, 30%, 50%, 70% and 90%) of one continuum ("A happy" to "A fear"). The intersection of the two curves indicates the point where half of the subjects would respond "happy" and the other half "fear" (56% in this example). This point was taken as the subjective categorical boundary of the continuum "A happy to A fear".

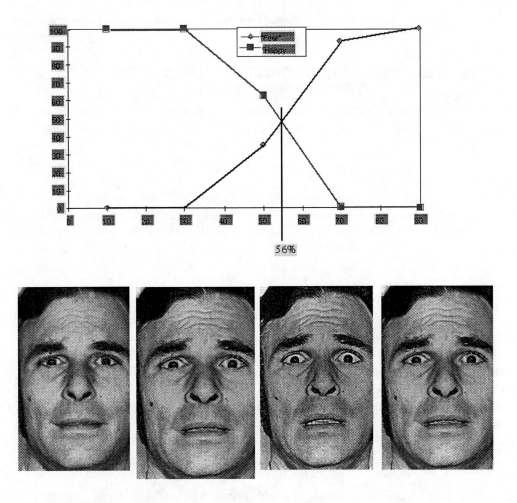

56%

Figure 2. On the basis of the identification task, a categorical boundary can be
computed for each single continuum. Then, pairs of morphed faces crossing
(between) or not (within) this boundary are submitted to subjects in a discrimination task.
Even if these pairs of faces are separated by an identical amount of physical distance, subjects
discriminated more easily between-differences than within-ones.

The same procedure was applied to each of the three continua in order to obtain their own
categorical boundary. For the three continua, categorical boundaries were 56% for "A happy
to A fear", 42% for "B happy to B fear" and 41% for" C happy to C fear". Each continuum
gave rise to three kinds of pairs of morphed faces. First, four BETWEEN pairs (for example,
a pair in which the first image was a morph identified as happy and the second one as fear)
were pulled out of the continuum "A happy to A fear", i.e. pairs "36%-66%", "38%-68%",
"40%-70%" and "42%-72%" while BETWEEN pairs pulled out of the continua "B happy to
B fear" and "C happy to C fear" are "30%-60%", "32%-62%", "34%-64%" and "36%-66%",
in order to respect the categorical boundary for all the three continua. Second, four WITHIN
pairs (two different morphed images both identified as fear, for instance) were created. These
pairs were for continua A, B and C "1%-31%", "8%-38%", "64%-94%" and "69%-99%".

Third, eight SAME pairs were generated for methodological purpose (the same image presented twice). Indeed, we made SAME pairs in order to have an equivalent number of same and different pairs to present to subjects. These SAME pairs are for continua A, B and C "10%-10%", "20%-20%", "30%-30%", "40%-40%", "60%-60%", "70%-70%", "80%-80%" and "90%-90%". Note that the physical difference between the stimuli of BETWEEN and WITHIN pairs was fixed (30%).

Forty-eight pairs were available (24 SAME pairs and 24 different pairs with 12 BETWEEN and 12 WITHIN pairs). In order to increase the signal-to-noise ratio, these pairs were repeated 6 times, so that 288 trials (144 SAME, 72 BETWEEN and 72 WITHIN) were recorded. All stimuli were used equally often in each of the three conditions.

During the EEG recording, subjects sat on a chair in a dark room with their head restrained by a chin rest. Their heads were placed one meter from the screen, and stimuli were 6cm horizontal and 8cm vertical; stimuli thus subtended a visual angle of 3°*4°. Subjects were presented with 12 blocks of 24 pairs of stimuli, the BETWEEN, WITHIN and SAME pairs being randomly intermixed within each block of trials. The order of the 12 blocks was also counterbalanced across subjects. A small white cross lasting 300ms on the centre of the screen followed then by a black screen for 400ms signalled the beginning of each trial. Then, the first image was presented for 400ms. A black screen was displayed for 1300ms before the onset of the second image for 400ms. The intertrial interval lasted 1500ms (black screen), but subjects had 1200ms after the second stimulus onset to answer. The participants had to decide as quickly and as accurately as possible whether the second image of the pair was exactly the same as the first one (delayed same-different matching task). This task shares the same goal with the ABX discrimination task used in the categorical perception literature, i.e. to show an enhanced discriminability for BETWEEN-categorical differences as compared to WITHIN-categorical differences; with the advantage that memory load component is reduced (Campanella et al., 2000). Subjects had to press the right or left key on a mouse with the right finger. The labeling (same/different) of the buttons was counterbalanced across subjects.

Subjects

Twelve new participants (right-handed males, 21-26 years, without neurological disease and with normal/corrected vision) volunteered for cash in the ERP experiment.

Results

The main result of this study is that the perceptual categorization of happiness and fear facial expressions takes place early in the perceptual face processing system, at around 170ms following stimulus onset, in the bilateral occipito-temporal regions.

Indeed, several ERP visual studies have evidenced a negative occipito-temporal component, the N170 (e.g., Bentin, Allison, Puce, Perez, & McCarthy, 1996), recorded around 170 ms after stimulus onset. The N170 responds preferentially (and maximally at the right hemisphere) to faces as compared to objects and was functionally referred to the structural encoding stage of the Bruce and Young's model (1986). This stage was usually considered as allowing subjects to generate a configurational representation of the observed face. In our study, we showed that, following the second face onset in the pair, the amplitude of the bilateral occipito-temporal negativities (N170) was reduced for WITHIN and SAME pairs relative to BETWEEN ones (Figure 3).

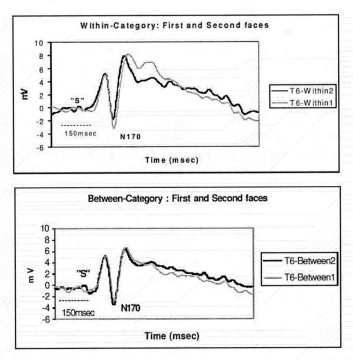

Figure 3. The N170 (recorded at occipito-temporal sites, right electrode T6 and left T5) presents a lower amplitude in response to the second faces of WITHIN and SAME pairs, as compared with the one evoked in response to the second faces of BETWEEN pairs (note that no difference emerged when first faces of the pairs were compared). This was true as in the right than in the left hemisphere, and was interpreted as a "priming" effect.

The higher amplitude of the N170 for the second face of BETWEEN pairs as compared to WITHIN and SAME pairs can be understood by the fact that subjects are confronted with two faces (in BETWEEN pairs) perceived as different expressions (happiness and fear) by the perceptual system. Two different configurational facial analyses have thus to be performed successively in the BETWEEN condition, whereas in the WITHIN and SAME conditions, the second facial expression belongs to the same expression as the first one. Several ERP studies have shown that successive repetitions of words, objects and faces lead to a reduction in ERPs amplitudes (Schweinberger, 1996; Paller & Gross, 1998). Concerning face processing in particular, repetition-priming effects on ERPs, indexed by a lower amplitude to the second face presentation, have already been observed (Begleiter, Porjesz & Wang, 1995; Ji, Porjesz & Begleiter, 1998; Henson, Shallice & Dolan, 2000).

Considering these evidences, we proposed that the striking reduction in the N170 amplitude to the second face of the SAME and WITHIN pairs reflects a *repetition priming effect*. In fact, BETWEEN pairs are constituted by two faces showing two different emotional expressions, while SAME and WITHIN pairs refer to the same one. These results indicate that the categorical perception of human facial emotional expressions has a perceptual origin in the bilateral occipito-temporal regions, while typical prior studies found emotion-modulated ERP components considerably later.

DISCUSSION

The hallmark of categorical perception is that subjects hardly discriminate two different morphed faces representing a same emotional expression as compared with two different faces representing two different facial expressions (the physical distance inside each pair being kept constant). Several studies have investigated this phenomenon at a behavioral level (Etcoff & Magee, 1992; Calder et al., 1996; Young et al., 1997). In a first ERP study (Campanella et al., 2002a), we showed that CP of facial expressions -characterized by a latency delay in the discrimination of within-differences- does not only affect the P3b component, a neurophysiological component functionally related to a decisional-motor stage of subjects' response, but also an earlier component (around 270ms), the N2/P3a, which is more related to an attentional orienting complex (Halgren & Marinkovic, 1995). At this point, a question arises: could CP of emotional expressions affect early perceptive stages of face processing? In the present ERP experiment (Campanella et al., 2002b), we showed that the temporal course of the perceptual categorization of happiness and fear facial expressions takes place early in the perceptual face processing system, at around 170ms following stimulus onset, in the bilateral occipito-temporal regions. However, whether the results so far suggest that face expression affects structural encoding if the task requires face emotional matching, we have to note that some ERP studies showed no perceptual priming effects, regardless of whether the task was a simple oddball or a speeded face recognition (Bentin & Deouell, 2000). In other words, tasks requiring explicit emotion identification involved later ERP components modulations. Then, we put forward the hypothesis that, unlike explicit identification, (implicit) emotional face matching is a shallow perceptual task that is probably based on shallow (structural encoding) processes. This is particularly important as we showed in this experiment that our brain was able as early as about 170 ms to discriminate between fearful and happy facial emotional representations. We suggest that this effect has a primordial adaptive value, as failing to allocate special attention to potentially dangerous stimuli (such as fearful faces) could result in no coping or in inappropriate coping. A better understanding of the neural mechanisms implied in the decoding of emotions (and particularly, in this case, of the fear emotion) could help us to put light on the deficits shown by many psychiatric disorders in the decoding of emotions. To illustrate this point of view, we can refer for instance to Clark (1999), who has proposed several mechanisms -one of them directly pertaining to the deployment of attention- that can account for the persistence of anxiety disorder. According to the sustained vigilance model (Beck, Emery and Greenberg, 1985), anxious individuals would be characterized by an overactive fear cognitive representation, leading them to over-perceive threat in their environment. An alternative view is proposed by the sustained avoidance model (Clark & Wells, 1995), suggesting that anxious individuals are actively avoiding threat stimuli when such a cognitive avoidance might provide them an escape from the feared situation. Establishing which model is would be of particular importance, not only for theoretical reasons, but also for applied concerns. In fact, while the sustained vigilance model implies that anxious individuals should be trained to redirect their attention on non-threatening information in order to have a less biased perception of reality, the sustained avoidance model suggests that anxious individuals should focus their attention on stimuli initially perceived as threatening in order to disconfirm this initial impression, or to develop their abilities to confront anxious situations. Another example could be furnished by psychopathy. This generally referred to anti-social behaviors, which are principally defined by DSM IV as agressive behaviors directed to animals or humans, aggravated theft and disrespect of the laws, and which is typically correlated to the ADHD deficit (Attention Deficit - Hypercativity Disorder) (Mc Ardle et al., 1995). Studies investigating the recognition of emotional facial expressions showed as main result that psychopathics have a reduced experience of the fear emotional expression (Ogloff & Wong, 1990). We suggest that understanding the functional origin of these deficits and their neural correlates will help us to have a better understanding of the clinical symptomatology of these patients, the final goal being to optimize our therapeutical approach.

CONCLUSIONS

The main result of the present experiment consists in showing that our brain was able as early as about 170 ms to discriminate between fearful and happy emotional facial expressions. This suggests that the categorical discrimination of these emotions has an early perceptual origin, around 170 ms, in the bilateral occipito-temporal regions. Bilateral activations in the occipito-temporal cortex during unpleasant emotions have also been observed (e.g., Lane, Reiman, Bradley, Lang, Ahern, Davidson & Schwartz, 1997). It is suggested that the amygdala may be playing some role in tuning the visual system to become more sensitive to threat cues (Davidson & Irwin, 1999) by means of efferent projections to primary sensory areas (Amaral, Price, Pitkanen & Carmichael, 1992; Ledoux, 1995). Indeed, several studies have shown that the human amygdala is processing the emotional salience of faces, with a specificity of the left amygdala response to fear faces (Morris, Frith, Perrett, Rowland, Young, Calder & Dolan, 1996; Breiter, Etcoff, Whalen, Kennedy, Rauch, Buckner, Strauss, Hyman & Rosen, 1996), even if they were not perceived consciously (Whalen, Rauch, Etcoff, McInerney, Lee & Jenike, 1998).

We have to outline that the amygdala seems to have a key role in the decoding of threatening stimuli, such as fearful faces, by tuning for instance our visual system in order to *quickly* re-orient our attention to furnish fast and adapted reactions. However, a recent functional magnetic resonance imaging (fMRI) study demonstrated that the engagement of the right prefrontal cortex during the cognitive evaluation of angry and fearful facial expressions is associated with an attenuation of the response of the amygdala to these same stimuli, providing evidence for a functional neural network for emotional evaluation (Hariri et al., 2003). These results point to the importance of neocortical regions, including the prefrontal and anterior cingulate cortices, in regulating emotional responses mediated by the amygdala through conscious evaluation and appraisal. This clearly suggests that we have to consider psychiatric disorders as resulting from the dysfunction of a neural network, represented by dynamic interactions, and not as being related to a single deficit of a specific neural mechanism (Davidson et al., 2002).

ACKNOWLEDGMENTS

We thank Professors Raymond Bruyer, Xavier Seron, Marc Crommelinck, Jean-Michel Guérit and Dr. Damien Debatisse for their helpful suggestions and comments. We also thank all the students and PHD students who participated in our experiments.

The author was supported by the Belgian National Fund of Scientific Reserach (F.N.R.S.).

REFERENCES

Almassy, N., Edelman, G.M., & Sporns, O. (1998). Behavioral constraints in the development of neuronal properties: a cortical model embedded in a real-world. *Cerebral Cortex*, 8(4), 346-361.

Amaral, D.G., Price, J.L., Pitkanen, A., & Carmichael, S.T. (1992). Anatomical organization of the primate amygdaloid complex. In *The Amygdala- Neurobiological Aspects of Emotion, Memory and Mental Dysfunction*, ed. J. Aggleton. Wiley, New York, pp 1-66.

Beck, A.T., Emery, G. & Greenberg, R.L. (1985). Cognitive structures and anxiogenic rules. In A.T., Beck, G., Emery & R.L. Greenberg (Eds), *Anxiety disorders and phobias* (54-66). New York: Basic books.

Begleiter, H., Porjesz, B., Wang, W.Y. (1995). Event-related brain potentials differentiate priming and recognition to familiar and unfamiliar faces. *Electroencephalography and Clinical Neurophysiology*, 94(1), 41-49.

Bentin, S., Allison, T., Puce, A., Perez, E., McCarthy, G. (1996). Electrophysiological studies of face perception in humans. *Journal of Cognitive Neuroscience*, 8, 551-565.

Bentin, S., & Deouell, L.Y. (2000). Structural encoding and identification in face processing: ERP evidence for separate mechanisms. *Cognitive Neuropsychology*, 17 (1/2/3), 35-54.

Bimler, D., & Kirkland, J. (2001). Categorical perception of facial expressions of emotion: Evidence for multidimensional scaling. *Cognition & Emotion,* 15(5), 633-658.

Bornstein, M.H., Korda, N.O. (1984). Discrimination and matching within and between hues measured by reaction times : Some implications for categorical perception and levels of information processing. *Psychological Research*, 46, 207-222.

Bornstein, M.H., & Monroe, M.D. (1980). Chromatic information processing: rate depends on stimulus location in the category and psychological complexity. *Psychological Research*, 42, 213-225.

Breiter, H.C., Etcoff, N.L., Whalen, P.J., Kennedy, W.A., Rauch, S.L., Buckner, R.L., Strauss, M.M., Hyman, S.E., & Rosen, B.R. (1996). Response and habituation of the human amygdala during visual processing of facial expression. *Neuron*, 17, 875-887.

Bruce, V., & Young, A.W. (1986). Understanding face recognition. *British Journal of Psychology*, 77, 305-327.

Calder, A.J., Young, A.W., Perrett, D.I., Etcoff, N.L., Rowland, D. (1996). Categorical perception of morphed facial expressions. *Visual Cognition*, 3, 81-117.

Calder, A.J., Keane, J., Cole, J., Campbell, R., & Young, A.W. (2000). Facial expression recognition by people with Möbius syndrome. *Cognitive Neuropsychology*, 17 (1/2/3), 73-87.

Calder, A.J., Burton, A.M., Miller, P., Young, A.W., & Akamatsu, S. (2001). A principal component analysis of facial expressions. *Vision Research*, 41, 1179-1208.

Campanella, S., Hanoteau, C., Dépy, D., Rossion, B., Bruyer, R., Crommelinck, M., & Guerit, J.M.(2000). Right N170 modulation in a face discrimination task : an account for categorical perception of familiar faces. *Psychophysiology*, 37(6), 796-806.

Campanella, S., Gaspard, C., Debatisse, D., Bruyer, R., & Guérit, J.M. (2002 a). Discrimination of emotional facial expressions in a visual oddball task: an ERP study. *Biological Psychology*, 59, 171-186.

Campanella, S., Quinet, P., Bruyer, R., Crommelinck, M., & Guérit, J.M. (2002 b). Categorical perception of happiness and fear facial expressions : an ERP study. *Journal of Cognitive Neuroscience*, 14(2), 210-227.

Clark, D.M., & Wells, A. (1995). A cognitive model of social phobia. In R. Heimberg, M. Liebowitz, D.A. Hope, & F.R. Schneier (Eds.), *Social phobia: diagnosis, assessment and treatment*. New York: Guilford Press.

Clark, D.M. (1999). Anxiety disorders: why do they persist and how to treat them. *Behavior Research and Therapy*, 37, 5-27.

Davidson, R.J., & Irwin, W. (1999). The functional neuroanatomy of emotion and affective style. *Trends in Cognitive Sciences*, 3(1), 11-21.

Davidson, R.J., Pizzagalli, D., Nitschke, J.B., & Putnam, K. (2002). Depression: Perspectives from Affective Neuroscience. *Annual Review of Psychology*, 53, 545-574.

De Gelder, B., Teunisse, J.P., Benson, P.J. (1997). Categorical perception of facial expressions : categories and their internal structure. *Cognition and Emotion*, 11, 1-23.

Ekman, P., & Friesen, W.V. (1976). *Pictures of facial affect*. Palo Alto, CA: Consulting Psychologists Press.

Etcoff, N.L., Magee, J.J. (1992). Categorical perception of facial expressions. *Cognition*, 44, 227-240.

Granato, P., Bruyer, R., & Revillon, J.J. (1996). Etude objective de la percpetion du sourire et de la tristesse par la méthode d'analyse de recherche de l'intégration des émotions "MARIE". *Annales Médico-Psychologiques*, 154 (1), 1-9.

Hariri, A.R., Mattay, V.S., Tessitore, A., Fera, F., & Weinberger, D.R. (2003). Neocortical modulations of the amygdala response to fearful stimuli. *Biological Psychiatry*, 53, 494-501.

Harnad, S. (Ed.) (1987). *Categorical Perception : The groundwork of cognition*. Cambridge : Cambridge

Hautecoeur, P., Debruyne, P., Forzy, G., Gallois, P., Hache, J.-C., Dereux, J.-F. (1993). Potentiels évoqués visuels et reconnaissance des visages. Influence de la célébrité et de l'expression émotionnelle. *Revue Neurologique (Paris)*, 149(3), 207-212.

Henson, R., Shallice, T., & Dolan, R. (2000). Neuroimaging evidence for dissociable forms of repetition priming. *Science*, 287, 1269-1272.

Ji, J., Porjesz, B., Begleiter, H. (1998). ERP components in category matching tasks. *Evoked Potentials-Electroencephalography and Clinical Neurophysiology*, 108(4), 380-389.

Kotsoni, E., de Haan, M., & Johnson, M.H. (2001). Categorical perception of facial expressions by 7-months old infants. *Perception*, 30(9), 1115-1125.

Kunst-Wilson, W.R., & Zajonc, R.B. (1980). Affective discrimination of stimuli that cannot be recognized. *Science*, 207, 557-558.

Lane, R.D., Reiman, E.M., Bradley, M.M., Lang, P.J., Ahern, G.L., Davidson, R.J., & Schwartz, G.E. (1997). Neuroanatomical correlates of pleasant and unpleasant emotion. *Neuropsychologia*, 35(11), 1437-1444.

Ledoux, J. E. (1995). In search of an emotional system in the brain: Leaping from fear to emotion and consciousness. In *The Cognitive Neuroscience*, M.S. Gazzaniga (Editor), MIT Press, Cambridge, Massachusetts, pp. 1049-1061.

Liberman, A.M., Harris, K.S., Hoffman, H.S., Griffith, B.C. (1957). The discrimination of speech sounds within and across phoneme boundaries. *Journal of Experimental Psychology*, 53, 368-385.

McArdle, P., O'Brien, G., & Kolvin, I. (1995). Hypercativity: Prevalence and relationship with conduct disorder. *Journal of Child psychology and Psychiatry*, 36(2), 279-303.

Morris, J.S., Frith, C.D., Perrett, D.I., Rowland, D., Young, A.W., Calder, A.J., & Dolan, R.J. (1996). A differential neural response in the human amygdala to fearful and happy facial expressions. *Nature*, 383, 812-815.

Münte, T.F., Brack, M., Grootheer, O., Wieringa, B.M., Matzke, M., & Johannes, S. (1998). Brain potentials reveal the timing of face identity and expression judgments. *Neuroscience Research*, 30, 25-34.

Murphy, S.T., & Zajonc, R.B. (1993). Affect, cognition, and awareness: affective priming with optimal and suboptimal stimulus exposure. *Journal of Personality and Social Psychology*, 64, 723-739.

Ogloff, J.R., & Wong, S. (1990). Electrodermal and cardiovascular evidence of a coping response in psychopaths. *Criminal Justice and Behaviour*, 17, 231-245.

Orozco, S., & Ehlers, C.L. (1998). Gender differences in electrophysiological responses to facial stimuli. *Biological Psychiatry, 44,* 281-289.

Paller, K.A., & Gross, M. (1998). Brain potentials associated with perceptual priming vs. explicit remembering during the repetition of visual word-form. *Neuropsychologia*, 36(6), 559-571.

Pizzagalli, D., Regard, M., & Lehmann, D. (1999). Rapid emotional face processing in the human right

Potter, D.D., & Parker, D.M. (1989). Electrophysiological correlates of facial identity and expression processing. In: Crawford, J.R., Parker, D.M. (Eds), *Developments in Clinical and Experimental Neuropsychology*. Plenum Press, New York, pp 143-155.

Schweinberger, S.R. (1996). How Gorbachev primed Yeltsin: Analyses of associative priming in person recognition by means of reaction times and event-related potentials. *Journal of Experimental Psychology-Learning, Memory and Cognition*, 22(6), 1383-1407.

Treue, S., & Maunsell, J.H.R. (1996). Attentional modulation of visual motion processing in cortical areas MT and MST. *Nature,* 382, 539-541.

Whalen, P.J., Rauch, S.L., Etcoff, N., McInerney, S.C., Lee, M.B., & Jenike, M.A. (1998). Masked presentations of emotional facial expressions modulate amygdala activity without explicit knowledge. *Journal of Neuroscience*, 18, 411-418.

Woodworth, R.S., & Schlosberg, H. (1954). *Experimental Psychology: Revised edition.* New York: Henry Holt.

Young, A.W., Rowland, D., Calder, A.J., Etcoff, N.L., Seth, A., Perrett, D.I. (1997). Facial expression megamix : Tests of dimensional and category accounts of emotion recognition. *Cognition*, 63, 271-313.

Chapter 11

EVOLVED COGNITIVE ARCHITECTURE MEDIATING FEAR: A GENOMIC CONFLICT APPROACH

*William Michael Brown**

Dalhousie University

ABSTRACT

Recent theoretical and empirical work in evolutionary biology suggests that mammalian neurocognitive architecture is not necessarily a unified whole designed to further the interests of an individual organism (Haig, 2000; Trivers, 2000). For example intragenomic conflicts may influence brain development and behaviour in accordance with probabilistic conflicts of interest between parental genomes over resources encountered by the descendant's mammalian ancestors. The phenomenon of genomic imprinting may be explained in part by conflicts of interest between parental genomes over developmental resources (e.g. growth). Genomic imprinting is differential gene expression depending upon the parental origin in which a gene was transmitted. This chapter argues that psychological resources may be a battleground for intragenomic conflicts. Motivations and cognitions are instrumental resources for the production and suppression of fitness-related behaviours, which potentially have divergent costs for parental genes. For example, the traditional view of the fear response is that it is good for individual or species survival because it allows individuals to confront or avoid threats. This hypothesis is known as the "Fight-or-Flight" (FOF) response. Neuroscientists have located particular neural systems mediating FOF. A genomic conflict view may help elucidate FOF computational machinery. Specifically it is expected that when relatedness asymmetries exist intragenomic conflicts over FOF may occur due to the divergent costs for parental genes expressed in fearful offspring. In conclusion genomic conflicts may have selected for the functional compartmentalization and manipulative interactions between brain components mediating fear.

KEYWORDS: Genomic conflict; Fear; Genomic imprinting; Cognitive neuroscience; Neuroethology

---

* Correspondence: William Michael Brown, Department of Psychology, Life Sciences Centre, Dalhousie University, Halifax, Nova Scotia, B3H 4J1, CANADA, email: wmbrown@is2.dal.ca

Fear is a psychoneuroendocrinological mechanism mediating avoidance and/or aggression. One definition of fear in the psychological literature is: "An emotional state in the presence or anticipation of a dangerous or noxious stimuli" (Reber, 1985). A common view of fear in the neuroscience literature is that fear triggers the "fight or flight" response, characterized by increased heart rate, breathing, and muscle tension, which allows the individual to escape from danger or defend itself against a predator or conspecific (LeDoux, 1995; McEwen, 1995; Armory & LeDoux, 2000; Ohman & Mineka, 2001). Based on the presence or absence of a stimulus, the brain regulates the strength and duration of this apparent coping mechanism. When this regulatory system malfunctions, however, it can lead to excessive fearfulness in certain individuals. Excessively fearful individuals appear to have difficulty suppressing the body's response to stress (Armory & LeDoux, 2000).

An evolutionary perspective may assist our conceptual understanding of fear and when it is expressed. A revised definition of fear based on evolutionary considerations is: Fear is a modulator of risk (i.e. from aversion to seeking risk) that evolved to be responsive to reliably occurring cross-generational contexts. However, fear may also be defined as an Achilles' heal of the brain that can easily be triggered (like a smoke alarm – see Nesse & Young, 2000). This chapter argues that intragenomic conflict theory (Haig, 2000; Trivers, 2000) may facilitate our understanding of the evolved neurocognitive architecture mediating fear. If fear is an evolved psychoneuroendocrinological resource producing differential costs to maternally and paternally derived genes, intragenomic conflicts may occur over individual responses. Unlike previous psychological analyses of fear I will make explicit for whom (i.e. what evolutionarily unit) fear is good for given particular ecological conditions (e.g. relatedness asymmetries within families). The reason it is necessary to be specific regarding the inclusive fitness costs and benefits across levels of selection is due to genomic imprinting, a phenomenon that 'violates' a particular Mendelian law (i.e. a gene's expression should not vary by parent of origin) and has been implicated in mammalian brain and behaviour (Lefebvre et al., 1998; Isles & Wilkinson, 2000, Davies et al., 2001; Isles et al. 2001; Keverne, 2001).

GENOMIC IMPRINTING AND GENOMIC CONFLICT

The vast majority of mammalian genes are biallelically expressed. Biallelic expression is when both parents' genes are actively transcribed in offspring. Genomic imprinting is the inactivation of a particular gene dependent upon the sex of the parent from which it was transmitted (Haig, 2000). The genomic conflict hypothesis proposes that multiple paternity favours the differential expression of maternal and paternal alleles so that (a) paternal alleles increase costs to the offspring's mother; and (b) the maternal alleles decrease these costs. Haig (1999; 2000) suggests that genomic conflict could apply to all costs imposed on a mother that benefit offspring. Indeed the genomic conflict hypothesis applies to all interactions between relatives with different maternal and paternal coefficients of relatedness (Haig 1997a).

GENOMIC CONFLICT AND FEAR

If parental genes consistently find themselves in a non-natal environment with non-kin it could be beneficial to be weary of and aggressive toward others. The dispersing sex has a distinct advantage in manipulating the fear response of offspring since dispersal can have an effect of relatedness asymmetries among collateral kin (e.g. cousins). Relatedness asymmetries may be defined as the differences between coefficients of relatedness for parental genomes (Haig, 1997a). Specifically an individuals kin can be categorized as *symmetric* relatives (with *equal* probabilities of sharing copies of an individuals maternally and paternally derived genes) and *asymmetric* relatives (with *unequal* probabilities of sharing an individuals maternally and paternally derived genes). Inclusive fitness theory (Hamilton, 1964) generally deals with the issue of asymmetric kin by employing an average coefficient of relatedness (i.e. the probability that a rare gene is shared from a recent common ancestor). Average coefficients of relatedness are based on the assumption that maternally and paternally derived alleles are constrained to have the same effects. However, when this assumption is relaxed, relatedness asymmetries influence the chances of internal conflicts within individuals over cognition and behaviour (Haig, 1997a; 2000). Another pathway to relatedness asymmetries is multiple paternity. For example if mother produces several offspring with different males, paternal genetic relatedness decreases between siblings, increasing the potential for internal conflict. However even if intragenomic conflicts over fear occur, what are the neurobiological mechanisms involved?

Brain Development and Genomic Imprinting

Evidence suggests that imprinted genes influence brain development, behaviour and cognition (Isles & Wilkinson, 2000; Davies et al., 2001; Goos & Silverman, 2001; Keverne, 2001). For example, human females with Turner's syndrome who inherit an X chromosome from their mother have higher scores on social cognitive dysfunction than females who inherit an X chromosome from father (Skuse et al., 1997). This suggests that mother's X-chromosome plays a role in human social cognitive capacities. Interestingly, findings in mice show that imprinted genes are involved in neural development (e.g. the neocortex and hypothalamus – see Keverne et al., 1996) and maternal investment (e.g. grooming offspring – see Lefebvre et al., 1998; Li et al., 1999). See Table 1 for some of the brain areas related to imprinted genes.

Table 1. Brain areas and genomic imprinting (by parental origin)

BRAIN AREA	PARENTAL ORIGIN
Hypothalamus	Paternal gene expression
Amygdala	Paternal gene expression
Cortex	Maternal gene expression
Hippocampus	Maternal gene expression
Striatum	Maternal gene expression

Specifically, maternal genes are over-expressed (relative to paternal) in the neocortex and hippocampus while paternal genes (relative to maternal) are over-expressed in the hypothalamus and amygdala (Isles & Wilkinson, 2000; Keverne, 2001). Interestingly these brain components are implicated in fear responses (Fischer et al., 2000; Armory & LeDoux, 2000; Kim at el., 2001; Lathe, 2001).

Neurobiology of Fear

When an animal receives sensory input that is recognized as dangerous, the neurons from the sensory organ send signals to the amygdala (Black, 1998). The amygdala then influences the hypothalamus to produce corticotropin-releasing hormone (CRH). CRH release triggers discharges of adrenocorticotropic hormone (ACTH) from the pituitary gland. ACTH then to stimulate the adrenal gland to produce cortisol. Cortisol levels in the blood cause increases in glucose production (Black, 1998).

Studies of neuronal activity in response to fearful stimuli suggest that the prefrontal cortex (i.e. a cognitive and emotional learning center that helps interpret sensory stimuli) is involved in the conscious assessment of threat. After sensory information passes through the amygdala it is transmitted to the cortex. There, the threat is examined in detail presumably to determine whether or not a real danger exists. This is potentially one of the steps in the processing of fear in which the manipulation of sensory information could occur. If paternally derived brain components respond to a paternal-specific threat (i.e. where behavioural output benefits paternal genes at a cost to maternal genes) there may be an 'arms race' between neural responses. Based on information generated in the cortex regarding the content of the threat, the amygdala could be either signalled to perpetuate or to abort the fear response (Le Doux, 1995). Whether or not the amygdala 'complies' may have been influenced by ancestral evolutionary conflicts. Game theoretical considerations on reliable signalling and reciprocity could play some role in the 'decisions' made by the amygdala. These speculations regarding internal computational conflicts over fear may be orchestrated via the elaborate connections within the neural system mediating fear (See Figure 1).

Why are there different brain areas involved in fear responses? Furthermore, if fear responses were designed by natural selection to solely benefit individual survival and reproduction why would maternal and paternal genes exhibit differential expression in the areas mediating in fear? A simply proximate answer is that paternal and maternal genes are cooperating for the collective good (i.e. the individual organism's survival and reproduction). However intuitive this 'answer' appears, cooperation cannot be assumed, rather synergism (even within organisms) must be rigorously explained evolutionarily (Haig, 1997b). Cooperation between brain components cannot be assumed when conflicts of interest between maternal and paternal genes could arise over information-processing. Figure 1 shows the afferents and efferents facilitating interaction between the brain components moderating fear responses. Specifically it appears that there are ample opportunity within the brain for cooperation and conflict over emotional and cognitive responses to threats. It appears that maternal genes are linked to cognitive appraisals of threat, while paternal genes influence the initial emotional response to threat.

Anatomical Organization - Afferents And Efferents

Intragenomic conflicts over fear could modulate: a) the so-called 'fight-or-flight' response; b) the activation / suppression of fear; and c) fear memory consolidation.

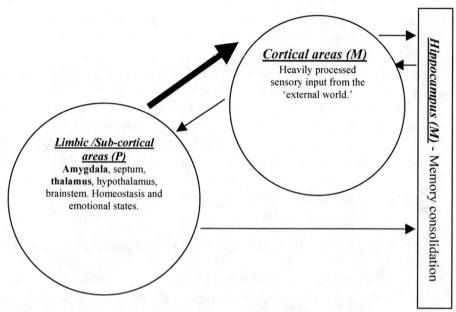

Figure 1. Possible influences of parental genes and inter-relationships between global brain areas mediating fear. Heavier arrow denotes stronger connections. "M" is maternal gene expression, while "P" denotes paternal gene expression. Since there appears to be a division of labour among brain components (of different parental origins) the possibility of manipulation of sensory input, emotional response, and memory consolidation is possible.

Interestingly LeDoux et al (1985) have suggested that the amygdala has a greater number of efferent (compared to afferent) connections transmitting information to the cortex. Furthermore, this is not the case between the thalamus and amygdala. Perhaps the amygdala 'trusts' information sent from the thalamus more than the highly modified (or adaptively filtered from the point of view of mother's genes) cortical information. This speculation implies that increased or highly processed information allows for sensory biases (Holland & Rice, 1997).

In Figure 1 a hypothesized system for how genomic conflicts over fear are implemented in the brain is presented. Maternal genes may be involved the social cognitive activation and suppression of the fear response. Paternal genes could manipulate emotional machinery to be fast acting and impulsive to avoid cognitive manipulation or adjust information that was modified in the hippocampus and/or cortex to favour maternal genes. This does not necessarily imply that paternal genes will always strategically activate fear responses. However under conditions where relatedness asymmetries are high, paternal genes could favour aggression while maternal genes could favour conciliatory cognitions. For example, imagine a family conflict between half-siblings (e.g. physical aggression). Presume that the two siblings have different fathers (i.e. paternal relatedness = 0) but the same mother (i.e.

maternal relatedness = 1.00). Relatedness in this case is the likelihood that the two siblings share a particular gene for cooperating with one another that they received from their mother. Based on this relatedness asymmetry it would be predicted that paternally derived brain areas (e.g. the hypothalamus and the amygdala) might activate an aggressive response in situations where a paternally unrelated sibling is the transgressor. However, since maternal relatedness is high the hippocampus and cortex may 'downplay' the transgression (e.g. "your sister did not mean to steal your radio"; "she was just teasing you, forgive her"; "your brother did not intend to punch you that hard"). Such cognitions could be orchestrated to de-escalate conflict and thus the costs to maternal genes.

Based on genomic conflict theory it is predicted that relatedness asymmetries may select for intragenomic conflict over all information that has differential costs for maternal and paternal genes. In the case of sibling aggression one may predict that paternal genes would influence the decoding of sensory information during sibling conflict in such a way as to facilitate retaliation. However, maternally derived brain areas may attempt to suppress anger (e.g. by placing the transgression in a forgivable context). In cases where relatedness is more symmetrical (two siblings share the same mother and father) it is predicted that internal conflicts between brain and cognitive components are minimized.

FIGHT OR FLIGHT: GOOD FOR WHOM?

Why fight or flight? What evolutionary forces modulate choices for one strategy over the other? One obvious response to these questions is that you should only fight when you are going to succeed in the competition. This would be a conventional approach to the problem and does not take into account relatedness asymmetries between individuals during a within-family conflict. Table 2 depicts a hypothesized conflict mediating divergent fear responses within an individual.

Table 2. Internal conflicts over fight or flight within a family context

SENSORY INPUT *Maternally related half-sibling attacks you.*	
DIVERGENT NEURAL RESPONSE	**DIVERGENT OUTPUT**
Paternal - Amygdala and hypothalamus coordinate anger response.	*Paternal* - 'Fight' response / retaliation toward paternally unrelated half-sibling.
Maternal - Hippocampus / cortex counter-response places transgression in maternally beneficial context (e.g. "you deserved the attack").	*Maternal* - 'Flight' response and/or reconciliation between maternal relatives.

OUT OF CONTROL FEAR

Are there examples of hyper- or hypo-fear states relating to imprinted genes? Imprinted genes influencing serotonin reuptake could be involved. Raine et al (1998) suggest that fearlessness may be associated with larger body size, abnormal functioning of both the amygdala and the prefrontal cortex. Interestingly, children with hypothalamic hamartomas (tumour like but non-neoplasmic overgrowth of tissue that is disordered in structure) show higher incidences of oppositional defiant disorder (Weissenberger et al. 2001). Individuals who are particularly violent appear to have greater activity in the hypothalamus / amygdala and have blunted cortical activity (e.g. orbital frontal and anterior cingulate – see Davidson, 2001). Bunzel et al. (1998) and Kato et al. (1996) have shown that imprinted genes (maternally derived) may be implicated in the serotonin-2A (5HT-2A) receptor gene in humans. Serotonin is involved in the stress response (specifically in reducing impulsive aggression (Davidson et al., 2000). These findings appear consistent with theoretical work suggesting that maternal genes would benefit from contributing to the collective good; while paternal genes may benefit from exploiting the collective good (Haig & Wilkins, 2000).

FEARFUL ASYMMETRY: PATERNAL
AND MATERNAL X CHROMOSOMES

Females get an X-chromosome from their heterogametic father (XY) and an X-chromosome from their homogametic mother (XX). Therefore there is a 100 percent chance that a father with X-linked anxiety will pass this trait to daughters. When anxiety is X-linked on the paternal side, the probability that a son received an 'anxiety-related gene' from his father is zero. However, a mother who has X-linked anxiety has a 50 percent chance of passing the disorder to sons or daughters. This asymmetry may account for sex differences in anxiety (females outnumber males). This speculation entertains the possibility of a paternal basis to anxiety. Interestingly boys with fragile X syndrome (X inherited from mother) appear to have social cognitive deficits (Hessel et al., 2001). This finding is consistent with the hypothesis that maternal genes may be contributing to social cognitive capacity in humans. Paternal genes may contribute to the fear response. Girls with fragile X syndrome share an entire X-chromosome with their father. Daughters with a paternally derived fragile X syndrome exhibit higher levels of anxiety and avoidance compared to boys with a maternally derived X-chromosome (Hessel et al., 2001).

Searching the National Institute of Health's Online Mendelian Inheritance in Man (http://www3.ncbi.nlm.nih.gov/Omim/searchomim.html) suggests that anxiety-related mental dysfunction may be linked to imprinted genes. Anxiety and panic symptoms appear to vary with imprinting effects dealing with maternal deletions and or variants (i.e. disrupted function of maternal version of the gene). Perhaps the presence and absence of anxiety in individuals with imprinting disorders could be due to differences in brain components regulating fear (e.g. amygdala and/or cortical areas).

Table 3. Presence or absence of fear symptoms in individuals with commonly imprinted disorders (by parental origin). "P" is paternal and "M" is maternal basis

Fear symptoms	Disorder	Imprinted basis (P vs. M)
No	Prader-Willi syndrome	P loss
Yes	Angelman syndrome	M loss
No/Yes	Turner's syndrome	P loss / M loss
Yes/No	Uniparental disomy	P loss / M loss
Yes/No	Tourette's syndrome	Potentially P or M transmission *

*Tourette's syndrome may have parent of origin effects. However imprinting still has not been *unequivocally* established in the peer-reviewed literature.

SOCIAL TRANSMISSION AND FEAR: EME-GENE CONFLICT?

According to Brown (2001a) maternal genes may play a role in the social cognitive capacities for culture (i.e. the social transmission of information and behaviour). Indeed this may help explain why there is reduced mtDNA variability in whale species with matrilineal cultural inheritance of dialect (Whitehead, 1998). Social information from mother may be more reliable due to relatedness asymmetries (Haig, 2000; Brown, 2001a). In the case of fear it can be imagined that socially learned rules (designed to evoke a fear of punishment) might be more in the domain of maternal than paternal genes. Indeed one could argue that socially learned prohibitions may be specifically designed to reduce the threat of paternal genes exploiting the collective good in cases where paternal relatedness is lower than maternal relatedness (Haig, 1999).

Interestingly some phobias (e.g. snake) may be socially transmitted in primates, including humans (Mineka & Cook, 1988; Fredrikson, Annas, & Wik, 1997). Fear of snakes may be culturally transmitted from mother to offspring. That is, a mother's repeated exposure to snakes appears to increase the likelihood of phobia in her offspring (Frdrikson, 1997). If behavioural modeling of fear is occurring in humans, perhaps this occurs matrilineally.

The fossil record (Armstrong, 1982) and comparative ethological research suggests that that the neocortical expansion evolved a social navigational environment (Dunbar, 1992). Keverne (2001) suggests that genomic conflict may have influenced the exponential increase in neocortex size. Maternal genes (via the neocortex) could be responsible for navigating through social relationships largely made up of unrelated dispersing males and closely related collateral kin. Keverne (2001) envisions neocortical expansion as a strategy in which maternal genes escape the "emancipation" of paternally mediated endocrine determinism. To support this hypothesis there has been a decrease in size of the hypothalamus, medial preoptic area and septum, while at the same time there has been an increase in the striatum and neocortex in mammals (Keverne et al., 1996; Brown, 2001b; de Winter & Oxnard, 2001).

CONCLUSIONS

This paper is the first to speculate regarding the relative roles of genomic imprinting and potential conflicts between maternal and paternal genes over the modulation of fear. Perhaps it is time that we view an organism as a parliament of interests. Evolved psychological mechanisms may be great problem-solvers while at the same time creating new adaptive problems for conflicting lower-level evolutionary units (e.g. paternal vs. maternal genes). When we find a coordinated fear response in an organism designed by paternal and maternal genes this could be due to coinciding fitness interests of lower-level evolutionary units.

The numerous anxiety disorders found in modern populations could be due to imprinting gone awry. Specifically perhaps the balanced tug of war between paternal and maternal genes has given way to one side winning the battle due to the ultimate detriment of the afflicted individual. However, there are numerous conditions when maternal and paternal genes may 'agree' over fear responses (e.g. predator avoidance, visual cliff, fear of infection, dangerous conspecific etc.).

A genomic conflict approach to fear may be worthwhile. For example, particular developmental disorders with an imprinted basis appear to modulate stress responses in humans. Furthermore, as seen in mice imprinted genes affect some of the neural areas involved in fear responses (e.g. amygdala, hippocampus, cortex and hypothalamus). Theoretically it may be justifiable to see fear as a psychological resource that is capable of altering an individual's behaviour in fitness-enhancing, fitness-reducing and fitness-neutral directions. Relatedness asymmetries complicate what is fitness enhancing and reducing. Therefore it may be necessary for evolutionarily minded fear researchers to consider how fear benefits (and costs) lower level evolutionary units when there are conflicts of interest over particular courses of action.

ACKNOWLEDGEMENTS

I would like to thank Boris Palameta and Pete Richerson for their helpful comments. Scholarship funding for this research was from the Natural Sciences and Engineering Research Council (CANADA) and the Isaak Walton Memorial Trust.

REFERENCES

Allen, N.D., Logan, K., Lally, G., Drage, D.J., Norris, M.L., & Keverne, E.B. (1995). Distribution of parthenogenetic cells in the brain development and behavior. *Proceedings of the National Academy of Sciences, 92,* 10782-10786.

Armory, J.L., & LeDoux, J.E. (2000). How danger is encoded: Toward a systems,cellular, and computational understanding of cognitive-emotional interactions in fear. In M.S. Gazzaniga (Ed.) *The New Cognitive Neurosciences* (pp1067-1080). Cambridge, MA: MIT Press.

Barton, R.A. & Harvey, P.H. (2000). Mosaic evolution of brain structure in mammals. *Nature, 405,* 1055-1058.

Black H. (1998). Investigators Pinpointing Fear's Activity in the Brain. *The Scientist, 2,* 10.

Brown, W.M. (2001a). Genomic imprinting and the cognitive architecture mediating human culture. *Journal of Cognition and Culture.* 1: 251-258.

Brown, W.M. (2001b). Natural selection of mammalian brain components. *Trends in Ecology and Evolution, 16,* 471-473.

Davies, W., Isles, A.R., & Wilkinson, L.S. (2001), Imprinted genes and mental dysfunction. *Annals of Medicine, 33*, 428-436.

Dunbar, R.I.M. (1992). Neocortex size as a constraint on group size in primates. *Journalof Human Evolution, 20*, 469-493.

Fischer H, Andersson JLR, Furmark T, Fredrikson M (2000). Fear conditioning and brain activity: A positron emission tomography study in humans. *Behavioral Neuroscience, 114*, 671-680.

Fredrikson, M., Annas, P., & Wik, G. (1997). Parental history, aversion exposure, and thedevelopment of snake and spider phobia in women. *Behavior Research and Therapy, 1*, 23-28.

Goos, L.M. & Silverman, I. (2001). The influence of genomic imprinting on brain development and behavior. *Evolution and Human Behavior, 22*, 385-407

Haig D., & Wilkins, J.F. (2000). Genomic imprinting, sibling solidarity and the logic of collective action. *Philosophical Transactions: Biological Sciences (The Royal Society, 355*, 1593-1597

Haig, D. (1997). Parental antagonism, relatedness asymmetries, and genomic imprinting. *Proceedings of the Royal Society of London Series B-Biological Sciences, 264*, 1657-1662.

Haig, D. (1997). The social gene. In J.R. Krebs and N.B. Davies (Eds), *Behavioural ecology: An evolutionary approach*, Fourth edition, (pp. 284-304). Oxford, UK: Blackwell Science.

Haig, D. (1999). Multiple paternity and genomic imprinting. *Genetics, 151*, 1229-1231.

Haig, D. (2000). Genomic imprinting, sex-biased dispersal, and social behavior. *Annals of the New York Academy of Sciences, 907*, 149-163.

Isles, A.R. & Wilkinson, L.S. (2000). Imprinted genes, cognition and behaviour. *Trends in Cognitive Sciences*, 4, 309-318.

Isles, A.R., Baum, M.J., Ma, D., Keverne, E.B. & Allen, N.D. (2001). Parent of origin effects on odour preference in mice. *Nature, 409*, 783-784.

Kalin, N.H. (1993, May issue). The Neurobiology of Fear. *Scientific American*, 94-101.

Keverne, E.B. (2001). Genomic imprinting, maternal care, and brain evolution. *Hormones and Behavior, 40*, 146-155.

Keverne, E.B., Fundele, R., Narasimha, M., Barton, S.C., & Surani, M.A. (1996). Genomic imprinting and the differential roles of parental genomes in brain development. *Developmental Brain Research, 92*, 91-100.

Kim, J.J., Lee, H.J.J., Han, J.S., & Packard, M.G. (2001). Amygdala is critical for stressinduced modulation of hippocampal long-term potentiation and learning. *Journal of Neuroscience, 21*, 5222-5228.

Lathe, R. (2001). Hormones and the hippocampus Journal of Endocrinology, 169, 205231.

LeDoux, J.E. (1995). In search of an emotional system in the brain: Leaping from fear to emotion and consciousness. In M.S. Gazzaniga (Ed.) *The Cognitive Neurosciences* (pp 1049-1061). Cambridge, MA: MIT Press.

LeDoux, J.E., Ruggiero, D.A., & Reis, D.J. (1985). Projections to the subcortical forebrain defined regions of the medial geniculate body in the rat. *Journal of Comparative Neurology, 242*, 182-213.

Lefebvre, L., Viville, S., Barton, S.C., Ishino, F., Keverne, E.B. & Surani, M.A. (1998). Abnormal maternal behaviour and growth retardation associated with loss of the imprinted gene *Mest. Nature Genetics, 20,* 163-169.

Li, L.L., Keverne, E.B., Aparicio, S.A., Ishino, F., Barton, S.C. & Surani, M.A. (1999). Regulation of maternal behaviour and offspring growth by paternally expressed *Peg3. Science, 284,* 330-333.

McEwan, B.S. (1995). Stressful experience, brain, and emotions: Developmental, genetic, and hormonal influences. In M.S. Gazzaniga (Ed.) *The Cognitive Neurosciences* (pp 1117-1135). Cambridge, MA: MIT Press.

Mineka, S., & Cook, M. (1988). Social learning and the acquisition of snake fear in monkeys. In T.R. Zentall & B.G. Galef (Eds.) *Social Learning: Psychological and Biological Perspectives* (pp 51-73). Hillsdale, NJ: Lawrence Erlbaum Publishers.

Murphy, S.K., Wylie, A.A. & Jirtle, R.L. (2001). Imprinting of *PEG3* the human homologue of a mouse gene involved in nurturing behavior. *Genomics, 71,* 110-117.

Ohman, A., & Mineka, S. (2001). Fears, phobias, and preparedness: Toward and evolved module of fear and fear learning. *Psychological Review, 108,* 483-522.

Reber, A.S. *Dictionary of psychology.* Middlesex, England: Penguin.

Rice, W.R. & Holland, B. (1997). The enemies within: Intergenomic conflict, interlocus contest evolution (ICE), and the intraspecific Red Queen. *Behavioral Ecology and Sociobiology, 41,* 1-10.

Skuse, D.H., James, R.S., Bishop, D.V.M., Coppin, B., Dalton, P., Aamodt-Leeper, G., Bacarese-Hamilton, M., Creswell, C., McGurk, R., Jacobs, P.A. (1997). Evidencefrom Turner's syndrome of an imprinted X-linked locus affecting cognitive function. *Nature, 387,* 705-708.

Trivers, R. (2000). The elements of a scientific theory of self-deception. *Annals of theNew York Academy of Sciences, 907,* 114-131.

Whitehead, H. (1998). Cultural selection and genetic diversity in matrilineal whales. *Science, 282,* 1708-1711.

Wilson, D.S. & Yoshimura, J. (1994). On the coexistence of specialists and generalists. *American Naturalist, 144,* 692-707.

Chapter 12

THE ROLE OF THE HUMAN CEREBELLUM IN FEAR-CONDITIONING

Matthias Maschke, Markus Frings and Dagmar Timmann
Department of Neurology,
University of Duisburg-Essen, Hufelandstr.
55, 45122 Essen, matthias.maschke@uni-essen.de

1. ABSTRACT

The role of the cerebellum has been traditionally seen in coordination of limb movements and control of posture, gait, speech and gaze. However, results of the last decades of research suggest that the cerebellum is also crucially involved in implicit motor learning such as conditioning and habituation of specific aversive reflexes, adaptation of voluntary movements to external forces or changed visual cues and learning of complex motor skills. Recent studies provide evidence that specific cognitive processes may also rely on the integrity of the cerebellum. Moreover, it appears that the cerebellum is closely related to the autonomic nervous system. In animals, stimulation of the cerebellar vermis or fastigial nuclei, e.g., provoke changes in pupil diameter and a decrease in blood pressure. Therefore and from results of other animal experiments, it was hypothesized that the human cerebellum also modulates conditioning of unspecific aversive reactions. Here, patients with lesions involving the cerebellar vermis were tested for impairment of the fear-conditioned bradycardia and fear-conditioned potentiation of startle-reflex. Results demonstrated that controls, but not cerebellar patients, showed a significant decrease of heart rate during fear conditioning. In addition, the fear-conditioned potentiation effect of the blink reflex was significantly reduced in patients with medial cerebellar lesions compared with controls. To evaluate whether fear-conditioning or the potentiation itself are mediated by the cerebellum, a positron emission tomography (PET)- study of fear-conditioned potentiation of the startle reflex was performed in healthy human subjects. Results suggested that the left cerebellar hemisphere was activated by fear-conditioning, whereas the medial cerebellum showed a significant increase of the regional cerebellar blood flow attributable to the potentiation itself. In summary, different parts of the human cerebellum appear to be involved in conditioning of fear.

2. INTRODUCTION

2.1 The Traditional Role of the Cerebellum

In the 19th century, Rolando (1809), Fluorens (1824) and Luciani (1891) demonstrated in animals that cerebellar ablations resulted in disturbances of voluntary movements, gait and posture. Babinski (1899, 1902) and Holmes (1917, 1939) confirmed these observations in humans with lesions restricted to the cerebellum. Since then, there is a broad agreement that the main role of the cerebellum is coordination of voluntary movements, stance and gait and control of eye movements and speech. Moreover, the studies mentioned above led to the assumption that the cerebellum is not involved in perception of sensory signals and higher order functions such as attention, learning, memory and language. Additionally, it is well established that different functions are localized in different regions of the cerebellum indicating a functional compartmentalization of the human cerebellum (Dichgans and Diener 1985). Control of posture and eye movements are mediated by medial parts of the cerebellum (i.e., vermis). The lateral cerebellum (i.e., hemispheres) is especially important in coordination of goal-directed voluntary movements. Despite the prominent role of the cerebellum in motor control there were hints that the cerebellum might also take part in motor learning and cognition since the beginning of systematic cerebellar research (for review see: Schmahmann 1997).

2.2 The Cerebellar Involvement in Motor-Learning Processes

Nowadays there is little doubt that motor learning processes are mediated by the cerebellum (for review see: Thompson and Krupa 1994, Bloedel and Bracha 1995, Thach 1996, 1998). In addition to its involvement in learning of complex motor skills, it appears to be crucial for implicit learning such as habituation, adaptation and conditioning as shown by many studies in animals and humans. In particular in humans, cerebellar lesions in the territory of the posterior inferior cerebellar artery (PICA) but not in the territory of the superior cerebellar artery (SCA) led to an impairment of the adaptation of goal-directed voluntary arm movements to a visual feedback altered by prism glasses (Weiner et al. 1983, Martin et al. 1996). In contrast, classical conditioning of the eyeblink response was prevented by ischemic strokes in the SCA territory, but was preserved following lesions in the PICA territory (Gerwig et al. 2003). A similar differential impairment was demonstrated for conditioning of the limb flexion reflex, another specific aversive reaction. Patients with infarctions of the anterior lobe (SCA territory) showed absent or a low frequency of conditioned responses, whereas patients with lesions in the posterior lobe (PICA territory) revealed almost a normal frequency of conditioned responses (Timmann et al. 2000). As complement to these results functional brain imaging studies demonstrated that classical conditioning of specific aversive reactions such as the eyeblink response, limb flexion reflex and jaw opening reflex were associated with activations including the superior and intermediate parts of the cerebellum (Molchan et al. 1994, Logan and Grafton 1995, Blaxton et al. 1996, Timmann et al. 1996, Schreurs et al. 1997, Maschke et al. 2000a). Investigations of habituation processes revealed that the medial cerebellum might be critical for long-term habituation of the acoustic startle response (Timmann et al. 1998, Maschke et al. 2000b).

Together, these observations implied that different parts of the cerebellum contribute to distinct forms of associative and non-associative implicit motor learning in man. This led to an extension of the clinical functional compartmentalization of the cerebellum (Dichgans and Diener 1985) to motor learning paradigms in humans.

2.3 Does the Cerebellum Contribute to Cognitive Functions?

In contrast to the cerebellar involvement in motor learning, the contribution of the cerebellum to cognitive functions and behavior is still a matter of debate. Although some studies found only deficits in certain cognitive associative learning paradigms but not in broader cognitive functions such as attention, learning or memory (Daum and Ackermann 1995, Drepper et al. 1999, Timmann et al. 2002, Maschke et al. 2002a), others suggested a more general role of the cerebellum in cognition, affective behavior and/or personality (Fiez 1996, Thach 1998, Schmahmann and Sherman 1998). Schmahmann and Sherman (1998) labeled a symptom complex characterized by an impairment of working memory, planning, set-shifting, verbal fluency, abstract reasoning, difficulties in visuo-spatial organization, visual memory and logical sequencing and changes of affect as cerebellar cognitive affective syndrome. They found behavioral and cognitive changes most prominent in patients with lesions within the posterior lobe of the cerebellar hemisphere and the cerebellar vermis. Lesions within the posterior lobe of the cerebellum are usually not associated with severe deficits in motor control. Therefore, it may be that specific parts of the cerebellum are involved in non-motor functions and that these parts are different from those responsible for motor control.

2.4 Modulation of Autonomic Responses by the Cerebellum

Another non-motor system that might be influenced by the cerebellum is the autonomic nervous system. The pupil diameter is known to be dilated by sympathetic and decreased by parasympathetic stimulation mediated by areas within the brainstem. However, stimulation of the fastigial and interposed nuclei and the cerebellar anterior lobe resulted in changes of pupil size suggesting that the cerebellum might be part of the pathway that controls inner eye muscles (Sachs and Fincher 1927, Moruzzi 1947). Furthermore, stimulation of the vermis of the anterior lobe was followed by a decrease of blood pressure (Moruzzi 1938, Wiggers 1942). More recently it was demonstrated that the nodulus and the uvula of the cerebellum may play an important role in postural changes of blood pressure and heart rate (Nisimaru et al. 1998). Findings of these animal experiments were complemented by results of studies in humans. Critchley et al. (2000) reported that exercise and mental stressor tasks leading to increased blood pressure and heart rate were associated with activations in the cerebellar vermis, brainstem and right anterior cingulate in a positron emission tomography (PET) experiment. Activations were also observed in the lateral cerebellum. Moreover, a functional magnetic resonance imaging (fMRI) study, which investigated brain areas involved in respiratory control, further supported the cerebellar involvement in autonomic functions (Harper et al. 1998). Results showed that, in addition to expected activations within medullary and pontine areas and hypothalamus, cerebellar areas were activated related to respiratory control. Together, these studies suggest that the cerebellum may act as a functional relay between cortex and brainstem for regulation of autonomic responses, which may accompany cognitive, motor and emotional behavior.

2.5 The Role of the Cerebellum in Nociception and Fear-Conditioning

Changes of blood pressure, cardiac rhythm and pupil diameter are known to represent unspecific aversive reactions to fear- or painful stimuli. Given the results described above it was speculated that the cerebellum is involved in the modulation of these unspecific aversive reactions and nociception. Interestingly, recent functional imaging studies found activations of deep cerebellar nuclei, anterior vermis and bilaterally in the cerebellar hemispheric lobule VI evoked by noxious stimuli (Becarra et al. 1999, Bingel et al. 2002, Helmchen et al. 2003). The relationship of the cerebellum to neural circuits mediating fear was investigated by several animal and functional imaging studies (for review see: Büchel and Dolan 2000, Vazdarjanova 2002). In particular, the learning of an association between a neutral stimulus and a fear-eliciting stimulus is called fear-conditioning and is known to be mainly controlled by the amygdala (for review see: Fanselow and LeDoux 1999). In animal experiments ablation of the cerebellar vermis resulted in an impaired fear-conditioned bradycardia suggesting that the medial cerebellum is also involved in fear-conditioning (Supple and Leaton 1990a, 1990b, Sebastiani et al. 1992, Supple and Kapps 1993, Ghelarducci et al. 1996). However, others found no effect of cerebellar lesions on fear-conditioning if measured by the potentiated startle paradigm (Hitchcock and Davis 1986). Based on these animal experiments it was investigated whether the human cerebellum plays a critical role in fear-conditioning and, if so, whether fear-conditioning is mediated by a specific region of the cerebellum (Maschke et al. 2000c, Frings et al. 2002, Maschke et al. 2002b). In the following chapters, results of these experiments will be summarized and discussed.

3. FEAR-CONDITIONED BRADYCARDIA

Based on the animal experiments demonstrating an alteration of fear-conditioned bradycardia by lesions to the medial cerebellum (Supple and Leaton 1990a, 1990b, Sebastiani et al. 1992, Supple and Kapps 1993, Ghelarducci et al. 1996) a paradigm was designed to investigate whether the human cerebellum also plays a role in fear-conditioning bradycardia (Maschke et al. 2002b).

Patients (n=5) included in that study had medial cerebellar lesions including the cerebellar vermis due to surgery of cerebellar astrocytoma in childhood. Magnetic resonance images confirmed that vermal lesions predominantly affected lobules VI to VIII and to a lesser extent V and IX. Patients exhibited a mild to moderate cerebellar ataxia. Results of cerebellar patients were compared to those of healthy, age- and sex-matched control subjects (mean age: patients 19.6 years, controls 21.2 years).

Testing consisted of a delay paradigm, which is standard in Pavlovian conditioning. The conditioned stimulus (CS) was a tone (70 dB) that co-terminated with the unconditioned stimulus (US). As US a fear-eliciting painful electrical stimulus was applied at the subject's right index finger via ring electrodes (intensity in patients: 4.5±3.2 mA, in controls: 5.4±1.0

mA). The tone (CS) lasted for 6 seconds and preceded the US by 5900 ms. The procedure was characterized by 3 phases: (1) habituation phase, in which 6 CS alone trials were presented, (2) conditioning phase, in which 20 pairs of CS and US were applied, and, (3) extinction phase consisting of 6 CS alone trials. The mean intertrial interval was 25 seconds (range 22-28 s). Heart rate and skin conductance responses were obtained as dependent variables. Recordings were done from 6 seconds before start of the CS until 6 seconds after CS offset. Other conditioning studies revealed that conditioned changes of autonomic responses occur mostly in the interval from 4 to 6 seconds after onset of the CS (Öhmann 1974, Powell et al. 1974). Therefore, heart rate changes and electrodermal responses (second interval response, SIR) were analyzed within this time interval. For intraindividual normalization the mean heart rate in the last 2 seconds before CS onset was subtracted from the mean heart rate in the interval from 4 to 6 seconds after onset of the CS. This normalized heart rate was called meandiff/bpm. For statistical analysis, the means of meandiff/bpm and incidence of electrodermal responses (SIR) of five successive trials were calculated resulting in six blocks. Effects of fear-conditioning were assessed by comparing results of heart rate and electrodermal responses of the habituation phase (block 1) with those of the extinction phase (block 6).

In controls, the meandiff/bpm of the habituation phase was higher in the habituation phase compared to the extinction phase (mean±SD 2.5±5.5 vs. 0.1±3.7) (Figure 1A). In contrast, cerebellar patients showed an increase of the meandiff/bpm from the habituation phase to the extinction phase (mean±SD −1.8±5.7 vs. 0.6±3.4). However, probably due to high intersubject variability this different behavior was close to significance only (group by block interaction (ANOVA): p=0.06). To reduce intersubject variability the errors of the predicted heart rate (residuals) within the interval from 4 to 6 seconds after CS onset were calculated. Therefore, a linear regression analysis with heart rate of baseline as predictor variable and heart rate of the aforementioned CS-US interval as dependent variable was performed separately for each subject. Mean residuals were obtained by subtracting the predicted heart rate from the obtained heart rate within the interval from 4 to 6 seconds after CS onset. Using these mean residuals as dependent variable the univariate repeated measures analysis (ANOVA) revealed a significant group by block interaction (p=0.009) confirming the differences in fear conditioned bradycardia between groups (Figure 1B). In contrast, there was no significant difference in SIR incidence between groups.

The most important result of this study was the lack of fear-conditioned bradycardia in cerebellar patients when the habituation phase was compared to the extinction phase. Given that patients had midline cerebellar lesions results suggest that medial parts of the human cerebellum are involved in fear-conditioning as measured by heart rate changes. The missing differences in electrodermal response might have been due to the high intersubject variability and/or small study population. The lack of fear-conditioned bradycardia are supported by the results from animal experiments, which reported an impaired acquisition of conditioned bradycardic responses after removal of the cerebellar vermis (Supple and Leaton 1990a, 1990b, Sebastiani et al. 1992, Supple and Kapps 1993, Ghelarducci et al. 1996). A selective involvement of the medial cerebellum is also supported by findings of study by Lavond et al. (1984) revealing that lesions to the intermediate cerebellum did not have effects on fear-conditioned bradycardia.

Figure 1A

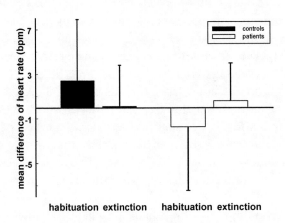

Figure 1B

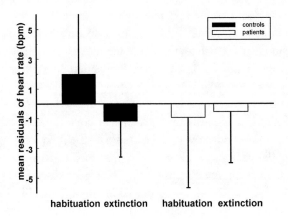

Fear-conditioned bradycardia. **(A)** shows the means±SD of heart rate differences (meandiff/bpm) and **(B)** the residuals of heart rate in the habituation and extinction phases in cerebellar patients. In controls, the difference in heart rate as well as the residuals decreased from the habituation to the extinction phase. The same difference could not be detected in cerebellar patients. (Maschke et al., J Neurol Neurosurg Psychiatry 2002; 72:116-8; with permission from the BMJ Publishing Group).

4. FEAR-CONDITIONED POTENTIATION OF THE STARTLE REFLEX

The startle reflex represents an unspecific aversive reaction that prevents animals from sudden attacks by stiffening the muscles of neck, body wall and limbs (Landis and Hunt 1939). The neural circuit controlling the startle reflex is located within the brain stem (for review see: Yeomans and Frankland 1996, Koch 1999). In experimental conditions the startle reflex is elicited by a sudden loud tone (acoustic startle reflex). The amplitude of the startle response can be increased or decreased by different experimental manipulations. Examples for the increase of the amplitude are sensitization, fear-conditioned potentiation and drug-induced enhancement, whereas habituation, prepulse inhibition, drug-induced inhibition and the attenuation by positive affect result in an amplitude decrease. Fear-conditioned potentiation, first described by Brown et al. (1951), is an augmentation of the startle amplitude by presenting the eliciting acoustic startle stimulus together with a cue, which has previously been paired with a painful shock. Whether the cerebellum is part of the pathway responsible for this fear-conditioned potentiation is a matter of debate. While stimulation of the anterior cerebellar vermis resulted in an increase of the startle reflex in the fear-conditioned potentiation paradigm in rats (Albert et al. 1985), others did not find an effect of bilateral transection of the cerebellar peduncles on this paradigm (Hitchcock and Davis 1986). Therefore, two studies were designed to test whether the fear-conditioned potentiation of the startle reflex is mediated by the human cerebellum. The first study tested the influence of cerebellar lesions on the potentiation in cerebellar patients (Maschke et al. 2000). The second study investigated whether the cerebellum is activated by fear-conditioned potentiation using PET (Frings et al. 2002).

4.1 Fear-Conditioned Potentiation of the Acoustic Startle Reflex in Cerebellar Patients

Ten patients with either circumscribed cerebellar lesions or generalized degeneration of the cerebellum (mean age 33.8 years) and 16 age- and sex-matched healthy control subjects (mean age 29.6 years) were tested. Six of the patients had lesions of the medial cerebellum including the vermis due to surgery for astrocytoma or medulloblastoma in childhood. These patients had a mild to moderate cerebellar ataxia. Two other patients presented with diffuse degenerative cerebellar disease (idiopathic cerebellar ataxia, spinocerebellar ataxia type 6). They showed moderate to severe cerebellar ataxia. Both the patients with midline lesions and the two patients with degenerative ataxia represented the group of cerebellar patients with medial lesions. The remaining two patients had lateral lesions within the cerebellar hemispheres due to hemorrhagic stroke or surgery for hemangioblastoma. Cerebellar ataxia was very mild in these two patients.

The paradigm was designed according to fear-conditioned startle paradigms used in previous studies (Brown et al. 1951, Lipp et al. 1994). The procedure was divided into three phases: (1) habituation of the startle reflex, (2) fear-conditioning, and (3) potentiation of the startle reflex. During the habituation phase subjects received 20 successive acoustic startle stimuli presented via stereophonic headphones (single tone burst, 80 dB, duration 50 ms). During the fear-conditioning phase 20 successive pairs of the CS and US were presented. The CS consisted of a white light, which was presented through blackened diving goggles with two small electric light bulbs that were fastened inside at the top of the goggles. The light increased in its intensity in a ramp form over 2 seconds. The US was a unpleasant electrical stimulus applied at the subject's right index finger via ring electrodes. The US co-terminated with the CS. The intensity of the US was similar for patients (mean±SD 3.1±1.5 mA) and controls (mean±SD 3.3±1.2 mA). The subsequent potentiation phase consisted of an alternating stimulus sequence of three different (pairs) of stimuli: (a) 6 pairs of CS and US ("light-shock", LS), (b) 12 CS paired with a single burst ("light-tone", LT) , and (c) 12 single tone bursts alone trials ("tone", T). These three types of stimuli were presented in a pseudorandom order. Intertrial intervals changed pseudorandomly (mean 16 seconds, range 13-19 seconds).

Measurements consisted of electromyographic (EMG), heart rate and electrodermal response recordings. EMG was obtained from the orbicularis oculi muscles during the habituation and potentiation phases. Peak amplitudes of orbicularis oculi responses were the principle measurement of the magnitude of the startle response. To allow intersubject comparisons peak amplitudes were intraindividually normalized to the mean of all 20 trials of the habituation phase and the 24 LT and T trials of the potentiation phase. Electrodermal response and heart rate changes were used to quantify possible differences in amount of fear during the fear-conditioning phase.

Both the cerebellar patients with medial lesions and control subjects revealed a significant habituation of the startle response (Figure 2). There was no significant difference between both groups as shown by univariate repeated measures analysis (group x block (mean of 4 successive trials) interaction: p=0.9). Electrodermal responses obtained during the fear-conditioning phase were significantly higher in the control group compared with the group of cerebellar patients with medial lesions. Likewise, the univariate repeated measures analysis with blocks of the mean maximal amplitude of electrodermal responses of 4 successive trials as dependent variable showed a significant group (p=0.03) and a significant block effect (p=0.006), but no significant group by block interaction (p=0.15). Moreover, there was no significant difference of the mean or change of heart rate comparing the two groups. In the potentiation phase, the normalized startle amplitude evoked by the pair of light and tone (LT) was higher than the startle amplitude evoked by the tone alone in controls (Figure 3). In contrast, in cerebellar patients startle responses evoked by the LT trials appeared to have the same magnitude as startle responses elicited by the tone alone. The potentiation effect was determined as the difference in the normalized peak amplitude of the acoustic startle reflex evoked by the LT pairs and the tone alone trials. The mean±SD potentiation effect in controls was 21.6±35.6%, whereas the group of patients with medial cerebellar lesions revealed no potentiation effect (mean±SD −6.4±15.3%). To underline these results a univariate repeated measures analysis with normalized peak amplitudes of the startle response as dependent variable was performed (group = between subject factor, condition (LT vs. T) as within subject factor). This analysis showed a significant group effect (p<0.001) and group by condition interaction (p=0.048) reflecting the higher potentiation effect in the control group compared to the cerebellar group. In contrast to patients with medial cerebellar lesions, the two patients with lateral cerebellar patients showed preserved potentiation effects, which were in the range of control subjects (12.8% and 34.8%).

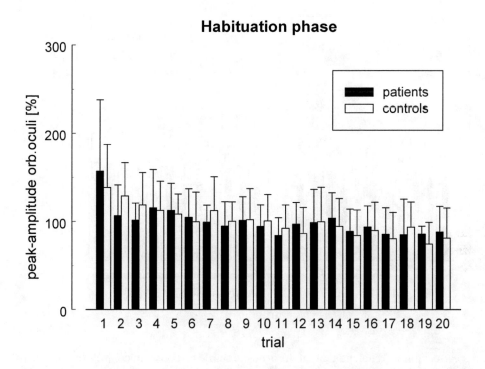

Figure 2. Habituation of the acoustic startle response. There was a provable habituation effect with no significant difference between the control group and the group of patients with medial cerebellar lesions as shown by the normalized peak amplitudes of the startle response (Maschke et al., J Neurol Neurosurg Psychiatry 2000; 68:358-64; with permission from the BMJ Publishing Group).

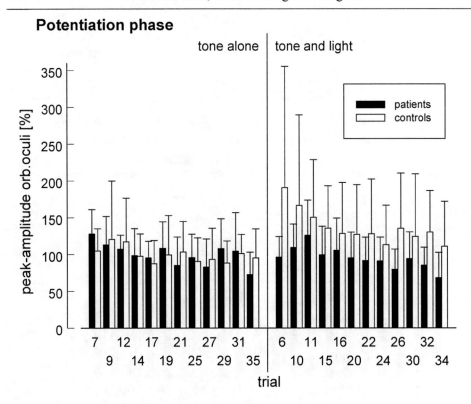

Figure 3. Fear-conditioned potentiation of the acoustic startle response. In controls, normalized peak amplitudes of the startle response appeared to be higher in the trials that presented pairs of light and tone in comparison to the responses evoked by the tone alone trials. In contrast, the magnitude of startle responses were the same in tone alone and paired trials in the group of patients with medial cerebellar lesions (Maschke et al., J Neurol Neurosurg Psychiatry 2000; 68:358-64; with permission from the BMJ Publishing Group).

The main result of this study was that medial cerebellar lesions prevented fear-conditioned potentiation of the startle response, whereas lateral cerebellar lesions had no effect. In contrast, habituation was similar comparing cerebellar patients and controls. Results of electrodermal responses and heart rate in the fear-conditioning phase were conflicting.

Depending upon the number of stimulus presentations and the time interval between two stimuli, the decrease in the response to the stimulus can last for minutes or hours (short-term-habituation), or can be retained for days or weeks (long-term-habituation) (Thompson and Spencer 1966, Davis 1972). Therefore, the habituation process tested in this experiment was a short-term habituation. The result of a preserved short-term habituation is in keeping with results of other studies, which investigated the habituation of the startle response in animals or humans with medial cerebellar lesions (Leaton and Supple 1986, 1991, Lopiano et al. 1990, Maschke et al. 2000b). In these studies, short-term habituation was normal, but the long-term habituation was impaired. Thus, the medial part of the cerebellum including the vermis appears to play a crucial role in long-term but not in short-term habituation of the startle response. Whether the medial cerebellum is involved only in the acquisition of the long-term habituation of the acoustic startle response or is also the site of its memory trace is a matter of debate. In animal experiments removal of the cerebellar vermis before training prevented the acquisition of long-term habituation, whereas long-term habituation was unaffected when the same lesion was made after training sessions (Lopiano et al. 1990). These results indicate that the cerebellar vermis is not the site of the retention of long-term habituation of the startle response. However, hippocampal lesions also did not prevent long-term habituation in rats (Leaton 1981). Therefore, it remains open which structures are essential for retention of long-term habituation of the startle response.

To obtain objective data of fear during the fear-conditioning phase electrodermal responses and heart rate changes were measured. The fact that patients with medial cerebellar lesions had significantly lower amplitudes of electrodermal responses supports previous findings showing that the medial cerebellum is involved in the modulation of autonomic responses (e.g., Nisimaru et al. 1998, Critchley et al. 2000). However, the time course of changes in amplitudes of electrodermal responses and heart rate were not different between patients and controls. These results agree with those of Daum et al. (1993), which revealed an intact electrodermal conditioning in an eyeblink conditioning paradigm in cerebellar patients, but they are in contrast with the results of impaired fear-conditioned bradycardia described above (Maschke et al. 2002b). How can these seemingly different findings be reconciled? The CS-US interval in fear-conditioning of the fear-conditioned startle paradigm was 2 seconds and that of the study of Daum et al. only 1 second, while the CS-US interval used in the fear-conditioned bradycardia paradigm had a duration of 6 seconds. Given that it is known that the best interval to obtain conditioning-related electrodermal responses (i.e., second interval responses, SIR) and heart rate changes is 4 to 6 second after onset of the CS (Öhmann 1974, Powell et al. 1974), the CS-US intervals used in the fear-conditioned startle paradigm and in the study of Daum et al. were not optimal for assessment of conditioning-related autonomic responses. Therefore, differences between patients and controls might have been missed.

The missing potentiation effect in patients with medial cerebellar lesions but preserved potentiation in patients with lateral cerebellar lesions suggests a selective involvement of the medial human cerebellum in this paradigm. This is in line with a study investigating the influence of electrical stimulation of the vermis on the magnitude of the fear-conditioned startle (Albert et al. 1985). That study revealed that the magnitude increased with stimulation of the vermis. However, Hitchcock and Davis (1986) bilaterally transected the cerebellar peduncles without any effect on startle potentiation. In contrast, new findings suggest that the functional integrity of the cerebellum is necessary for acoustic fear response memory formation (Sacchetti et al. 2002). Together, these findings imply that the medial cerebellum may be involved but may not be essential for fear-conditioned potentiation of the startle response. However, results of this study could not identify whether the impairment was due to disturbed potentiation (i.e., expression of fear-conditioning) and/or fear-conditioning (i.e., non-motor associative learning) itself.

4.2 Cerebellar Activations Due to Fear-Conditioned Potentiation of the Acoustic Startle Reflex as Revealed by PET

Based on the above findings of impaired fear-conditioned startle in patients with medial cerebellar lesions, we were interested if cerebellar activations were present in healthy subjects in a similar paradigm using PET (Frings et al. 2002). The aim of the study was to confirm the involvement of the human cerebellum in the potentiated startle paradigm and to investigate whether the cerebellum is differentially involved in fear-conditioning itself and in the motor expression of fear-conditioning, i.e. the augmentation of the startle reflex.

The study was performed in eight healthy young men (mean age 28 years). The fear-conditioned startle paradigm was slightly modified from the previous study. To habituate the startle response and the CS, subjects received 10 acoustic startle stimuli (single tone burst, 120 dB, 50 ms) and 10 light stimuli (same stimulus parameters as described above) in advance of PET scanning. In the subsequent fear-conditioning phase subjects received 10 paired presentations of the CS (i.e., the light) and the US consisting of an electric shock applied at the subject's right index finger (mean intensity 8 mA, duration 100 ms). Intertrial intervals changed pseudorandomly between 12 and 17 seconds. Thereafter, subjects underwent 12 PET scans. In 4 of these scans 6 acoustic startle stimuli alone were presented (T, startle response), in another 4 scans subjects received 6 paired presentations of the light and startle stimulus (LT, potentiation) and in the remaining 4 scans trials (n=6) consisted of the light stimulus alone (L). The sequence of conditions was the same for each subject: LT-T-L-T-LT-L-T-L-LT-L-LT-T. To obtain measurements of the magnitude of startle responses EMG was recorded from both orbicularis oculi muscles. Changes of regional cerebral blood flow (rCBF) were assessed using statistical parametric mapping (SPM99b, Wellcome Department of Cognitive Neurology, London, UK). After scans were realigned to each other, filtered and transformed into stereotactic anatomical space (Talairach and Tornoux 1988), differences in global blood flow were removed by ANCOVA with global blood flow as the confounding variable (Friston et al.1990). Results are displayed as statistical parametric maps showing the significance levels of areas of significant increase of rCBF. The average PET data were superimposed onto the standard MRI template of SPM. The right side of the image represents the right side of the brain. The MRI atlas of the human cerebellum (Schmahmann et al., 2000) was used to determine the localization of significant changes of rCBF within the cerebellum. Changes of rCBF obtained by subtraction of activation during condition T from those in the paired condition LT were regarded as measurements of fear-conditioning. Changes of rCBF revealed by subtraction of condition L from condition LT were taken as measurement for fear-conditioned potentiation.

Five of eight subjects revealed a significant potentiation effect (mean 15.6%). PET analysis of these subjects showed an increase of rCBF associated with fear-conditioning within the left cerebellar hemisphere in Crus I with an extension into hemispheral lobule VI (local maximum: x=-32 mm, y=-82 mm, z=-22 mm, Z-Score 2.96, Figure 4a). In contrast, rCBF changes related to fear-conditioned potentiation were found in vermal lobule III (x=-2 mm, y=-38 mm, z=-14 mm, Z-Score 2.99), vermal lobules IV/V (x=2 mm, y=-58 mm, z=4 mm, Z-Score 3.28, Figure 4b) and in left Crus I (x=-30 mm, y=-86 mm, z=-24 mm, Z-Score 2.86).

These findings imply that different parts of the cerebellum are involved in fear-conditioning and fear-conditioned potentiation of the acoustic startle response. The localization of fear-conditioning within the left cerebellar hemisphere (Crus I, lobule HVI) is supported by a recent PET study, which demonstrated an activation within the left cerebellar hemisphere during fear-conditioning in a paradigm using paired shocks to videotape cues (Fischer et al. 2000). Moreover, vermal activations associated with fear-conditioned potentiation are consistent with our previous findings of a missing potentiation effect in patients with medial cerebellar lesions (Maschke et al. 2000c) and with animal experiments

(Albert et al. 1985). The results suggest that vermal lesions may impair fear-conditioned potentiation because of changes in motor performance rather than the learning process itself.

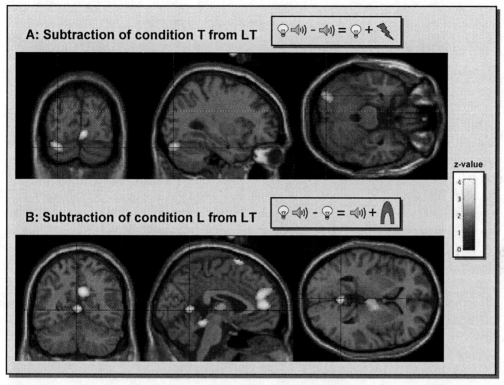

Figure 4. PET activations during (A) fear-conditioning and (B) fear conditioned potentiation of the acoustic startle response. An increase of rCBF associated with fear-conditioning (A) was shown within the left cerebellar hemisphere in Crus I with an extension to hemispheral lobule VI (local maximum: x=-32 mm, y=-82 mm, z=-22 mm, Z-Score 2.96). In contrast, rCBF changes indicating a cerebellar involvement in fear-conditioned potentiation (B) were found in vermal lobule III (x= x=-2 mm, y=-38 mm, z=-14 mm, Z-Score 2.99), vermal lobules IV/V (x=2 mm, y=58 mm, z=4 mm, Z-Score 3.28) and in left Crus I (x=-30 mm, y=-86 mm, z=-24 mm, Z-Score 2.86, not shown in this figure) (Frings et al. Neuroreport. 2002; 13:1275-8; with permission from Lippincott Williams and Wilkins).

5. SUMMARY

Results of the three studies described above suggest that the human cerebellum is part of the neural pathway that mediate fear-conditioning and the expression of responses evoked by fear-conditioning, i.e. potentiation of the startle reflex and bradycardia. Furthermore, different areas of the cerebellum appear to play distinct roles in these paradigms. The medial cerebellum including the vermis seems to mediate predominantly performance of motor and autonomic responses of fear-conditioning, whereas the cerebellar hemisphere (Crus I and lobule HVI) may be involved in the fear-conditioning process itself. Interestingly, hemispheral lobule VI is known to be crucial for the acquisition of conditioned eyeblink response (Yeo and Hesslow 1998, Attwell et al. 2001). In humans, the involvement of hemispheral lobules VI and Crus I in eyeblink-conditioning has been confirmed by a recent fMRI study (Ramnani et al. 2000). Thus, lobules HVI and Crus I may play a more general role in associative learning regardless of which stimuli and reflexes are associated. Furthermore, the results underline the existence of a functional compartmentalization within the human cerebellum.

6. REFERENCES

Albert TJ, Dempsey CW, Sorenson CA (1985). Anterior vermal stimulation: effect on behavior and basal forebrain neurochemistry in rat. *Biol Psychiatry* 20:1267-1276

Attwell PJ, Rahman S, Yeo CH (2001). Acquisition of eyeblink conditioning is critically dependent on normal function in cerebellar cortical lobule HVI. *J Neurosi* 21:5715-5722

Babinski JFF (1899). De l'asynergie cérébelleuse. *Rev Neurol 7:* 806-816

Becerra LR, Breiter HC, Stojanovic M, Fishman S, Edwards A, Comite AR, Gonzalez RG, Borsook D (1999). Human brain activation under controlled thermal stimulation and habituation to noxious heat: an fMRI study. *Magn Reson Med* 41:1044-1057

Bingel U, Quante M, Knab R, Bromm B, Weiller C, Büchel C (2002). Subcortical structures involved in pain processing: evidence from single-trial fMRI. *Pain* 99:313-321

Blaxton TA, Zeffiro TA, Gabrieli JD, Bookheimer SY, Carrillo MC, Theodore WH, Disterhoft JF (1996). Functional mapping of human learning: a positron emission tomography activation study of eyeblink conditioning. *J Neurosci* 16:4032-4040

Bloedel JR, Bracha V (1995). On the cerebellum, cutaneomuscular reflexes, movement control and elusive engrams of memory. *Behav Brain Res* 68:1-44

Brown JS, Kalish HI, Farber IE (1951). Conditioned fear as revealed by magnitude of startle response to an auditory stimulus. *J Exp Psychol* 41:317-328

Buchel C, Dolan RJ (2000). Classical fear conditioning in functional neuroimaging. *Curr Opin Neurobiol* 10:219-223

Critchley HD, Corfield DR, Chandler MP, Mathias CJ, Dolan RJ (2000). *Cerebral correlates of autonomic cardiovascular arousal: a functional neuroimaging investigation in humans.* 523:259-70

Daum I, Schugens MM, Ackermann H, Lutzenberger W, Dichgans J, Birbaumer N (1993). Classical conditioning after cerebellar lesions in humans. *Behav Neurosci* 107:748-756

Daum I, Ackermann H (1995). Cerebellar contributions to cognition. *Behav Brain Res* 67:201-210

Davis M (1972). Differential retention of sensitization and habituation of the startle response in the rat. *J Comp Physiol Psychol* 78:260-267

Dichgans J, Diener HC (1985). Clinical evidence of functional compartimentalization of the cerebellum. In: Bloedel JR, Dichgans J, Precht W (eds) *Cerebellar functions.* Springer, Berlin, 126-146

Drepper J, Timmann D, Kolb FP, Diener HC (1999). Non-motor associative learning in patients with degenerative cerebellar disease. *Brain* 122:87-97

Fanselow MS, LeDoux JE (1999). Why we think plasticity underlying Pavlovian fear conditioning occurs in the basolateral amygdala. *Neuron* 23:229-232

Fiez JA (1996) Cerebellar contributions to cognition. *Neuron* 16:13-15

Fischer H, Andersson JL, Furmark T, Fredrikson M (2000). Fear conditioning and brain activity: a positron emission tomography study in humans. *Behav Neurosci* 114:671-680

Flourens P (1824). Recherches expérimentales sur les propriétés et le fonctions due système nerveux dons les animaux vertébrés, Ed. 1, Paris: Crevot

Frings M, Maschke M, Erichsen M, Jentzen W, Muller SP, Kolb FP, Diener HC, Timmann D (2002). Involvement of the human cerebellum in fear-conditioned potentiation of the acoustic startle response: a PET study. *Neuroreport* 13:1275-1278

Friston KJ, Frith CD, Liddle PF, Dolan RJ, Lammertsma AA, Frackowiak RSJ (1990). The relationship between global and local changes in PET scans. *J Cerebr Blood Flow Metab* 10:458-466

Gerwig M, Dimitrova Λ, Kolb FP, Maschke M, Brol B, Kunnel Λ, Boring D, Thilmann AF, Forsting M, Diener HC, Timmann D (2003). Comparison of eyeblink conditioning in patients with superior and posterior inferior cerebellar lesions. *Brain* 126:71-94

Ghelarducci B, Salamone D, Simoni A, Sebastiani L (1996). Effects of early cerebellar removal on the classically conditioned bradycardia of adult rabbits. *Exp Brain Res* 111:417-23

Harper RM, Gozal D, Bandler R, Spriggs D, Lee J, Alger J (1998). Regional brain activation in humans during respiratory and blood pressure challenges. *Clin Exp Pharmacol Physiol* 25:483-486.

Helmchen C, Mohr C, Erdmann C, Petersen D, Nitschke MF (2003). Differential cerebellar activation related to perceived pain intensity during noxious thermal stimulation in humans: a functional magnetic resonance imaging study. *Neurosci Lett* 335:202-206

Hitchcock JM, Davis M (1986). Lesions of the amygdala, but not of the cerebellum or red nucleus, block conditioned fear as measured with the potentiated startle paradigm. *Behav Neurosci* 100:11-22

Holmes G (1917). The symptoms of acute cerebellar injuries due to gunshot injuries. *Brain* 40: 461-535

Holmes G (1939). The cerebellum of man (Hughlings Jackson memorial lecture). *Brain* 62: 1-30

Koch M (1999). The neurobiology of startle. *Prog Neurobiol* 59:107-28

Landis C, Hunt WA (1939). *The startle pattern*. New York: Farrar and Rinehart

Lavond DG, Lincoln JS, McCormick DA, Thompson RF (1984). Effect of bilateral lesions of the dentate and interpositus cerebellar nuclei on conditioning of heart-rate and nictitating membrane/eyelid responses in the rabbit. *Brain Res* 305:323-330

Lipp OV, Sheridan J, Siddle DA (1994). Human blink startle during aversive and nonaversive Pavlovian conditioning. *J Exp Psychol Anim Behav Process* 20:380-389

Leaton RN (1981). Habituation of startle response, lick suppression, and exploratory behavior in rats with hippocampal lesions. *J Comp Physiol Psychol* 95:813-826

Leaton RN, Supple WF (1986). Cerebellar vermis: essential for long-term habituation of the acoustic startle response. *Science* 232:513-515

Leaton RN, Supple WF (1991). Medial cerebellum and long-term habituation of acoustic startle in rats. Behav Neurosci 105:804-816

Logan CG, Grafton ST (1995). Functional anatomy of human eyeblink conditioning determined with regional cerebral glucose metabolism and positron-emission tomography. *Proc Natl Acad Sci U S A*. 92:7500-7504

Lopiano L, De'Sperati C, Montarolo PG (1990). Long-term habituation of the acoustic startle response: role of the cerebellar vermis. *Neuroscience* 35:79-84

Luciani L (1891). Il cervelletto: nuovi studi di fisiologia normale e pathologica. Firenze: Le Monnier. German translation, Leipzig: E. Besold, 1893

Martin TA, Keating JG, Goodkin HP, Bastian AJ, Thach WT (1996). Throwing while looking through prisms. I. Focal olivocerebellar lesions impair adaptation. *Brain* 119:1183-1198

Maschke M, Kolb FP, Drepper J, Peper M, Lachauer S, Muller SP, Diener HC, Timmann D (2000a). A possible role of the human cerebellum in conditioning of the jaw-opening reflex. *Neurosci Lett* 285:213-217

Maschke M, Drepper J, Kindsvater K, Kolb FP, Diener HC, Timmann D (2000b). Involvement of the human medial cerebellum in long-term habituation of the acoustic startle response. *Exp Brain Research* 133:359-367

Maschke M, Drepper J, Kindsvater K, Kolb FP, Diener HC, Timmann D (2000c). Fear conditioned potentiation of the acoustic blink reflex in patients with cerebellar lesions. *J Neurol Neurosurg Psychiatry* 68:358-364

Maschke M, Drepper J, Burgerhoff K, Calabrese S, Kolb FP, Daum I, Diener HC, Timmann D (2002a). Differences in trace and delay visuomotor associative learning in cerebellar patients. *Exp Brain Res* 147:538-548

Maschke M, Schugens M, Kindsvater K, Drepper J, Kolb FP, Diener HC, Daum I, Timmann D (2002b). Fear conditioned changes of heart rate in patients with medial cerebellar lesions. *J Neurol Neurosurg Psychiatry* 72:116-118

Molchan SE, Sunderland T, McIntosh AR, Herscovitch P, Schreurs BG (1994). A functional anatomical study of associative learning in humans. *Proc Natl Acad Sci U S A*. 91:8122-8126

Moruzzi G (1940). Paleocerebellar inhibition of vasomotor and respiratory carotid sinus reflexes. *J Neurophysiol* 3:20-32

Moruzzi G (1947). Sham rage and localized autonomic responses elicited by cerebellar stimulation in the acute thalamic rat. In: Proceedings XVII International Congress of Physiology Oxford, pp. 114-115

Nisimaru N, Okahara K, Yanai S (1998). Cerebellar control of cardiovascular responses during postural changes in conscious rabbits. *Neurosci Res* 32:267-271

Öhmann A (1974). Orienting reactions, expectancy learning, and conditional responses in electrodermal conditioning with different interstimulus intervals. Biol Psychol 1:189-200

Powell DA, Lipkin M, Milligan ML (1974). Concomitant heart rate and corneoretinal potential conditioning in the rabbit (Oryctolagus cuniculus): effects of caudate lesions. *Learning and Motivation* 5:532-547

Ramnani N, Toni I, Josephs O, Ashburner J, Passingham RE (2000). Learning- and expectation-related changes in the human brain during motor learning. *J Neurophysiol* 84:3026-3035

Rolando L (1809). Saggio sopra la vera struttura del cerebello dell´uome e degli animali e sopra le funzioni del sistema nervosa. Sassari: Stamperia da S.S.R.M. Privilegiata.

Sacchetti B, Baldi E, Lorenzini CA, Bucherelli C (2002). Cerebellar role in fear-conditioning consolidation. *Proc Natl Acad Sci U S A* 99:8406-11

Sachs E, Fincher EF (1927). Anatomical and physiological observations on lesions in the cerebellar nuclei in Macacus rhesus. *Brain* 50:350-356

Schmahmann JD (1997). Rediscovery of an early concept. *Int Rev Neurobiol* 41:3-27

Schmahmann JD, Sherman JC (1998). The cerebellar cognitive affective syndrome. *Brain* 121:561-79

Schmahmann JD, Doyon J, Toga AW, Evans AC, Petrides M (2000). MRI atlas of the human cerebellum. Academic press, San Diego

Schreurs BG, McIntosh AR, Bahro M, Herscovitch P, Sunderland T, Molchan SE (1997). Lateralization and behavioral correlation of changes in regional cerebral blood flow with classical conditioning of the human eyeblink response. *J Neurophysiol* 77:2153-2163

Sebastiani L, LaNoce A, Paton, JF, Ghelarducci B (1992). Influence of the cerebellar posterior vermis on the acquisition of the classically conditioned bradycardia response in the rabbit. *Exp Brain Res* 88:193-198

Supple WF Jr, Leaton RN (1990a). Lesions of the cerebellar vermis and cerebellar hemispheres: effects on heart rate conditioning in rats. *Behav Neurosi* 104:934-47

Supple WF Jr, Leaton RN (1990b). Cerebellar vermis: essential for classically conditioned bradycardia in the rat. *Brain Res* 509:17-23

Supple WF Jr, Kapp BS (1993). The anterior cerebellar vermis: essential involvement in classically conditioned bradycardia in the rabbit. *J Neurosi* 13:3705-3711

Talairach J, Tournoux P (1988). *Co-planar stereotaxis atlas of the human brain*. Georg-Thieme-Verlag, New York.

Thach WT (1996). On the specific role of the cerebellum in motor learning and cognition: clues from PET activation and lesion studies in man. *Behav Brain Sci* 19:411-431

Thach WT (1998). What is the role of the cerebellum in motor learning. *Trends Cogn Sci* 2:331-337

Thompson RF, Spencer WA (1966). Habituation: a model phenomenon for the study of neuronal substrates of behavior. *Psychol Rev* 73:16-43

Thompson RF, Krupa DJ (1994). Organization of memory traces in the mammalian brain. *Annu Rev Neurosci* 17: 519-54

Timmann D, Kolb FP, Baier C, Rijntjes M, Müller SP, Diener HC, Weiller C (1996). Cerebellar activation during classical conditioning of the human flexion reflex using positron emission tomography (PET). *NeuroReport* 7:2056-2060

Timmann D, Musso C, Kolb FP, Rijntjes M, Jüptner M, Müller SP, Diener HC, Weiller C (1998). Involvement of the human cerebellum during habituation of the acoustic startle response: a PET study. *J Neurol Neurosurg Psychiatry* 65:771-773

Timmann D, Baier PC, Diener HC, Kolb FP (2000). Classically conditioned withdrawal reflex in cerebellar patients. 1. Impaired conditioned responses. *Exp Brain Res* 130:453-470

Timmann D, Drepper J, Maschke M, Kolb FP, Böring D, Thilmann AF, Diener HC (2002). Motor deficits cannot explain impaired cognitive associative learning in cerebellar patients. *Neuropsychologia* 40:788-800

Vazdarjanova A (2002). Chasing "fear memories" to the cerebellum. *Proc Natl Acad Sci U S A* 99:7814-7815

Weiner MJ, Hallett M, Funkenstein HH (1983). Adaptation to lateral displacement of vision in patients with lesions of the central nervous system. *Neurology* 33:766-772

Wiggers K (1942). *De invloed van het cerebellum op de vegetatieve functies*. J.H. Kok, N.V., Kampden

Hesslow G, Yeo C (1998). Cerebellum and learning: a complex problem. *Science* 280:1817-9

Yeomans JS, Frankland PW (1996). The acoustic startle reflex: neurons and connections. *Brain Res Rev* 21:301-314.

Chapter 13

CULTURAL ASPECTS OF FEAR FACTORS IN EGYPTIAN COLLEGE STUDENTS[1,2]

Ahmed M. Abdel-Khalek
Kuwait University

ABSTRACT

Five hundred and twenty male and female Egyptian undergraduate students completed the 108 items of the Wolpe and Lang (1977) Fear Survey Schedule III in its Arabic version (A - FSS III). The correlation matrix was subjected to principal components analysis, followed by Varimax rotation. Three criteria for retaining factors were: (a) eigenvalue greater than one; (b) 0.4 or higher for a salient loading, and (c) a minimum of four variables with salient loadings. According to these criteria, nine interpretable factors were retained, which explained 40.3% and 40.5% of the variance for males and females, respectively. These factors are the fear of: (1) social inadequacy, (2) responsibility and authority, (3) death and surgical operations, (4) noise and violence, (5) sexual acts, (6) medical procedures, (7) agoraphobia, (8) heights and deep water, and (9) small animals. The factor of noise and violence in males becomes "noise" only in females. These factors were compared with both Wolpe and Lang's six conceptual categories and the five fear factors model of Arrindell (1980) and Arrindell et al. (1984). The nine factors were discussed in the light of specific characteristics of the Arabic culture.

* * *

For more than three decades, the Fear Survey Schedules (FSSs) have enjoyed considerable prestige among behavior therapists and among researchers in clinical psychology, and personality assessment, as well as in cross-cultural studies. These tools have been used in several different countries (see for example: Abdel-Khalek, 1988, 1994; Granell

[1] Address reprint requests to Ahmed Abdel-Khalek, Department of Psychology, College of Social Sciences, Kuwait University, P.O. Box 68168 Kaifan, Code No. 71962, Kuwait.

[2] I thank Dr. Antony Johae, Associate Professor, Department of English Literature, Faculty of Arts, Kuwait University for his assistance in proofing the manuscript.

de Aldaz, 1982; Spinks, 1980). The FSSs can be used clinically to assess general fears, to target specific fears for treatment, to measure changes in the patient's fear-related behavior, and as a starting point for discussion with the patient (Roberts & La Greca, 1981). It is particularly noteworthy that the success of treatment is reflected in the reduction of the total FSS score, inasmuch as the treatment effects are generalized to other fears. Wolpe & Lang (1964) pointed out that:

> In all cases, it is a necessary preliminary to have a full picture of the stimulus antecedents of the neurotic reactions. While many such antecedents are easily discernible, and indeed may be brought forward by the patient among his presenting complaints, others may be quite obscure, recognized only after a great deal of questioning and observing the patient - and sometimes not even then (p. 27).

Over the last three decades, there has emerged an extensive body of empirical work dealing with varied aspects of the FSS in different countries. However, research on the FSS in Arabic samples is scarce. Abdel-Khalek (1988, 1994) investigated specific psychometric parameters of the Arabic FSS III (A - FSS III), especially its reliability, validity, and norms, as well as its relationship with personality scales. Nevertheless, the factorial structure of the FSS III in its Arabic version has not been systematically explored in published research so far.

Factor analysis is a major statistical procedure for describing relationships between various abilities and behavior. One of its aims is to explore basic dimensions and to organize a large variety of stimuli or items into a small number of clusters or meaningful classes. Factor analysis has been used systematically to determine the structure of the FSSs. Most of these analyses were carried out mainly on Western Ss (see for example: Agathon & Brouri, 1983, Arrindell, Emmelkamp & van der Ende, 1984, Brown & Crawford, 1988, Kartsounis, Mervyn-Smith & Pickersgill, 1983, Oei, Cavallo & Evans, 1987, Tejero, Avila, San & Torrubia, 1989). Several studies have analyzed Wolpe and Lang (1964) FSS III both in normal and psychiatric samples (Holmes, Rothstein, Stout, & Rosecrans, 1975, Agathon & Brouri, 1983; Brown & Crawford, 1988, Tejero, Avila, San, & Torrubia, 1989).

The replicated findings of these analyses on Western Ss can be summarized in light of the comprehensive studies which were carried out by Arrindell and his colleagues. That is, over 98% of the fear factors identified in 38 studies have been classified under the following categories: (I) Interpersonal events or situations, (II) Death, injuries, illness, blood and surgical procedures, (III) Animals, and (IV) Agoraphobic fears (Arrindell et al., 1991). Arrindell (1980) identified a fifth factor referred to as sexual and aggressive scenes. It can be said that the aforementioned five factor paradigm has been widely accepted. There is no doubt, however, that the Western analyses cannot be taken for granted and applied directly to Arab samples.

Egypt, as a developing country, has a different state of affairs than the Western world. There are economic factors, given Egypt's nascent industrial base, and there are differing percentages of religious groups (91% Muslims, 8% Christians (mainly Copts), 1% Jews and others). There are historical differences as well. Egypt's longest recorded history in the world is replete with invaders and occupiers. Foremost among them are Assyrians, Persians, Greeks, Ptolemies, Romans, Byzantines, Ottomans, French, and British. One can hypothesize that these invasions and occupations have left deep scars on Egyptians. It is worth noting that in the recent history of Egypt, there have been four bitter wars with Israel (1948, 1956, 1967, and 1973).

From the present writer's personal point of view, the main factors that mould the behavior and personality of Egyptians nowadays are as follows: the longest recorded history, different invaders, wars with Israel, religion, mediocre economic development and growth, unique geographical position, and both Arabic and Pharaonic roots.

Based on a personal impression as an Egyptian citizen, I can speculate about the main characteristics of behavior and personality among Egyptians in recent years as: conservative, traditional, reserved, favoring authoritarian attitudes in socialization, cynical, ironical, satirical, humorous, tolerant, subjective, peaceful, and guilt prone.

On the basis of empirical research, Egyptians show themselves as having high mean scores on fear, neuroticism, trait anxiety, and death anxiety (Abdel-Khalek, 1981, 1986, 1989, 1994), in comparison with Western counterparts. There is also a consistent finding for Egyptians, i.e. females attained higher mean scores in the aforementioned psychopathological scales than their male peers. In the same vein, these sex-related differences among Egyptians are higher than that found in Western samples (Templer, 1991).

The present investigation tried to address the question: to what extent can these characteristics of the Egyptian culture as well as the empirical findings based on Egyptian Ss predict a patterning of fear that could differ from the clustering found to date in studies that have been conducted in mostly Western nations?

Thus, the aim of the present study was to: (1) determine the factorial structure of the A-FSS III (108 item) among Egyptian male and female undergraduate students, (2) to compare this factor structure with structures reported in other studies in order to examine the cross-cultural generalizability of the FSS III dimensions, and (3) to compare the factors of the present study with both the conceptually-related categories of Wolpe and Lang (1977) as developers of the scale, and the five factor model of Arrindell (1980) and Arrindell et al. (1984).

METHOD

Subjects

Two samples of male (N=282) and female (N=238) undergraduate students of Egyptian nationality were recruited from six different faculties: Agriculture, Arts, Commerce, Education, Engineering, and Science, in the University of Alexandria, Egypt. The mean age for males was 23.7 years (SD = 1.6), and that for females was 22.9 (SD=1.3). The 282 and 238 subjects (Ss) to 108 items ratio is not a high one. A lower ratio, however, would be acceptable, since there are testable models of both Wolpe and Lang (1977) and Arrindell et al. (1990).

All Ss who were approached for participation in the study volunteered to do so. The participants were assured of the complete confidentiality of their responses. Information on the socioeconomic status of the sample was unfortunately not available. However, Egyptian universities would account for all social classes. It is worth mentioning that the present study is based on the same sample used in previous research (see: Abdel-Khalek, 1994).

Instrument

The FSS-III (Wolpe & Lang, 1977) contains 108 items. Each item denotes an object, experience or situation which may be feared by an S. Ss were requested to rate their aversion (felt fear or anxiety) to each of the 108 phobic items, on a 5 - point Likert - type scale, i.e. 0 (Not at all), 1 (A little), 2 (A fair amount), 3 (Much), and 4 (Very much). The questionnaire was translated into Arabic and adapted by Abdel-Khalek (1988). Coefficients of reliability (test-retest and internal consistency), concurrent validity, and norms for the A-FSS-III in the Egyptian context have been previously documented (Abdel-Khalek, 1988, 1994). Korayem (1987) carried out a back translation of the 108 A-FSS -III items. That is, he translated the Arabic version into English and then compared it to the original English version. This procedure gave very good results ensuring accuracy. In the present Arabic study, the content, number of items, instructions, and response options are identical to the original (American) version of the scale.

Procedure

The 108 items of the A-FSS- III were administered during regular classroom sessions. Upon completion of each questionnaire, the response sheet was checked carefully. A few Ss had to be asked to fill in omitted items.

Statistical Analysis

Correlation coefficients were computed between each of the FSS items. Then, the resultant 108 by 108 correlational matrix was subjected to principal components factor analysis with iteration, followed by orthogonal rotation of axes by normalized Varimax procedure. Unities were inserted in the diagonal cells of the correlational matrix. Guttman's lower - bound criterion was followed, i.e. the eigenvalue $\geq$ 1.0, to determine the number of factors to be extracted (SPSS, 1990).

In determining the significance level of factor loadings, an arbitrary level of at least 0.4 or higher was adopted as salient loading. The criterion for retaining a factor was a minimum of 4 variables with accepted loadings (i. e. $\geq$ 0.4), and eigenvalue greater than one.

RESULTS AND DISCUSSION

Using the above-mentioned criteria, i.e. the eigenvalue $\geq$ 1.0, and at least 4 variables with loadings $\geq$ 0.4, ten factors were kept for interpretative purposes at first. Communality (h^2) values were quite high, i.e.103 (95.4 %) and 100 items (92.6%) had h^2 over 0.3 for males and females, respectively. Since the tenth factor in males and the eighth factor in females were uninterpretable inasmuch as they contained miscellaneous items, it was decided to delete them. The nine factors explained 40.3% and 40.5% of the variance in both sexes, respectively. Table 1 sets out the eigenvalues and the percent of variance accounted for by the nine factors before rotation.

Table 1. Eigenvalues and percentages of explained variance for the 9 factor solution

(Eigen.)	Males		Females	
Factor	Eigenvalues	% Variance	Eigenvalues	% Variance
1	19.9	18.4	18.4	17.1
2	5.8	5.4	6.3	5.8
3	3.5	3.3	4.1	3.8
4	2.7	2.5	3.2	3.0
5	2.8	2.6	2.9	2.6
6	2.4	2.3	2.6	2.4
7	2.3	2.1	2.4	2.2
8	2.0	1.9	1.9	1.8
9	1.9	1.8	1.9	1.8
		40.3		40.5

It is worth mentioning that the visual inspection of the Scree test provided only three significant factors. They explained 27.04% and 26.7% of the common variance for males and females, respectively. In proportion to the 108 item of the FSS-III, three factors are an unacceptable solution. Based on the accepted loading ≥ 0.4, the three factor solution classified only 34 items (31.5%) and 36 items (33.3%) for males and females, respectively out of the 108 items. This solution was caused by underfactorizing and it obscured the effective distribution of the items into a pattern which clearly and appropriately reflects the scales built into the questionnaire by its developers as Arrindell et al. (1984, p. 242) pointed out. For all these reasons, the most parsimonious solution of three factors based on the Scree test was discarded.

According to the 0.4 criterion of the salient loading, nine factors classified 74 (68.5%) and 76(70.4%) of the items. Thus, 34 (31.5%), and 32 (29.6%) items out of the 108 items FSS-III have no salient loading on any one of the nine factors in males and females, respectively.

Table 2. Orthogonal (Varimax) 9 factors of the A - FSS III and loadings in males

Factor 1: Fear of social inadequacy	Loadings
76. Looking foolish	.67
67. Being ignored	.63
77. Losing control of yourself	.62
75. Making mistakes	.61
64. Feeling disapproved of	.59
61. Feeling rejected by others	.57
96. Hurting the feelings of others	.57
16. Failure	.54
83. Thoughts of being mentally ill	.50
94. Being dressed unsuitably	.50
79. Becoming nauseous	.49
93. Ideas of possible homosexuality	.48
26. Feeling angry	.43
12. Being teased	.42

54. Angry people	.40
Factor 2 : Fear of responsibility and authority	**Loadings**
107. Responsibility (being in charge)	.60
81. Being responsible for decisions	.55
104. Marriage	.54
95. Ministers or priests	.51
84. Taking written tests	.50
85. Being with a member of the opposite sex	.45
27. People in authority	.42
17. Entering a room where other people are already seated	.40
6. Speaking in public	.40
Factor 3 : Fear of death and surgical operations	**Loadings**
66. Cemeteries	.66
5. Dead people	.62
98. Undertakers	.57
57. Animal blood	.55
56. Human blood	.54
53. Witnessing surgical operations	.53
41. Weapons	.46
90. Taking medicine	.45
55. Mice or rats	.43
60. Prospects of a surgical operation	.42
Factor 4 : Fear of noise and violence	**Loadings**
33. Crowds	.60
15. Sirens	.59
30. Sudden noises	.55
35. One person bullying another	.55
42. Dirt	.53
4. Loud voices	.52
40. Dead animals	.52
1. Noise of vacuum cleaners	.51
36. Tough looking people	.45
101. Masturbation	.44
106. Vomiting	.43
Factor 5: Sexual fears	**Loadings**
71. Nude women	.70
91. Becoming sexually aroused	.60
89. Being seen unclothed	.51
85. Being with a member of the opposite sex	.49
97. Kissing	.44
Factor 6: Fear of medical procedures	**Loadings**
34. Cats	.53
73. Doctors	.51
29. Seeing other people injected	.50
108. Hospitals	.48
63. Medical odors	.45
22. Receiving injections	.43
103. Physical examinations	.42
90. Taking medicine	.40

Factor 7: Agoraphobia	Loadings
31. Journeys by car	.61
7. Crossing streets	.54
11. Automobiles	.51
9. Being in a strange place	.48
25. Journeys by train	.46
37. Birds	.42
Factor 8: Fear of heights and deep water	**Loadings**
92. Being punished by God	.49
18. High places on land	.47
19. Looking down from high buildings	.45
38. Sight of deep water	.40
Factor 9: Fear of small animals	**Loadings**
44. Crawling insects	.58
24. Bats	.57
28. Flying insects	.55
50. Strange shapes	.53
88. Germs	.45
55. mice or rats	.44
65. Harmless snakes	.42
87. Dogs	.41
80. Harmless spiders	.40

Table 2 gives the loadings of the nine factors after Varimax rotation in males. The items are presented in a descending order according to the size of the saturation. Table 2 shows that factor 1 contains fifteen salient loadings (≥ 0.4). It was labeled "fear of social inadequacy". The same factor was extracted by Kartsounis et al. (1983), and factors with similar names were reported in previous studies: fear of being socially unacceptable (Holmes et al., 1975, Rothstein et al., 1972), fear of interpersonal events (Brown & Crawford, 1988, Granell de Aldaz, 1982, Landy & Gaupp, 1971), fear of social disapproval (Meikle & Mitchell, 1974), fear of social rejection (Bamber, 1977), fear of social criticism (Goldberg, Yinon, & Cohen, 1975), fear of negative social evaluation (Oei et al., 1987, Tejero, et al., 1989), fear of interpersonal situations (Agathon & Brouri, 1983, Spinks, 1980), and social phobia (Arrindell et al., 1984).

Factor 2 is characterized by "fear of responsibility and authority". Rothstein et al. (1972) extracted the fear of authority factor among psychiatric inpatients. Granell de Aldaz (1982) obtained a factor called "responsibility" among Venezuelan females only. Most of the variables in her factor are the same as in the present one.

Factor 3 was labeled "fear of death and surgical operations". It contains ten salient saturations (≥ 0.4). The first sub-component in this factor is represented by items such as "cemeteries", "dead people", and "undertakers". The second sub-component in this factor is represented by items such as "witnessing surgical operations", and "prospects of a surgical operation". Items such as "animal blood", "human blood", "weapons", and "taking medicine" can be considered as stimuli which have some kind of relation to "death". Fear of "mice or rats" is the only variable that loads high on this factor; however, that does not seem to fit in conceptually. Some items in this factor such as those relating to "surgical operations" and "blood" were clustered in the tissue damage factor in Bamber's (1977) analysis. Holmes et al. (1975) extracted the death and illness factor among nonpsychiatric male population.

However, the only items shared by the two studies refer to "death". Stratton and Moore (1977) also extracted (by four different methods of factorization) separate factors for fear of blood, death and injury, dead animals, and weapons.

Factor 4 represents the "fear of noise and violence". It contains eleven salient saturations. Items contributing to the first sub-component of this factor include "crowds", "sirens", "sudden noises", "loud voices", and "noise of vacuum cleaners". In the meantime, this factor contains a subcomponent pertaining to violence, and includes the following items: "one person bullying another", and "tough looking people". One can speculate on a subtle relationship between noise and violence. Still, this factor incorporates variables with high loadings that do not appear to fit conceptually, such as "dirt", "dead animals", and "vomiting". The factor of "noise" has been previously extracted by different researchers (Landy & Gaupp, 1971, Meikle & Mitchell, 1974, Rothstein et al., 1972, Stratton & Moore, 1977). The present factor would have a relation to Arrindell et al.'s (1984, 1990) fears of sexual and agrresssive scenes. It is important to note that the present factor contains a sex-related item, namely "masturbation".

Factor 5 is characterized as "sexual fears". Five salient saturations loaded on this factor. Items contributing to it are highly consistent and include "nude women", "becoming sexually aroused", and "kissing". The same factor was extracted by Tejero et al. (1989) with Spanish university students. Arrindell (1980) identified a factor of sexual and aggressive scenes. Rubin et al. (1969) extracted a factor of morally-related fears and sexual fears. In the same vein, Holmes et al. (1975) obtained a factor pertaining to fears of primitive, moralistic, and sexual stimuli. Meikle and Mitchell (1974) found a factor assessing fear of nude bodies.

Factor 6 was labeled "fear of medical procedures". Eight items have significant saturations on this factor. It is represented by items such as "doctors", "hospitals", and "physical examinations". Nevertheless, "fear of cats" might be considered, conceptually, as a misfit in this factor. Tejero et al. (1989) have extracted the same factor. Other somewhat different names to the same factor are as follows: medical intervention (Goldberg et al., 1975), medical-surgical procedures (Brown & Crawford, 1988, Landy & Gaupp, 1971, Stratton & Moore, 1977), fear of medical treatment (Bamber, 1977), fear of doctors (Meikle, & Mitchell, 1974), and fear of doctors and hospitals (Granell de Aldaz, 1982).

Factor 7 is characterized by "agoraphobia". Six items have high loadings on this factor. It is concerned mainly with travel and means of transportation such as "journeys by car", "automobiles", "journeys by train", and "crossing streets". The same factor was frequently extracted by different researchers (Arrindell et al., 1984, Arrindell & van der Ende, 1986, Agathon & Brouri, 1983, Kartsounis et al., 1983, Oei et al., 1987, Tejero et al., 1989). In addition, Merbaum & Stricker (1972) obtained a fear of travel factor, while Meikle and Mitchell (1974) extracted a minor factor (the fourth) of surface travel. However, the variables in the last two factors overlapped well with the agoraphobic factor. The present factor among students is consistent with the findings of Arrindell et al. (1987, 1990). However, it conflicts with Hallam and Hafner's (1978) results which state that agoraphobia is either an all or none phenomenon, not a graded one.

Factor 8 was labeled "fear of heights and deep water". It has four salient loadings: "being punished by God", "high places on land", "looking down from high buildings", and "sight of deep water". The first item, i.e. "being punished by God" may be considered as inconsistent with the factor label. Nevertheless, the vast majority of Egyptian Muslims view God as the only powerful creator situated in a high and great place. In referring to God (Allah), some

Egyptian Muslims made an involuntary expressive movement, i.e. pointing upward. Hallam and Hafner (1978) extracted the same factor as the present one. Meikle and Mitchell (1974), and Stratton and Moore (1977) have extracted the factor of heights, while Goldberg et al. (1975), and Rothstein et al. (1972) named the factor: fear of high places.

Factor 9 is characterized by the "fear of small animals". Nine items load highly on this factor. It seems that "fear of strange shapes "does not fit conceptually in this factor. A sizeable number of studies have extracted the same factor (see: Bamber, 1977, Hallam & Hafner, 1978, Holmes et al., 1975, Oei et al., 1987, Rubin et al., 1969, Spinks, 1980). Other studies used somewhat different names such as the following: fear of irrational non human objects (Agathon & Brouri, 1983), fear of animals and insects (Goldberg et al., 1975, Granell de Aldaz, 1982, Brown & Crawford, 1988), fear of animals (Arrindell et al., 1991, Tejero et al., 1989), fear of harmless animals (Merbaum & Stricker, 1972), fear of flying animals (Meikle & Mitchell, 1974), fear of insects (Stratton & Moore, 1977), fear of animate nonhuman organisms (Landy & Gaupp, 1971), and fear of nuisance animals (Wade, 1978).

Table 3 presents the factors of females. By and large, there is a good similarity between the factors of males and females. However, some differences are to be expected. Regarding the comparison between factors, different and sophisticated methods are available. Nevertheless, the simple method of comparing the percentages of the salient loaded items in a given pair of factors will be followed. Table 4 shows the results. The percentages of common items ranged from 45.5 to 88.9, with a mean of 69.3, denoting similarity.

Table 3. Orthogonal (Varimax) 9 factors of the A - FSS III and loadings in Females

Factor 1: Fear of social inadequacy	Loadings
67. Being ignored	.71
76. Looking foolish	.69
77. Losing control of yourself	.67
61. Feeling rejected by others	.64
64. Feeling disapproved of	.64
75. Making mistakes	.59
96. Hurting the feelings of others	.59
94. Being dressed unsuitably	.53
79. Becoming nauseous	.51
35. One person bullying another	.50
106. Vomiting	.46
78. Fainting	.45
93. Ideas of possible homosexuality	.45
83. Thoughts of being mentally ill	.43
16. Failure	.40
Factor 2: Fear of responsibility and authority	**Loadings**
107. Responsibility (being in charge)	.69
81. Being responsible for decisions	.65
49. Being criticized	.50
104. Marriage	.48
84. Taking written tests	.46
27. People in authority	.44
95. Ministers or priests	.43

23. Strangers	.40
Factor 3: Fear of small animals	**Loadings**
24. Bats	.65
65. Harmless snakes	.63
55. Mice or rats	.62
44. Crawling insects	.58
80. Harmless spiders	.55
28. Flying insects	.53
40. Dead animals	.53
88. Germs	.50
21. Imaginary creatures	.49
20. Worms	.48
41. Weapons	.42
57. Animal Blood	.41
87. Dogs	.40
Factor 4: Fear of medical procedures	**Loadings**
90. Taking medicine	.64
22. Receiving injections	.61
108. Hospitals	.58
73. Doctors	.55
63. Medical odors	.52
29. Seeing other people injected	.49
103. Physical examinations	.41
Factor 5: Fear of noise	**Loadings**
4. Loud voices	.66
15. Sirens	.64
30. Sudden noises	.55
33. Crowds	.54
1. Noise of vacuum cleaners	.51
26. Feeling angry	.42
Factor 6: Sexual fears	**Loadings**
91. Becoming sexually aroused	.58
70. Nude men	.54
51. Being touched by others	.52
85. Being with a member of the opposite sex	.51
71. Nude women	.45
89. Being seen unclothed	.41
Factor 7: Agoraphobia	**Loadings**
31. Journeys by car	.64
100. Fish	.56
43. Journey by bus	.54
34. Cats	.52
37. Birds	.50
25. Journeys by train	.41
87. Dogs	.41
Factor 8: Fear of death and surgical operations	**Loadings**
53. Witnessing surgical operation	.70
48. Sick people	.67
56. Human blood	.65
57. Animal blood	.51
2. Open wounds	.48

74. Crippled or deformed people	.45
5. Dead people	.42
45. Seeing a fight	.40
98. Undertakers	.40
Factor 9: Fear of heights and deep water	**Loadings**
14. Thunder	.71
72. Lightening	.66
19. Looking down from high buildings	.59
7. Crossing streets	.49
18. High places on land	.47
38. Sight of deep water	.42

Table 4. Comparison of factors derived from the samples of males (M) and females (F)

The factor in males	No. of the factor in females	No. of sig. loadings		Common items	
		M	**F**	**No.**	**%**
1. Fears of social inadequacy	1	15	15	12	80
2. Fear of responsibility and authority	2	9	8	6	66.7
3. Fear of death and surgical operations	8	10	9	5	50
4. Fear of noise and violence*	5	11	6	5	45.5
5. Sexual fears	6	5	6	4	80
6. Fear of medical procedures	4	8	7	7	87.5
7. Agoraphobia	7	6	7	3	50
8. Fear of heights and deep water	9	4	6	3	75
9. Fear of small animals	3	9	13	8	88.9
Mean of the percentages of common items**					69.3

* This factor in the female group was named "Fear of noise" only.

** The percentage of the common items was computed in reference to the number of significant loadings in the male group.

GENERAL DISCUSSION

The present study has achieved its aims. First, the factorial structure of the 108 items of the FSS III (Wolpe & Lang, 1977) in its Arabic form (A - FSS III; Abdel-Khalek, 1988, 1994) among Egyptian undergraduate students (N = 520) has been identified. Second, the cross-cultural comparability of this factor structure has been studied in relation to previous findings. The third aim (i.e. comparing the present factors with both Wolpe and Lang's (1977) conceptual categories, and the five factor model of Arrindell (1980) and Arrindell et al. (1984)), will be discussed below.

Factor analysis revealed that, in general, around two thirds of the 108 items formed nine dimensions (according to the 0.4 criterion of the salient loading). The majority of the factors of the present study constitute meaningful dimensions of close relevance to the phenomenon of phobic stimuli.

It is of interest to compare the present findings with the conceptual categories of fear according to the developers of the scale (Wolpe and Lang, 1977, see figure 1). They classified the items of their FSS III into six categories: (1) social or interpersonal, (2) tissue damage, illness, and death, (3) animal, (4) noises, (5) other classical phobias, and (6) miscellaneous. Two categories in Wolpe and Lang's (1977) conceptualization (i.e. 1 and 2) have been divided respectively into four factors (i. e. 1, 2, 3 and 6). Another two categories (i.e. 3 and 4) are the same as two factors (i. e. 4 and 9). The last two categories (i.e. 5 and 6) were not extracted in the present factorial analysis. In summary, four out of the six conceptual categories of Wolpe and Lang (1977) were obtained in the present analysis. However, the last two categories, i.e. classical and miscellaneous phobias, were not extracted in previous well-planned factor analytic studies.

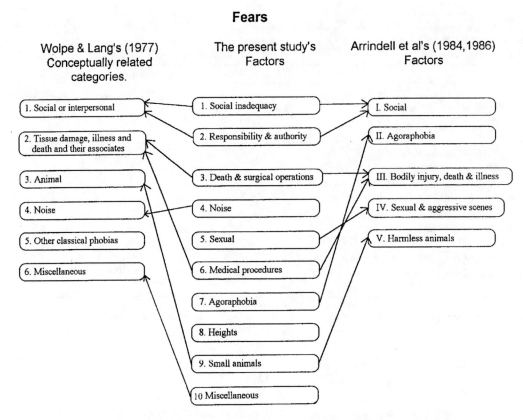

Figure 1. Comparison between the present study's factors and both
Wolpe & Lang (1977) classes and Arrindell et al's (1984, 1986) factors

All of the nine factors of the present study, in some way or another, have been reported previously in the literature. Nevertheless, the number of factors varied among the vast majority of previous studies including the present one. Ammerman (1988) reported that the number of factors ranged between five and 17, while Wade (1978) reported a range from three to 28 factors. The number of factors extracted is a function of the number of input stimuli inserted in the fear schedule, as well as the variety of these items. Unfortunately, the factorial analyses of the fear schedules were not carried out with the same measure. Moreover, the vast diversity, the wide range, and the ease of gathering plenty of these phobic stimuli have tempted many writers to add new items to the already existing schedules. Thus, the comparison between studies (and cultures) becomes tentative and inaccurate, inasmuch as any comparison has to run between schedules containing items of the same number and content. The comparison between factors obtained from different studies is also hampered by differences in methods of analysis, criteria to stop factorization and rotation, and the size and characteristics of the sample (see: Arrindell et al., 1984, Wade, 1978).

In spite of the uncontrolled determinants of the factorial structures, certain factors have regularly emerged; that is, social, animal, and injury fears (Hallam & Hafner, 1978); while Tasto (1977) stated that the most frequent clusters are fears related to: (1) small animals, (2) death, physical pain and surgery, (3) aggression, and (4) interpersonal events (social evaluation vs. social interaction). Based on an extensive empirical series of studies, Arrindell and van der Ende (1986) and Arrindell et al. (1987, 1990) concluded that there are at least five fear components which can be used to describe an individual's idiosyncratic patterning of his / her experienced irrational fears, that is, social fears, agoraphobic fears, bodily injury, death and illness fears, fears of sexual and aggressive scenes, and fears of harmless animals. Arrindell et al. (1984, 1987, 1990) have demonstrated the retrievability and generalizability of these factors across samples, gender, and nations (American, British, Canadian and Dutch Ss). In an Australian sample, however, Arrindell et al. (1991) advocated a four-dimensional taxonomy, since two interpersonal factors were merged to one factor.

Comparing the five factors of Arrindell et al. (1984, 1990) to the nine factors of the present study respectively reveals certain similarities (see: figure 1). The social fears factor has been divided into two components: (a) social inadequacy, and (b) responsibility and authority. The two separate factors of agoraphobia and harmless animals are the same. Fear of sexual and aggressive scenes has been broken down into two components: (a) fear of noise and violence in males and noise in females, and (b) sexual fears. The factor pertaining to fear of bodily injury, death and illness fears has been reclassified in the present analysis into two separate factors: (a) fear of death and surgical operations, and (b) fear of medical procedures. However, a factor of "heights and deep water", was not obtained in the study of Arrindell et al. (1990). By and large, the major factors previously identified in clinical and non-clinical Ss were fully replicated. However, there are two precautions or limitations: (a) three of the factors of Arrindell et al. factors (i.e. I, III and IV) have been broken down respectively into six factors (i.e. 1, and 2; 3 and 6; 4 and 5), and (b) only one factor in the present study (No. 8: heights) was not obtained in the analysis of Arrindell et al.

Of greater importance is differentiating between the methodologies, Arrindell and his colleagues used in their series of studies on the one hand and the present study on the other in at least two respects. First, the number of items used in the FSS III version in the present study is larger than that of Arrindell et al. (1984, 1990) (108 vs. 76 respectively). The number of factors identified - other things being equal - is a function of the number of input items for the scale. Thus, it was expected that more factors would be extracted in the present study. Second, the statistical procedures in the series of studies by Arrindell et al. are more solid, robust and parsimonious than in the present study. In particular, Arrindell et al. (1984) criticized the eigenvalue > 1.00 criterion in producing a large number of factors, in leading to over extraction of factors, and producing non-replicable factors. They agreed with Walkey (1983) on the importance of using the theoretical structure of the pattern of scales under examination when determining the number of factors to be rotated to simple structure.

Nevertheless, two criteria were used in the present study in addition to the eigenvalue of > 1.00. They were the level of the salient loading (i.e. > 0.4), and a minimum of four salient loadings in any given factor. There are also two important points in the present endeavor. On the one hand, it is the contention of the present writer that nine factors sufficiently account for the 108 items of the A-FSS III. On the other hand, all of the nine factors (see Tables 2 and 3) are interpretable, and meaningful to the phenomenon of phobic stimuli, and have been previously reported in the literature.

It is particularly noteworthy that two out of the five factors of Arrindell (1980), and Arrindell et al. (1984) were replicated in the present study. However, three out of their five factors have been divided into six factors. Is this partition or breaking down of the factors a characteristic of the Egyptian sample? The answer to this question deserves closer scrutiny. However, the following are merely preliminary contemplations.

One of the main findings of the present investigation is the extraction of two social/interpersonal factors rather than one. These two factors could be seen as the most important, considering the order of their appearance (the first two, see Tables 2 and 3), their high eigenvalues, (see Table 1), and the large number of salient loadings ≥ 0.4 included in them. This could be seen as congruent with the results of Chaleby (1987) pertaining to the social phobia in Saudis. He found that social phobia is a notably common disorder among Saudis, constituting approximately 13% of all neurotic disorders seen in his clinic. In spite of the clinical nature of his sample, he introduces interpretations of his results in the light of the so-called Saudi culture as follows:

> The Saudi culture is heavily disciplined with rigid moral codes and highly valued customs and rituals. Even small deviations from the rules are unacceptable and individuals who do not conform are quickly outcast. It is important to stress that the rules might apply to minor social rituals, such as the manner of greeting somebody, or how to start a conversation by asking about the health of every member of the family, naming only the males and referring to the females by symbols (p. 169).

Indeed, a good deal of similarity between Saudis and Egyptians existed. Foremost among these similarities are the language and Islam. They share a sizeable portion of the Arabic heritage. Both speak the Arabic language. All Saudis are Muslims, while 91% of Egyptians are Muslims. The vast majority of people in both countries are orthodox (Sunni) Muslims. Last but not least, there are good relations and mutual respect between the people of the two countries. Notwithstanding, there is room for some differences. The national income of Saudi Arabia is much higher than that of Egypt, while the rate of social change is faster in Egypt. In comparison to Saudis, Egyptians in general are less conservative. This could be seen in manifold respects pertaining to the degree of following customs, and traditions. However, it would appear that similarities overshadow the differences. In summary, it is a matter of different but near positions on the same continuum. All in all, one of the notable results of the present analysis in Egyptians is the extraction of two rather than one factor of fear of social/interpersonal stimuli, i.e. "Social inadequacy" and "Responsibility and authority". The last-mentioned element deserves closer scrutiny.

"Authority", especially of a political kind, has played an important role throughout history in the lives of Egyptians. Through the centuries, Egypt has been the target of colonization by different invaders (see the introduction). Those invaders, of course, carried out coercive practices, used tough power, and ruled tyrannically and autocratically. So, it could be said that the fear of authority was deeply-rooted in some Egyptians. At the same time, authoritarianism plays an important role in family, school and in everyday life in a sizeable portion of the Egyptian society. Thus, the fears which centered around authority and also "responsibility" seemed warranted.

"Death", the first component in the third factor in males and in the eighth factor in females, also has a unique status among Egyptians since the dawn of civilization. Thus, death may be a source of a good deal of fear among them. This could be seen as congruent with the results showing a high mean score of Egyptians' death anxiety (Abdel-Khalek, 1986).The inclusion of an element of "surgical operations" with a component of death in one factor has a significant meaning. Surgery and death are in one aversive package in the minds of some Egyptians especially among low socio-economic classes.

Beshai and Templer (1978) speculated that "a developing country such as Egypt is more likely than a society such as that of the U. S. A. to find itself in the throes of compound threats to human life, in the absence of adequate medical and technological means of coping with such threats..." They added that "the Egyptian culture has been described as preoccupied with mourning, bereavement, and edification of death by Egyptologists and anthropologists. While the modern culture of Egypt is Arabic, it is also influenced by ancient Egyptian customs regarding death and funeral rites" (p. 155f).

Fakhr El-Islam (1994) studied the morbid fears in a sample of Qatari women in which all of them were Muslims. He commented on the fear of death as follows:

Muslims, believe that death is foreordained, and that it must find a means in order to take place e.g. disease or accident... Patients fear unexpected and 'untimely' death or fatal disease, which overtakes them before they have the time and opportunity to repent and replace their wrongdoings with goodness, piety and worship. Fear of death is usually greatest at bedtime: sleep, which is considered a 'minor' reversible death, is fearfully anticipated to continue into the full final death. Death is regarded as the major pleasure destroyer (Hazem Ul Laththat), and thinking about death is considered the best warning reminder to man of his accountability to God in the afterlife that follows. It is not surprising, therefore, that morbid fears involving death and fatal disease should follow bereavement (139).

It is particularly noteworthy that in the series of investigations by Arrindell et al. (1990), there is no separate factor of fear of sex. Otherwise this factor was fear of "Sexual and aggressive scenes". Thus, one may speculate that in Western culture, there is no fear of "sex" per se, but in its conjunction with "aggression". In the West, there is stress on individual liberty including a liberal attitude toward sexual acts and practices. This attitude may be considered as a reflection of the sexual revolution and the loosening of social mores regarding sexual behavior. So, what fearful is the aggressive sex. Foremost among it, is rape. Recent community surveys in the West revealed that:

prevalence of rape estimates range from 5% to 22% of adult women. Between 1981 and 1991 the rate of rape in the U. S. A. increased four times as much as the overall crime rate. In the U. S., 12.1 million adult women have been forcibly raped during their lifetime. Of these, 39% had been raped more than once. One in four females experience rape sometime in their lifetime. Every six minutes a women is raped in the U. S... 57% of women in a community sample who had been raped developed post-traumatic stress disorder (PTSD) at some point in their lives. While traumatic events generally led to PTSD less than 25% of the time, 80% of rape victims evidence PTSD symptomatology. The degree of violence experienced during rape affected the severity of the PTSD symptoms (Meichenbaum, 1994, p. 70).

In contexts like this, it is predictable that what is fearful in the West is aggressive sex and not sex itself. Contrary to this, there is a separate and pure factor in the present study pertaining to sex per se. In a traditional, conservative, and mainly Muslim society like Egypt, it is predictable to fear sex. To quote yet again from Fakhr El-Islam (1994), "...Traditional methods of child rearing and upbringing emphasize chastity and prohibit premarital sexual relationships, which count as a major sin... [and emphasize] its socially disgraceful and eternally punishable consequences according to Islamic code" (p. 139).

For different reasons, it can be hypothesized that culture may be one of the determinants of morbid fears (Chaleby, 1987; Fakhr El-Islam, 1994), as well as the FSS III factors. That is, social learning plays a role in fears and phobias. Arrindell et al. (1987, 1990, 1991) compared Ss belonging to a Western culture. But Egypt has a different culture, history, language, and situation as compared to the Western World. As a consequence, problems of life as well as environmental cues are different in Egypt than in the West. So, the differences between the extracted factors of the FSS may be attributed to culture, and may reflect variation in stimulus conditions across Western and Arab cultures.

However, there is a possibility that similarities between the factors extracted in the present analysis on Egyptians and previous studies on Western Ss overshadow the differences. All of the present factors have been previously extracted in one Western analysis or another, notwithstanding different samples, morbidity, number of items, statistical analysis, and procedures, etc. In comparison with the parsimonious model of Arrindell et al. (1990), all of their factors are represented in the present analysis. Thus, someone may say that it could then appear as though there is cross-cultural inconsistency when in fact it is due to other factors as mentioned above. In the present writer's view, nevertheless, the breaking down of three of the unitary factors in that model into six components or factors in the present analysis is a unique phenomenon which characterizes the responses of the Egyptian sample. The typical example in this endeavor is the breaking down of the social factor to two factors, i.e. fear of "Social inadequacy" and "Responsibility and authority". By and large, it is the contention of the present writer that this analysis yields a unique structure of the factors among Egyptians, denoting a cultural specificity and effect. Foremost among these results are the phobic and noxious natures of: authority, death, and sex as separate factors.

The possible clinical application of the present results on Egyptian Ss has to wait the judgment of the present nine factors regarding their internal consistency reliability in terms of Cronbach's coefficient alpha, and the correlations between the factors. There is also a need to carry out a second-order factorizing of the present nine factors.

REFERENCES

Abdel-Khalek, A.M. (1981) Extraversion and neuroticism as basic personality dimensions in Egyptian samples. *Personality & Individual Differences, 2,* 91-97.

Abdel-Khalek, A.M. (1986) Death anxiety in Egyptian samples. *Personality & Individual Differences*, 7, 479 - 483.

Abdel-Khalek, A M. (1988) The Fear Survey Schedule III and its correlation with personality in Egyptian samples. *Journal of Behavior Therapy & Experimental Psychiatry*, 19, 113-118.

Abdel-Khalek, A.M. (1989) The development and validation of an Arabic form of the STAI: Egyptian results. *Personality & Individual Differences, 10*, 277-285.

Abdel-Khalek, A.M. (1994) Normative results on the Arabic Fear Survey Schedule III. *Journal of Behavior Therapy & Experimental Psychiatry*, 25, 61 - 67.

Agathon, M., & Brouri, R. (1983) Analyse factorielle d' une échelle de peurs, la FSS III (89 items), sur une population psychiatrique. *Revue de Psychologie Appliquée, 33*, 203 - 214.

Ammerman, R. T. (1988) Fear Survey Schedule III. In M. Hersen & A. S. Bellack (Eds.), *Dictionary of behavioral assessment techniques.* New York : Pergamon Press, pp. 216 - 218.

Arrindell, W.A. (1980) Dimensional structure and psychopathology correlates of the Fear Survey Schedule (FSS-III) in a phobic population: A factorial definition of agoraphobia. *Behavior Research & Therapy,* 18, 229-242.

Arrindell, W. A., Emmelkamp, P. M. G., & van der Ende, J. (1984) Phobic dimensions: I. Reliability and generalizability across samples, gender, and nations. *Advances in Behavior Research & Therapy,* 6, 207 - 254.

Arrindell, W. A., & van der Ende, J. (1986) Further evidence for cross - sample invariance of phobic factors: Psychiatric inpatient ratings on the Fear Survey Schedule - III. *Behavior Research & Therapy*, 24,289 - 297.

Arrindell, W. A., Pickersgill, M. J., Bridges, K. R., Kartsounis, L. D., Mervyn - Smith, J., van der Ende, J., & Sanderman, R. (1987) Self - reported fears of American, British and Dutch university students : A cross - national comparative study. *Advances in Behavior Research & Therapy*, 9, 207 - 245.

Arrindell, W. A., Solyom, C., Ledwidge, B., van der Ende, J., Hageman, W., Solyom, L., & Zaitman, A. (1990) Cross - national validity of the five - components model of self-assessed fears: Canadian psychiatric outpatients data vs. Dutch target ratings on the Fear Survey Schedule III. *Advances in Behavior Research & Therapy,* 12, 101 - 122.

Arrindell, W. A. Oei, T. P. S., Evans, L., & Van der Ende, J. (1991) Agoraphobic, animal, death-injury-illness and social stimuli clusters as major elements in a four dimensional taxonomy of self-rated fears: First-order level confirmatory evidence from an Australian sample of anxiety disorder patients. *Advances in Behavior Research & Therapy,* 13, 227-249.

Bamber, J. H. (1977) The factorial structure of adolescent responses to a Fear Survey Schedule. *Journal of Genetic Psychology* 130, 229 - 238.

Beshai, J. A., & Templer, D. I. (1978) American and Egyptian attitudes toward death, *Essence, 2,* 155-158.

Brown, A. M., & Crawford, H. J. (1988) Fear Survey Schedule III: Oblique and orthogonal factorial structures in an American college population. *Personality & Individual Differences*, 9, 401 - 410.

Chaleby, K. (1987) Social phobia in Saudis. *Social Psychiatry 22,* 167-170.

Fakhr El-Islam, M. (1994) Cultural aspects of morbid fears in Qatari women, *Social Psychiatry & Psychiatric Epidemiology, 29*, 137-140

Goldberg, J., Yinon, Y., & Cohen, A. (1975) A factor analysis of the Israeli Fear Survey Inventory. *Psychological Reports*, 36, 175 - 179.

Granell de Aldaz, E. (1982) Factor analysis of a Venezuelan Fear Survey Schedule. *Behavior Research & Therapy*, 20, 313 - 322.

Hallam, R. S., & Hafner, R. J. (1978) Fears of phobic patients: Factor analyses of self- report data. *Behavior Research & Therapy*, 16, 1 - 6.

Hersen, M. (1973) Self - assessment of fear. *Behavior Therapy*, 4, 241 - 257.

Holmes, G. R., Rothstein, W., Stout, A. L., & Rosecrans, C. J. (1975) Comparison of four factor analyses of the Fear Survey Schedule. *Journal of Clinical Psychology*, 31, 56 - 61.

Kartsounis, L. D., Mervyn-Smith, J., & Pickersgill, M. J. (1983) Factor analysis of the responses of British university students to the Fear Survey Schedule (FSS III). *Personality & Individual Differences*, 4, 157 - 163.

Korayem, A.S.M. (1987) A factorial study of the Fear Survey Schedules and their relation to personality dimensions. Unpublished MA Thesis, Alexandria University, Egypt.

Landy, F. J., & Gaupp, L. A. (1971) A factor analysis of the Fear Survey Schedule- III. *Behavior Research & Therapy*, 9, 89 - 93.

Meichenbaum, D. (1994) *A clinical handbook/practical therapist manual for assessing and treating adults with post-traumatic stress disorder.* Waterloo, Ontario: Institute Press.

Meikle, S., & Mitchell, M. C. (1974) Factor analysis of the Fear Survey Schedule with phobics. *Journal of Clinical Psychology*, 30, 44 - 46.

Merbaum, M., & Stricker, G. (1972) Factor analytic study of male and female responses to the Fear Survey Schedule. *Journal of Behavior Therapy & Experimental Psychiatry*, 3, 87 - 90.

Oei, T. P.S., Cavallo, G., & Evans, L. (1987) Utility of Fear Survey Schedule with Australian samples of anxiety disorder patients. *Journal of Behavior Therapy & Experimental Psychiatry*, 18, 329 - 336.

Roberts, M. C., & La Greca, A. M. (1981) Behavioral assessment. In C. E. Walker (Ed.), *Clinical practice of psychology : A guide for mental health professional*, New York : Pergamon Press, pp. 293 – 346.

Rothstein, W., Holmes, G. R., & Boblitt, W. E. (1972) A factor analysis of the Fear Survey Schedule with a psychiatric population. *Journal of Clinical Psychology*, 28, 78 - 80.

Rubin, S. E., Lawlis, G. F., Tasto, D. L., & Namenk, T. (1969) Factor analysis of the 122 item Fear Survey Schedule. *Behavior Research & Therapy*, 7, 381 - 386.

Spinks, P. M. (1980) An item and factor analysis of the FSS III. *Personality & Individual Differences*, 1, 363 -370.

SPSS Inc. (1990) *SPSS : Statistical data analysis*. Chicago : SPSS.

Stratton, T. T., & Moore, C. L. (1977) Application of the robust factor concept to the Fear Survey Schedule. *Journal of Behavior Therapy & Experimental Psychiatry*, 8, 229 -235.

Tasto, D. L. (1977) Self - report schedules and inventories. In A. R. Ciminero, K. S. Calhoun, & H. E. Adams (Eds.) *Handbook of behavioral assessment*, New York : Wiley.

Tejero, A., Avila, C., San, A., & Torrubia, R. (1989) Estructura factorial de la version Catalan del Fear Schedule III. *Revista de Psiquiatria de la Facultad de Medicina de Barcelona*, 16, 283 - 294.

Templer, D. I. (1991) Comment on large gender differences on death anxiety in Arab countries. *Psychological Reports, 69,* 1186.

Wade, T. C. (1978) Factor analytic approaches to the investigation of common fears: A critical appraisal and reanalysis. *Behavior Therapy*, 9, 923 - 935.

Walkey, F. H. (1983) Simple versus complex factor analyses of responses to multiple scale questionnaire. *Multivariate Behavioral Research*, 18, 401 - 421.

Wolpe, J., & Lang, P. (1964) A Fear Survey Schedule for use in behavior therapy. *Behavior Research & Therapy*, 2, 27 - 30.

Wolpe, J., & Lang, P. (1977) *Manual for the Fear Survey Schedule*. San Diego, CA : Educational & Industrial Testing Service.

Chapter 14

REVIEW OF THE FEAR OF
PAIN QUESTIONNAIRE – III

Augustine Osman, Mei-Chuan Wang and Francisco X. Barrios
University of Northern Iowa
Cedar Falls, Iowa 50614-0505

RATIONALE FOR THE DEVELOPMENT OF THE
FEAR OF PAIN QUESTIONNAIRE – III

In the past decade, research in the area of how individuals respond to pain has focused extensively on the cognitive and behavioral response domains. Consequently, most self-report instruments that are currently available to researchers and clinicians are limited to the assessment of pain-related cognitive and behavioral responses. For example, the Pain Catastrophizing Scale (PCS; Sullivan, Bishop, & Pivik, 1995; Osman et al., 2000) taps cognitive dimensions of rumination, magnification, and hopelessness. The Survey of Pain Attitudes Scale (SOPA-35; Jensen, Turner, & Romano, 2000) evaluates attitudinal dimensions of disability and beliefs about pain. To date, adequate attention has not been given to the development and validation of instruments for the assessment of emotional responses to pain. In the initial conceptualization of the Fear of Pain Questionnaire –III (FPQ-III), McNeil and Rainwater (1998) made extensive conceptual distinctions between the constructs of *fear of pain* and *anxiety related to the experience of pain* (see pp. 390-391). Indeed, research has also established strong relationships between pain and a range of emotional states (e.g., see Knotek, 2001; Kremer & Atkinson, 1984), indicating the need to develop and validate pain-specific measures of emotional distress such as fear.

FEAR OF PAIN QUESTIONNAIRE - III: DEVELOPMENT AND SCORING

The Fear of Pain Questionnaire-III was designed by McNeil and Rainwater (1998) to assess three emotional components of pain-related responses: fear related of severe pain, fear related to minor pain, and fear related to medical pain. The authors generated the FPQ-III items from multiple sources to reflect the multidimensionality of the fear of pain response construct. Specifically, the initial items were designed to describe eight specific painful situations, as recommended in the behavioral-analytic principles. Items that were generated in response to these situations were submitted to content validity analyses by four independent judges. Additional items were developed and included in the initial pool of 151 potential items. The authors conducted two additional studies, with unselected undergraduates, to derive the final 30-item version of the FPQ-III. The factor-analytic study identified three correlated factors, each characterized by 10 items. Items on this instrument are scored on a 5-point Likert-type rating scale ranging from 1 (*not at all*) to 5 (*extreme*) in terms of how fearful the individual experiences pain associated with each item. The total score is obtained for each factor scale by summing ratings on the related items within the scale. For the FPQ-III total scale, scores range from 30 to 150.

FACTOR STRUCTURE OF THE FPQ-III

Osman et al. (2002) conducted two factor analytic studies to replicate systematically the factor structure of the FPQ-III. Participants were 300 (120 men and 180 women) unselected undergraduate students. The average age of this sample was 21.1 years (*SD* = 3.8 years; range = 18-37 years). An iterated principal-axis factoring (PAF) with direct oblimin (oblique) rotation procedures were employed to replicate factor structure. The Velicer's minimum average partial (MAP; Velicer, 1976; Gorsuch, 1991) procedure was used to determine the number of factors to extract. Items were considered relevant for a primary factor when they loaded .35 or higher on the target factor. Results provided support for the three-factor solution accounting for approximately 49.8% of the total variance in the sample data. In a second factor analytic study, the authors conducted confirmatory factor analyses (CFA) to establish stronger construct validity for the FPQ-III. Participants were 250 unselected undergraduate students (90 men and 160 women) ranging in age from 18 to 44 years. Results of the Robust Maximum-likelihood estimation procedure provided excellent fit for the 3-factor oblique model when compared with the null, one-factor, and three-factor orthogonal models. The CFA analyses were conducted using both the individual FPQ-III items and the rationally-derived parcels as measured variables.

INTERNAL CONSISTENCY AND
STABILITY OF SCORES ON THE FPQ-III

The FPQ-III has adequate test-retest reliability and internal consistency reliability estimates. For their normative undergraduate sample (N = 275), McNeil and Rainwater (1998) reported coefficient alpha estimates ranging from .87 to .88 for the FPQ-III factor scales, and an alpha estimate of .92 for the FPQ-III total score. In addition, in a sub-sample of 186 undergraduates, these authors reported 3-week test-retest reliability correlations ranging from .69 to .76 for the FPQ-III factor scale scores, and a stability coefficient of .74 for the FPQ total score. In a sample of 250 unselected undergraduates, Osman et al. (2002) provided additional support for the internal consistency of the FPQ-III factor scales: Severe Pain (alpha

= .90), Minor Pain (alpha = .87), and Medical Pain (alpha = .89). The alpha estimate for the FPQ-III total score was high, .93. For men, the alpha estimates ranged from .85 to .89; and for women, the alpha estimates ranged from .85 to .90 for the FPQ-III scale scores. Overall, scores on the FPQ-III total and scale scores have good internal consistency and stability.

NORMATIVE (MEANS AND STANDARD DEVIATIONS) DATA FOR THE FPQ-III

McNeil and Rainwater (1998) reported normative data of the FPQ-III for samples of chronic pain inpatients (N = 40; M age = 47.2 years, SD = 13.6), general medical outpatients (N = 40; M age = 45.3 years, SD = 11.8) and unselected sample of undergraduates (N = 660; M age = 19.8 years, SD = 3.6). The range of scores across these independent samples were from 18.4 (SD = 6.0) to 37.1 (SD = 7.4) for the FPQ-III factor scale scores; the range of scores for the FPQ-III total scale was from 78.1 (SD = 25.1) to 79.0 (SD = 16.2). Osman et al. (2002) provided additional normative data for 250 unselected undergraduates ranging in age from 18-44 years, and a sample of 131 non-clinical adults comparable in age to the McNeil and Rainwater's (1998) medical and clinic pain inpatients. For the non-clinical adult sample, the range of scores on the FPQ-III factor scales were from 17.6 (SD = 5.49) to 34.2 (SD = 8.57); the mean FPQ-III total score was 78.2 (SD = 18.01). Separate normative data were presented for men and women in studies by McNeil and Rainwater (1998) and Osman et al. (2002). Overall, scores on the Severe and Medical scales were sensitive in differentiating between the responses of the chronic pain inpatients and the non-clinical adult samples.

VALIDITY ANALYSES OF THE FPQ-III SCORES

Correlations among the three FPQ-III factor scale scores range from .73 to .49 (see McNeil & Rainwater, 1998), suggesting moderate overlap among these factor scales. Osman et al. (2002) provided adequate convergent and discriminant validity evidence for the FPQ-III, using confirmatory factor analytic procedures. Specifically, for a sample of 250 unselected undergraduates, these authors reported a strong positive relationship between the FPQ-III scores and the Pain Anxiety and Symptoms Scale (coefficient = .45) scores (PASS; McCracken et al., 1992) supporting evidence of convergent validity. A low relationship was obtained between the FPQ-III scores and related measures of distress including anxiety and depression (coefficient = 16; Negative Affect), indicating evidence of discriminant validity. In a follow-up study that included 131 non-clinical adults, results of the regression analyses showed that scores on the Severe Pain scale (coefficient = .22, p < .02) and the Minor Pain scale (coefficient = .21; p < .03) were useful in predicting scores on a measure of pain catastrophizing, providing support for criterion-related validity.

DISCUSSION

Results of the studies conducted to date with the FPQ-III show that this instrument has replicable factor structure across independent samples. In addition, preliminary psychometric properties including internal consistency, test-retest reliability, and concurrent validity are strong for this newly developed self-report instrument. In terms of its clinical utility, scores on the FPQ-III total and scales are useful in differentiating the responses of clinic pain patients and non-clinical adults. The instrument is brief, easy to administer and score in applied and clinic settings. Scores on the FPQ-III can compliment scores on cognitive and behavioral pain measures. Additional studies with a range of clinic samples, however, are needed to attempt to replicate these preliminary findings.

REFERENCES

Gorsuch, R. L. (1991). *UniMult Guide.* Altadena, CA: UniMult.

Jensen, M. P., Turner, J. A., & Romano, J. M. (2000). Pain belief assessment: A comparison of the short and long versions of the Survey of Pain Attitudes. *The Journal of Pain, 1,* 138- 150.

Knotek, P. (2001). Pain and time in rheumatic patients: Changes of pain threshold, pain affects, and stress in family. *Studia Psychologia, 43,* 49-58.

Kremer, E. F., & Atkinson, J. H. (1984). Pain language: Affect. *Journal of Psychosomatic Research, 28,* 125-132.

McCracken, L. M., Zayfert, C., & Gross, R. T. (1992). The Pain Anxiety Symptoms Scale (PASS): Development and validation of a scale to measure fear of pain. *Pain, 50,* 67-73.

McNeil, D. W., & Rainwater, A. J. (1998). Development of the Fear of Pain Questionnaire – III. *Journal of Behavioral Medicine, 21,* 389-410.

Osman, A., Barrios, F. X., Gutierrez, P. M., Kopper, B. A., Merrifield, T., & Grittmann, L. (2000). The Pain Catastrophizing Scale: Further psychometric evaluation with adult samples. *Journal of Behavioral Medicine, 23,* 351-362.

Osman, A., Breitenstein, J. L., Barrios, F. X., Gutierrez, P. M., & Kopper, B. A. (2002). The Fear of Pain Questionnaire – III: Further reliability and validity with nonclinical samples. *Journal of Behavioral Medicine, 25,* 155-173.

Sullivan, M. J. L., Bishop, S. C., & Pivik, J. (1995). The Pain Catastrophizing Scale: Development and validation. *Psychological Assessment, 7,* 524-532.

Velicer, W. F. (1976). Determining the number of components from the matrix of partial correlations. *Psychometrika, 41,* 321-327.

INDEX